ENERGY SECURITY
IN THE GULF
CHALLENGES AND PROSPECTS

ENERGY SECURITY
IN THE GULF
CHALLENGES AND PROSPECTS

**THE EMIRATES CENTER FOR STRATEGIC
STUDIES AND RESEARCH**

THE EMIRATES CENTER FOR STRATEGIC STUDIES AND RESEARCH

The Emirates Center for Strategic Studies and Research (ECSSR) is an independent research institution dedicated to the promotion of professional studies and educational excellence in the UAE, the Gulf and the Arab world. Since its establishment in Abu Dhabi in 1994, the ECSSR has served as a focal point for scholarship on political, economic and social matters. Indeed, the ECSSR is at the forefront of analysis and commentary on Arab affairs.

The Center seeks to provide a forum for the scholarly exchange of ideas by hosting conferences and symposia, organizing workshops, sponsoring a lecture series and publishing original and translated books and research papers. The ECSSR also has an active fellowship and grant program for the writing of scholarly books and for the translation into Arabic of work relevant to the Center's mission. Moreover, the ECSSR has a large library including rare and specialized holdings, and a state-of-the-art technology center, which has developed an award-winning website that is a unique and comprehensive source of information on the Gulf.

Through these and other activities, the ECSSR aspires to engage in mutually beneficial professional endeavors with comparable institutions worldwide, and to contribute to the general educational and academic development of the UAE.

The views expressed in this book do not necessarily reflect those of the ECSSR.

First published in 2010 by
The Emirates Center for Strategic Studies and Research
PO Box 4567, Abu Dhabi, United Arab Emirates

E-mail: pubdis@ecssr.ae
Website: http://www.ecssr.ae

ISBN: 978-9948-14-299-7 hardback edition
ISBN: 978-9948-14-300-0 paperback edition
ISBN: 978-9948-14-301-7 electronic edition

CONTENTS

FIGURES

TABLES

ABBREVIATIONS AND ACRONYMS

ADEC	Abu Dhabi Future Energy Company
APICORP	Arab Petroleum Investments Corporation
Aramco	Arab American Oil Company (Saudi Arabia)
bbl	barrel
bcm	billion cubic meters
bcfpd	billion cubic feet per day
BOT	build–operate–transfer
bpd	barrels per day
Btu	British thermal units
CCGT	combined-cycle gas turbine
CCS	carbon capture and storage
CDM	Clean Development Mechanism (Kyoto)
CERs	Certified Emissions Reductions
CFBC	circulating fluidized bed combustion
CFR	Council on Foreign Relations (US)
CFTC	Commodity Futures Trading Commission
CIEC	Conference on International Economic Cooperation
CIF	cost, insurance, freight
CNOOC	China National Offshore Oil Corporation
CNPC	China National Petroleum Corporation
CSP	concentrated solar power
CTL	coal-to-liquids
CTS	Cap and Trade systems
DB	Deutsche Bank
DIFC	Dubai International Financial Center
DoE	Department of Energy (US)
DSM	demand side management
E&P	exploration and production

EHR	enhanced hydrocarbon recovery
EIA	Energy Information Administration (US)
EITI	Extractive Industries Transparency Initiative
EOR	enhanced oil recovery
EPC	engineering, procurement and construction
ESPO	East Siberia–Pacific Ocean
ETS	emission trading scheme
EU	European Union
Eurodif	European Gaseous Diffusion Uranium Enrichment Consortium.
FEC	fuel and energy complex (Russia)
FGD	flue gas desulfurization
FID	final investment decision
FOB	free-on-board
FSA	fuel supply agreement
G-2	Group of Two
G-8	Group of Eight
G-20	Group of Twenty
GHG	greenhouse gas
GJ	gigajoule
GoM	Gulf of Mexico
GDP	gross domestic product
GRC	Gulf Research Center
GRP	Global Research Partnership (KAUST)
$GtCO_2$	billion tons of CO_2
GTL	gas-to-liquids
Gtoe	billion tons of oil equivalent
GW	gigawatts
HEU	highly enriched uranium
HFO	heavy fuel oil
HPAD	Hydrogen Power Abu Dhabi
IAEA	International Atomic Energy Agency

ICCS–NTUA	Institute of Communications and Computer Systems of the National Technical University of Athens
IEA	International Energy Agency
IEF	International Energy Forum
IEO	International Energy Outlook (DOE)
IGCC	integrated gasification combined cycle
IMF	International Monetary Fund
IOC	international oil company
IPCC	Inter-governmental Panel on Climate Change
IPIC	International Petroleum Investment Company (UAE)
IPP	independent power producer
IRENA	International Renewable Energy Agency
IRR	internal rate of return
IWPP	integrated water and power plant
KAUST	King Abdulaziz University for Science and Technology
kbpd	thousand barrels per day
KIA	Kuwait Investment Authority
KISR	Kuwait Institute for Scientific Research
KPC	Kuwait Petroleum Corporation
KPIZ	Khalifa Port and Industrial Zone
kW	kilowatt
LIBOR	London Inter-bank Offered Rate
LNG	liquefied natural gas
mbpd	million barrels per day (also mmb/d)
mBtu	million British thermal units
MEA	monoethanolamine
MENA	Middle East and North Africa
MIST	Masdar Institute of Science and Technology
MIT	Massachusetts Institute of Technology

mmb/d	million barrels per day (also mbpd)
mpg	miles per gallon
mt	million tons
mtoe	million tons of oil equivalent
MWh	megawatt hour
NGCC	natural gas combined cycle
NIMS	nano-particle ionic materials
NOx	nitrogen oxide
NOC	national oil company
NPT	(nuclear) Non-Proliferation Treaty
NPV	net present values (model)
NPVPFR	net present value of petroleum fiscal revenues
NPVPFV	net present valve of petroleum fiscal value
NYMEX	New York Mercantile Exchange
OECD	Organization for Economic Cooperation and Development
OF	oil-fired
OIES	Oxford Institute for Energy Studies
OPEC	Organization of the Petroleum Exporting Countries
PF	pulverized fuel
PIH	permanent income hypothesis
ppm	parts per million
PTSA	pressure and temperature swing adsorption
PV	photovoltaic
QIA	Qatar Investment Authority
QPC	Qatar Petroleum Company
R&D	research and development
RD&D	research, development and demonstration
SABIC	Saudi Arabian Basic Industries Corporation
SCO	Shanghai Cooperation Organization
SCR	selective catalytic reduction (SCR

SDR	Special Drawing Rights
SLR	sea level rise
SNCR	selective non-catalytic reduction
SPR	Strategic Petroleum Reserve
SWF	sovereign wealth fund
tcf	trillion cubic feet
tcm	trillion cubic meters
toe	tons of oil equivalent
TWh	terawatt-hours
UAE	United Arab Emirates
USGS	United States Geological Survey
WEO	World Energy Outlook (IEA)
WTI	West Texas Intermediate
WTO	World Trade Organization

Energy is essential to the process of development in the Gulf region, both in terms of its direct use and in the allocation of the proceeds from its export. Hence, there is an ever-present need to achieve the maximum level of energy security possible for producers and consumers alike, especially in light of today's various geo-strategic developments and escalating security-related and economic challenges.

The need to ensure energy security for producing countries, and the challenges this task presents, should not blind us to our commitment to the requirements of consumers and the need to ensure a reliable flow of energy resources at acceptable prices. This, however, demands concerted efforts by all to ensure appropriate levels of supply and demand, and maintain both regional and international peace and stability.

To discuss this vital issue, the Emirates Center for Strategic Studies and Research (ECSSR) convened its 15th Annual Energy Conference under the title 'Energy Security in the Gulf: Challenges and Prospects' on November 16–18, 2009 in Abu Dhabi, hosting a group of distinguished energy experts from various academic, professional and technical backgrounds.

This book comprises a valuable collection of the papers presented at the conference, providing a scholarly, strategic examination of energy security in a region characterized by instability and conflict. The papers presented in this volume identify energy security challenges in a globalized economy in view of global consumption uncertainties, oil price preferences and the diversification of energy sources. The interplay between oil prices and fiscal sustainability in the Gulf states is examined, as well as the politicization of markets and the relationship between energy resources and regional conflict. Russian and Asian perspectives on energy security are also discussed, as is the role of new technology in achieving energy sustainability for both producers and consumers.

It is fitting at this juncture to express my gratitude to all the speakers for their participation in the ECSSR 15th Annual Energy Conference. Their informative presentations compiled in this volume offer sound insight and informed perspectives on various aspects of energy security in the Gulf. I would also like to express my appreciation to the distinguished academics who served on the referee panel, reviewing the conference papers prior to publication and offering their critical assessment.

Finally, thanks are due to the Editor, Francis Field, for coordinating the publication of this book, as well as to the other members of the ECSSR Department of Publications, Translation and Distribution who assisted during the course of the project.

Jamal S. Al-Suwaidi, Ph.D.
Director General
ECSSR

INTRODUCTION

Gulf Energy Security: Challenges and Prospects

An issue of great concern to all nations, energy security stands at the forefront of the international agenda. Thus, a recurring theme throughout this volume is the dramatic change which has occurred in the view and definition of the concept of energy security.

In the past, substantial emphasis has been placed on the perspectives of consumer nations, but little attention has been paid to the concerns of energy producers, whose interests are equally served by maintaining security of supply. José Maria Botelho de Vasconcelos highlights this fact and stresses the ongoing commitment of the Organization of the Petroleum Exporting Countries (OPEC) to the efficient, economic supply of petroleum to consumers. OPEC members, he writes, seek to sell oil and gas to support their development and improve living standards in producing countries; "Hydrocarbons provide our main source of income, in some cases accounting for more than 90 percent of our export revenue ... Thus, we are firmly committed to maintaining security of supply." Indeed, while oil-producing and oil-consuming countries share a broad range of interests in promoting global energy security, Ali Aissaoui reminds us that producers consider themselves to be much more vulnerable to the instability and volatility of global oil markets. In tackling this problem the first and most obvious option of Gulf producers, he suggests, would be for GCC governments to capture the rent from *total* petroleum production – not just exports – which would involve a re-evaluation and adjustment of current domestic petroleum pricing policies. He concludes that changing the domestic pricing regime, diversifying the economy and extending domestic taxation are among the hard policy choices facing governments in the region.

Riyad Hamzah highlights another keenly-felt vulnerability in the Gulf—in an area that collectively possesses more than two-fifths of global oil reserves and constitutes as much as one-fifth of total global production, the past investments made in the development of science and technology in the Gulf have not been proportional to their significance to the economy. Although he concedes that numerous initiatives have been launched recently to strengthen the role of universities and research centers, and to overcome the obstacles to technology transfer in the areas of short-term energy security, he states that the region requires more graduate programs focused on the different aspects of energy – particularly capacity-building and scientific advancement – as it has been dependent for too long on the international purchase of technologies that are vital to its survival.

Other internal factors that negatively affect energy markets and Gulf security, according to Mohammed Al-Sahlawi, include "the lack of real democracy, the existence of corruption, and the unstructured nature of labor markets which has led to high national unemployment in the Gulf countries." These problems, he states, create barriers to economic and managerial reform, adversely affecting energy security. Furthermore, he argues that supply security, demand security and oil price stability in relation to the US dollar are important concerns when achieving energy security in the Gulf. The state of the world economy and supply and demand prospects, as well as interdependence between producers and consumers – particularly those with high demand growth rates – are also factors which will ensure that energy security in the Gulf remains an issue of international importance, but one in which the role of the Gulf countries themselves should not be underestimated.

[4]

The importance of energy interdependence is further illustrated by Anas Alhajji, who describes it as "the key to energy security for any nation." While energy independence might improve some aspects of energy security, he writes, it does not shield a country from energy shocks, so consuming countries can only enhance their energy security through "reciprocal energy security." Thus, he defines energy security as *the steady availability of energy supplies that ensures economic growth in both producing and consuming countries with the lowest social cost and the lowest price volatility.* Based on his 'energy star' model, he states that energy security can be achieved via diversification of energy sources, imports and exports for consumers, and income diversification and reduced dependence on energy exports for producers. Above all, however, he highlights the fact that without accurate measurement and assessment to produce up-to-date data on the various factors determining energy security – data which is largely lacking in the Gulf states – decision-makers are unable to make the necessary policy recommendations to avoid energy crises and price instability.

Vincent Lauerman's exploration of the producer–consumer gap yields a model for a producer–consumer administered price band mechanism. He argues that such a mechanism – administered by both oil producers and consumers – would generally be able to keep prices relatively stable and at reasonable levels. The ideal basis for the mechanism, he posits, would be a treaty between members of OPEC, the International Energy Agency (IEA) and the G-20 to create a 'Global Oil Agency' with a governing structure similar to that of the IEA. Such a body would be in a position to stabilize prices at reasonable levels, which would contribute to relatively stable investment flows and capacity additions all along the supply chain, including spare OPEC production capacity to help protect against supply shocks.

The need for more effective controls is seconded by Nodari Simoniya, who criticizes the West for being unable to accept the idea of an 'equitable' and 'mutually beneficial' solution for energy cooperation between exporters and importers, and warns that if an equitable approach to energy security is not found the world will face an epoch of continued energy conflict. He states that Russia supports an agreement on fair oil pricing, which would release energy pricing from the "whims of uncontrolled speculation" and create "an international regulating mechanism with strict controls and wide-ranging powers"; this would not only preserve energy security, he writes, but also foster greater peace worldwide.

On the demand side, Raad Alkadiri warns that a combination of sustained slower global economic growth, high prices, concerns about the environmental impact of hydrocarbon emissions and faster-than-expected technological innovation could limit the rising demand for hydrocarbons. Under these circumstances, the call on OPEC crude could be as low as 25 mbpd in 2020. Moreover, with more sluggish demand the difficulties of OPEC market management are likely to be amplified. Anemic demand growth, or worse still demand destruction, will complicate OPEC price defense efforts, particularly if Iraqi production increases significantly. Under those circumstances, the outlook for prices, and therefore for the finances of the Arab Gulf states, will look much bleaker over the next ten years. However, he suggests that the Arab Gulf states have time to manage this transition, assuming they start early enough, but they must begin with a recognition that it is not the scale of their resource base that is ultimately most important, but rather the scale of global demand for those commodities. In that sense, the Gulf states will continue to live with the energy insecurity; how they manage this insecurity, and the long-term policy measures they take to mitigate the risks, will determine how much pain they feel as world energy use transforms in the years to come.

Philip Andrews-Speed suggests that success in developing a growing flow of oil and exports from the Middle East to Asia will be critical to the economic development of the countries of the Middle East. However, he concludes that this success depends on a wide range of factors over which Middle Eastern states have varying degrees of control. At the extreme, he suggests, Gulf countries can take steps to ensure that production capacity in the region for both oil and gas grows ahead of global demand, thus assuring that they are able to supply Asia's demand; but this of course runs the risk of prices falling to unacceptable levels. They must also consider the extent to which the capacity of Middle Eastern states to export oil and gas will be constrained by their own domestic demand for energy as their economies grow over the coming decades.

Furthermore, a possible shift in energy exports to Asia will result in a deepening political and economic engagement with the Gulf, which will "bring new strategic players into the Middle East who have in the past been bystanders to political events in the region, notably China and India." Should this occur, Ronald Soligo and Amy Myers Jaffe's investigation of the implications of oil market politicization on conflict suggests that while consuming countries may compete for access to resources, and producers and consumers will struggle over the distribution of oil rents, such conflicts can be handled within the context of the current global economic system. Despite some turbulent history, they conclude that countries will probably continue to use oil as a means for pressuring other states to alter policies they disagree with, but that their actions are constrained by the existence of both a global market for oil and substitutes for oil.

In terms of price volatility, they suggest that at the very least a framework for consultations between exporters and importers of oil and gas should be established to deal with price volatility and financial flows. This can be achieved within the context of existing institutions (G-20, IEA, Energy Charter) or in a new, more specialized institution that would develop rules and procedures to prevent energy-related crises in the future or to deal effectively with crises when they occur.

They also call for a mechanism to coordinate the use of strategic inventories held by consuming countries and excess capacity held – primarily by producers – to deal with unusual spikes in prices. Since all countries benefit from price stability, they posit that all countries should participate in the cost of maintaining these buffers—the exception being those countries with very low per capita income.

In the long term, they conclude that all countries should work to slow the growth in the demand for oil by encouraging efficiency and new automobile technologies in order to keep the share of oil coming from the Middle East at "reasonable levels"; and that the United States should impose a tax on oil (and other fossil fuels) both to capture some of the rents that now accrue to producers and to find measures to deal with GHG emissions.

Indeed, Hisham Khatib points out that today, energy security must be viewed in a much broader context, incorporating "a wider diversity of forms and quantities of energy, and a need to meet environmental challenges, all within constrained budgets." Energy security, he states, is now entwined with environmental management.

In this context, Leila Benali explores the possible makeup of the future Gulf energy mix. Diversification of the fuel mix, she states, is rising ever higher on government agendas for a number of reasons, including strained fuel supplies, environmental concerns and geopolitics. She writes that, in theory, the main alternatives to hydrocarbons considered in the region are coal, renewables and (long term) nuclear power, but that natural gas will likely be the fuel of choice for Gulf electricity generation in the future. Hydrocarbon producers used to be of the opinion that the emphasis on clean technologies and CO_2 emissions caps could only end up harming long-term demand for their main export. Today, however, the scale of regional investment in renewables and clean energy ventures is estimated at around US$33 billion between 2009 and 2013, and: "after reviewing the options, GCC countries appear to have identified solar and carbon capture and storage (CCS) as the main focus areas of their involvement in the clean energy scene."

Sa'ad Al-Jandal suggests that the deployment of CCS is increasingly seen as an attractive option within a portfolio to mitigate climate change. Although he concludes that there is no "final answer" to the question of whether CCS is beneficial to a sustainable transformation of the energy production sectors in the GCC countries and beyond, there are various reasons why CCS could be seen as a 'bridging technology' that allows for a smooth transition away from the current carbon focus of industrial-level electricity generation and others towards a more environmentally sustainable future. National deployment of CCS, he states, will allow GCC oil companies and power institutions to take on a pioneering role with regional pilot and demonstration projects which may lead to forefront expertise advantages. However, he warns that the most important precondition for any further engagement in CCS is the creation of a reliable and stringent regulatory and climate policy framework in the Gulf which considers all the different mitigation options.

The over-riding consensus of the papers presented in this volume is that energy security should be – and is increasingly – viewed as a common concern to both producers and consumers around the world. This interdependence necessitates the comprehensive adoption of a broader, more equitable view of energy security as a whole. Furthermore, while the differences among states abound, there is enough common concern to provide scope for the creation of an international mechanism to regulate pricing and defend against supply shocks.

Diversification of both supply and demand is inevitable in the decades ahead, as new and alternative energy sources increase their penetration of the global energy mix. In this context, there is a need in the Gulf states to invest in education, science and technology, and R&D in order to bolster self-sufficiency and cement their position as major producers. Also, policies concerning domestic use and pricing of energy in the Gulf states may require re-evaluation and adjustment to meet the challenges ahead.

Ultimately, energy security is an issue of mutual concern to all, and as such can only be sustained through inclusive, multi-lateral approaches to achieving an energy mix and supply–demand balance that supports the interests of both energy-dependent consuming countries and rapidly developing producers.

KEYNOTE ADDRESS

Energy Security in the Gulf: An OPEC Perspective

H.E. Eng. José Maria Botelho de Vasconcelos

OPEC has a strong presence in the Gulf. Indeed, the Organization was established in this region – at Baghdad in September 1960 – and half of our twelve Member Countries hail from this part of the world, including four of our five founding members.

Locally, Abu Dhabi joined OPEC in 1967 and transferred its membership to the United Arab Emirates in 1974, while overall the six Gulf members account for 65 percent of OPEC's crude oil output and 60 percent of its marketed production of natural gas. Their share of proven reserves is slightly higher, at 72 and 79 percent respectively, which testifies to the Gulf region's global importance. It possesses 57 percent of the world's crude oil reserves and 40 percent of its natural gas. The fact that its share of world output is just a fraction of this – 30 percent of oil and 11 percent of gas – suggests that these reserves will last longer than most of those located elsewhere in the world.

The oil-producing developing countries share many challenges and prospects both in the oil industry and elsewhere. These include the need to ensure that the world at large has a clear understanding of these countries' positions on important energy issues. Naturally, energy security is one such issue.

Many consumers view energy security from a very narrow perspective, limiting the concept to the security of oil supply. However, as we all know here in the Gulf, there are no justifiable grounds for such a limitation.

Time and again, OPEC has demonstrated its commitment to maintaining the security of oil supplies in both normal and abnormal circumstances. In 2005, for example, prompt assurances concerning OPEC supplies helped to prevent the output disruptions caused by Hurricanes Katrina and Rita in the Gulf of Mexico from developing into major energy crises.

In this regard, the OPEC Statute – which has guided the Organization's policy for nearly half a century – clearly articulates the Organization's stance when it states that: "Due regard shall be given at all times ... to the necessity of securing ... an efficient, economic and regular supply of petroleum to consuming nations."

We have abided by this principle and will continue to do so in the future. Ultimately, we want to sell our oil and gas on world markets, to help develop our economies and improve the living standards of our peoples. Hydrocarbons provide our main source of income, in some cases accounting for more than 90 percent of our export revenue. Why should we seek to restrict this process? Surely that would not make sense; thus, we are firmly committed to maintaining security of supply.

What really concerns the members of OPEC is the 'other side of the coin': security of demand. We strongly believe that this should be given equal weight to security of supply for consumers.

There is too much uncertainty in the market over matters such as future world economic growth levels, policies in consuming countries, and technological advances. This makes it almost impossible to devise effective investment strategies for future production capacity to meet forecast rising levels of demand.

The latest projections in OPEC's reference case see world oil demand rising by 20 million barrels per day (mbpd) to 106 mbpd by 2030. However, these are only projections, based on present trends and expected patterns of behavior. The reality may turn out to be very different in what

[14]

is an uncertain world. Therefore, every effort must be made to avoid adding to this inherent uncertainty in an unnecessary way as, in the long run, this will prove most counterproductive.

As all of us in this industry know, producers cannot afford to invest heavily in capacity that may not be needed. It is, indeed, an expensive business maintaining idle capacity. Neither producers nor consumers want excessive, volatile oil prices in the future, and this can be best avoided by committing the correct levels of investment today.

This is why OPEC has repeatedly encouraged consumer governments to ensure transparency, predictability and consistency in their policy-making, as this is one key area where efforts can be made to reduce uncertainty.

OPEC, however, has a broader vision of energy security, as our Gulf members know. Energy security should be universal, benefiting rich and poor nations alike. It should apply to the entire supply chain and cover foreseeable time-horizons, as well as enable all consumers to benefit from the most modern energy products. Furthermore, it should apply to all energy sources in a manner that is free from prejudicial regulatory and legislative constraints. Here I refer in particular to the very high levels of taxation imposed on oil products in numerous consuming countries.

We welcomed the real progress that was achieved in 2006 when energy security topped the agenda at the G8 summit in St. Petersburg. This appeared to lead to a better understanding by all parties of the true, broader nature of energy security.

The BBC summed this up well: "The point of putting energy security top of the agenda was to require the Western world to examine the problem not just from their own viewpoint as energy consumers, but consider also the needs and concerns of those who produce the stuff and transport it."

We thought we had finally got the message across about the true, collective nature of energy security; and so we have been saddened by recent calls from influential parties in richer nations to reduce their dependence on imported oil. We cannot see where this is leading, nor what these nations hope to gain from such calls.

One of the clear lessons from recent events – and the global financial crisis provides and apt example of this – is that the world economy performs best in a climate characterized by interdependence among nations. This is especially true for the energy industry. The infrastructure and trading patterns of this industry are well-established and global in nature, and the challenges facing it extend well beyond basic market economics; they also include universal issues affecting the advancement of mankind, such as the preservation of the environment and the pursuit of sustainable development. These issues are too big to be handled at the national level; however, they are also very difficult to confront at the international level—as can be seen in the build-up to the Copenhagen climate negotiations.

No country can afford to 'go it alone' in the energy industry today; therefore, we should all recognize the true value of interdependence among nations and the comprehensive nature of energy security. This will help the energy industry – and particularly the oil and gas sector – to develop in an orderly manner which, in turn, will support sound world economic growth and benefit mankind as a whole.

ENERGY SECURITY
AND THE GULF REGION

1

Global Energy Security: Implications for the Gulf

Hisham Khatib

In general, the world has seen considerable development and progress in the past 50 years. Living standards have improved, people have become healthier and live longer, and science and technology have considerably enhanced human welfare. No doubt the availability of abundant and cheap sources of energy, mainly in the form of crude oil from the Gulf, has contributed to these achievements. The availability of adequate energy supply – for the world as a whole as well as for individual countries – is essential for sustainable development, the proper functioning of the economy, and human well-being. Thus, the continuous availability of energy in the quantities and forms required by the economy and accepted by society must be ensured and secured.[1]

In the past, and especially since the early 1970s, energy security has been narrowly interpreted as being synonymous with the adequate and stable availability of crude oil at an acceptable price, and reduced dependence on oil consumption and imports—particularly in the states of the Organization for Economic Cooperation and Development (OECD) and other major oil-importing countries; but changes in oil and other energy markets have altered that view. Suppliers have increased, as have proven reserves and stocks, and prices (although volatile) have become flexible and more transparent, dictated by market forces rather than by cartel arrangements. Global tensions and regional conflicts exist, but trade is flourishing and becoming freer. Suppliers have not imposed any oil sanctions since the early 1980s, nor have there been any real shortages anywhere in the world, and emergency stocks have rarely been used by the International Energy Agency (IEA). Instead, the United Nations and other actors have applied sanctions to some oil suppliers, but without affecting world oil trade or creating shortages. All this points to the present availability of abundant oil supplies, which have been greatly enhanced thanks in large part to technological advances. Our new oil age is characterized by globalization of demand for oil, the growing importance of environmental considerations which will shape how we use energy and oil, as well as new technologies that will slowly but dramatically affect oil as well as the whole energy portfolio.[2]

Energy security can be briefly defined as the continuous availability of energy in many forms, in sufficient quantities and at reasonable prices. Of course, fulfilling such a definition is a major challenge that many countries experience every day. Such a requirement is made more difficult by environmental constraints which are likely to further complicate an already challenging situation.

Today, energy security is viewed in a wider spectrum; it is characterized by not only availability of oil but a wider diversity of forms and quantities of energy, and a need to meet environmental challenges, all within constrained budgets. Energy security is now entwined with energy and environmental management. Simultaneously, the bulk of demand has shifted from North America and the European Union (EU) to some large developing countries like China and India which demand high energy intensity in their economies.

This paper will tackle energy security on four fronts. First of all it will review the future world energy outlook and its resource base. Second, it will refer to environmental challenges and their implications for the energy market and energy security. The third section will deal with the challenges to energy security through energy management and diversified energy forms. The last section will consider how this outlook and the related challenges will affect the Gulf countries.

The Future of World Energy

The world energy sector is characterized by significant features that will shape, or at least influence, its long term future. By 'long term' we mean the middle of this century. These characteristics are:

- Very high inertia; although the energy sector is willing (even anxious) to develop, the change is very slow. This is a result of the high capital nature of the required investments in the sector as well as the lengthy life of its facilities. Power stations are usable for thirty to forty years, pipelines and refiners much more and all energy facilities are quite expensive and cannot be cheaply or easily replaced. A gas pipeline built today will almost certainly be delivering gas in 2050, a coal power station committed in year 2010 will survive until the mid-century, burning coal and emitting carbon. Therefore the medium- (up to 2030) and even long-term future of the energy sector is being shaped by decisions being made today. Owing to its capital nature, lengthy execution of facilities and their long life, the sector has an invariable inertia to continue as it is with slow development and limited change. There are no revolutions in the energy sector, only a slow evolution.

- Globally there are sufficient fossil fuel reserves to meet long term demand. They are abundant, versatile, highly concentrated, relatively cheap, storable and tradable. Proven reserves, in spite of annual consumption, are maintained (or even increased) through evolving technologies and new discoveries. Also, some important and viable alternatives – particularly nuclear power – are receiving increasing public opposition and decreasing market share. Simultaneously, alternatives (other than hydro) and new forms of energy, although gaining in strength, still suffer from many inherent weaknesses. They are intermittent, dispersed with low concentration, require storage and are not tradable. All this means that, in most cases, they require heavy investment and are expensive. Even the most economical and promising alternative – wind power – owing to its intermittent nature, can only constitute a limited share of any national or regional power supply system (say 15 percent) and its incorporation in the electricity system is not easy and does not obviate the need for further investments to compensate for its intermittent nature. Alternative energies like wind and solar, in contrast to fossil fuels, are not easily stored or traded. Most alternatives are only available commercially in the form of electrical power which has inherent limitations as an energy form. Alternatives will continue to slowly grow and steadily become economically more viable but they will be mainly driven by the need for energy security and environmental concerns, rather than their ability to commercially compete or satisfy substantial global energy needs.

• Oil will continue to remain the most important and tradable form of energy for the medium- and long-term. This is thanks to its versatile nature (in use), its established markets and relative ease in transport. Land and air transport will continue to depend on liquid forms of energy for decades to come. Simply, there is no alternative in sight. In spite of the unrelenting talk of peak oil and exhaustible reserves, proven reserves of conventional oil are now higher than at any other time in the past. They stand at around 1,260 billion barrels of crude, 18 percent and 26 percent higher than proved reserves of a decade and two decades earlier, respectively.[3] Gulf countries' reserves are rising faster than the world average (see the Statistical Review at the end of this paper). This is without adding Canadian oil sands – another 150 billion barrels – and non-conventional oil—referred to later. Of course, there are no fossil resources that are not ultimately exhaustible, but what this paper argues is that oil in its different forms and its derivatives will continue to dominate the global energy scene in the long term. Assisted by technology, new discoveries and huge amounts of non-conventional sources, oil will not peak soon. However, oil reserves are increasingly becoming limited to fewer countries, some of which exist in unstable parts of the world—that is a fact that can have serious implications for future global energy security.

- Environmental concerns, whether actual or exaggerated, are increasingly being considered in planning future energy investments. These concerns can be local, regional or global. It is the global concerns, caused by the emission of green house gases (GHGs) – mostly CO_2 emissions – which are important to us. Environmental concerns, however exaggerated, will moderate the global energy path, but not halt or reverse it. The world, and in particular large developing countries which are still in their early stages of development, will continue to require increasing amounts of energy to cater for their growing economies and increasing populations. Developing countries, in particular, are more concerned with their short term economies and growth rather than with long term future global environmental concerns. Correspondingly, global energy use will be moderated through efficiency, conservation, cleaner technologies and new alternatives. Environmental management is going to be a slow, lengthy, painful process of mitigation and adaptation.

The years 2008 and 2009 have been tectonic years for energy. They were the first years in history that non-OECD commercial energy consumption (at 51.2 percent) exceeded that of the OECD. In 2008, probably for the first time in history, electrical power generation in the OECD fell. Now, China's power generation exceeds that of the EU and its carbon emissions surpass those of the United States. Coal (the most polluting fuel) is the world's fastest growing energy fuel; in 2008 it grew 3.1 percent, more than twice global primary energy growth of 1.4 percent, while oil consumption fell 0.6 percent to an average of 84.45 million barrels per day (mbpd). US oil consumption fell by the large margin of 6.4 percent, i.e., 1.3 mbpd, while that of China rose by 0.26 mbpd. Simultaneously,

2008 witnessed unusual swings in oil prices from US$147.27 per barrel of oil in mid-year to less than $32.40 at year end, then up to $60 by mid-2009. Coal prices witnessed greater swings from $219 per ton to $58 per ton. Volatility, to such extent, has not been witnessed before and most likely exacerbated the financial crisis of 2008–2009.

Just as important, in early 2009 a new administration was instituted in the United States that appears to be genuinely concerned about global environmental challenges—particularly growing emissions of CO_2. This reorientation, together with the rising environmental concerns of EU countries, is likely to have an impact on the usage and future of energy. The Copenhagen meeting at end of 2009 was a demonstration of this.

Energy Security through Energy Adequacy

Energy security can be ensured by local adequacy, i.e., availability of abundant and varied forms of indigenous energy resources. In the case of local shortages, which occur in most countries, energy security can be enhanced through:

- The ability of the state, or of market players, to draw on foreign energy resources and products that can be freely imported through ports or other transport channels and through cross-boundary energy grids (pipelines and electricity networks).
- Adequate national (or regional) strategic reserves to address any transient interruption, shortages, or unpredictable surge in demand.
- Technological and financial resources and know-how to develop indigenous renewable sources and power generation facilities to meet a portion of local energy requirements.
- Adequate attention to environmental challenges.

Energy security can also be enhanced through energy management and efficiency measures. Reducing energy intensity will reduce the dependence of the economy on energy consumption and imports.

To achieve energy security first of all requires ensuring global energy adequacy—the existence of enough energy resources, or other prospects, to meet long term world energy needs.

Energy Adequacy

Energy security depends, to a great extent, on the availability of an adequate resource base. The resource base is the sum of reserves and resources. Reserves (of all types and forms of hydrocarbon deposits, natural uranium, and thorium) are known and economically recoverable with present technologies. Resources are less certain, are not economically recoverable with present technologies, or are both. In the future, with advances in technology and geophysics, many of today's resources are likely to become reserves. It is the contention of this paper that most of the world's future energy requirements, at least until the middle of the 21st century, will be met by fossil fuels (see Figure 1.1). Many attempts have been made to assess the global fossil fuel resources base; this is detailed below.

In 2008, world consumption of primary energy totaled almost 11,300 million tons of oil equivalent (Mtoe) – 9,960 Mtoe of fossil, 620 Mtoe of nuclear energy, and 720 Mtoe of hydropower. To this should be added around 1,120 Mtoe of biomass and other renewables, for a total around 12,420 Mtoe. The world's huge resource base of fossil and nuclear fuels will be adequate to meet global requirements for decades to come.

Crude Oil

Proven oil reserves have increased steadily over the past 20 years, and have almost doubled, mainly thanks to technology and because oil companies have expanded their estimates of existing reserves in already discovered fields. This optimism stems from better knowledge of the fields, increased productivity, and advances in technology. New technologies have led to more accurate estimates of reserves through better seismic (three, four and five dimensional) exploration, have improved drilling techniques (such as horizontal and offshore drilling), and have increased recovery factors – the share of oil that can be recovered – from 30 percent to 40–50 percent and higher.[4]

Figure 1.1

Share of Fuels in Global Energy Supply (1980–2030)

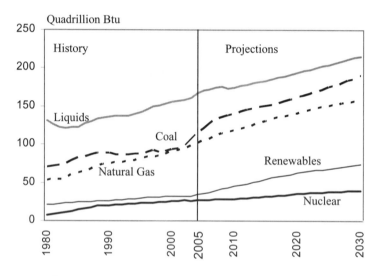

Source: IEO 2009.[5]

Huge amounts of untapped unconventional oil also exist, augmenting conventional oil reserves. Some 1.2 trillion barrels of heavy oil lie in the Orinoco oil belt in Venezuela. And the tar sands of Canada and oil shale deposits of the United States and the Russian Federation may contain 300 billion barrels of oil.

The global, ultimately recoverable stocks of conventional oil and NGLs, as they stood at end of 2007, are presented in Table 1.1.

Table 1.1
World Ultimately Recoverable Conventional Oil and NGL resources,
end-2007 (mean estimates, billion barrels)

	Initial reserves	Cumulative production	Reserves growth	Undiscovered resources	Ultimately recoverable resources	Remaining reserves	Remaining recoverable resources
	[1]	[2]	[3]	[4]	[5 =1+3+4]	[6 = 1-2]	[7 = 5-2]
OECD	458	363	27	185	670	95	307
North America	368	300	22	95	485	68	185
Europe	77	56	3	80	160	20	103
Pacific	13	7	2	10	25	6	18
Non OECD	1,911	765	375	620	2,907	1,147	2,142
Europe/low Asia	355	171	67	140	562	184	391
Asia	134	79	20	30	184	55	105
Middle East	986	312	204	257	1447	674	1,135
Africa	206	102	40	85	331	104	229
Latin America	229	100	44	108	381	129	281
World	2,369	1,128	402	805	3,577	1,241	2,449

Source: WEO 2008.

The above 2.45 trillion barrels refer to conventional oil and NGL resources. The total, long term, potentially recoverable oil resource base – including extra-heavy oil, oil sands and oil shale – depends on investment and is estimated at 4.8 to 6.5 trillion barrels. Adding coal-to-liquids (CTL) and gas-to-liquids (GTL) increases this potential by about 50 percent. Of these totals, nearly 1.1 trillion barrels have already been produced, for the most part at a cost of up to $30 per barrel in 2008 dollars (excluding taxes and royalties). The cost of exploiting remaining conventional resources typically ranges from $10 to $40 per barrel, while exploitation of oil sands costs between $30 and $80. Enhanced Oil Recovery (EOR) costs vary between $10 and $80 per barrel and oil shale from $50 to well over $100 (see Figure 1.2)

Figure 1.2
Production Costs of Oil Alternatives

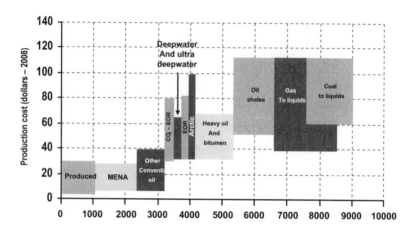

Source: WEO 2009.

The following is the minimum estimated West Texas Intermediate (WTI) oil price (2008) to justify investment in new projects in various world locations.

Table 1.2
Minimum Estimated WTI Oil Price to Justify Investment in Projects

Project Location / Type	US$ / b
Middle East	20
China	28
Libya	42
Mexico	55
Brazil	61
US Deepwater	65
Angola	71
Nigeria	78
Canadian Oil Sands	87
Venezuela Heavy Oil	114

Source: MEES, 2009.[6]

Natural Gas

As with the case of oil, ultimate natural gas reserves doubled over the last twenty years. Global proven reserves at the end of 2008 stood at close to 185 trillion cubic meters (tcm) – i.e., 167,000 Mtoe, similar to that of oil – and are equal to around 60 years of use at current production.

The US Geological Survey (USGS)[7] estimates remaining, ultimately recoverable resources of conventional natural gas at 436 tcm (390,000 Mtoe). This includes proven reserves, reserves growth and undiscovered resources, with cumulative production to 2008 amounting to only 13 percent of total initial resources. We must also consider the much larger non-conventional gas resources of over 900 tcm (810,000 Mtoe), a quarter of which are in North America, in terms of their significance to future energy security.

Taking all this together, the remaining ultimately recoverable resources of conventional and non-conventional gas can exceed 1,300 tcm, which is huge considering a consumption in 2008 of only 3 tcm.

Coal

Coal is the world's most abundant fossil fuel, with proven reserves estimated at almost 826 billion tons, equivalent to 550,000 Mtoe. At the present rate of production, these reserves should last for more than 122 years. Thus, the resource base of coal is much larger than that of oil and gas. In addition, coal reserves are more evenly distributed across the world, and coal is cheap. Efforts are being made to reduce production costs and to apply clean coal technologies to reduce the environmental impact of its use.

Coal demand is forecast to grow at a rate slightly higher than global energy demand growth. Most of this growth will be for power generation in non-OECD countries—mostly in Asia. Although trade in coal is still low, it is likely to increase slowly over time. Long-term trends in direct coal utilization are difficult to predict because of the potential impact of climate change policies. Coal gasification and liquefaction will augment global oil and gas supplies in the future.

Fossil Fuels Resource Base

To summarize, there is a considerable fossil fuels resource base, both in terms of reserves and resources, which is capable of satisfying global energy requirements for many decades to come. This is briefly summarized in Table 1.3:

Table 1.3
Fossil Fuels Resource Base (2008)
(in thousand Mtoe)

	Remaining reserves	Remaining, ultimately recoverable resources
Conventional Oil & NGL	170	335
Natural Gas	167	390
Coal	550	620

The remaining proven resources of fossil fuels amount to almost 900,000 Mtoe, with remaining, ultimately recoverable resources probably one and a half times that amount. When this is viewed against present annual consumption of fossil fuels (2008) of around 6,700 Mtoe, the future of global energy security seems secure; but it is not as simple as that.

Fossil fuels present challenges to energy security in the form of their uneven regional distribution, volatility of oil prices, increasing cost of extraction and environmentally detrimental impacts of their use. These will be dealt with in more detail later.

Nuclear Energy

Although nuclear energy is sometimes grouped with fossil fuels, it relies on a different resource base. In 2008, nuclear energy production amounted to 2,760 terawatt-hours (TWh) of electricity, replacing 620 Mtoe of other fuels, which is practically no different from figures ten years ago. Uranium requirements amounted to 67,000 tons in 2008, against reasonably assured resources (reserves) of 4.7 million tons (at $130 per kg). Ultimately recoverable reserves amount to almost 17 million tons.

Considering the relative stagnation in the growth of nuclear power, the enormous occurrences of low-grade uranium and the prospects for recycling nuclear fuels, such reserves will suffice for many decades.

Renewables

Renewable energy sources – especially hydroelectric power, biomass, wind power, and geothermal energy – account for a growing share of world energy consumption. Today hydropower and biomass together satisfy around 15 percent of global requirements.

The contribution of renewable energy – although the most fostered new form of energy – is still modest. Owing to its renewable nature it is not practical to talk about a resource base, rather to figure out the possible future energy contribution prospects of this energy source.

When dealing with renewable energy we have to consider three different resources: biomass, hydropower, and new and renewable sources like wind power, solar, bioenergy, etc.

Biomass is an important source of energy. Traditional biomass includes fuel wood – the main source of biomass energy – dung, and crop and forest residues. Lack of statistics makes it difficult to accurately estimate the contribution of renewables to the world's primary energy consumption, but it is estimated that the world consumed around 1.2 billion tons of oil equivalent (Gtoe) in 2008.[8] About two-thirds of this was from fuel wood, and the remainder from crop residues and dung. Of this around 7 percent was used to produce 240 TWh of electricity. Much of this contribution is sustainable from a supply standpoint, but the resulting energy services could be substantially increased by improving conversion efficiencies, which are typically still very low.

The contribution of biomass to world energy consumption is expected to increase slightly. It is mainly used as an energy source in low income developing countries. Today there are almost 2.5 billion people in developing countries depending on biomass for their cooking. While energy demand in these countries is steadily increasing, some of the demand is being met by switching from traditional to commercial energy sources. Biomass energy technology is rapidly advancing. Besides direct combustion, techniques for gasification, fermentation, and anaerobic digestion are all increasing the potential of biomass as a sustainable energy source.

Hydroelectricity is a valuable source of energy. It is renewable, clean and in most cases economical. Its contribution towards world electricity production is now 16 percent, more than that of nuclear (15 percent). It is not easy to estimate the future value of hydroelectricity in global energy consumption; still more difficult is to assess the economical resource base.

In 2008, hydroelectricity contributed 3,340 TWh of electricity. The efficiency of hydroelectricity production is almost 100 percent. The calorific value of this electricity accounts for 280 Mtoe, but in actual energy accounting we are more concerned with what this production saved in other energy forms. At an average efficiency of 38 percent of electricity generation this is equivalent to almost 735 Mtoe,[9] and whereas the contribution of nuclear has steadily decreased during the last three years, that of hydroelectricity increased at almost three percent annually in recent years, mostly as a result of increased production in Asian countries (China, India, Vietnam).

Hydroelectric power has still more potential. Technically exploitable hydro resources could potentially produce more than 14,000 TWh of electricity per year, equivalent to most of the world's total electricity requirements.[10] For environmental and economic reasons, however, most of these resources will not be exploited. Still, hydropower will continue to develop slowly. Hydropower is the most important among renewable energy sources. It is a clean and – in the right locations – a cheap source of energy, requiring only minimal running costs. However, owing to a shortage of potentially economically-viable sites, its annual growth will not exceed the annual growth of global energy demand.

Wind energy, in particular, has grown swiftly over the past decade, from 11 gigawatts (GW) of net installed capacity at the beginning of 2000 to 121 GW at the end of 2008—a trend that is projected to continue into the future. In 2008 its contribution is estimated to be 230 TWh rising to 660 TWh in 2015. However, wind energy suffers from many weaknesses. Beside its capital-intensive nature, it is an intermittent source of energy and can only augment existing power production facilities rather than replace them. Because of this limitation and the difficulty of incorporating wind facilities into existing power generation grids, as well as its high transmission costs, the wind power contribution to the energy resource base will continue to be limited and is not expected to exceed 1,500 TWh by 2030, which is around five percent of the world's projected electricity demand at that time. Wind power growth in most OECD countries is fostered by "feed-in tariffs," which are a form of subsidy to suppliers of wind power. Without such subsidies, its contribution and future will be in jeopardy.

The same applies to other forms of new and renewable energy sources: tidal power and waves, geothermal, concentrating solar thermal power (CSP), solar photovoltaic (PV); these will be dealt with more intensively in the study of future energy requirements. According to IEA and US Department of Energy (DOE)/Energy Information Administration (EIA) predictions, renewables can only increase their contribution to a maximum of 23 percent of total electricity generation in 2030 from the present level of 18 percent. Other than hydro, new and renewable energy will contribute nine percent in 2030 compared to three percent now.

Biofuels are a renewable source of energy and are used mainly in road transport. They take the form of ethanol and biodiesel. Biofuels contributed around 25 Mtoe in 2008 and their contribution is projected to be around 120 Mtoe in 2030, almost one fifth will be biodiesel. Their contribution as a fuel for road transport can be expected to increase from the present 1.5 percent to five percent in 2030. But their benefits and environmental worthiness are being increasingly questioned. They consume a lot of water and infringe on valuable agricultural land and food production.

Peak Oil

One of the main issues relevant to energy security is the challenge of "peak oil." Peak oil refers to the apex of production capacity, after which there will be a gradual global reduction in output. Productive capacity is the maximum sustainable level at which liquids can be produced and delivered to market. In the controversial Hubbert's[11] approach of 1982, peak production occurs when half of the global inventory of supply has been produced. However, this approach errs by considering only proven plus probable conventional reserves, which amount to around 2.3 trillion barrels, ignoring the remaining categories of conventional and unconventional reserves and resources, which could ultimately double the earlier amounts.

In a recent study by Cambridge Energy Research Associates (CERA),[12] global oil resources could amount to approximately 4.8 billion barrels, of which 1.1 billion barrels has already been produced. No doubt production of these ultimately limited resources will peak, but what is also important is sustainable production after the peak, which CERA calls an "undulating plateau of supply after the peak." This is demonstrated in Figure 1.3.

Figure 1.3

Oil Production Scenario

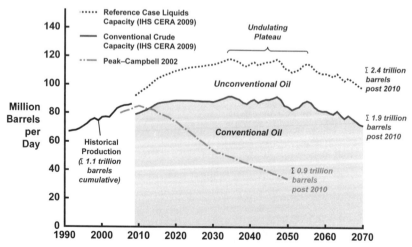

Source: CERA, see note 12.

To summarize, there will be no expected revolutions in the global energy scene but only a slow evolution. Fossil fuels, which presently dominate the global energy scene, will continue to do so for decades to come, with oil being the most important fuel in global energy use and trade. The increasing concentration of fossil resources (particularly oil) in only a few countries may pose challenges to global energy security, as will environmental concerns and potential global environmental agreements or legislation. All this will have important implications for the energy scene and world energy security. Owing to the high inertia of the sector, its extensive capital nature, abundant availability of fossil fuels and limitation of alternatives, the global energy scene up to year 2050 can be roughly determined.

In our quest for global energy security we should be concerned with "peak demand," rather than "peak oil," and with improving oil extraction to make more oil available to meet this peak demand. Presently, oil recovery factors are being improved from the traditional 35 percent to 50 percent, but by improved enhanced oil recovery (EOR) techniques an ultimate goal of 80 percent can be achieved in 2030.[13]

In terms of efficiency, only 39 percent of energy input is converted to useable energy, while 61 percent is lost in conversion. Similarly, only 13 percent of reservoir barrels are converted to usable energy. This can be doubled by 2030. If this is achieved, oil requirements, at that date will be almost halved, thus stretching usable oil reserves decades into the future.

Future Challenges to Global Energy Security

In the previous section this paper demonstrated that the world is not likely to face insurmountable shortages in energy resources for decades to come. The global fossil fuel resource base is huge, conventional resources of oil, gas and coal are abundant and not likely to peak in the near future, any depletion is being replaced by new discoveries, and advances in technology. Once existing conventional resources peak, they will be supplemented by non-conventional resources, mostly still untapped. Renewables – other than traditional biomass and hydro – although still modest, are growing at a fast rate and will augment existing resources to meet future demand. The growth of future demand is being greatly moderated by efficiency and energy management technologies, spearheaded not only by the need for economy but also by important environmental concerns.

Therefore, it does not seem that there will be a looming energy shortage crisis, resource wise, until the end of this century. The energy security challenges most likely lie elsewhere: in geography, volatility of markets and environment. This is what will be dealt with in this section.

Geography: The Uneven Distribution of Resources

Fossil fuels, which are the most important energy resource, are not evenly distributed worldwide. This particularly applies to oil, which is the most versatile energy fuel. Almost 60 percent of proven oil reserves exist in a limited number of countries of the Middle East, a geographical area not renowned for its stability. This poses a challenge to world energy security. More than half of the world's proven reserves of natural gas (53 percent) exist in three countries (Russia, Iran and Qatar) which are far from consumption centers. Coal is more evenly distributed geographically, but still there are heavy concentrations of reserves in certain geographical areas. Almost two thirds of proven coal reserves exist in the United States, Russia and China, all of which are heavy users of coal. This diversity between the location of resources and centers of demand poses a serious challenge to energy security from the perspective of most countries, particularly large economies, driving them to diversify their resources as much as possible and to seek alternatives. This only partially eases the problem. Oil, which is the most important and versatile energy source, is the most uneven in terms of geographical location and distribution, as we see in Table 1.4.

Table 1.4

Geographical Distribution of Proven Reserves of Fossil Fuel

	Reserves	World Population	Consumption
Oil			
North America	05.6%	6.6%	27.4%
Europe & Eurasia	11.3%	13.3%	24.3%
The Middle East	60.0%	3.2%	7.8%
Natural Gas			
North America	04.8%		27.6%
Europe & Eurasia	34.0%		37.8%
The Middle East	41.0%		10.8%
Coal			
North America	29.8%		18.4%
Europe & Eurasia	33.0%		15.8%
The Middle East	04.0%		0.3%

Source: BP Statistical Review 2009.

An important 40 percent of world proven oil reserves and one third of proven gas reserves exist in six Arab Gulf countries, which account for less than one percent of the world population (see the Statistical Annex). This demonstrates the crucial importance of the Gulf countries to global energy security. It also demonstrates the security issues facing major users in ensuring adequate and sustainable supplies—particularly oil for transport, for which there is no practical alternative for the foreseeable future.

Prices: Volatility and Uncertainty

Historically speaking, all fossil fuels have witnessed volatility and large swings in prices. This not only applies to the spot prices of crude oil, but also to trade in coal and LNG. But at no time have energy prices witnessed the extreme volatility they experienced in 2008 and the first half of 2009. Prices of crude oil swung from a peak of $147 per barrel in mid-2008 to less than $40/b at the end of the year. Prices of natural gas and LNG, which were relatively stable through the 1990s, doubled during the last few years and almost redoubled once more on average during 2008. The same applies to coal, a fuel which was known for its stability and low price—it reached unprecedented highs in 2008, averaging $150 per ton in Europe, but actually swinging between $219/ton to $58/ton. What has happened in oil prices since beginning of 2004, but particularly since 2007, has been unexpected. Prices which averaged $28/b at the end of 2003 rocketed to $74/b in mid-2006. In July 2008, WTI prices were over $147/b, an all-time record in nominal as well as in real terms. This was a second oil shock, as important as that of the first in 1974, but for different reasons.

It is not intended here to analyze the reasons behind this volatility, which was mainly caused by the disappearance of oil production reserve margins, and by market fundamentals, as demand – particularly of middle distillates – exceeded oil-refining capacity. Price rises were also assisted by depreciation in the value of the dollar versus other currencies, as well as by some speculation and panic price overshooting. What we are concerned with is the impact of this volatility on global energy security as well as its economic and strategic implications for both importing and exporting countries. Volatility in energy prices affects production costs as well as the social costs to importing countries. Energy costs can amount to as high as five percent of the GDP of large economies and more than twice that in smaller energy-importing countries. The implications of volatility on such a significant part of the world's economies are tremendous, leading to difficulties in budgeting, increases in the cost of outputs and services, unemployment, as well as variations in prices in the local market and social strains. The global financial crisis of 2008 was deepened by high energy prices.

The following figure displays the volatility of oil expenditures as a share of GDP:

Figure 1.4

Oil Expenditures as a Percentage of GDP[14]

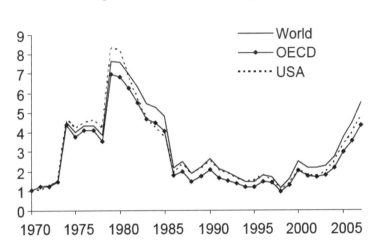

Source: OIES-WPM35.

Volatility is also a problem for energy exporters; budgeting becomes precarious, low prices will cause income shortages and high prices pose a problem in dealing with and managing surpluses, often leading to overspending. Such income and budgeting problems are not only restricted to the oil exporters but also affect their neighbors and labor exporting countries, which depend on remittances as well as on revenues from exports of goods and services to oil-rich countries. For energy-exporting countries, export security is becoming as important as import security is to resource-short countries. All this enhances the prospects for global energy cooperation and security.

In energy prices we need to be concerned with annual averages or a two- to three-year period rather than peaks or troughs which only persist for weeks or even days. Still, the volatility of 2008, not only in oil prices but also in all fossil fuels, is unprecedented and is unlikely to be repeated.

It is not possible to predict future oil prices but most importing countries are learning how to mitigate negative and high volatility by increasing local and regional strategic reserves, diversifying sources and forms of energy and reducing energy intensity in their economies. This paper relies on two price predictions detailed in Table 1.5. One of them was made by the IEA during the height of the energy price volatility of 2008; the other is that of the DOE/EIA and was made during first half of 2009.

Table 1.5
2030 Predicted Oil Prices ($2007 per barrel)

IEA	DOE/EIA
125 Reference	130 Reference
	200 High
	50 Low

Sources: International Energy Assessment (IEA), *World Energy Outlook* 2008; US Dept. of Energy, Energy Information Administration (DOE/EIA), *International Energy Outlook* 2009.

The IEA and DOE/EIA reference prices are almost identical, and with the present state of knowledge such a price is the most likely outcome. A $130/b price in 2030 (in 2007 dollars), implies a price of around $230/b in 2030 (in that year's dollars).

In view of the DOE/EIA prices, in the long term on a worldwide basis, the projections for economic growth are not greatly affected by oil price assumptions. There are, however, some relatively large regional impacts. The most significant variations are that for some oil-short regions outside the Middle East, annual GDP decreases by around 2.0 percent in the high price case relative to the reference case in 2015, leading to a 5.5 percent increase in GDP in 2015 in the oil-exporting Middle East region. The regional differences persist into the long term, with annual GDP in the Middle East about 6.2 percent higher in 2030 in the high oil price case than in the reference case, and GDP in some oil-importing regions (such as OECD Europe and Japan) between 2.0 percent and 3.0 percent lower in the high price case than in the reference case. This is not insignificant, and demonstrates the impact of long term high oil prices on economies of importing countries.

Environmental Policies and Energy Security

This paper does not intend to explore the environmental debate in detail—this is now well documented in most energy and environmental literature and reported almost daily in the quality press. It ranges from scientific and meaningful analysis to exaggerated doomsday scenarios of extreme rising temperatures, melting of glaciers, disappearing islands and coastal cities, etc. However there is a consensus that GHGs, particularly CO_2, are gradually concentrating in the atmosphere. This is caused both by anthropogenic emissions – mainly the use of fossil fuels (75%) – as well as deforestation.

In its 2007 Assessment Report,[15] the Inter-governmental Panel on Climate Change (IPCC) concluded that: "warming of the climate system is unequivocal, as is now evident from observations of increasing global average air and ocean temperatures, widespread melting of snow and ice, and rising global average sea level." The report claims "very high confidence" (more than 90 percent probability) that anthropogenic carbon dioxide (CO_2) emissions are driving climate change. According to the IPCC report, the global average surface temperature of the Earth has increased by approximately 0.8 degrees Celsius (or 1.4 Fahrenheit) since 1750, and the rate of warming has increased in recent decades. GHG concentrations in the atmosphere have increased since the 1700s owing to increasing GHG emissions. The report also states that CO_2 is the most important GHG. The concentration of CO_2 in the atmosphere has increased from 280 parts per million (ppm) in pre-industrial times to 379 ppm in 2005. Recent growth rates are a result of CO_2 emission increases of 1.9 ppm/year. Over the past 30 years alone, CO_2 emissions have increased by 70 percent.

IPCC findings and predictions have lately come under increased calls for review from different academic and scientific groups. However, IPCC projects global warming at the rate of 0.2 degrees per decade over the next 20 years, under a variety of world economic scenarios. Even if the emissions of CO_2 and other GHGs were halted today, the climate would continue to change and sea levels would continue to rise, since the Earth's surface is slow to respond to changes in atmospheric concentrations of GHGs. But without effective global policy intervention, greater warming and more dramatic levels of climate change can be expected, including additional ice melting, higher sea level rises (in the magnitude of anywhere from 0.18 to 0.59 meters, depending on the levels of future GHG concentrations), and alterations of natural systems such as ocean acidification, changes in wind patterns, and increased heat extremes.

The implications of all of this on energy security will be significant. It will encourage national policies and global agreements to limit carbon emissions through reducing the use of fossil fuels. It will also encourage the development of carbon-free renewables and similar forms of energy, particularly hydropower, wind power, nuclear and solar. However, we have already indicated that the potential of these sources is limited, to ensure energy security the world will have to continue to depend for decades to come on fossil fuels. This is the dilemma of the environmental debate.

Fossil fuels differ in their carbon content. Coal has the highest carbon content, while natural gas is relatively the cleanest as detailed in Table 1.6.[16]

Table 1.6

Global Carbon Emissions of Fossil Fuels
(tons per ton of oil equivalent [TOE])

	Tons of carbon per TOE	CO_2
Coal	1.08	3.96
Fuel Oil	0.84	3.07
Natural gas	0.64	2.34

Each ton of emitted carbon releases 3.67 tons of CO_2 into the atmosphere. Therefore of all fossil fuels it is coal which is the most polluting. Still, it is the fuel that is vastly rising in demand. This only indicates that most countries still place more emphasis on meeting their immediate energy security and short term economy requirements than long term environmental impacts.

Since 1990, world energy-related CO_2 emissions increased in almost all regions of the world, as demonstrated in Table 1.7.

Table 1.7

Growth in Energy-Related CO_2 Emissions (1990–2010)
(billion metric tons)

	1990	**Expected 2010**	**Average Annual Growth in Emissions**
North America	5.8	6.8	0.80%
Europe	4.1	4.3	0.24%
Asia	5.3	12.7	4.47%
Other	6.3	7.2	0.66%
Total World	21.5	31.0	1.84%

Source: IEO 2009.

The IEO 2009 estimates that over the period 2006–2030 the CO_2 emissions related to energy use will grow annually at a rate of 1.4 percent, which is much reduced from the 1.9 percent over the 1990–2006 period, mainly thanks to rationalization and efficiency in energy use inspired by environmental considerations. Of all countries it is only Japan that is expected to reduce its emissions by an average of 0.3 percent annually over the period to 2030, while those of the USA will likely continue to grow by 0.3 percent annually and those of China by 2.8 percent.

It is coal, with its high carbon content, that is expected to increase its contribution to meet world energy demand from the present 27 percent to around 28 percent in 2030, contributing more to world energy-related CO_2 emissions than any other energy-form as demonstrated in the following figure.

Figure 1.5

Contribution of Different Fossil Fuels to CO_2 Emissions

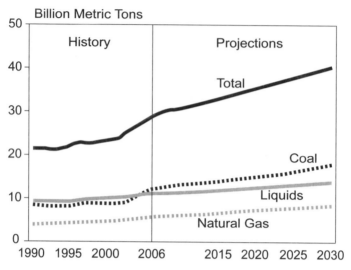

Source: IEO 2009.

It must be acknowledged that most coal resources exist in the world's most intensive energy-consuming nations: United States (29.8 percent), Russia (19.0 percent), China (13.9 percent) and India (7.2 percent). These countries, in order to improve their energy security, will increasingly rely on their indigenous coal resources to satisfy their energy needs. This national interest will possibly take precedence over any other consideration or environmental long-term implication. In spite of any future international agreements about emissions, it is decisions being made today, in the real world of the energy sector, rather than environmental considerations that will shape the future of energy. A coal power station built today will be there in 2050, emitting large amounts of CO_2; cars running on liquids will survive for decades to come; and a gas pipeline of today will continue to be carrying gas to consumption centers well into the middle of this century. The extent of future emissions is being decided by investment made today and in the near foreseeable future.

Environmental considerations have, and will continue to steadily affect the world energy sector. This will lead to more efficient utilization of energy sources, conservation by solicitation, taxation and legislation, and the promotion of alternatives to fossil fuels whenever possible. But it will be a slow, lengthy and a painful process. There is no escape from the fact that for decades to come, increased emissions of carbon into the atmosphere through energy-related activities will continue. The world needs not only to concentrate on processes for mitigation but also adaptation to this fact.

Energy efficiency is a very important source of emissions reduction which can reduce the overall costs of mitigation since gains from energy savings can offset some of the capital cost of such measures. To a lesser extent, the technologies of carbon capture and storage (CCS) hold great promise, in the long term, particularly in terms of the use of coal in electrical power generation. However, progress in this regard has, until recently, been slow. In order to assess the value of these technologies, as well as other promising energy efficiency practices, it will be useful to assign a value for CO_2 abatement. A figure of $50 per ton of CO_2 was recently proposed.[17] This figure can be used to assess and prioritize technologies for abatement. However, its accuracy depends on the future discount rate used.

Several fiscal options for reducing CO_2 measures have been proposed and some of them already adopted. The most important are "Cap and Trade" systems (CTS), which have already been adopted by the European Union through its emission trading scheme (ETS). Other measures have been proposed in the United States, such as regulation of the transportation sector, a carbon tax, an energy tax, or a hybrid approach.[18]

All these measures have implications for energy technologies and interfere in markets. They are clearly biased against intensive use of fossil fuels and favor mitigation measures as well as lower-carbon sources. Gradually these measures will be adopted in OECD countries, leading to lower growth rates of emissions. However, it is unknown how and when such measures will be adopted by countries outside the OECD – particularly China, India and Russia – where most of the world's growth in CO_2 emissions is occurring. This was debated at the UN environmental conference in Copenhagen in December 2009, but without a conclusive agreement.

A number of studies have been undertaken to determine ways to reduce GHG emissions, one of the most important of these is *Energy Technology Perspectives 2008* by the IEA.[19] Looking ahead to 2050 it includes two basic scenarios:[20]

- ACT Scenario: Global energy-related emissions are returned back to the current (i.e., 2005) level by 2050 and the CO_2 concentration in the atmosphere is stabilized at the level of some 520 ppm (corresponding to a global temperature increase of more than 2.4°C according to the IPCC [2007]).

- BLUE Scenario: Global energy-related emissions are reduced by 50 percent over the current level by 2050 and the CO_2 concentration in the atmosphere is stabilized at the level of some 450 ppm (corresponding to a global temperature increase of 2.0–2.4°C [IPCC]).

It does not now look possible to implement a scenario like that of the BLUE, and it will take all the goodwill in the world with international agreements, mitigation measures, etc., to implement the ACT scenario. It is based on a marginal CO_2 abatement cost of $50 per ton of CO_2 (against a present EU/ETS CO_2 price of 14 Euros per ton). It will involve an extra global investment of $17 trillion over the next four decades. More than that, it will mean reaching global agreements, consensus and cooperation—none of which are easy to achieve.

How Secure is our Energy Future?

It is not intended here to go into intensive predictions or scenarios of the path that the world energy industry is expected to take. Instead we shall refer to work already conducted by three energy study groups in the IEA,

DOE–EIA and WEC.[21] These studies mostly undertake predictions into the medium-term (2030); what we should be concerned with is outlook in the long-term, i.e., to year 2050.

As has been emphasized throughout this study, the future behavior of the energy sector is very much influenced by its inertia. Energy facilities (power stations, refineries, pipelines, exploration, etc.) are highly capital-intensive and have long lives. Thirty to forty years is the normal life of an energy facility. So they are not easily or economically replaced. The energy sector is not like the telecommunications sector with its rapid technological change, innovation, and cheap and easily replaceable gadgets. In energy we are dealing with the other extreme. Owing to the capital-intensive and long-life nature of these facilities, a good part of the future of the sector is being decided today.

These decisions will, however, be influenced and moderated by a number of important factors, including world economic growth, availability of resources, technological development, and environmental concerns.

Concerning the availability of resources, this has already been covered thoroughly in the first section. Fossil fuels, in their three main forms, are abundant, highly efficient and concentrated, tradable and relatively cheap. There is no foreseeable alternative to oil for transportation. New and renewable energy sources (other than hydro) are rapidly growing but from a low base. Therefore their short- and medium-term contributions, although very much publicized, will continue to be modest. They suffer from their small size, low concentration, intermittency of sources, need for storage and difficulty in collection and transmission. Nuclear energy, although a viable and safe source of energy in the right hands, faces a lot of popular opposition, particularly in European countries. This, beside its high capital requirements, will serve to restrict its short- and medium-term outlook.

One of the most important factors that will affect future world energy security and outlook is the growing influence of environmental considerations—whether justified or exaggerated. These considerations encourage renewables, and discourage growth or dependence on fossil fuels. They also call for mitigation mainly through technology and improvement in efficiency of energy production and utilization. Such improved efficiency would assist in de-coupling economic growth from mirror increases in energy consumption. In past periods of cheap energy – before the mid-1970s – economic growth was tightly coupled with an equal growth in energy consumption. This 1:1 gearing has now been tremendously reduced through energy efficiency, thus significantly reducing energy intensity in the world economy. A leading cause of this is not only the rising price of energy but also environmental concerns. This is a factor which will significantly influence the field of energy in the future.

These are facts that are recognized by forward-looking energy studies produced by high-quality study groups and institutions such as the IEA, DOE–EIA and WEC. The following future outlook benefits from their work. Here we shall deal with the three main energy components: consumption (and regional location), prices and investment.

Predication of Medium-Term Energy Consumption

The WEC study[22] looks ahead to 2050, and is therefore less definitive than medium-term studies. It presents many scenarios, the most likely of which envisages an average annual energy demand growth of 1.6 percent.

The following is a brief summary of both the IEA and the DOE–EIA energy consumption predictions for the medium-term. These both relate to the period 2006–2030, and refer to the basic scenario.

The IEA and DOE–EIA consumption predictions are quite similar. The EIA figures in IEO 2009, being more recent, present a fairly moderate annual growth figure for consumption—1.5 percent compared to 1.6 percent. Both assume that coal will register the higher growth figure among fossil fuels (almost twice that of oil), closely followed by natural gas. Nuclear is expected to grow under both scenarios, but at a rate lower than that of fossil fuels. Others (biomass, hydro and other renewables) are expected to grow at almost three percent annually, i.e., twice world energy growth. However, the new and other renewables (wind, solar, etc.), in spite of the publicity they receive, will only satisfy six percent of global electricity consumption in 2030; demonstrating their limitations, as already explained.[23]

Table 1.8

Future World Energy: Mid-Term Predictions

	IEA		DOE–EIA	
	Mtoe 2030	Annual Growth % (2006–2030)	Mtoe 2030	Annual Growth % (2006–2030)
Coal	4,908	2.0%	4,750	1.7%
Oil (liquids)	5,109	1.0%	5,393	0.9%
Gas	3,670	1.8%	3,950	1.6%
Nuclear	901	0.9%	1,005	1.6%
Hydro	414	1.9%	1,852	3.0%
Biomass	1,662	1.4%		
Other Renewables	350	7.2%		
World Total	**17,014**	**1.6%**	**16,960**	**1.5%**

Sources: IEO 2009; WEO 2008.

The most important conclusion of these predictions is that in the mid-term – year 2030 – fossil fuels will still satisfy 83 percent of world energy consumption, almost identical to that of 2006 consumption, indicating the inertia of the energy system. Still, there are shifts in usage of fossil fuels; coal use will grow to almost twice that of oil because of the abundant availability of indigenous coal resources in the large consumption centers of the United States, China, India and Russia. In spite of global worries about CO_2 emissions, coal – the dirtiest of fuels – is expected to continue to be the strongest in terms of demand growth owing to its geographic locations. This indicates that it is economic considerations and countries' energy security interests that will continue to be the most important factor in determining future energy consumption considerations.

The most recent DOE–EIA predictions (May 2009) are based on an average real world gross domestic product (GDP) growth of 3.5 percent annually over the period 2006–2030. When this is compared with the 1.5 percent expected annual increase in global energy consumption, it implies an estimated two percentage points drop in annual energy growth owing to efficiency improvements over the same period. Therefore, the implied elasticity in demand for energy in the world economy (unity in the period preceding 1973), dropped to 0.59 during the period 1990–2006, and is now expected to drop further to 0.43, a trend that is likely to continue (see Table 1.9).

Table 1.9

Growth in Energy Consumption and World Economy

	Average annual GDP growth %		Average annual growth in energy consumption (%)		Elasticity Energy/ Economy	
	1990– 2006	2006– 2030	1990– 2006	2006– 2030	1990– 2006	2006– 2030
OECD	2.5	2.2	1.3	0.6	0.52	0.27
Non-OECD	4.4	4.9	2.7	2.3	0.61	0.47
World	3.2	3.5	1.9	1.5	0.59	0.43

Source: IEO 2009; WEO 2008.

When the estimated energy consumption increase of 1.5 percent annually in 2006–2030 is compared to that of growth in world population (growth of around one percent annually), we notice an increase of almost 0.5 percent annually in energy consumption per capita over the same period. This is mainly a result of improving worldwide living standards, particularly in developing countries, and the conversion to commercial energy forms from biomass and other non-commercial forms of energy.

What is of concern to us in here is the predicted growth of CO_2 emissions, which – according to IEO 2009 – are expected to grow at a rate of 1.4 percent over the period 2006–2030, from 29 billion tons of CO_2 in

2006 to 40.39 billion tons in 2030. The conclusions are clear: in spite of environmental concerns, mitigation efforts and the outcry against emissions, these are predicted to continue to grow at a high rate of almost 1.4 percent annually in the coming two decades. The world must adapt to this fact.

Future Price Predictions

In this section we are concerned with predicting future oil prices. Oil prices, particularly as we have seen over the period 2008–2009, can be somewhat volatile. This is caused by: low OPEC production margins; limited refining capacity; local and regional political and security considerations; as well as the weakness of the US dollar. Limited oil price volatility over the coming years can be expected and this will affect world energy security.

In the following short analysis we are concerned with future oil price trends. The IEO 2009 considers three cases of world oil prices, over the period up to 2030. In the reference case, world price rises from an average $61 per barrel in 2009 (in real 2007 dollars) to $110 per barrel in 2015 and $130 per barrel in 2030 ($189 per barrel in nominal terms), for an average consumption of 112 mbpd in 2030. In the low price case, oil prices average $50 per barrel in 2030 ($73 per barrel in nominal terms), compared with $200 per barrel ($289 per barrel in nominal terms) in the high price case. The projections for total liquids consumption in 2030 range from 90 mbpd in the high price case to 120 mbpd in the low price case, reflecting a substantial range of uncertainty in the projections.

In the WEO 2008, the IEA import crude oil prices are assumed in the reference scenario to average $100 over the period 2008–2015 and linearly rise to $122 in 2030 (all in real 2007 dollars). When considerations are taken of different prices of oil between IEA import crude and WTI, there are only minor differences in the two predicted price estimates. Realizing that IEO 2009 predictions were undertaken early in 2009, after the 2008 volatility, they represent sound estimates in view of the prevailing circumstances. These imply that oil prices will slowly increase in real terms from the present $65–75 range in 2009 dollars to an average of $130 per barrel in 2030 (also in 2009 dollars). This implies a doubling over twenty years, i.e., an average increase in oil prices of 3.5 percent annually in real terms. This is a significant price increase.

Oil prices lead the energy markets with real annual increases; the other fuels in the energy market are expected to follow. However, the price of gas by pipeline is mostly restricted by long term supply contracts, while LNG deliveries have more price freedom. This is also likely to apply to trade in coal which has recently exhibited extreme volatility.

Future Energy Investment Forecast

Adequate investments in the energy sector are imperative to ensure global energy security. The energy sector, as has been emphasized throughout this paper, is highly capital-intensive. Investments are needed to expand supply capacity, develop new resources and build facilities as well as to replace aging equipment or depleted wells. Recently, in the period 2000–2008, costs of investment in the energy sector have almost doubled, mainly as a result of the rising costs of metals and materials (see Figure 1.6), although some easing in these material costs has taken place in recent months.

Figure 1.6

Prices of Metals (2000–2008)

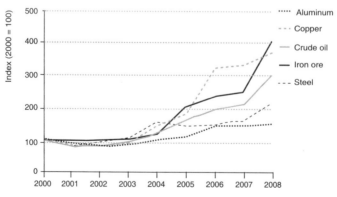

Source: IMF, WEO 2008.

The IEA estimates energy sector investment requirements to be $26 trillion (2007 dollars) over the period 2007–2030, that is slightly more than a trillion dollars per year. Over the same period world GDP will average $70 trillion annually. Assuming 10 percent as being the average world gross capital formation, this will be $7 trillion on average during that period. With such figures energy investments will constitute almost 1.5 percent of the world's GDP and almost 15 percent of its investments, which is an impressive figure.

More than half of this will go into the electrical power sector. The ratio was even higher during the 1990s—almost 60 percent to two thirds. Half of the power sector investments will be devoted to power generation, the rest to network and control. The WEO 2008 estimates investments to be allocated as in Table 1.10.

Table 1.10
Estimate of Future Energy Sector Investments (2008–2030)
(US$ Trillion [2007])

	OECD	Non-OECD	World
Power	5.7	7.9	13.6
Oil	1.4	4.6	6.0
Gas	2.3	3.0	5.3
Coal	0.2	0.5	0.7
Inter-regional transport	–	–	0.4
Total	9.6	16.0	26.1

Source: WEO 2008.

As expected, oil will receive the larger share of energy resource investment; closely followed by natural gas. Coal investments – owing to limited mining requirements – are normally minor compared to that of oil and gas.

The availability of adequate funds for energy investments, particularly considering the present world financial crisis, is becoming more difficult both for national oil companies (NOCs) and international companies.

Procurement of such investment is a major challenge. Shortages in investment funds, which are not unlikely, will only lead to energy shortages, pushing up the price of oil and other forms of energy, and leading to world energy insecurity.

Electrical Power and World Energy Security

Owing to its significance to global energy security, a special section is allocated here to electrical power, its availability and the value of its security.

Electrical power generation constitutes an important component in the energy chain. Electricity is the most important energy carrier—as it provides the means to convert fossil fuels as well as renewables and nuclear energy into a useful energy for utilization in industry, commerce and in homes. Electricity is the only form in which the primary energy of most renewables and nuclear can be conveyed and utilized. Thanks to its usefulness and versatility, electricity consumption is growing at a faster rate than that of primary energy consumption, as is detailed in Table 1.11.

Table 1.11

Electrical Energy Generation and Growth Prospects to 2030 (trillion kWh)

Fuels	2006	2010	2030	Average Annual Growth % (2006–2030)
Coal	7.4	8.7	13.8	2.5
Natural Gas	3.6	4.2	6.8	2.7
Hydro & other renewables	3.4	4.1	6.7	2.9
Nuclear	2.7	2.8	3.8	1.5
Liquids	0.9	0.9	0.9	-0.1
Total World Electricity	18.0	20.6	31.8	2.4
Fuels Equivalent (Mtoe)	4,500	5,000	7,100	1.9
World Energy (Mtoe)	11,800	12,700	17,000	1.5
Electricity Fuels/ Energy	38%	39%	42%	–

Source: IEO 2009 and author calculations.

Notes: Assumption: average generation efficiency 34% (2006); 35% (2010); 38% (2030).

It is obvious from the above table that electricity production will soon claim 40 percent of world primary energy fuels, making it the most important user of primary energy—more than transport or industry. Of primary importance in the electricity production business is:

- The relatively low conversion efficiency of electricity production. At most, of one unit of primary energy input only one third is converted to useful electrical output. The rest is wasted heat, emitted through the chimney and in cooling. Improving electrical generation efficiency will go a long way towards reducing fuel input as well as carbon emissions.

- Electricity production accounts for the world's major use of coal, which is the main global pollutant. Table 1.12 shows the share of electricity in global coal consumption.

Table 1.12

Share of Coal Usage in Electricity Production

Year	Coal for Electricity (Mtoe)	Total Coal (Mtoe)	Electricity %
2006	1860	3042	61%
2010	2160	3400	63%
2030	3260	4800	68%

- Investment in electrical power facilities is the most capital intensive investment in the energy sector and presently constitutes more than half of total world energy investments.

- By present trends, and by the middle of this century, almost half of the world's primary energy will be targeted towards electricity generation. Furthermore, by that time electricity will meet most of the final energy use in OECD countries.

Consequently, electricity production is crucial to world energy security issues. Still, as of today there are almost 1.5 billion people in developing countries worldwide who have no access to electricity and still depend on biomass, thus impeding their development and global well-being.

To summarize, the future risks and challenges to global energy security are serious and should not be underestimated. They call for understanding and global cooperation to ensure a steady and sustainable supply of energy sources to world economies in order to maintain development and improve people's welfare. In the following list we summarize these challenges and offer proposals for meeting them:

- The world now depends (over 80 percent) on fossil fuels to supply its energy requirements. These are depletable in the long term. There is no foreseeable medium-term alternative to fossil fuels to satisfy world energy consumption. However, there are enough oil, gas and coal resources in conventional and non-conventional form to supply the required fuels well into second half of this century.

- Fossil fuel supplies – particularly crude oil which is the most versatile of energy resources – are not evenly distributed throughout the world. More than half of global oil resources are situated in the Gulf region, a part of the world which has experienced security threats and challenges during recent years, many of them caused by its oil wealth. It is essential to work towards security in this strategic part of the world, and also along the sea routes of oil and LNG tankers.

- New renewable energy sources suffer – and will continue to do so for some time – from inherent weaknesses (technical and economical) that handicap their credibility as a dependable energy source, even in the medium term. Nuclear power, which is a proven and viable energy source, is not accepted by the people of most developed economies, which delays its mobilization as a badly needed energy source.

- Fossil fuel utilization is the main source of anthropogenic emissions of GHGs into the atmosphere. In spite of all efforts to curtail increasing emissions, they will continue to rise in the foreseeable future, calling for mitigation and efficiency measures, as well as development of carbon sinks. The global economy, which is expected to grow at an average of 3–3.5 percent annually over the next two decades, is expected to witness less than half that growth (1.5% annually) in energy consumption, the rest will be absorbed by improved efficiency in use. These efficiency measures need to be encouraged and extended to cover all forms of energy consumption since they represent the most economical means to limit emissions. Development of sinks and reflectors (forests, white roofs, etc.) as well as CCS technologies, regulation, taxation and similar mitigation measures are likely to lead to the stabilization of CO_2 emissions by mid-century.

- Oil prices, owing to limited alternatives, are expected to increase steadily in real terms over the next few decades and to witness some volatility (hopefully not as serious as that during the 2008–2009 period). This will put a serious economic strain on many developing countries, where energy imports constitute a significant portion of their budgets. These countries in particular should attempt to phase out any subsidies (other than life-line tariffs) in their economies to avoid any unnecessary energy imports.

- Development of energy resources is a high-capital investment business. Most upstream development of the oil and gas business is now being undertaken by national oil and gas companies. The ability of these national companies to mobilize state funds or attract other financial resources to finance expansion and development to meet global future demand is a genuine source of worry in terms of world energy security.

Global Energy Security: Implications for the Gulf

In the previous three sections we reviewed the world's energy resources, their forms, locations and adequacy, the future global economy and its energy linkages, as well as environmental challenges to world energy security. In this section we review their implications for the Gulf, mainly the six GCC states of the Arabian Peninsula (Saudi Arabia, Kuwait, UAE, Qatar, Bahrain and Oman). In this regard, the following considerations are particularly relevant:

- The Gulf countries contain almost 500 thousand million barrels of proven oil reserves (40 percent of the world's proven oil reserves and half of OPEC reserves) and 42 tcm of proven reserves of natural gas (23 percent of world and 45 percent of OPEC reserves). The population of the Gulf represents less than one percent of the world population. This disparity breeds geographical, security, wealth, political and other issues. (See Statistical Annex for the Gulf's energy endowment.)

- There will be no alternative to fossil fuels for decades to come— well into the middle of this century. New alternative and renewable energy resources have not lived up to their promise and are unlikely to do so in the foreseeable future. Oil, thanks to its versatility and its tradability, is the most important energy resource, particularly for transportation. Therefore this resource will remain the center of attention – politically as well as in terms of security – of major energy consuming countries, and particularly the United States, EU and China, which are major importers of oil.

- The Gulf region has a relatively large area but it is sparsely populated, with large deserts. The Middle East region has a history of instability.

- The Gulf countries and their limited populations depend, to a large extent, on vast numbers of foreign workers and skilled expatriate staff, many of whom are single. The dependability on such a large and varied foreign labor force during possible future regional disturbances should be a source of concern to the Gulf countries and those who consume their energy resources.

- The Gulf countries, in their endeavor to preserve their wealth, are rightly anxious to develop their energy resources through state-owned national oil and gas companies. Their oil wealth is guarded by sometimes overzealous legislative councils. The world oil and gas industry and its future development require a lot of capital, expertise and sophisticated technology. The ability of Gulf countries to mobilize financial, technical and human resources – nationally or internationally – on their own in order to achieve the necessary increase in oil output as demanded by world markets, is a major concern to world energy security as well as to the countries concerned.

- Much of the world trade in oil (almost 25 percent) passes through the straits of Hormuz and Bab El-Mandeb and is likely to continue to do so for the foreseeable future. These two waterways are surrounded by not always friendly neighbors and have recently been subject to piracy. This is a source of alarm for major importing countries, who have called for a stronger land and seaborne military presence in the region.

- Global environmental awareness is gaining strength and targeting crude oil in particular (in spite of the fact that it is less polluting than coal, which is abundant in some major consuming countries). This has led to calls for carbon taxation and other fiscal means to rationalize future consumption. Oil is the most heavily taxed commodity in Europe, with taxation exceeding the cost of imports by many times. These high prices, which benefit only marginally the oil exporters, are breeding negative publicity for the oil exporters and their commodity.

- Gulf countries are depleting their main – and for some, sole – resource in order to fuel the world economy and maintain the welfare of economies and communities mainly in OECD countries. Are these efforts (and long term sacrifices) appreciated and properly compensated or rewarded?

[59]

- Are Gulf countries building their indigenous capabilities – particularly manpower and infrastructure – for a long term sustainable future in the second half of this century and beyond, when their natural resources will be mainly depleted? Are they employing their surpluses and managing their wealth funds wisely to cater for possibly difficult future years?

- Are Gulf countries wisely consuming their own energy resources internally? Subsidized internal consumption of oil, gas and electricity is leading to overuse and the wastage and diversion of scarce recourses away from the more lucrative export market. These practices are creating a culture of wastefulness that is difficult to correct in difficult times.

- Gulf countries are creating large fiscal surpluses. Countries with surpluses tend to overspend. Correspondingly, there are large allocations to defense and military expenditure. Are these allocations justified?

- Also, financial surpluses are creating a strong tendency to invest in highly capital intensive nuclear power—this in a region over-rich in natural gas, which is the cheap and ideal fuel for electricity production. Is this a rational approach?

- The Gulf is the world's driest in terms of water resources. Desalination is dependent on energy utilization and combined power–water production is presently the only means to produce desalinated water. A long term sustainable water strategy and outlook are required.

- Most importantly, are Gulf oil and gas production policies and export strategies sustainable? Are they in the right quantities and prices to balance medium- and long-term Gulf budgets and allow for investments in developing new resources and replenishing depletable ones, as well as adding to wealth funds? Are the Gulf policies of acting as "residual oil producers" correct? How will the fortunes of Gulf countries, highly dependent on depletable oil and gas exports, fare in the medium- and long-term?

These are all issues which should be of concern to Gulf countries, governments and people, which require long term planning; they are briefly reviewed below.

We shall begin with the future of the oil and gas industry, its sustainability in the Gulf countries and the incomes these countries can expect to generate from their exports in the future. As has been emphasized throughout this paper, there are no viable alternatives to oil and gas in fuelling the world economy for decades to come. The reality of the world economy and its demand for energy implies a slow growth in demand for oil and gas. The main, abundant, long term reserves available are those of OPEC, particularly the Gulf members. With the gradual depletion of non-OPEC reserves, and the relatively abundant oil and gas reserves available in the Gulf, there will be positive annual growth in the demand for Gulf oil.

Owing to the scarcity of this resource, its prices are expected to grow in real terms, even in the conservation scenarios, from an average of $60–70 per barrel in 2009 to double that in 2030—possibly even higher (see: IEO 2009, WEO 2008).[24] This means a doubling of oil prices in over two decades, an average price increase of 3–3.5 percent per year, for many years to come. This is assuring to producers, but demands discipline, solidarity and fair pricing and production polices within OPEC. OPEC's recent performance has been encouraging. A three percent real growth in oil price is not an exaggerated prospect. The world economy is expected to grow at this average rate, or even higher in the future.[25] Therefore, the oil burden (with its very slow growth in demand) to the world economy will be constant or even decreasing.

Will future oil income and prices be sufficient to balance Gulf budgets? Presently the Saudi budget break-even oil price is set at below \$60 per barrel, and that of Kuwait, the UAE and Qatar at \$50 per barrel, while Bahrain and Oman need a price of \$70 to balance their budgets (see Statistical Annex)

In 2008, world oil prices averaged \$97/b and Gulf countries achieved very high oil export incomes (see Table 1.13). Based on these trends, this paper estimates the value of Gulf energy exports in 2030 to exceed one trillion dollars (in 2009 dollars).

Table 1.13

Estimated Value of Gulf Oil Exports (2000–2030)

Year	Gulf crude production (kbpd)	Value of Gulf exports (US\$ bn in 2007\$)
2000	12,913	123
2007	14,764	380
2008	15,289	509
2015	18,000 (exports)	720
2030	22,000 (exports)	1,040

Notes: Assuming US\$110 and US\$130 real price of oil in 2015 and 2030 respectively in 2007 dollars.

In 2007, the combined GDP of the Gulf countries was around \$770 billion (see Statistical Annex), of which energy exports accounted for exactly half.

Prices of oil in 2008 were high and not explained by fundamentals. If we consider the IEA and DOE/EIA reference scenario production for the future price of oil we can expect an export income to the Gulf of \$720 billion in 2015 and over one trillion in 2030 (2007 dollars), which is quite healthy. This should be studied against a backdrop of Gulf budget requirements which in 2009 were around \$40–60 per barrel for most Gulf countries.[26] Therefore, predictions of future income, under the present situation, seem to be quite healthy. What is required is wise management of this income to sustain future prosperity. In the past two years the Gulf surpluses invested in the United States were the world's highest, and exceeded that of China.

Defense Aspects

The current US and European military and naval presence in some smaller Gulf countries will likely continue in the future; it may also be strengthened if there are signs of instability in the Middle East region. Oil is of vital value to the United States, the EU and China, and they are increasingly dependent on imports. Thus, it is vital for economic and social welfare worldwide that the oil exports of Gulf countries increase. The United States and a number of European countries will continue to station small contingents of armed forces in the Gulf and exhibit a strong presence in the oil sea-lanes in the region. This is apparently of mutual security benefit to the large oil consumers and the small resource-rich energy exporters in the region.

Controversial Spending: Armaments and Nuclear Power

Owing to their high energy income surpluses, the Gulf countries are often tempted to over spend. Here we shall briefly analyze two examples of this tendency: armaments and nuclear technology. Gulf defense expenditure is estimated to be around eight percent of Gulf GDP, i.e., $60 billion in 2007, compared to an average of three percent of global GDP worldwide. In 2008, the global arms bazaar was $55 billion, of this the UAE spent $9.4 billion and Saudi Arabia $8.7 billion.[27] This means that these two Gulf countries alone accounted for one third of the world's arms trade.

The other controversial aspect is the plan to build nuclear power stations in the Gulf region (in the past the idea of introducing coal power plants was muted, which I understand has since been discarded). Nuclear energy is the most expensive means of electricity production worldwide. Recent costs have risen to $5,000–8,000 per KW (considering the cost of the Olkiluoto Finish plant).[28] Correspondingly, cost of production (cents per kWh) is very high.[29] In the UAE, investment in 5–6 1,000 MW reactors is estimated at $40 billion. Such plants will be mainly manned by foreign expatriate staff (probably Europeans) who are unlikely to remain during any serious security crisis in the Gulf—as distinct from the case of orthodox power plants which can continue to be run by nationals or regional Arab staff. Therefore, besides the cost, nuclear may present a risk to power availability during a security emergency. The Gulf is rich in relatively cheap gas, which is the ideal fuel for electricity generation. A regional gas network in the Gulf will offer the cheapest and most secure source of fuel supplies to power stations.

The Demographic Challenge

With the exception of Saudi Arabia and Oman, the indigenous population base in the Gulf is small. Population numbers in some Gulf countries change rapidly as a result of the movement of expatriates. The indigenous populations of small Gulf countries are only around 20 percent – and in some cases less – of the population residing in these countries. Most of the foreign labor now comes from South Asia (the Philippines, India, Bangladesh, Pakistan, Sri Lanka) and to a lesser extent from Arab countries.[30] These are mostly young people, unmarried or residing as singles in the Gulf. They no doubt present serious demographic and long term problems, particularly if the security situation changes in the region. Increasing and widening the demographic base should be a target for some of the smaller Gulf countries.

Environmental Aspects: Emissions and Subsidies

The economies of the Gulf are the most energy intensive in the world, owing to the nature of their economies, their extreme weather conditions and also because of subsidies. Oil products are sold relatively cheaply and at a much lower price than in countries of similar income. Electricity tariffs are also quite cheap and are heavily subsidized, and in some countries electricity is provided almost free to the indigenous population.

Cheap energy prices and subsidies lead to wastage, over spending and unnecessary use as well as misallocation of resources. They also lead to the diversion of valuable resources from exports. Correspondingly, energy use and emissions in the Gulf region are the world's highest per capita. The world average CO_2 emissions per capita is around 4.25 tons, while that of the UAE is 58, Qatar 48, Bahrain 34, Kuwait 32, and Saudi Arabia 17 tons.[31] Although population numbers change rapidly, thus making emission calculations rather uncertain, it is clear that per capita Gulf emissions are the world's highest. Also, Gulf states' per capita electricity usage are the world's highest (as high as 10,000 kWh per capita) and are still growing at a rate that averages 7–9 percent annually, which is more than three times the world average. This is not only caused by the requirements of economic growth and a rapidly increasing population, but also by wastage and overuse owing to subsidies.

It is often argued in the Gulf that indigenous energy wealth is a God-given resource for the population to freely enjoy. This is an incorrect argument. What we are concerned with is energy services, of which fuel only constitutes a part—often a minor part. The real cost of electricity and energy services is not only the fuel cost but also the huge investment costs of power stations, refineries and energy networks, apparatus and facilities. Mobility is not only achieved by burning fuel but also through investing in transport facilities, refining and fuel distribution networks which often constitute a value higher than that of the fuel itself. All these investments in facilities and equipment are imported via foreign currencies and at high prices, thus sapping the Gulf's wealth. A good amount of it is unnecessarily wasted through overuse, which also unnecessarily adds to Gulf emissions. (The Statistical Annex details Gulf energy and electricity use and its emissions.)

It is estimated that Saudi and Iranian oil product subsidies in 2007 reached a staggering $53 billion; they have risen further in 2008 and 2009. Such huge subsidies do not give incentives to national oil companies to achieve financial efficiency and cut costs.

Energy Investment and Technology

Gulf oil and gas is the world's lowest cost to produce (per unit of output), thus calling on relatively moderate investments, but sophisticated technology is still needed to attain high standards of efficiency and output. Prospecting and developing costs per barrel of new additions to oil production in Gulf countries amount to less than $10,000 per barrel of daily production capacity—one third of the world average and one tenth of some offshore US projects.

Recent years have seen the emergence of a 'new world order for oil,' dominated by national oil and gas companies, sometimes to the exclusion of IOCs—restricting their role to assisting NOCs or acting as oil field services companies. It is estimated that in 2030, more than 60 percent of the world's oil production will be by NOCs.[32] The Gulf is dominated by NOCs, where government ownership is 100 percent: Saudi Aramco (SA), ADNOC (UAE – Abu Dhabi), KPC (Kuwait). The big question remains, however: are these NOCs capable of raising the large investments required to expand their exploration and production activities to meet growing demand and replace depleted fields? Are they in a position to acquire the sophisticated technologies and skilled personnel (usually developed by IOCs and service companies) to reach the efficiencies required? Are these companies operating in a subsidized market and, with no competition, capable of matching the financial and managerial levels already achieved by IOCs? These are vital questions not only for the Gulf countries, but also for global energy security requirements.

Some of the NOCs like Aramco are believed to have reached technological levels like that of the best IOCs (although this is not always the case). The issue is complicated in some Gulf countries by the zeal to protect national oil wealth by restricting the involvement of foreign companies or their partnership with NOCs, thus delaying investments and deployment of new technologies. Few NOCs are required by law to hand over their surpluses to their governments, thus restricting their ability to invest. These are issues which can restrict the development of future production that need to be addressed by certain Gulf countries.

Realizing these restrictions, strategic partnerships have been developed between some Gulf NOCs and IOCs, mainly in Abu Dhabi, Oman and Qatar. More will be needed in the future to allow Gulf NOCs access to sophisticated new technologies, skilled manpower, corporate culture as well as the investments needed for adequate and efficient future expansion.

The WEO-2008 estimates worldwide oil and gas cumulative upstream investments, over the period 2007–2008, to be \$8.36 trillion (in 2007 dollars), of this only \$1.12 trillion (13 percent) is needed in the Middle East, mainly in Gulf countries. Although this amount seems to be modest compared to expected oil export income, it may not always be readily available in some countries thanks to the legislative and budgetary restrictions mentioned above. This spells a need for careful consideration by Gulf countries.

Water Challenges

The Gulf faces grave water shortage challenges as one of the world's driest regions. Owing to economic development and demographic changes, its water requirements are rapidly increasing. They can no longer be secured from renewable sources or limited natural water resources. All Gulf countries have resorted to desalination in the past few decades, with Kuwait pioneering this effort in the 1950s. Increasingly, water is desalinated through a process of combined electricity and water production. The energy–water nexus is more prominent in the Gulf region than anywhere else, with desalination becoming an increasing part of all electricity generation projects, thus increasing costs by a large margin. Gulf electricity generation is growing at a sustainable rate of 7–9 percent annually, and this is accompanied by growing amounts of desalinated water. Water security in the Gulf region has become an integral part of local energy/electricity security, thus posing yet another challenge to the energy security of the region.

Sustainability: A Summary

Gulf oil production policies are dictated by global demand, OPEC allocations and budgetary requirements. It is not intended here to advise Gulf countries as to their production policy, which is an independent national decision for each country to take. However, the above analysis points out to the following:

- Oil is and will remain for decades to come the world's most important and desired fuel. Its value, in real terms, is likely to significantly increase over the long term.

- Income from oil and gas exports will likely exceed Gulf budgetary requirements. Surpluses will be generated in the future; some of them are likely to be large. This provides a temptation to overspend. The challenge will be to wisely manage these surpluses to meet the requirements of a "rainy day."

- The real long term wealth of any nation lies in its educated and cultured population, i.e., its human wealth. This is what needs to be bolstered in the Gulf in the long term. This is a major challenge, particularly in some Gulf countries which have a narrow national demographic base.

Statistical Annex

Gulf Proven Crude Oil Reserves by Country 2000–08
(Million Barrels)

	2000	2001	2002	2003	2004	2005	2006	2007	2008
Kuwait	96,500	96,500	96,500	99,000	101,500	101,500	101,500	101,500	101,500
Qatar	13,157	15,207	15,207	26,089	25,494	25,288	26,185	25,090	25,405
Saudi Arabia	262,766	262,697	262,790	262,730	264,310	264,211	264,251	264,209	264,063
UAE	97,800	97,800	97,800	97,800	97,800	97,800	97,800	97,800	97,800
Oman	5,400	5,400	5,400	5,500	5,500	5,500	5,600	5,600	5,600
Gulf	475,623	477,604	477,697	491,119	494,604	494,299	495,336	494,199	494,368

Source: OPEC Annual Statistical Bulletin 2008.

Gulf Proven Natural Gas Reserves by Country, 2000-08 (BCM)

	2000	2001	2002	2003	2004	2005	2006	2007	2008
Kuwait	1,557	1,557	1,557	1,572	1,572	1,572	1,780	1,784	1,784
Qatar	14,443	25,783	25,783	25,783	25,783	25,636	25,636	25,636	25,466
Saudi Arabia	6,301	6,456	6,646	6,754	6,834	6,900	7,154	7,305	7,570
UAE	6,060	6,060	6,060	6,060	6,060	6,060	6,040	6,072	6,091
Oman	570	600	650	700	750	800	850	900	980
Bahrain	100	100	100	100	100	95	95	90	90
Gulf	29,031	40,556	40,796	40,969	41,099	41,063	41,555	41,787	41,981

Source: OPEC Annual Statistical Bulletin 2008.

Gulf Crude Oil Production by Country, 2000–08 (kbpd)

	2000	2001	2002	2003	2004	2005	2006	2007	2008
Kuwait	1,996	1,947	1,746	2,108	2,289	2,573	2,665	2,575	2,676
Qatar	648	633	569	676	755	766	803	845	843
Saudi Arabia	8,095	7,889	7,093	8,410	8,897	9,353	9,208	8,816	9,198
UAE	2,175	2,115	1,900	2,248	2,344	2,378	2,568	2,529	2,572
Gulf	12,914	12,584	11,308	13,442	14,285	15,071	15,243	14,765	15,289

Source: OPEC Annual Statistical Bulletin 2008.

Gulf Member Countries' Value of Petroleum Exports, 2000–08 ($Million)

	2000	2001	2002	2003	2004	2005	2006	2007	2008
Kuwait	18,185	14,969	14,060	19,005	26,675	42,441	53,178	60,019	84,438
Qatar	7,834	6,964	6,885	8,814	11,694	17,585	23,350	29,130	38,950
Saudi Arabia	70,866	59,788	63,815	82,271	110,896	161,784	188,468	206,480	283,215
UAE	26,148	23,909	22,806	29,183	38,801	55,079	70,100	84,390	102,500
Gulf	123,033	105,630	107,566	139,273	188,066	276,889	335,096	380,019	509,103

Source: OPEC Annual Statistical Bulletin 2008.

Budget Oil Price Assumptions for Selected Oil-Producing Countries ($/b)

	2002	2003	2004	2005	2006	2007	2008	2009
Kuwait	15	15	15	21	36	36	50	35
Qatar	16	17	19	27	36	40	55	40
Saudi Arabia	15.5	18	18.5	25	38	42.5	48	40
Bahrain	15-18	20-21	20-21	30	30	40	40	60
Oman	18	20	21	23	32	40	45	45

Source: MEES.

Nominal Gulf GDP, 1996–2007 (US$ billion)

	1996–99	2000–04	2005	2006	2007
Kuwait	29.5	48.7	80.8	98.7	111.4
Qatar	10.8	22.0	42.5	52.7	65.8
Saudi Arabia	157.5	205.3	315.8	349.1	375.3
Bahrain	6.3	9.0	13.4	15.8	19.8
Oman	15.2	21.3	30.7	38.4	42.4
UAE	50.7	80.7	117.5	136.3	159.7
Gulf	270.0	387.0	600.7	691.0	774.4

Source: National agencies and World Bank estimates.

Gulf Energy Consumption and Emissions (2007/2008)

	Consumption (Mtoe)						Emission Mt CO_2		
	2007			2008			2008		
	Oil	Gas	Total	Oil	Gas	Total	Oil	Gas	Total
Kuwait	13.6	10.9	24.5	15.3	11.5	26.8	47	26	73
Qatar	4.0	17.7	21.7	4.6	17.9	22.5	14	42	56
Saudi Arabia	96.1	67.0	163.1	104.2	70.3	174.5	321	165	486
UAE	20.7	44.4	65.1	22.9	52.3	75.2	71	123	194
Gulf			274.4			299.0			809

In the Eye of the Beholder: Global Consumption Uncertainties and Energy Security in the Gulf States

Raad Alkadiri

For the past century, energy security has been overwhelmingly viewed from the standpoint of consumers of hydrocarbons, and especially of oil. The growing importance of crude oil as a source of energy for transport and industry throughout the twentieth century ensured that it rapidly became a strategic commodity whose uninterrupted supply was considered vital to the national security of consumer states in the developed world. Whether through commercial investment, imperialism or brute force, these states sought to ensure the steady flow of cheap oil to fuel their economies. The battle for control of reserves and production worldwide was the stuff of high politics, shaping the evolution not just of the producing states themselves, but also of the international systems that have emerged over the past hundred years. The British Empire, the post-World War II *Pax Americana*, the Cold War and Third World anti-colonial struggles; all owed their contours in part to the desire for energy security.[1]

Over the past forty years, consumer concerns regarding the security of oil supplies have become even more acute. The Arab oil embargo of 1973 and the Islamic revolution in Iran in 1979 brought with them not only a sudden sharp rise in prices and a resultant economic downturn in the industrialized world, but also a reinforced sense that production was vulnerable to political risks in inherently unstable parts of the world where a large proportion of crude reserves were situated. Since the 1990s, the sense of threat has become stronger still as a result of the growing concentration of oil reserves in countries that restrict international oil company (IOC) investment, and where national oil companies (NOCs) are prevalent. The rapid rise of consumption in China in the 2000s, and the competition for worldwide upstream assets that IOCs have faced from Chinese NOCs (not to mention the steep rise in oil prices that occurred in the latter half of the decade), have added yet another dimension to the energy insecurity felt by developed states.

This view of energy security misses a simple but crucial point, however. For most producing states, crude oil exports are the backbone of the economy and of public finances. Consequently, it is imperative they get their commodity to market, admittedly at the highest price possible. Furthermore, the area where a large proportion of global oil supplies are located – the Arab states of the Gulf region – has remained relatively stable over the past twenty years. These states have been buffeted by the ill-winds of regional politics from time to time, although ironically the most potentially destabilizing of late – the US-led invasion of Iraq in 2003 – was a war of choice by the world's largest consumer. On the whole, however, the Arab Gulf states have gone through a process of political and economic evolution that has not only ensured their own domestic stability, but has also gone a long way toward guaranteeing the stable supply of crude oil globally at a price that both their own economies and those of consumers can sustain. As Arab Gulf leaders have made clear, for these countries the critical national security question is not whether they can hold the developed world to ransom by interrupting supplies, but rather whether there is a guaranteed market for their principal commodity, both now and in the future, which will justify the massive investments they have to make to ensure that the flow of oil continues. Looking forward, the question for these states is not whether the world will have enough oil, but rather whether there will be sufficient consumption in the future to meet the supplies that will be available.

Energy Security for Producers

What gives these concerns greater urgency is precisely the political and economic changes that the Arab Gulf states have undergone over the past decade, and the evolution in the way that they have come to view their prime commodity. The Gulf states have learned the lessons of the 1970s and the 1980s. High prices then not only translated into ill-conceived and largely unproductive profligate spending at home and large-scale investment overseas, it also facilitated IOC investment in areas outside the Organization of the Petroleum Exporting Countries (OPEC) member states that ultimately served to bring world crude oil prices down and to test the cohesion of OPEC. The result was a combination of massive internal and external deficits (that eventually left some key producers – notably Saudi Arabia – on the brink of bankruptcy), rising debt, real falling incomes and growing unemployment, especially among the young.

However, the reaction of the Arab Gulf states to the latest oil boom, which began in 2003 – and arguably continues today despite the fall in prices from the heady levels of US$147 per barrel witnessed in mid 2008 – has been different. On the financial front, governments in the region resisted the impulse to spend on a massive scale, at least initially, focusing instead on paying down domestic debt and shoring up their treasuries. Foreign reserves were built up to historic high levels, with Saudi Arabia's alone reaching over $500 billion. The Kingdom, together with Kuwait, Qatar and the UAE, amassed combined reserves of well over $1.2 trillion during the boom years (although this figure has fallen as a result of investment losses and deficit spending in the wake of the recent global downturn). Spending did rise over this high oil price period, but at a slower rate than revenue gains from higher oil prices. Moreover, much of it was targeted at physical and human infrastructure, two long-neglected areas.

But it was not merely the relative fiscal rectitude of Arab Gulf governments and the restoration of macro-economic stability that marked this latest boom as being different to its predecessors. The states of the region have clearly sought to change the nature of their economies

[73]

through a series of significant policy changes aimed at establishing the basis for a new, 'developmentalist' state to emerge, modeled on the Asian Tigers.[2] Three areas were particularly critical. The first was improving the regulatory environment that opened up new industries and bolstered investor confidence in local economies. In Saudi Arabia, a new insurance law introduced in 2004 as part of the process of World Trade Organization (WTO) accession provided the basis for a nascent insurance industry. In Bahrain, policies were introduced to bolster the growing financial services industry, leading to a burgeoning Islamic finance sector; and in a number of countries of the region, including Qatar and Bahrain, labor laws were either passed or updated.

This legislation was designed to underpin and bolster the second area of change—the development of closer public–private sector partnerships between states and local entrepreneurs. In some cases, this has involved tie-ups between ruling families in each state and private sector partners, with the former providing finance and the latter providing business management. In other cases, the state has provided land for the establishment of government-mandated 'economic cities,' which are designed as incubators for private-sector financed infrastructure and productive investment ventures. Governments have also reached out directly to foreign investors in a bid not just to create revenue for the state, but also to establish industrial development and diversification (the $25 billion deal between Saudi Aramco and Dow Chemicals being a recent example of this strategy).

Governments in the Arab Gulf states were assisted in this approach by the fact that they found far more willing local partners than had been the case in the past. In the aftermath of the September 11, 2001, terrorist attacks in New York and Washington, DC, many Gulf investors liquidated their assets in the United States and Europe (partly out of fear that they would be seized or face interference) and sought investments closer to home. These repatriated funds provided a massive boost to the liquidity of local markets and precisely the springboard that Gulf governments needed to launch their ambitious new agendas. Thus, it was not simply that the ruling families of

Arab Gulf states were providing more space for local private sector investment under this new strategy (thereby alleviating the "crowding out" syndrome that had characterized these economies in the past); the private sector itself was actively looking for new opportunities at home.

However, it was not simply private sector money that was being invested differently. The Gulf states themselves were also finding new ways to leverage their own assets. The primary approach was through sovereign wealth funds, long-standing government savings vehicles that adopted a much more active and visible strategy, broadening their asset base (including, in some cases, the purchase of more exotic – and riskier – assets) and focusing their investment at home as well as abroad. Funds such as Mubadala and the International Petroleum Investment Company (IPIC) in Abu Dhabi, the Qatar Investment Authority (QIA), Kuwait Investment Authority (KIA) and Istithmar in Dubai took direct equity stakes in local ventures, providing the capital – and in some cases the technology and expertise – needed to develop new local industries. However, Gulf governments have also sought to expand their investments through other means, principally hybrid companies such as Dubai World. Although operated as commercial entities, these companies are state funded and controlled by members of the ruling families, providing a bridge between productive investment and the creation of additional state revenue streams. The financial crisis that engulfed Dubai World in late 2009 has cast a pall over these ventures, raising concerns over their internal governance. Nevertheless, the fact that there was little spillover from the crash illustrated the relative robustness of such investment vehicles elsewhere in the region.

Energy Security in Oil Exporting States

The overall goal of the Arab Gulf states during this period has been to change the strategic focus of their economies, moving from simply relying on the monetization of their primary commodity – hydrocarbons – to using these assets as the foundation for economic diversification, employment creation and raising the standard of living for their populations. But not even those governments that are the least endowed with oil and gas resources have readjusted away from their economic and financial dependence on hydrocarbons completely. Oil and gas, as a source of revenue and an industrial input, continue to underpin the economic development of the Arab Gulf states, and that situation will not change for the foreseeable future. As such, the dependence on the market for, and revenue from, these resources will remain significant and will be a critical factor in determining the success or failure of the economic development strategy.

Indeed, while spending has not been as profligate as in the past, this does not mean that it has not risen as the Gulf states have embarked on their ambitious ventures over the past decade. Saudi Arabia increased its spending by over 100 percent in nominal terms between 2004 and 2009, and Qatar by almost 300 percent. Moreover, as expenditures have risen, so has the crude oil price that these states need to ensure balanced internal and external accounts. In 2000, most Arab Gulf states needed a crude oil price of under $20 per barrel (for West Texas Intermediate [WTI] grade) to avoid deficits, with Kuwait and the United Arab Emirates (UAE) needing $10 per barrel or less. By 2009, the break-even point had risen to around $45 per barrel for Saudi and Kuwait, and over $20 per barrel for the United Arab Emirates. Only Qatar, which benefited from massive gas export revenues, remained at a low level.[3]

This change points to one of the major threats to the success of the developmentalist project in the Arab Gulf states looking forward, and to the core of energy security fears among producer states: the sustainability of current crude oil prices into the future. On at least two levels, there is cause for optimism. First, as far as OPEC dynamics go, the Gulf states can feel far more comfortable than they did in the past of managing prices in their current $70 per barrel range. While a divide exists between the Arab Gulf states and OPEC members such as Venezuela and Iran that need a break-even price in the $80–90 per barrel range, the deep schisms between price hawks and doves that marked earlier periods of the organization's history are no longer present. It is not simply that the fear that prices in the current range would lead to a massive economic downturn has proven false, leaving states with lower break-even levels to enjoy continued windfalls without concerns about demand; much of the politics that characterized OPEC decision-making in bygone eras has disappeared. The memory of the last price collapse in 1998 and OPEC's subsequent success in managing the recovery, have served to refocus both the debate and strategy of the organization over the past decade. Disagreements still surface, but none are fundamental enough to scupper the overall strategy or the uncontested leadership of Saudi Arabia within OPEC. Higher prices, and therefore higher revenue, have also eased the pain of production cuts that have been necessary to manage the market over the past few years. Indeed, as the unprecedented quota compliance levels witnessed early in 2009 showed, there is a broad understanding within the organization that the key to market management during periods of crisis is collective action. OPEC's strategy of being proactive and cutting production in the face of price-fall threats, and being reactive when prices rise again, has served all its member states well.

Figure 2.1

Selected OPEC External Account Threshold Prices

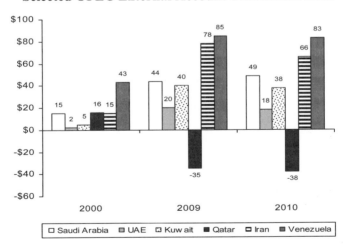

Source: PFC Energy Market Intelligence Service.

Second, OPEC members, including the Arab Gulf states, have faced a relatively fortuitous set of supply–demand dynamics over the past few years. Rising demand, especially in China and the developing world, has occurred at a time when non-OPEC production has either struggled to grow or in many places has been in decline. Thus, the threat to market share posed by new non-OPEC production during previous price spikes (in the North Sea, Mexico and Asia, for example) has not materialized during this latest boom. Non-OPEC production has risen only marginally since 2004 (by 350,000 barrels per day [bpd]), thereby facilitating much smoother market management by OPEC, and without forcing it to cut back too much production to keep prices firm.

This pattern looks set to continue for the most part. Conventional crude production in various non-OPEC provinces (the North Sea, United States and Canada, parts of Latin America and South East Asia) is in decline owing to the maturity of reservoirs or lack of investment.[4] There are only a few major bright spots, including Kazakhstan and Brazil, where major increases are expected. In Kazakhstan, production is expected to rise by 1.8 million barrels per day (mbpd) over the next ten years, reaching around 3 mbpd. Meanwhile, the pre-salt discoveries in Brazil, while not yet officially quantified, are thought to be huge, possibly in the order of 50–80 billion barrels. However, they will be extremely costly to develop, and major incremental production increases (amounting to as much as around 2 mbpd in total) are not expected to begin until 2012 at the earliest, with the bulk hitting around 2020–25.[5]

Indeed, the biggest challenge to OPEC's market management is likely to come from within the organization, principally from Iraq. Having successfully completed two licensing rounds in 2009, the country could theoretically raise its production to over 11 mbpd within a decade. In fact, Iraqi leaders now see their country as potentially on a par with Saudi Arabia as the largest producer in the world within ten years. The awards made to foreign oil companies in the licensing rounds certainly promise much, but whether the reality matches the potential remains to be seen. Prospective producers will have to overcome major challenges in the country to reach even a fraction of the output target that they claim is achievable. The infrastructure to process and carry the new crude volumes has yet to be built, import bottlenecks are inevitable, water resources are already in short supply, the local human resource capacity is extremely limited and politics is likely to continue to interfere with smooth decision-making in the oil and gas sector. The potentially explosive questions of where authority to manage the sector will reside (with the central or regional governments), how revenue will be distributed, and which institutions will have ultimate decision-making authority have all yet to be answered with any clarity. How these issues are resolved will go a long way toward determining whether the improvement in security witnessed during 2008 and 2009 can be sustained, or whether a more pyrrhic cycle of Iraq's civil war will resume once more, with nascent foreign investment by IOCs and NOCs proving a tempting target for trouble-makers.

These challenges have convinced the rest of OPEC that Iraq is an issue that needs to be monitored, but not addressed for the time being. Members, including the Arab Gulf states, maintain a sanguine view, believing that the obstacles to a rapid increase in Iraqi output make a quick ramp up unlikely in the medium term. Moreover, they believe that an agreement can ultimately be reached with Iraq that will reincorporate it into the organization's quota mechanism relatively smoothly. Baghdad's rhetoric has suggested otherwise, with Iraqi leaders insisting that the country will no longer be judged on a par with Iran as it was before when it comes to setting its output quota; instead, they regard only Saudi Arabia as Iraq's peer. Moreover, rather than accepting a quota when its production rises above 3 mbpd as OPEC expects, Iraqi officials insist that it will not accept output restrictions until its production hits 6 mbpd at least.

Time will tell whether OPEC's relative sense of comfort is justified, but in the short term the additional crude that Iraq is likely to bring on-line will be small. Even under the best of circumstances, Iraqi production is unlikely to rise by much more than 200,000 barrels per day (kbpd) over the next two years, a volume that OPEC should be able to manage. Thereafter, that figure could be much higher, reaching 1.5–2.0 mbpd within seven years at least.

The Demand Equation

How much of a problem the additional volumes from Iraq and non-OPEC states create for OPEC's market and price management will depend to a large extent on those factors that determine global consumption moving forward. Ultimately, the combination of three key elements will shape this demand equation in the medium- to long-term: economic growth; policy; and technology. How they play out, and how prepared the Arab Gulf governments are to respond to these changes, will determine the extent of the energy security threat that the producing states of the region face moving forwards.

Economic Growth

The impact of the global economy on demand, and on the economic well-being of the Arab Gulf states, has been clearly illustrated by the 2008–09 downturn. For the first time since the early 1980s, the world has witnessed demand destruction over this period, with average demand falling by 1.5 mbpd between 2007 and 2009.[6] Massive fiscal stimulus measures by governments in the United States, China and other major economies have steadied the economic ship, but the prospects for economic growth over the medium term still look relatively anemic. After contracting by 1 percent in 2009, the IMF expects the global economy to expand by no more than 3 percent in 2010. Moreover, it forecasts growth of only 4 percent per annum in 2010–14, a full percentage point below the pre-downturn trend.[7] In part, this is a result of the paucity of coordinated policy measures that the world's biggest economies have introduced in response to the economic crisis. Rather than coming together to address the underlying structural causes that helped to precipitate the global downturn – notably the imbalance between deficit and surplus states – the major economies of the world sought instead to focus internally, introducing domestic measures designed to stimulate growth in the short term.

This response carries with it both short- and longer-term dangers. In the immediate term, the strength of the global recovery, and especially the recovery in the United States, remains in question. With no prospect of a new US government stimulus package once the present one runs its course, support for economic growth in the United States will remain fragile given the continued absence of private sector demand growth and high levels of unemployment. Forecasts of a double dip recession may prove unduly pessimistic, but a steep, V-shaped recovery is not on the cards either. This will translate into continued weak final demand for oil products, something that will threaten prices unless OPEC takes tough production-cut measures to provide price support.

The Arab Gulf states in OPEC have relatively healthy balance sheets, however, courtesy of a number of years of strong prices. So any short-term downturn is likely to be manageable. But the absence of a coordinated response to the economic downturn, and the persistence of major structural imbalances, pose a risk of relatively weak economic growth over the longer term, even with a return to trend growth in the major developing economies, including China. PFC Energy's most pessimistic scenario forecasts average annual global growth of around 2.5 percent between 2013 and 2020. Under these circumstances, global liquids demand would take until 2013 to recover its 2007 levels, and average annual demand growth thereafter would be less than one percent for the rest of the decade.

This pessimistic economic and demand growth picture would create a major dilemma for the Arab Gulf states of OPEC. On the one hand, slow growth would be likely to limit the amount of non-OPEC upstream investment and lead to the delay or cancellation of a number of projects, thereby reducing the competition for market share that OPEC will face over the course of the next decade. Nevertheless, OPEC states would be forced to maintain significant levels of spare capacity – at least 4–5 mbpd – for much of the decade. Indeed, this figure could be significantly higher if Iraq or a non-OPEC producer such as Brazil comes close to meeting its production potential in a speedy fashion.

Sustained high levels of spare capacity pose two distinct challenges for Arab Gulf producers and the rest of OPEC. Firstly, they would test

OPEC's hard-won cohesion by making market management harder. The prospect of lower prices for a long period of time may be enough to keep the organization's more recalcitrant quota busters in check, especially as many of those have the least spare capacity. Nevertheless, relations among the main OPEC members could become more tense—even more so if Iraqi output is on a significant and unrestrained uptick.

Secondly, and perhaps more importantly, the prospect of higher levels of spare capacity will lessen the incentive for the main OPEC producers to invest in new production. This is particularly the case for Saudi Arabia which, as the effective swing producer in the organization, must inevitably carry the biggest burden of output cuts if OPEC cohesion is to be maintained. Projects to increase the Kingdom's production capacity to 12.5 mbpd will be complete by 2011, but beyond that figure, Saudi leaders face a difficult decision: whether to invest vast sums of money to raise capacity further to 15.5 mbpd or simply to keep the incremental oil in the ground in case of an emergency.[8] Saudi Arabia's willingness to maintain spare capacity has been key to its strategic importance globally, but some Saudi officials have already made clear their reluctance to invest in new capacity that may not be needed. If the prospects for long-term demand growth are relatively dim, this reticence is likely to grow.

Policy Changes

The Saudi dilemma is exacerbated by other possible storm clouds on the horizon, notably those linked to policy measures to reduce consumption in the developed world, particularly in light of concerns over energy security, rising energy prices and – more importantly – climate change. The energy security debate continues to rage in the United States, focused particularly on the dependability of supplies from Middle East producers, including the Arab Gulf states. As mentioned earlier, the fact that disruptions of supply from these states have been minimal, and the fact that Saudi Arabia has taken the leading role (at considerable financial cost) to ensure sufficient spare capacity is maintained, has done nothing to dampen the prevailing sentiment. If anything, energy security concerns have grown stronger in the aftermath of September 11, 2001, as some US national security hawks have sought to make a causal link between the purchase of oil from the Arab Gulf and the financing of terrorism. Reducing the United States' dependence on Middle East oil has become a mantra of both Republican and Democratic administrations, even while US Presidents seek to encourage Saudi Arabia to expand its spare capacity. President George W. Bush in his 2006 State of the Union address called for a 75 percent reduction in US oil imports from the Middle East by 2025 as part of efforts to wean the United States off what he called its "addiction" to oil.[9] The statement caused consternation and some anger among Saudi officials. Similarly, Barack Obama, both during his campaign and as President, has repeatedly emphasized the imperative of significantly reducing US oil imports. In his speech accepting the Democratic presidential nomination in August 2008, he promised to end US imports from the Middle East within 10 years. Securing US energy independence has been one of the principal justifications he has used for his policy drive to improve energy efficiency in the United States.[10]

The rise in energy prices in the United States over the past decade has given arguments for cutting consumption – and hence the need for Middle East oil – even greater salience. Structural factors, including the rise of so-called "ex-urb" residential communities around major cities that necessitate long commutes, have limited the changes in consumption behavior that have occurred. Nonetheless, there is a palpable change in the mindset of US consumers, for whom fuel efficiency is becoming far more of a consideration than it has been since the oil shock of the 1970s. At the same time, the Obama administration has come to office determined to adopt a more activist policy approach to changing US consumption habits designed ultimately to reduce the US demand for gasoline.

However, the greatest impact on policy moving forward is likely to come as a result of concerns over climate change in the United States and elsewhere around the world. The relative failure of the Copenhagen Summit, which was unable to reach an accord mandating uniform and universal green house gas (GHG) emission standards, revealed the limits of multilateral policy measures that can successfully be negotiated and introduced. On both bilateral and unilateral levels, however, it is clear that the tide is turning, and that the need to introduce measures to combat climate change is being taken far more seriously by governments, including in Washington. Indeed, the United States has witnessed a significant and apparently irreversible shift in opinion regarding the reality of climate change and the need to confront it.[11] Industry, the financial community and the public at large support these efforts, making the debate about policy part of the mainstream—something that was not the case as little as two years ago.

That is not to suggest that change – either in consumption habits or in policy – will be immediate. On the contrary, as both the Copenhagen Summit and the fate of US climate change legislation in Congress illustrate, the political obstacles to change are significant. New policies will eventually be enacted, but it will take a lot longer than optimists hope. Moreover, the initial focus – in countries such as the United States at least – will be on linking any efforts to job creation and economic growth initiatives. As such, hydrocarbons will continue to fuel the economies of the world for some time to come.

Nevertheless, when they do eventually come to fruition, the raft of policies and initiatives proposed in the United States and elsewhere to deal with climate change will be game-changers for the use of hydrocarbons, and therefore for the states that produce oil and gas. Thus, while change in consumption habits is likely to be gradual, the direction is clearly set. Moreover, the most cost effective – and potentially the easiest and most immediate – measures to introduce are in the area of efficiency, and these are likely to be the main focus of policy for most big oil-consuming governments in the short- to medium-term.

This trend is already evident in the United States, where the Obama administration is seeking to create a "clean economy" via a series of innovative programs and policies essentially designed to improve efficiency while also touted to boost employment and economic growth.

Investments committed to improving the insulation of federal buildings were included as part of the government 2009 stimulus package, and proposals to encourage similar measures in commercial and residential buildings – including financial incentives – have also been proposed. Energy efficiency mandates have also been laid down for electrical appliances. Perhaps more importantly, new national fuel economy standards have been mandated that aim to raise the fuel efficiency of new car fleets from 25 miles per gallon (mpg) in 2009 to an average of 35.5 mpg by 2016, a change that the White House insists would cut consumption by 1.8 billion barrels of oil during the life of the program.[12] Moreover, the standard was passed with the support of the big US automobile makers.

Similar measures have also been put in place elsewhere in the world. Energy efficiency has been a goal in China since the mid 2000s, and in 2009 the Chinese government imposed even tougher fuel efficiency standards than the United States, mandating that vehicle fleet efficiency rise from 35.8 mpg to 42.2 mpg by 2015. The government also pledged to reduce the energy intensity of the economy by 40–45 percent per unit of gross domestic product (GDP) by 2020.[13] While these efficiency gains will amount to less in absolute terms than the US measures, and will impact other fossil fuels as well as oil, they nonetheless have a longer-term significance for the Arab Gulf oil and gas producers. It is the developing world that these states are looking to in order to sustain demand growth in the future, not the developed world economies, where oil demand is forecast to stagnate or go into decline. Given its huge population and the anticipated pace of its economic growth – both in absolute terms and on a per capita basis – China in particular is regarded as an important engine for this demand growth, and a key market for Arab Gulf producers. Indeed, major producers such as Saudi Arabia are already seeking to lock in supplies to this market through investments in downstream assets in China.

According to PFC Energy forecasts, Chinese crude oil demand will rise from around 7.5 mbpd in 2009 to over 11 mbpd in 2020, and to almost 13 mbpd by 2030. Driving this forecast growth is the anticipated rise in demand for transport fuels, as rising per capita GDP and the consequent growth in purchasing power of China's burgeoning middle class lead to greater vehicle penetration. The number of cars per capita is presently around 50 per 1,000 people (compared with around 800 per 1,000 people in the United States). However, historical evidence suggests that the relationship of per capita GDP and car ownership follows an s-curve rather than a linear pattern, with China close to the point where a rise in per capita GDP leads to a more accelerated increase in vehicle penetration. Indeed, a recent study suggests that if Chinese per capita economic growth continues on its present trend, the vehicle fleet is forecast to double by 2014, and to double again by 2019; in absolute terms, the Chinese car fleet would match the United States' fleet today within a decade.[14] Naturally, along with the rise in number of cars will come a rise in demand for gasoline.

Faced with this potentially steep rise in gasoline demand and its associated energy security threats, the Chinese government is already examining measures that could ease the rising crude oil import burden. Government initiatives have been launched to encourage consumers and businesses to buy hybrid and electric cars, including subsidies and in some cases direct cash-payment programs. Beijing has also offered financial incentives to the automobile industry to encourage the research and development of an electric car fleet. Finally, the Chinese authorities are beginning to construct the infrastructure necessary to facilitate such a fleet. The government's initial targets remain modest: the goal is to sell 500,000 hybrids and electric cars per year by 2011, which amounts to around 3 percent of annual car sales. These targets may prove difficult to achieve in the short- to medium-term, despite the perceived malleability of China's first-time car buyers and the government's ability to impose centrally planned mandates; but in the longer term, the objective is clearly to ease the burden of crude oil demand growth, and Beijing's efforts could well allow China to make an evolutionary jump in the technology its chooses for its transport fleet, leap-frogging far more rapidly to more fuel efficient vehicles – possibly even using hydrogen-based fuel cells – than has been the case in the developed world. This, in turn, would alter the traditional relationship between oil demand growth and vehicle penetration that underpins many of the scenarios for Chinese demand moving forwards.[15]

Technological Developments

The uncertainties that China faces in transforming its car fleet points to the final major factor that will determine the demand equation over the coming decades, namely how technological developments will impact oil consumption habits and how quickly. While policy changes will undoubtedly have an impact on the demand picture, technological change – both in hardware and in fuels used to power economies – will be the major determinant of the role of hydrocarbons in the future.[16] Indeed, policy and technological change go hand-in-hand, in part by determining the third element that will drive innovation and the implementation of technology: cost.

The emerging culture of greater environmental awareness and the response of both governments and business to this societal change is driving innovation to enhance energy efficiency and to replace hydrocarbons and fossil fuels as the main sources of energy in the future. A variety of alternatives have been proposed, from biofuels to replace conventional oil and gas, to the greater use of nuclear power and renewable energy, which would dispense with hydrocarbons altogether.[17] While research and development has delivered the technology to make this switch possible in many cases, however, costs – including sunk investment costs in new infrastructure – remain a prohibitive barrier to their large-scale commercial use.

This cost barrier is likely to change in the future, however, owing to a combination of factors. First, rising demand for crude oil, if it continues at its present rate, will ultimately drive up the costs of the commodity. These increased prices will almost certainly alter consumption behavior, making current patterns of oil use ever-more uneconomical. As Christopher Steiner has noted, the innovation spur that a significant rise in prices would bring could re-shape ways of life and "bring with it all the global impact of a World War and its inherent technology evolutions—minus all the death."[18] The impact of higher costs is already evident in the different consumption habits of the United States compared to Europe, where taxation on gasoline makes it much more expensive. Steiner estimates that a rise in US gasoline costs to $6 per gallon would spur a shift to the use of European-style diesel fuel in the United States.

The second factor that would increase the penetration of new technology and alternative energies is a fall in the price of both. Part of this is likely to be the product of greater economies of scale as technologies and alternative energies are used more widely, and the sunk costs of infrastructure can be shared more broadly. But technological innovation could also lead to a drop in prices, thereby making new systems more commercially viable. The recent steady increase in unconventional gas production in the United States offers a good example of this dynamic: technical breakthroughs in hydraulic fracturing and horizontal drilling over the past decade have allowed difficult reservoirs to be developed in a more commercial fashion, and a rise in prices has added further economic support for the process. As a result, production has grown by almost 50 percent over the past two years, from a base of about 15 billion cubic feet per day (bcfpd) in 2007 to around 23 bcfpd in 2009. As this technology is transferred worldwide, unconventional gas production is being seen as increasingly viable elsewhere, easing both energy supply and environmental concerns in various parts of the globe.[19] Similar advances are being seen in other technologies, such as hydrogen-based batteries to fuel electric cars and in the development of renewable energy sources such as wind and solar, all of which could dampen the growth in demand for oil in the future.

Just how far away this future is, however, remains uncertain. The interplay of technological innovation, policy drivers and costs will change consumption behavior and promote a shift to more efficient and eventually alternative energy use; but in the early years the pace of any change is likely to be gradual, certainly slower than optimists believe, and could amount to slower demand growth rather than destruction of demand for oil. In a May 2008 study on US energy policy and fuel demand in the transportation sector, Kenneth Medlock and Amy Myers Jaffe conclude that improved vehicle fuel efficiency standards mandated by the Bush administration would slow oil demand growth over the next decade, but not reduce overall consumption. According to Medlock and Jaffe's research, while overall oil dependency in the US transport sector would be reduced by 9.5 percent by 2017 if the on-road efficiency of motor vehicles in the United States reached 20.5 mpg (which they calculated as the impact of the Bush administration's mandate), actual demand would still grow by 800 kbpd over 2006 levels. The gains in efficiency would be slightly greater over a longer period, but it would take a much more significant improvement in fuel efficiency to reduce demand to below 2006 levels.[20] A PFC Energy study of the impact of tougher fuel efficiency targets announced by the Obama administration in May 2009 similarly found that the demand savings from these policy initiatives would be relatively modest. It forecast that the new initiative could net a reduction in consumption of around 150 kbpd by 2016 compared to saving under existing Bush-era regulations, although the study did conclude that this would amount to an actual fall in US gasoline consumption of 1.12 mbpd compared to 2008 levels.[21]

These studies suggest that, even under the most propitious of policy and technological circumstances, hydrocarbons look likely to remain the mainstay of global energy demand for the next decade at least. Furthermore, as the supply of liquids – conventional crude, condensates and increasingly biofuels – from non-OPEC sources declines over the next 15 years, so the demand for OPEC crude oil will increase. By 2020, PFC Energy forecasts suggest that the call on OPEC crude could be as much as 36 mbpd, compared to 27 mbpd today.[22] The bulk of the additional supplies would have to come from Arab Gulf producing states, notably

Saudi Arabia. Indeed, the question under those circumstances would not be whether oil demand will be sufficient to meet supplies, but whether the world – and the Arab Gulf states in particular – can produce enough oil to meet burgeoning consumption.

In that case, the energy security picture for the Arab Gulf producing states would look more benign over the coming decade. Not only would there be a continued market for oil, but the supply–demand dynamics would make OPEC's target of around $75 per barrel sustainable while increasing the organization's share of supply. Indeed, under this best-case scenario, the pressure on prices is likely to be upwards over the next decade, although this would probably serve to increase policy and technology changes designed to enhance energy efficiency among consumers, and ultimately to destroy oil demand in the longer term.

Figure 2.2

Long-Term Supply/Demand Forecasts and the Call on OPEC Crude

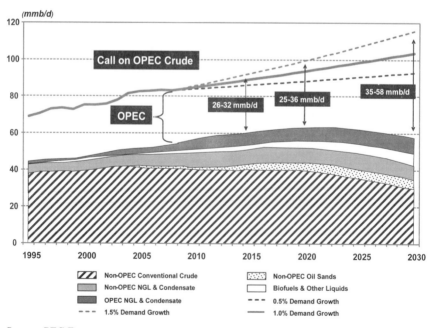

Source: PFC Energy.

The Energy Security Future for the Arab Gulf States

However, as suggested earlier, this picture is fraught with uncertainty. This high level of consumption forecast for OPEC crude oil under the best-case scenario assumes relatively strong demand growth (1.5 percent per annum) throughout the coming decade. OPEC defense of prices in their current range could probably be sustained at slightly lower demand-growth levels (say 1 percent per annum); but a combination of sustained slower global economic growth, high prices, concerns about the environmental impact of hydrocarbon emissions and faster-than-expected technological innovation could push in a different direction that will not back out hydrocarbons from the market altogether, but certainly limit the rise in demand for them. Under these circumstances, the call on OPEC crude could be as low as 25 mbpd in 2020. Moreover, with more sluggish demand, the difficulties of OPEC market management are likely to be greater. Anemic demand growth, or worse still demand destruction, will complicate OPEC price defense efforts, particularly if Iraqi production does increase significantly. Under those circumstances, the outlook for prices, and therefore for the finances of the Arab Gulf states, will look much bleaker over the next ten years. The current range of around $75 per barrel certainly looks out of reach, and even the $50 per barrel that is the broad financial break-even line may prove unattainable on a sustained basis. The Arab Gulf states would have to learn to live with much lower revenues than at present, which would probably force them to eat into their reserves. Furthermore, it will test the limits of the developmentalist reforms that are underway.

In the longer term, a fall in demand for crude looks even more inevitable. Indeed, with the exception of non-OECD Asia (essentially China and India), PFC Energy forecasts a fall in demand across the globe after 2020, including in regions such as the Middle East, which is anticipated to be one of the fastest growing areas of consumption over the next ten years. Just how precipitous this fall in consumption will be will depend on how much efficiency and fuel switching takes place in the interim.

This does not necessarily spell doom and gloom for the Arab producer states of the Gulf. For one thing, any immediate switch away from crude oil is likely to be in favor of natural gas, abundant reserves of which exist in the region. The financial and economic boom that LNG exports have brought Qatar – which holds the third largest gas reserves in the world with 891 trillion cubic feet (tcf) – over the past decade is testament to this fact. With abundant gas resources of their own, Saudi Arabia and the UAE (fourth and fifth largest, respectively, in terms of global reserves) will be able to take advantage of increased world demand for this fuel.

More importantly, gas will provide one of the means for the economic diversification that the Arab Gulf states will have to undergo in the coming decades if they are to be able to adjust their economies to the shift away from oil, in particular, and hydrocarbons in general. The Gulf states have already initiated ambitious policies that seek to take advantage of their rich resource endowments as industrial inputs (providing them with a competitive edge in areas such as petrochemicals, for example). By moving further downstream in the production chain, these states are aiming to capture more of the value-added benefits of their prime resources, as well as promoting wider job creation. There are also lessons to be learned from the experiments of less resource-rich entities like Dubai and Bahrain, which have sought to take advantage of globalization to establish themselves as global centers of finance and commerce.

Ultimately, the Arab Gulf states have time to manage this transition, assuming they start early enough. This will begin with a recognition that it is not the scale of their resource base that is ultimately the most important thing, but rather the scale of global demand for those commodities. In that sense, the Arab Gulf states will continue to live with the energy insecurity of a producer; but how they manage this insecurity, and the long-term policy measures they take to mitigate the risks, will determine how much pain they feel as world energy use transforms in the years to come.

3

Energy Security in the Gulf and the US Dollar: An Overview

Mohammed A. Al-Sahlawi

The Gulf littoral states, consisting of Iran, Iraq and the six members of the Gulf Cooperation council (GCC) – Bahrain, Kuwait, Oman, Qatar, Saudi Arabia and the United Arab Emirates – comprise major world suppliers of energy. Securing energy in the Gulf is therefore a major priority both for these countries and for the international community.

Energy security in general, and in the Arabian Gulf in particular, is a matter of great concern to policy makers and specialists alike. Historically speaking, the Gulf has been – and continues to be – a major trading route between East and West, but its strategic importance was increased considerably upon the discovery of substantial oil and gas reserves in the region. Currently, the Gulf region contains the largest oil and gas reserves in the world, and offers unquestionable cost and location-related advantages. Most of the existing literature on Gulf oil and gas focuses on those aspects of supply security that concern the maintenance of reliable supplies at reasonable prices, with less attention paid to demand security from the perspective of the producers themselves. Furthermore, an important dimension of energy security in the Gulf is the price of oil and its relation to the US dollar as the established oil pricing unit.

This paper will discuss the different aspects of energy security, including demand security and the economic and geopolitical impact of US dollar movements on energy security in the Gulf. The security of the states of the Gulf and its significance to the energy industry will be discussed, followed by an exploration of energy security parameters. Finally, a number of conclusions will be provided.

The Gulf in the Global Energy Scene: Essential Facts

It was the oil price shock of 1973–74 which drew attention to the issue of energy security and highlighted the widespread global dependence on Gulf energy resources. As a result, new energy policies were adopted by industrialized consuming countries – including the United States, Western European states and Japan – in order to reduce their dependence on imported oil and gas from the Gulf. Among other policies are those related to energy conservation, development of alternative energy including renewables and nuclear, and investing in exploration in high production-cost areas such as the North Sea and Alaska when oil prices are high enough to justify such investments. Despite these structural and organizational developments, the Gulf remains the world's major energy producer and exporter, without much competition from other areas, especially in terms of oil. Table 3.1 shows oil reserves and production in the Gulf as compared to the world and other regions in 2008.

The Gulf possesses around 60 percent of world oil reserves. The physical reliability of these reserves and their expected life can be measured (for oil) by their reserve to production ratio, which is 81 years, compared to 43 years worldwide at 2008 production rates. This indicates the Gulf's long-term potential as the main oil supplier.

As far as natural gas is concerned, the Gulf holds about 40.6 percent of world gas reserves, and produced only 12 of percent of total world production in the year 2008 as shown in Table 3.2.

Table 3.1
Proven Gulf Oil Reserves and Production, 2008

Region/Country	Proved reserves (thousand million barrels)	% of World Reserves	Production (kbpd)	% of total
Iran	137.6	10.9%	4,325	5.3%
Iraq	115.0	9.1%	2,423	3.0%
Kuwait	101.5	8.1%	2,784	3.4%
Oman	5.6	0.4%	728	0.9%
Qatar	27.3	2.2%	1,378	1.7%
Saudi Arabia	264.1	21.0%	10,846	13.3%
United Arab Emirates	97.8	7.8%	2,980	3.6%
Total Gulf	748.8	59.5%	25,465	31.1%
Total Middle East	754.1	59.9%	26,200	32.0%
Total North America	70.9	5.6%	13,131	16.0%
Total S. & Cent. America	123.2	9.8%	6,685	8.2%
Total Europe & Eurasia	142.2	11.3%	17,591	21.5%
Total Africa	125.6	10.0%	10,285	12.6%
Total Asia-Pacific	42.0	3.3%	7,928	9.7%
Total World	1,258.0	100.0%	81,820	100%

Source: *BP Statistical Review of World Energy 2009.*

Table 3.2
Proven Gulf Natural Gas Reserves and Production, 2008

Region/Country	Proven reserves (trillion cubic meters [tcm])	% of world Reserve	Production (billion cubic meters [bcm])	% of total
Bahrain	0.09	0.05%	13.4	0.4%
Iran	29.61	16.0%	116.3	3.8%
Iraq	3.17	1.7%	—	—
Kuwait	1.78	1.0%	12.8	0.4%
Oman	0.98	0.5%	24.1	0.8%
Qatar	25.46	13.8%	76.6	2.5%
Saudi Arabia	7.57	4.1%	78.1	2.5%
United Arab Emirates	6.43	3.5%	50.2	1.6%
Total Gulf	75.09	40.6%	371.6	12.1%
Total Middle East	75.91	41.0%	381.1	12.4%
Total North America	8.87	4.8%	812.3	26.7%
Total S. & Cent. America	7.31	4.0%	158.9	5.2%
Total Europe & Eurasia	62.89	34.0%	1,087.3	35.4%
Total Africa	14.65	7.9%	214.8	7.0%
Total Asia-Pacific	15.39	8.3%	411.2	13.4%
Total World	185.02	100.0%	3,065.6	100%

Source: *BP Statistical Review of World Energy 2009.*

Table 3.3
Gulf Oil and Natural Gas Consumption, 2008

Region	Oil Consumption (kbpd)	% of total	Natural Gas Consumption (bcm)	% of total
Iran	1730	2.05%	117.6	3.90%
Iraq	295*	0.35%	9.4*	0.31%
Kuwait	300	0.35%	12.8	0.42%
Oman	69.1*	0.08%	11*	0.36%
Qatar	104	0.12%	19.8	0.66%
Saudi Arabia	2224	2.63%	78.1	2.59%
United Arab Emirates	467	0.55%	58.1	1.92%
Total Gulf	5188	6.14%	306.8	10.16%
Total Middle East	6423	7.61%	327.1	10.84%
Total North America	23753	28.12%	824.4	27.31%
Total S. & Cent. America	5901	6.99%	143.0	4.74%
Total Europe & Eurasia	20158	23.87%	1143.9	37.89%
Total Africa	2881	3.41%	94.9	3.14%
Total Asia-Pacific	25339	30.00%	485.3	16.08%
Total World	84455	100.00%	3018.7	100.0%

Source: *BP Statistical Review of World Energy 2009.*

* CIA World Factbook (estimated 2007).

The oil and gas consumption of the following main consumer regions is expressed in Table 3.3 as a percentage of global consumption: North America, represented mainly by the United States; Europe; and the Asia-Pacific represented by China and India. These three regions account for more than 80 percent of total oil and gas demand. Comparing production with consumption data, the Gulf almost consumes what it produces in natural gas. This is a result of use in energy intensive industries such as petrochemicals, power generation and water desalination that have been built on a large scale in the Gulf.

A comparison between the Gulf and the three main regions in terms of oil and gas reserves, production and consumption is presented in Figures 3.1 and 3.2, which are derived from previous tables. It is clear that the Gulf states possess the highest proportion of oil and gas reserves and account for the highest oil production.

In addition to these facts, energy security in the Gulf is very closely related to Gulf security in general.[1] Iran and Saudi Arabia are the most influential Gulf countries, and they continue to compete for regional power and leadership on several political and energy-related fronts. Iraq, meanwhile, is plagued by its internal problems and is therefore considered to be a destabilizing factor in the Gulf security equilibrium. Indeed, Iraq is one of the points of conflict between Iran and Saudi Arabia, largely as a result of the different religious schools of thought in the Gulf.

Another controversial issue that has implications for energy security not only at the Gulf level but also internationally is suspicion over Iran's nuclear program, which persists despite Iranian claims of its civilian nature. Any escalation of this issue to the point where the United States – individually or collectively with Israel – were to launch military action would severely jeopardize Gulf security.

The relations between the GCC countries themselves, on the other hand, appear harmonious, but there have been a lack of tangible achievements since the establishment of the Council in 1980. Needless to say, the recent windfall of oil revenues has improved socio-economic stability in the region, increased spending on arms, and served to expand oil production capacity. Finally, the Arab–Israeli conflict, Palestinian tensions, and the issue of internal political and economic reform are still pending issues.

Figure 3.1

Gulf Oil Reserves, Production and Consumption, 2008

(% of World)

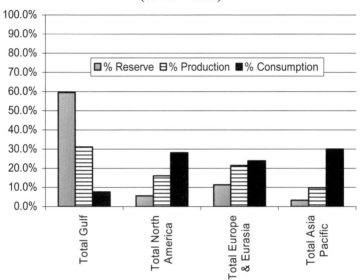

Figure 3.2

Gulf Natural Gas Reserves, Production and Consumption, 2008

(% of World)

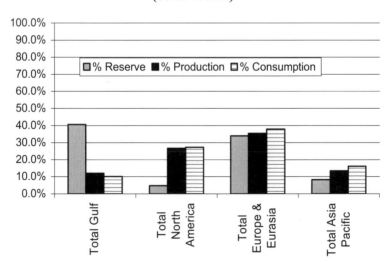

Energy Security in the Gulf

After World War II, the United Kingdom and the United States were the sole powers responsible for protecting the Gulf and securing the accessibility of oil supplies. This unilateral view of energy security – which was based merely on supply security without considering demand security – began to be challenged by the evolution of nationalism in the 1950s. As a result, the Gulf came under threat both internally and externally. Internal threats included the 1951 Iranian revolution which nationalized the country's oil sector, and the independence movements in countries such as Iraq. Both Iran and Iraq are dominant Gulf oil producers and their influence on world and gulf energy security was immediate. On the other hand, external threats included the dramatic events surrounding the 1956 nationalization of the Suez Canal, and its political and military consequences. Another challenge was posed by the structural market changes brought about by the establishment of the Organization of the Petroleum Exporting Countries (OPEC) in 1960. The founders were Venezuela and four Gulf oil producers: Saudi Arabia, Iraq, Iran, and Kuwait. The aim of OPEC was to safeguard the interest of its member states by coordinating pricing and oil production policies among them, and to reduce the market power of the major international oil companies. This strategic move by Gulf oil producers changed the world oil market with respect to prices, giving more power to the newly founded OPEC over its oil supply and pricing. However, the substantial rise in oil prices in 1973–74 was a market reaction to the Arab–Israeli war of October 1973 and the subsequent Arab oil embargo against those countries supporting Israel, notably the United States.

Rising oil prices have encouraged investment in exploration in non-traditional areas such as West Africa, the North Sea, the Caspian Sea, and Central Asia, and at the same time created broader awareness of energy conservation and environment protection. The increase in oil supply from non-Gulf regions was motivated by supply security, and with stable oil prices and rapidly advancing technologies more oil will be pumped into the market. Despite new oil discoveries, the Gulf remains the dominant supplier, able to meet fast-growing global demand and keen to stabilize oil markets—even if this means reducing its output to maintain reasonable oil price levels. In light of these developments, energy security in the Gulf has become a pressing issue for both consumers and producers. The interdependence between buyers and sellers in competitive and integrated energy markets has made energy security an issue of international responsibility.

Supply Security

The core conceptual understanding of energy security in the Gulf relates to the pursuit of a secure flow of oil and gas supplies to consuming countries. Since the middle of the last century, this objective has been achieved by the direct political influence and military presence of the United States in the Gulf.[2] The United States imports almost half of its daily consumption of oil, which amounts to 20 mbpd, and 20 percent of these imports are from the Gulf. Therefore, the United States is dependent on Gulf oil and greatly concerned about the region's stability and the sustainability of its oil supplies. Recently, the role of the United States in securing the Gulf began to be questioned by US policy makers, given the human and financial costs associated with such a commitment.[3] Thus, the security of energy supplies from the Gulf began to be advocated as an 'international' mission. However, it is worth noting that security of supply cannot be achieved without the support and involvement of the Gulf oil producers themselves. Excluding Iran and Iraq, the Arabian Gulf countries led by Saudi Arabia hold the highest share of the supply security burden. They contribute financially to protecting the Gulf, and influence OPEC's decisions regarding higher production and relatively low prices for the sake of oil market stability and to stimulate world economic growth— thus ultimately fulfilling supply security objectives. This policy preserves the market share of OPEC and the Gulf. At the same time, importantly, it also increases the share of oil in the global energy mix, a matter of some concern given the increasing importance of other forms of energy, especially natural gas.

Oil consuming countries also have an interest in securing energy supplies from the Gulf, but this differs according to their energy needs and their political and economic considerations. For example, EU energy policy is essentially driven by energy security.[4] Although the EU encourages diversification of energy sources and suppliers, its energy mix is dominated by fossil fuels, with oil and gas constituting around 70 percent of its energy consumption. Owing to its limited oil and gas resources and suppliers, the EU considers the Gulf as a long-term energy supplier and is therefore keen to maintain economic and political stability in the Gulf. To facilitate this objective, the EU is playing an influential role in the Arab–Israeli negotiation process, and acting as an important economic partner of the Gulf countries in the energy and industrial sectors.

On the other hand, the growing Asian economies – mainly China and India – are facing increasing demand for oil and gas. In the 1970s, most of these countries were self-sufficient in terms of energy,[5] but now they are vulnerable to oil and gas supply disruptions which have placed energy security high on their list of policy priorities. China and India in particular are keen to secure oil and gas supplies from the Gulf and maintain stability in the region to promote mutual economic interests such as opening their markets to Gulf investments in energy and petrochemical projects. Meanwhile, the Gulf guarantees access to oil and gas resources, which leads to demand security from the Gulf perspective.

Demand Security

Until recently, demand security has been a neglected issue in academic circles in spite of the downstream activities that have been undertaken by Gulf energy producers in major consuming regions. For many years, attention was focused on supply security through identifying energy supplies and maintaining their accessibility by all means necessary,

[102]

while the producers' role was hardly recognized. As important as supply security is, demand security – from the producers' viewpoint – deserves more attention. Economically speaking, the demand for oil and gas is affected mainly by prices, but other factors include internal and external political considerations and regulations, particularly those pertaining to energy resource conservation and the preservation of the environment. Econometric studies show that the price and income elasticities of oil and gas demand are low in the short run. Furthermore, the price elasticities of oil and gas demand in the developing countries tend to be less than in the developed countries.[6] These findings are affected by technological and financial developments as well as consuming countries' energy taxation regimes. On that basis, the Gulf seeks to bolster security of demand by promoting oil and gas as the major and prominent fuels. To enforce such a policy, oil production should be at levels that allow prices to remain acceptable, so as not to encourage a shift towards alternative energies or exploration in other regions. The price should also stimulate demand and economic growth in consuming countries, and at the same time provide sufficient funds for the Gulf producers to invest in expanding their production capacities to meet growing demand and offset any disruption or shortage. As a further step to enhance demand security, Gulf oil and gas producers have devised investment programs – solely or jointly with oil and gas consuming countries – to build refineries, petrochemical complexes and gas stations near the epicenters of consumption in order to secure markets for their oil and gas.

The real challenge with respect to demand security is how to cope with sudden increases or drops in demand. Based on a business-as-usual assumption, it is estimated that global oil demand will increase by more than 1.5 percent annually from its current 87 mbpd, with higher annual growth rates of about five percent in developing Asian states such as China and India. Most of this demand will be met by oil from the Gulf. This emphasizes the necessity of maintaining Gulf security and the stability of oil prices.

Energy Security and the US Dollar

Energy security goes beyond simply securing supply and demand as it involves achieving stable energy prices. Oil price stability also implies global and Gulf economic security owing to its impact on oil producers' revenues. Oil price is essentially determined by market forces: supply and demand. Other factors include exchange rates, inflation, taxes and financial speculation. The price of oil is quoted in US dollars and is therefore affected by dollar exchange rates. The impact of dollar fluctuations on real oil export earnings and producers' terms of trade is therefore highly significant.[7] Any depreciation in the dollar will reduce the real value of the oil revenues of Gulf producers and destabilize oil prices. Meanwhile, denominating oil trade in US dollars strengthens the political and economic power of the United States and its position in the Gulf. While shifting away from the dollar to any other pricing scheme such as the Euro, Special Drawing Rights (SDRs), or a basket of currencies might create currency market shocks, it might improve the Gulf oil producers' trade accounts with other major oil consumers.

Variations in the dollar's value against other currencies will destabilize Gulf oil producers' economies and may reduce essential funding for investment in exploration and the development of petroleum resources to satisfy expected demand growth. In mid-2007, oil prices reached a record high of more than US$140/b, which thereby increased oil producers' foreign assets. The value of these assets was eroded by a weak dollar, and the investments in generation capacities to add more supply contributed to the price reduction. The volatility of oil prices as a result of dollar fluctuations has added to global financial uncertainty and contributed to the current economic and financial crises. Thus, the US dollar plays a key role in energy security and, by extension, in broader Gulf security. It magnifies the geopolitical power of the United States in the Gulf and affects oil producers' investment decisions aimed at managing supply and demand security.

Concluding Remarks

Energy security in the Gulf is integral to the broader security of the region. Several hot spots in the Middle East pose real threats to Gulf security; there is the prolonged Arab–Israeli conflict – in which peace seems a distant prospect – the miserable situation in Iraq, internal Palestinian tensions and, last but not least, the social and political fragmentation of Lebanon. Furthermore, on the Gulf front there is the international and GCC confrontation with Iran over its nuclear program.

Internal factors that negatively affect energy markets and Gulf security include the lack of real democracy, the existence of corruption, and the unstructured nature of labor markets which has led to high national unemployment in the Gulf countries. These problems create barriers to economic and managerial reform.

From an energy security perspective, supply security, demand security, and oil price stability in relation to the US dollar are important concerns. The state of the world economy and supply and demand prospects, in addition to the policies of consumer nations concerning environmental protection and energy efficiency are also important interacting factors. The interdependence between producers and consumers – particularly those with high demand growth rates – will ensure that energy security in the Gulf remains an issue of international importance, but one in which the role of the Gulf countries themselves should not be underestimated.

4

GCC Oil Price Preferences: At the Confluence of Global Energy Security and Local Fiscal Sustainability

Ali Aissaoui

The dramatic oil market developments of recent years – which spurred a steep increase of oil prices to nearly US$150 per barrel in the summer of 2008, followed by their precipitous fall to under $35 per barrel the following winter – have brought unprecedented attention to oil prices. The causes and severe consequences of these sharp swings have come under intense scrutiny around the world. Regrettably, the polarization of views concerning the cause of these sharp price movements has not informed the debate. What these discussions have most likely achieved, however, is a collective challenge to policy rigidity and inertia. Coming together first in Jeddah in June 2008 and then in London in December, key energy policy makers from both the oil-importing and oil-exporting countries moved to recapture the debate and discuss measures to stabilize the market. Unfortunately, in focusing on the mechanisms and functions of the oil market, these and subsequent meetings have so far failed – or deliberatley avoided – to forge a common view on oil price levels that could anchor market expectations, despite the announcement by Saudi Arabia and other key producers within the Gulf Cooperation Council (GCC) of their price preferences.

The GCC region, which comprises, in order of their hydrocarbon weight, Saudi Arabia, Qatar, the United Arab Emirates (UAE), Kuwait,

Oman and Bahrain, holds 39 percent of the world's proven conventional reserves of crude oil and condensate, and 23 percent of natural gas reserves. As such, the region has become the center of attention with regard to global energy security. Therefore, while "[t]he world needs to anticipate what forces may throw the region off track,"[1] the region also needs to convince the world that low oil prices are a potential driver of such forces. Saudi Arabia's assertion that $75 per barrel should be a fair price for oil, and subsequent suggestions by other GCC countries of a price range around that target, was met with great skepticism before gaining some currency. In essence, two arguments have been put forward to justify these price targets. The first reiterates the importance of sustaining the world's energy investment requirements to ensure global energy security; the second stresses the need to secure oil-producers' fiscal sustainability, which is key to their socio-economic stability. In keeping with these arguments, we propose to validate the asserted price ranges by reframing the issue beyond the market and focusing on the long-term determinants of oil prices, i.e., technology, economics and politics.

This paper is organized into five parts. The first provides a brief perspective on the apparent shift in policy towards global energy markets and highlights the dual perception of oil prices in the context of the producer–consumer dialogue. The second part examines what prompted the GCC countries to assert their own price preferences. The third part establishes that such preferences cannot be revealed by the market and takes a non-market perspective to justify them. The fourth and fifth parts demonstrate that these prices could be set at the confluence of the economic cost of producing a marginal barrel of oil and the fiscal value of the petroleum assets. This is followed by a brief discussion on the resulting inter-temporal distribution of GCC petroleum fiscal revenues and the extent to which their currently preferred prices could achieve fiscal sustainability.

The Oil Price Dimension of Global Energy Security

Policy Shift towards Energy Markets

Energy security has emerged as a more prominent theme in recent years, permeating news, views and current affairs around the world. To be sure, different people have different opinions on the subject, but one fact is clear: most views have tended to reflect the predominant concern of the oil-importing countries with regard to their security of supply. Few have considered the producers' viewpoints and their legitimate apprehension regarding the other side of the coin—security of demand.[2] A more politically-informed view of the issue is that energy security is a multidimensional concept. The recognition of its global nature and the growing interdependence between the various stakeholders have provided the basis for a new paradigm, which encompasses three main issues: a) improving the energy investment climate and enabling funding; b) addressing the environmental challenges posed by different energy supply mixes; and c) enhancing the producer–consumer dialogue to achieve greater market transparency and stability. These issues became the pivotal components of the St. Petersburg's declaration on global energy security (2006 G8 Summit). Although putting price volatility at the top of the list of challenges to be dealt with, oil prices were left to the market. The credibility of the resulting action plan, which identified "increasing transparency, predictability and stability of global energy markets" as a priority action, has been seriously eroded by the wild swings in prices that have occurred since.

Three years after St. Petersburg, and in the wake of these market upheavals, the G8 Summit meeting in July 2009 in L'Aquila (Italy) had no choice but to abandon its priority action; but it was not in the way one might expect. The International Energy Agency (IEA), which was charged with evaluating the progress made in implementing the St. Petersburg Plan of Action, delivered its "key message" to the Summit in the form of a statement of ideals according to which, "[w]ell-functioning energy markets require free market prices and data transparency, independent regulators, effective non-discriminatory operations of networks and good physical and market integration across borders."[3] This was well-meaning but ultimately unhelpful. Participants at the Summit realized that they had probably better consider the progress and the follow-up initiatives of the Jeddah and London meetings. Their call on the International Energy Forum (IEF) – the institutional underpinning of the producer–consumer dialogue – to take the case of market stability, marks a clear shift in their thinking about policy-making in the field. Among the main issues, which have since been identified as priorities for the forthcoming producer–consumer dialogue (Cancun, March 29–31, 2010), is the urgent need to gain a deeper understanding of the functioning of energy markets and to consider ways and means to improve their performance. However, the focus on the functioning of energy markets might lead to the neglect of a key dimension of global energy security: oil price levels.

The Dual Price Perception of the Producer–Consumer Dialogue

Until recently, oil prices have been a taboo topic of the Producer–Consumer dialogue. Since it was formally initiated in 1991 by France and Venezuela, this unique gathering of the world's top energy policy makers has sought to further a set of common objectives geared towards achieving global energy security and market stability. This has been made possible in large part by three key developments: a) the tolerance by the major energy players – in particular the United States – of a certain degree of multilateralism in oil matters; b) the progressive shift from rivalry to cooperation between the IEA and the Organization of the Petroleum Exporting Countries (OPEC); and c) the establishment of the IEF to frame and lead the dialogue. With energy security issues permeating their discussions, the focus on reliable and affordable supply by the oil-importing countries and on stable and remunerative markets by the oil-exporting countries has resulted in a duality of perceptions about price levels, which is fraught with tensions. However, while the dialogue has been instrumental in defusing some of these tensions, it has until recently tended to shy away from discussing price issues. That is, it conformed to the now-discredited Washington Consensus and its neoliberal agenda: talks on prices were decried as interference with the functioning of free markets and regarded – politically *de facto* if not *de jure*[4] – as tantamount to price-fixing. The recent dramatic manifestation of the oil market dysfunction (or "betrayal" as some put it more vehemently) has brought oil prices to the top of policy agendas: first by oil-consuming countries expressing concerns about the record price levels reached in the summer of 2008; then by oil-producing countries trying to contain the price collapse the following winter; and finally by both producers and consumers seeking to promote market stability and explore mechanisms to contain oil price volatility.

Oil Prices Preferences

Structural Anomalies

The vulnerability of the energy-importing and energy-exporting countries to international oil prices is non-uniform and asymmetrical. In reviewing the literature on the macroeconomic impact of oil prices, some authors have recently reinterpreted the resulting analyses to question the magnitude of such an impact and explain today's minimal impact of high oil prices. In support of their arguments, they observed that up to mid-2008 there had been "a steady rise in the price of oil to historically high levels with no observable negative impact on macroeconomic indicators."[5] The global downturn was, instead, caused by global current account imbalances rather than oil prices. According to the conventional empirical analyses these authors have challenged, oil prices are key determinants of the macroeconomic cycle, and sustained high oil prices significantly affect external accounts, growth, inflation and, ultimately, employment. It is not denied, however, that energy-importing developing countries generally suffer the distributional effects of high oil prices, and that they have limited fiscal capacity to moderate the effects of international oil prices on domestic energy prices. Whatever the case, the degree of magnitude and diverse pattern of impact may explain why, as a group, the energy-importing countries have been intentionally vague about their price preferences. In contrast, and for reasons developed more fully below, the petroleum-exporting countries, and notably those of the GCC, share important economic similarities and are almost to the same degree disproportionately vulnerable to lower oil prices. As a result, they have been more forthcoming in revealing their own price preferences.

At the core of the asymmetry between energy-exporting and energy-importing countries are several macro-economic anomalies related to the structures of trade, gross domestic product (GDP) and governments' budget receipts. In the IEA countries, for instance, energy imports represented about 21 percent of total imports in 2008, and energy trade (both imports and exports) represented some seven percent of aggregate GDP (see Table 4.1). By stark contrast in OPEC countries, petroleum exports (i.e., crude oil, oil products, natural gas and natural gas liquids [NGLs]) represented about 85 percent of total exports, whilst petroleum trade represented some 44 percent of aggregate GDP. Similarly, despite the fact that the IEA countries receive more revenue from taxing final petroleum consumption than OPEC countries get from taxing primary production, the share of these respective revenues in total budget resources was seven percent for the IEA and 72 percent for OPEC.[6] Much of what is true of OPEC in this regard is equally true of the GCC countries, since Kuwait, Qatar, Saudi Arabia and the UAE contribute to a little more than half of OPEC's reported output.

Saudi and GCC Assertions

In the midst of a dramatic oil price collapse, Saudi Arabia moved towards a new concept without waiting for the upcoming London energy summit. In an exclusive interview with the Kuwaiti daily newspaper *Al-Seyassah* (Politics), dated November 29, 2008, and aimed at a larger GCC audience than just the Saudis, King Abdullah was reported to have said that Saudi Arabia wanted the price of oil to improve and stabilize at around $75 per barrel. The statement was intended to allay fears about the impact of twin credit and oil market crises on the GCC economies. However, the King's assertion of a Saudi oil preference was also a statement on fiscal policy: "In our view, $75 per barrel would be a fair price. Our budgets are not based on the earlier high price but on a lower one. What comes in excess goes to surplus reserves and sovereign wealth."[7] This statement emphasizes the fiscal argument and suggests the policy rule to deal with the instability of oil revenues. Not unexpectedly, the Saudi oil price preference was endorsed by the other key GCC producers, either directly or indirectly through a price band around that target.

Table 4.1

Macroeconomic Asymmetry between Oil-consuming Countries, Oil-producing Countries and the GCC (2008 estimates)

Main indicators	Unit	IEA Countries	OPEC Countries	GCC Countries
Average oil price	US$/bbl	97.19 (CIF)	94.45 (FOB)	
Share of energy imports in total imports	%	20.5	1.4	2.3
Share of energy exports in total exports	%	10.1	84.5	74.6
Share of energy trade in GDP	%	6.8	43.7	49.4
Share of petroleum taxes in budget revenues	%	7.1	72.3	79.7

Sources: Author's estimates using data from OECD/IEA, OPEC and GCC.

Notes: (CIF) cost, insurance, freight; (FOB) free-on-board.

The Saudi assertion should also be considered beyond the GCC context. Not only has it achieved wide acceptance within OPEC, but it has also been echoed by the industry at large. In debating the repercussions of the credit crisis and economic recession, a panel of energy industry leaders who gathered at the World Economic Forum (Davos, January 2009) highlighted the impact on the industry of reduced global demand, lower cash flows and insufficient funding. This panel, which the OPEC Secretary General was invited to join, called for an oil price in a range of $60–80 per barrel to stimulate investment,[8] a call consuming countries' top politicians could not ignore. The joint statement by President Nicolas Sarkozy and Prime Minister Gordon Brown that oil should be, "at prices that are not so high as to destroy the prospects of economic growth, but not so low as to lead to a slump in [energy] investment,"[9] suggests support for an as yet undetermined price range. At the same time, it confirms the earlier indication that energy-importing countries would refrain from stating their own oil price preferences.

The Determinants of a Fair Price for Oil

A Price the Market Cannot Reveal

Let us assume that the fundamentals of a market could steady, and that market expectations could be anchored. Then such a market might well move around an even price, which would be acknowledged as fair. But this is not the normal state of today's oil markets, and certainly not that of the US West Texas Intermediate (WTI)—the world's largest oil futures market at the New York Mercantile Exchange (NYMEX). Figure 4.1 shows the evolution of two series of WTI price indices in recent years. The first is the futures prices for nearby deliveries and the second is the spreads between the first and four-month contracts, approximated as the basis of futures (for the sake of statistic consistency, a one month contract is taken as a proxy for the spot price). The change in the pattern of the two indices is evident. For the first, it is not so much about the normal inter-day volatility of prices, but rather their sharp swings. For the second, it is not so much about the normal alternation of backwardation (positive basis) and contango (negative basis) as much as their depth. Obviously, several explanations of the factors responsible for such atypical changes have been offered. They include the evolution of demand and supply and how such parameters as price inelasticity, macro-economic variables, geopolitical uncertainties and producers' policies have interfered. These explanations have been extended to include the significant increase in trading activities in the futures market, and the effects of excessive speculation.[10] However, while generally persuasive, these *a posteriori* explanations are not completely convincing. A simple visual inspection of Figure 4.1 is sufficient to suggest that the swings in prices have been too sharp to be just the result of a shift in supply and demand, and that the futures spreads have been too wide to be merely a reflection of a shift in the economics of oil storage. This leads us to believe that oil markets have become dysfunctional and that dysfunctional markets can hardly reveal fair prices.

Figure 4.1
Daily Front Month WTI Prices and Futures Time Spreads
(2004–2009)

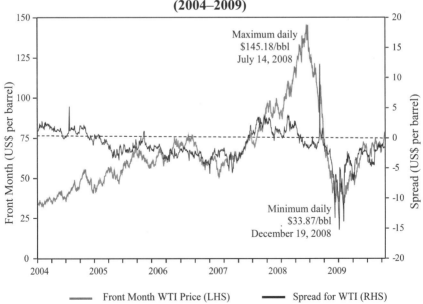

Source: Author, using DoE-IEA Futures Prices Database.

[115]

Therefore, can economic theory be of help? Unfortunately, not much. The formal debate over what constitutes a fair price stretches back to antiquity with the notion of a just barter in primitive exchanges. Later, the work of fourteenth century scholar Ibn Khaldun and subsequent work of the sixteenth century Spanish Salamanca school are important precursors. Ibn Khaldun – who was, admittedly, the first to cite utility as a source of the value and a determinant of the price of a product – probably paved the way to Martín de Azpilcueta's scarcity theory of value. In the Spanish medieval context where the cost of production was considered as the sole determinant of fair price, precious metals shipped from the Americas catalyzed new ideas and concepts. In that context, Luis de Molina, who was probably the most consistent in his view of economic value, contended that goods are valued not "according to their nobility or perfection," but according "to their ability to serve human utility."[11] Such views coincide with the free market theory grounded in classical liberal economic thinking, as propounded by nineteenth century economists such as John Stuart Mill. The above interpretation may, however, be partial. To fill the historical gap, one peer reviewer of this paper contributed the following:[12]

> My comment is to recall Saint Thomas Aquinas' 13th century pronouncements on "just prices" and "fair prices" – a question in the Roman empire and the medieval catholic church. According to Sedgwick's entry on "Just Prices" in Palgrave's Dictionary of Economics, it can be argued that the Saint came to the conclusion that a fair price was that which would emerge from a fair market—in which both sellers and buyers had choices (i.e. implicitly there was competition on both sides). This interpretation seems to me quite useful, since it raises practical questions, which can be answered, about what makes markets "fair" and whether the characteristics are present in the long or short term markets for oil, either as a commodity or as a capital asset (property).

Today's modern economists appear to avoid the issue of price fairness altogether, although the case is often made that actual market outcomes may depend on the initial distribution of resources. They often feel frustrated that, despite their efforts to move away from the ideals of efficient markets and rational expectations, they could not really come to grips with market imperfections. In the case of oil markets, these imperfections are indeed overwhelming. This comes as no surprise, however, given the strategic nature of this natural resource, the complex instruments used for its extraction and trading as a commodity, and the behavior and motivations of the main market participants. They include the impact of fiscal regimes in the host countries, OPEC output policies, strategic and commercial stockpiling, refining concentration, end-user taxation, environmental externalities, the speed of information and communication, and excess speculation in the futures market. In such conditions, and as most strikingly illustrated in Figure 4.1, the market can clear at any price, most likely between the marginal cost and the price of a substitute product, and prices today may differ from prices tomorrow.

Looking Beyond the Market

If a "fair price" cannot be revealed by the market, as we understand it, then we must look beyond. In a 1971 lead editorial published in *Science* magazine under the very title "What is a Fair Price for Oil?" Philip H. Abelson observed that, "in real life, such matters are decided not on the basis of abstract considerations but on an interplay of technology, economics, and politics."[13] The context of that time was the tough bargaining between the host countries of the Middle East and North Africa (MENA) and the major international oil companies on tax reference prices and tax rates, known in the industry as the Tripoli–Tehran–Tripoli agreements. Even in today's entirely different context and circumstances, however, petroleum fiscal revenue enhancement is topical. Furthermore, to the extent that fiscal regimes – in addition to technology and costs – remain a key determinant of oil prices, Abelson's remark is still relevant.[14]

Drawing on this remark, our assessment process of what level of oil price would be considered fair rests on three interrelated elements that directly impact the price and fiscal value of oil: technology, economics and politics/policy. These three elements of our analytical framework (Figure 4.2) are examined in more detail below.

Figure 4.2
Determinants of Oil Prices: A Framework beyond the Market

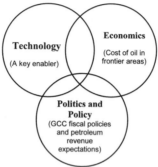

Source: Author, using Abelson's hint.

The technology element describes prospective developments in the field of geology, engineering and processes that could benefit exploration and development. These developments, which have been largely driven by concerns over energy security, increasingly factor in the perceived threat of climate change. Whatever the case, technology is likely to affect both costs and productivity and, as a result, put downward pressure on long term oil prices. As will be illustrtaed in later developments, this has been the case of deepwater and ultra deepwater technolgies. However, prolonged low oil prices, as was the case during most of the 1990s, may result in a loss of expertise amongst oil companies and technology providers. This was particularly true of enhanced oil recovery (EOR, also known as tertiary recovery) schemes, whose postponement left significant amounts of oil in the ground that could hardly be recovered in subsequent years. The expected outcome of this element of our framework is industry experts' perspective on the advances of energy technologies, the role they could play in the more efficient production of oil and the resulting impact on the cost of supply.

The economic element is concerned with the viability of different upstream projects under prevailing and forecasted geological, technological, environmental and market risk conditions. For any given project, the opportunity cost is the expected return needed to justify the investment. This should cover the costs of exploration, development and production, as well as the cost of capital and a risk premium. In this case, the outcome is the long-term economic cost of a barrel of oil produced from the project. The economic valuation can alternatively factor in taxation by the resource owner of the potential economic rent. In this case, the outcome is the breakeven oil price for the project. The breakeven price is the minimum price per barrel needed to recover all costs and yield a return sufficient to compensate for depreciation, the time value of money, and the risk premium. The project would only be economically viable if the expected market price over the life of the project is higher than the breakeven price. It should be noted that, by definition and construction, both the economic cost and the breakeven price are *ex-ante*, not *ex-post*.

The politics and policy element refers to the sovereign political arena of governments. It includes agenda setting, decision making, and implementation with regard to legislation, regulation and fiscal matters. The political arena may be extended to institutions such as OPEC, in order to coordinate petroleum policies, or the producer–consumer dialogue in order to strengthen their exchanges on policies. Our focus is the fiscal policies of the GCC countries. The outcome is the petroleum fiscal values derived from existing tax regimes and expected oil prices.

Of the three elements reviewed above, the technology element may challenge the efficacy of our framework. Indeed, technology cannot be addressed with precise analytical methods, and forecasting procedures commonly used in technology foresight, such as Delphi, are beyond our means.[15] Therefore, we assume that the cost of oil on which we build our economic argument in the next section factors in the industry experts' view on the impact of likely technological progress. With this postulation, we focus on the empirics of the two other elements.

The Long-Term Cost of Oil

The IEA's Economic Cost

The most comprehensive cost estimates available in the public domain are provided by the IEA in the form of long-term oil-supply cost curves, which show the availability of different oil resources as a function of their economic cost of production (Figure 4.3). The IEA's estimates have recently been updated to take into account developments in technology and costs.[16] Technology advances would have dramatically improved project economics if not for the surge of project costs. These costs, which had remained stable during most of the 1990s and early 2000s, have sharply increased in recent years, as a result of a combination of higher costs of industrial input factors, contractors' margins and project risk premiums. The magnitude of the surge in costs can be illustrated via one insightful example. According to the IEA's 2003 *World Energy Investment Outlook*, the capital costs of the first US Gulf of Mexico deep water fields developed in the 1970s were around $25 per barrel. Thanks to technological advances, however, fields in that region could be brought on line for less than $10 per barrel in 2003 (2002 dollars). Today, the lowest cost of similar projects is about $37 per barrel. Corrected according to the depreciation of the US dollar (using the US Federal Reserve major currencies index),[17] this would mean that the cost of these projects has risen by three times during the last six years. This is not an isolated example but rather reflects generic, across-the-board cost increases, which are coherent with our own findings on cost inflation of energy projects in the MENA region.[18]

Figure 4.3

Long-term Oil Supply Cost Curve

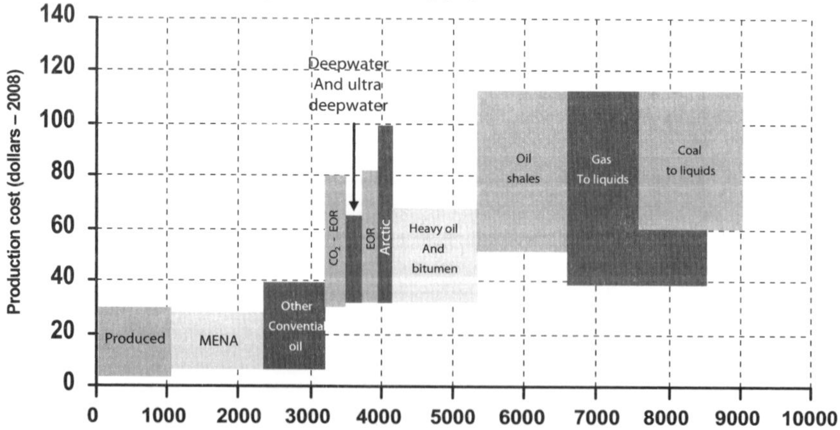

Source: International Energy Agency (IEA), 2008.

Figure 4.3 shows that, according to the IEA's cost methodology, a cumulative amount of some 1,100 billion barrels of oil has already been produced at a cost of $30 per barrel (2008 dollars). The economic cost of exploiting the remaining conventional oil is below $30 per barrel within MENA and is assumed to be even less within the lower-cost GCC area. In other conventional oil regions the cost of production may be as high as $40 per barrel. Non-conventional oil is obviously much more expensive. The cost for oil sands extraction falls between $30 per barrel and $70 per barrel, and that of oil production from new EOR projects between $30 per barrel and $80 per barrel. Oil shale is the most expensive, with extraction costs ranging from $50 to $110 per barrel. The upper cost of gas-to-liquids (GTL) and coal-to-liquids (CTL) is equally high (the overlap in the amount of these two resources denotes uncertainty in the full extent of their size).

We would be wise to caution against misinterpreting the IEA's long-term oil supply cost curve in two respects. Firstly, worldwide cumulative oil demand to 2030 and a little further beyond – which is currently estimated at some 900 billion barrels – could be easily covered by the remaining recoverable reserves of conventional oil at a cost of less than $40 per barrel (2008 dollars). The reason this will not happen is that the imperative of diversification of sources of petroleum supply – which is key to energy security – and the many political, legal and fiscal impediments to investments make it impossible to develop oil resources at increasing cost. As a result, oil companies already venturing into non-conventional oil, or contemplating doing so, should expect production costs to lie in the IEA's resource-weighted range of $45–95 per barrel. Secondly, there seem to be plenty of resources available at a cost below $110 per barrel—some 6.5 trillion barrels (9 trillion when adding CTL and GTL resources). The reason this is also potentially misleading is that the IEA's costs are significantly underestimated since environmental and other risk factors are very likely to affect the extent and speed with which these resources could be exploited. What is only explicitly stated for the moment is that the IEA's current cost estimates do not include petroleum royalties, nor do they account for the costs associated with the mitigation of CO_2 emissions.

Deutsche Bank's Breakeven Prices

More precise costs, within a relatively narrow range of potential production or activity volumes, can be obtained from currently planned projects. Deutsche Bank (DB), for instance, has managed to work out the cost of oil of deepwater and ultra deepwater projects involving major international oil companies (IOCs) in key growth areas around the world such as the US Gulf of Mexico (GoM), Brazil, Nigeria and Angola, using Wood Mackenzie's comprehensive database of capital and operating costs. Assuming an industry's internal rate of return (IRR) of 15 percent for each project, and working out royalties and taxes that reflect current understanding of the different fiscal regimes in place, DB found that, depending on the size of the oil field and on petroleum taxation, an oil price of between $60 and $83 per barrel is required to justify these investment projects (Table 4.2).[19] It is not clear what DB's methodology entailed; however, DB assures us that the breakeven prices it obtained proved to be consistent with estimates from the more sophisticated Wood Mackenzie's net present values (NPV) model.

Table 4.2
DB's Estimated Breakeven Prices for Key Oil Development Projects within Four Main Growth Deep Water Regions

Growth regions	Number of projects	Breakeven price for the lowest cost project (US$/bbl)	Breakeven price for the highest cost project (US$/bbl)
Brazil	5	39.05	59.59
US Gulf of Mexico	7	46.27	69.51
Angola	8	53.50	83.04
Nigeria	5	57.65	83.44

Source: Excerpted from Deutsche Bank's results.

It should be emphasized that even though these results seem pertinent, and consistent with the IEA's long-term supply cost approach (at least for the deepwater and ultra deepwater category), DB advise us to treat them with caution as other elements of uncertainty must be considered before a final decision to invest is taken:[20]

> Within the [above] growth regions, the rise in costs and taxes in recent years suggests that the average oil price necessary to achieve a 15 percent IRR in Angola is now $68/bbl, $62/bbl in the US GoM, $60/bbl in deep water Nigeria and around $60/bbl in Brazil (although this depends heavily on the scale of the development considered). Whilst this is in line with our estimate of the companies' long-run planning price, against the current economic backdrop it comes as little surprise that 2008 saw fewer final investment decisions (FIDs) taken than in any year since 1989 despite the surge in the oil price.

Notwithstanding DB's note of caution, we believe that current GCC price preferences of between $60 and $80 per barrel accommodate planned frontier projects and, as a result, are sufficient to support global energy investment requirements.

The Fiscal Value of GCC Petroleum Assets

Using a Simple Permanent Income Hypothesis (PIH) Framework

The third element of our framework is concerned, as explained earlier, with politics and policy. Since we are dealing with a case where petroleum resources are owned by sovereign states, the arguments should necessitate looking beyond the microeconomic or sectoral level. As with other owners of petroleum assets, the GCC governments rely on petroleum fiscal revenues (royalties and petroleum taxes), which as noted earlier (Table 4.1), currently represent 80 percent of their budget resources (the percentage is obviously higher when including governments' revenues from investment income associated with their external financial assets). As these revenues are quasi-exclusively levied on the value of exports, governments tend to associate the fiscal values of their petroleum assets with international oil prices. In such cases the key questions to answer are: what level of revenue does their preferred oil price range of $60–80 per barrel ensure, and will such revenues be sufficient to achieve fiscal sustainability?

The theoretical framework most often used to answer such questions is derived from Milton Friedman's permanent income hypothesis (PIH). The PIH stemmed originally from the theory that the choices made by consumers regarding their consumption patterns are determined not by current income but by their longer-term income expectations. When transposed to governments – assuming they are forward looking – it means that their spending decisions would be, similarly, determined not by current revenues but by longer-term revenue expectations as well. In our case, GCC governments are assumed to capture the petroleum rent, spend part of it on public goods (education, infrastructure, health and other social welfare programs) and save fiscal surpluses by investing in foreign assets (mostly financial assets), generally through Sovereign Wealth Funds (SWFs). In this case, a PIH for sustainable governments' spending would be approximated by an annuity value obtained as the sum of the net present value of petroleum fiscal revenues (NPVPFR) expected over the lifetime of their petroleum resources, in addition to their net revenues from financial assets.[21]

While the above formulation appears relatively simple, the key parameters involved in the quantification of future governments' petroleum fiscal revenues and corresponding annuity values are fairly complex and highly uncertain.[22] To establish a long-term framework analysis, assumptions must be made regarding governments' depletion policies,[23] i.e., the amount of proven recoverable reserves, likely addition to reserves, the allocation of these reserves between domestic markets and exports, and the associated production profile. These determinants, together with other important factors, which include the structure of export prices, and how petroleum revenues are shared between the government and the oil and gas industry, are summarized below.

- Current estimates of the GCC aggregate proven reserves of crude oil, natural gas and NGLs derived from Table 4.3 amount to 105.2 billion tons of oil equivalent (Gtoe) at the start of 2009. These reserves are 64 percent crude oil and condensate and 36 percent natural gas. The ratio of reserves over 2008 production (R/P ratio) is about 93 years for the region as a whole. This ratio, which can be interpreted as the static lifetime of proven reserves, has no consequence for the analysis but helps in deciding on a simulation horizon, which is set accordingly to 2100.[24] Furthermore, as we take a dynamic view of reserve and production, we assume a 20 percent addition to proven reserves in the form of contingent and yet-to-find volumes (potential additional volumes that could be discovered through exploration). These additions are key to depletion since they are assumed to lengthen the production plateau period.

- Petroleum exports, as well as intra-GCC petroleum supply (currently, Saudi crude oil to Bahrain or Qatari natural gas to the UAE and Oman) are valued on the basis of international market prices. Based on past trends, product export prices are assumed to continue moving together with the ratio of the average GCC petroleum export price to the price of Dated Brent (taken as a benchmark) set at 0.7.

- In contrast to hydrocarbon exports, domestic energy consumption, which includes feedstock to the petrochemical industry (basically oil products, natural gas and NGLs), is valued at average supply costs, which means that there is no petroleum rent to be extracted from the domestic sector.

- Owing to the lack of transparency surrounding petroleum fiscal regimes in the region, we have worked out GCC governments' takes through an average implicit petroleum tax rate, expressed as the quotient of petroleum fiscal revenues over total petroleum exports.[25] The calibration of most recent years' fiscal data results in a ratio of some 70 percent. This ratio is kept constant until 2020 then assumed to decline by half a percentage point each year during the production plateau phase to reflect much higher costs.

- The discount factor, which reflects both time preference and risk, is taken in the order of five percent, moderate enough to match the very long-term horizon set for the simulations.

- Finally, to factor in the effect of population dynamics, our results are expressed in per capita terms. In projecting the evolution of the GCC population we assume that future demographics will be affected by local population growth, as well as labor import policies. Decreasing rate of growth of the local population would combine with a more successful domestication of labor to temper long term population trends. As a result, the GCC population, which reached 38.6 million at the end of 2008, is likely to continue growing rapidly to nearly 50 million in 2020, before moderating to some 60 million in 2030. In the longer term, the population would stabilize around 120 million in 2100.

Table 4.3

Proven Petroleum Reserves, Production, and R/P Ratios of the GCC Countries in 2008

		Unit	Bahrain	Kuwait	Oman	Qatar	Saudi Arabia	UAE	2008 GCC Aggregate
Crude oil and NGLs	Reserves	Gt	0.1	14.0	0.8	2.9	36.3	13.0	67.1
	Production	Mt	13.5	137.3	36.0	60.8	515.3	139.5	902.4
	R/P Ratio	Year	7.4	102.0	22.2	47.7	70.4	93.2	74.4
Natural gas	Reserves	Gtoe	0.1	1.6	0.9	22.9	6.8	5.8	38.1
	Production	Mtoe	12.1	11.5	21.6	69.0	70.3	45.2	229.7
	R/P Ratio	Year	8.3	139.1	41.7	331.9	99.7	128.3	165.9
Total Petroleum	Reserves	Gtoe	0.2	15.6	1.7	25.8	43.1	18.8	105.2
	Production	Mtoe	25.6	148.8	57.6	129.8	585.6	188.7	1132.1
	R/P Ratio	Year	7.8	104.8	29.5	198.8	73.6	101.8	92.9

Source: Author's compilations using *BP Statistical Review of World Energy* (and own estimations for Bahrain).

On this basis, Figure 4.4 illustrates a baseline scenario where the GCC's production profile is characterized by three critical horizons:

- 2020: Combined commercial production of oil and gas would reach a maximum of 1,540 million tons of oil equivalent (toe) and, as a consequence, exports start declining.

- 2050: After a 30-year plateau, production will start falling off, leaving a post-2100 tail of about 35 percent of currently proven and yet-to-find reserves.

- 2060: Production ceases to meet domestic primary requirements of oil and gas, which would have by then more than tripled.

Figure 4.4
Base Case Scenario for GCC Petroleum Supply and Demand Profiles (1960–2100)

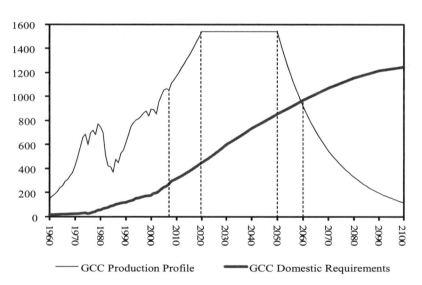

Note: Base year forecast: 2009. Future production profile based on aggregate proven remaining reserves of 105 Gtoe, with 35 percent of these reserves accounted for in a post-2100 tail.

Source: Author's simulations.

An alternative scenario consists of postponing the GCC production plateau to 2030 and consequently shortening it to 20 years. This assumption would lead to a higher production rate before 2030 and a faster depletion rate after 2050, resulting in a much lower post-2100 tail of about 20 percent. We dub this alternative an OPEC-based scenario. Indeed, as a quasi-core of OPEC (as noted earlier, four key members contribute a little more than half of OPEC output), the GCC region would be expected to produce within a particular framework. This framework assumes that global petroleum demand is first met by supply from non-OPEC producers, then by producers within OPEC acting as "residual" suppliers. The role of residual supplier stems from the ability of Saudi Arabia and, to a lesser extent, the UAE and Kuwait, to hold and use spare capacity to balance the market. Within this framework, the OPEC Secretariat indicates in its 2009 *World Oil Outlook* that despite revising its growth projections downwards on concerns of demand reduction and demand destruction, and further uncertainty about the extent of non-OPEC supply from non-conventional oil, it does not anticipate a plateau for OPEC crude oil and NGLS before 2030.[26] We would infer from this that the GCC production profile (deducting natural gas) would similarly not enter a plateau phase before that horizon. The resulting simulations of the GCC per capita NPVPFRs and associated annuity values for these two scenarios are summarized in Table 4.4. They correspond to the currently expressed oil price preferences being maintained constant. A further price preference assumption of $90 per barrel has been added. For reasons explained further below, this is the price needed to equalize the annuity value per capita of the base case scenario, with the average real per capita historical rent.

Obviously, the OPEC-based scenario increases the NPVPFRs; but would the GCC governments, if offered the option, prefer such a fast track production schedule? If their objective function were limited to maximizing the rent acruing to them, then they would choose – for any assumed domestic consumption profile, international oil price path and discount factor – the one that procures the highest NPVPFR per capita. However, as highlighted by Stevens and Mitchell, governments' choices should take into account broader social welfare function, which makes the choice of "what to count" in such a case far more complex: [27]

> The government should take account of the reduction of the oil reserve wealth ... including the forgoing of the option to produce later when oil price might be higher, and externalities such as environmental costs, and benefits which occur through direct linkages with the petroleum operation (inputs and outputs), the multiplier effect of these and of the government expenditure and the balance of payments effects of the revenues.

Table 4.4

GCC Net Present Value of Petroleum Fiscal Value (NPVPFV) Per Capita as a Function of Different Oil Price Preferences

Based on projections over the period 2009–2100		Units	Net present petroleum fiscal value (NPVPFV) based on a discount rate of 5 percent			
Oil price preferences		US$/bbl	60	75	80	90
Base-case Scenario	NPVPFR per capita	US$	74,435	93,045	99,250	111,650
	Corresponding annuity present value	US$	3,765	4,710	5,030	5,650
	Ratio to per cap historic rent	Unit	0.67	0.83	0.89	1.00
OPEC-based Sc.	NPVPFR per capita	US$	85,415	106,770	113,890	128,120
	Corresponding annuity present value	US$	4,320	5,400	5,740	6,480
	Ratio to per cap historic rent	Unit	0.76	0.96	1.02	1.15

Source: Author's simulations.

This being emphasized, we disregard the OPEC-based scenario for two reasons. The first is that by limiting its outlook to 2030, the OPEC Secretariat did not intend to access the resource finitude and depletion of its members. The second is that the GCC countries are more likley to resist pressure to produce at faster depletion rates. They need to defer some production and extend their production plateau so as to buy themselves the time needed for the long-term transition to a less petroleum-dependent economy.

Gauging the GCC's Fiscal Comfort

By adopting an infinite time horizon, it can formally be demonstrated that the annuity value per capita can be approximated by the product of the NPVPFR per capita and the discount factor. This simple formulation allows us to easily draw the annuity value as a function of constant oil prices and real interest rates, as illustrated in Figure 4.5 for the base-case scenario.

Figure 4.5
Permanent Petroleum Fiscal Revenue as a Function of Oil Prices and Interest Rates in the Base-case Scenario

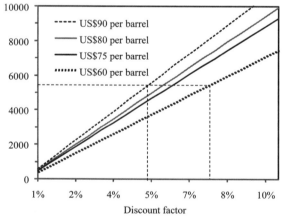

Source: Author's simulations.

Obviously, for a given interest rate the higher the price of oil the higher the annuity value. The converse is less evident. Indeed, it is far from intuitive that for a given annuity, higher interest rates should imply lower oil prices. As suggested by one reviewer of this paper, the difficulty in interpreting Figure 4.5 may also stem from the fact that our conceptual approximation overlooks the possible co-existence of two interest rates. One, which is used to discount future petroleum fiscal revenues, should reflect the opportunity cost of capital. The other is the rate of return earned from investing fiscal surpluses. Raising the first rate will lower the NPVPFR on which the annuity is based, whatever the investment return; raising the second will add to the annuity, whatever the NPVPFR.[28]

With these caveats in mind, Figure 4.5 raises the interesting question of whether or not current GCC oil preferences reflect their expectations of permanent petroleum fiscal revenues. To answer this question we need to form an opinion of what annuity values the GCC countries would be "fiscally comfortable" with. In other words, what are the amounts of annuity that would allow governments in the region to plan and execute desired socio-economic policies. Regrettably, there is no answer to this question in the absence of a clear indication of what such long-term plans might be. The historical record is even more difficult to establish. Over the last 50 years or so petroleum fiscal revenues in real terms (i.e., adjusted from inflation and the appreciation/depreciation of the US dollar) have exhibited large fluctuations around an average real rent per capita of about $5,650.[29] This is much higher than the annuity resulting from expected futures fiscal revenues under an oil price range of $60–80 per barrel. As hinted earlier, an equivalent annuity involves a price of at least $90 per barrel in the base case scenario. However, inferring a target income from an historic rent would not be reasonable without further analysis of the paths of domestic investment and savings and the extent to which the GCC countries have been accumulating financial assets.[30] This would require further research that is far beyond the scope of this study.

Before concluding, however, it should be stressed that in simulating the amount of the resource rent generated by the exploitation of hydrocarbons in the region, we have assumed that GCC governments would continue to favor levying the maximum rent from exports. They might also decide to tax domestic energy consumption. This could be achieved through a more appropriate domestic pricing of oil products, natural gas and NGLs. In the absence of competitive energy markets in the region, a domestic pricing regime can be established whereby prices reflect relevant opportunity costs. These can take the form of netback export market prices or, if such products are not exportable (the case of natural gas in Saudi Arabia), the form of long-run marginal cost of production plus a depletion premium.[31] Whatever the case, as an approximation to the complexities inherent to the simulation of the evolution of domestic prices, we can assume that the resource rent is captured by progressively taxing full production, starting with a rate of 50 percent, which procures the same fiscal revenues as the current 70 percent implicit tax on the value of petroleum exports. In a baseline scenario, where the GCC weighted average domestic price is assumed to increase from an estimated 20 percent of international oil prices in 2008 to some 50 percent by the year 2030, the implicit fiscal rate on total production would increase from 50 percent to 60 percent. Under this illustrative scenario the NPVPFV per capita would improve by approximately 25 percent under an international oil price assumption of $75 per barrel. This alternative fiscal prospect would change dramatically the GCC perception and preferences about international oil prices.

Conclusions

While oil-producing and oil-consuming countries share a broad scope of interests in promoting global energy security, they have different attitudes towards the oil price dimension. The producers, and particularly the more petroleum-dependent GCC countries among them, are much more vulnerable to the instability and volatility of global oil markets and, as a consequence, regard this dimension as critical. Their price preferences, however, cannot be revealed by the international oil market as it currently functions. A non-market perspective establishes that these preferences should lie at the confluence of the economic cost of developing petroleum projects in frontier areas and the expected fiscal value of their petroleum assets. Under this perspective, oil prices in the range of $60–80 per barrel should be appropriate to support energy investments worldwide. However, as long as fiscal revenues are derived from petroleum exports only, they would appear to be at the lower limit of what is required for long-term GCC fiscal sustainability.

Obviously, this conclusion should be interpreted with care given the challenges and limitations of the analysis. One implication is sure, however: improving petroleum fiscal revenues by other means could change current price preferences. The first and most obvious option would be for GCC governments to capture the rent from total petroleum production—not just from exports. This involves a re-evaluation and adjustment of current domestic petroleum pricing policies. A further, much more challenging avenue to fiscal sustainability resides in the diversification of the GCC economies and the taxation and redistribution of non-oil wealth. Changing the domestic pricing regime, diversifying the economy and extending taxation are among the hard policy choices facing governments in the region. As progress will likely be slow and protracted, GCC governments will continue for some time to associate the fiscal value of their petroleum assets and long-term fiscal sustainability with – and only with – international oil prices. Under these conditions, and given their development-based needs, the GCC, as an aggregate entity, may likely not achieve fiscal sustainability with an oil price below $90 per barrel.

[133]

RUSSIA AND ASIA:
PERSPECTIVES ON ENERGY SECURITY

5

Asia's Energy Demand and Implications for the Oil-Producing Countries of the Middle East

Philip Andrews-Speed

The Middle East holds about 60 percent of the world's proven conventional oil reserves and about 40 percent of the world's proven natural gas reserves. For at least the next twenty years the centers of growth in demand for both oil and gas will be located in non-OECD Asia, mainly in China and India. Over this period the demand for oil in OECD countries is likely to remain static or even fall, whilst demand for gas will continue to rise slowly. For these reasons the trade in both oil and gas from the Middle East to Asia is set to continue rising. This will result in a growing interdependence between the two regions, which will be enhanced by other forms of trade, cross-investments in energy and other sectors, and greater political engagement. At the same time, domestic demand within the Middle East will also rise substantially, especially for natural gas.

A critical challenge for the governments of the Middle East is to balance three sets of priorities. The first is to keep production levels sufficiently high and prices sufficiently low to ensure that Asian countries and other consumers continue to purchase oil and gas from international markets, rather than seek alternative forms of energy. The second priority is to ensure that the oil- and gas-exporting countries are able to gain a fair share of the economic rents from the extraction and export of their resources. This requires oil and gas prices not to fall too low. The third priority is to ensure that sufficient energy is available for domestic markets to support economic growth and development.

For these reasons, the future scale and nature of energy demand in Asia, and the reaction of Middle Eastern governments to this demand, are critical determinants of economic development among Middle Eastern states. The last few years have seen a rapid convergence of interests between certain Middle Eastern governments and large importing Asian states such as China. As each side seeks to address its own political and economic needs, cases of divergence in these interests may become more common.

The aims of this paper are to identify the factors which may determine the rate of growth of future Asian demand for oil and gas from the Middle East, and to examine the implications for the region. China will be used as an example – on account of the size of its potential import requirements – in order to examine the complexities surrounding energy relations between the Middle East and Asia.

Past and Future Patterns of Asian Demand

The aim of this section is to briefly document trends in relative demand for Middle East oil and gas from "The West" and "The East" (or Asia), and to examine likely future trends. By "The West" we mean the continents which lie to the west of the Middle East, namely Europe, Africa, and North and South America. By "The East" or Asia, we mean the Asian continent, excluding the Middle East itself and the Former Soviet Union, and also South-east Asia and Australasia.

Demand for Oil

The last twenty years have seen a steady but significant shift in the balance of demand for Middle Eastern oil from the West to Asia. Since 1990 the proportion of global demand accounted for by the West has declined from 75 to 63 percent. At the same time, Asia's share of demand has grown from 21 to 30 percent. Over this period the West's share of total oil production has declined from 63 to 58 percent, whilst that of the Middle East has grown from 27 to 32 percent. As a consequence, oil exports from the Middle East have risen by more than 40 percent.[1]

Rapid and sustained economic growth in Asia accompanied by slowing growth in oil production in the region has made Asia the major importer of oil from the Middle East (see Figure 5.1). The share of Middle East oil exports shipped to Asia has risen from 45 to 70 percent, whilst that shipped to the West has declined from 55 to 30 percent. China has been one of the main drivers of this growth, for its imports of oil from the Middle East have risen from 10,000 barrels per day (bpd) in 1994 to 1.8 million barrels per day (mbpd) in 2008 (see Figure 5.2). Although the total quantity of oil exported from the Middle East has doubled, the dependence of Asia on the Middle East for its imports of oil has declined from 77 to 63 percent.[2]

Figure 5.1

**Oil Exports from the Middle East to the West and to the East
(1990–2008)**

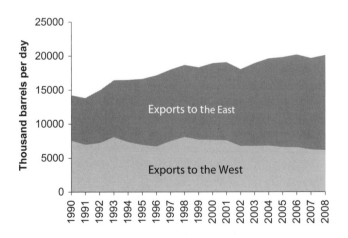

Source: *BP Statistical Review of World Energy*, various years.

The future growth of energy demand in Asia and the rest of the world depends on a variety of factors, such as economic growth rates, the structure of economies, and the energy efficiency of appliances. Transport is a key sector for oil consumption, as most countries are reducing the use of oil in industry and power. But within the transport sector, any attempt to forecast future demand is plagued by uncertainties, even within a single country. Although oil is the dominant fuel in the transport sector today, the longevity and degree of its dominance will depend on the nature of decisions which key oil-consuming and oil-producing countries may make in the coming years. On the consumption side, conventional transport fuels distilled from crude oil face potential challenges from natural gas, electricity and hydrogen. Furthermore, liquid fuels can be manufactured from coal, natural gas and plant materials (biofuels). On the production side, certain countries have yet to make firm decisions to press ahead with the extraction of abundant non-conventional oil reserves (oil shale, tar sand).

Figure 5.2

China's Oil Imports from the Middle East

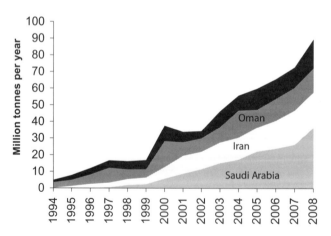

Sources: Chunrong Tian, "Review of China's Oil Imports and Exports in 1999," *International Petroleum Economics*, Vol. 8, No. 2 (2000), pp. 5–9 (in Chinese); Chunrong Tian, "Review of China's Oil Imports and Exports in 2004," *International Petroleum Economics*, Vol. 13, No. 3 (2005), pp. 10–16 (in Chinese); Chunrong Tian, "Review of China's Oil Imports and Exports in 2008," *International Petroleum Economics*, Vol. 17, No. 3 (2009), pp. 31–39 (in Chinese).

With these limitations in mind, the projections of the International
Energy Agency (IEA) to the year 2030 identify some important
considerations for this study.[3] First, non-OECD Asia plays a dominant
role in the future growth of world oil demand, and within this region
China and India are the main sources of demand growth. Second, the
alternative policy scenario for the year 2030 envisages substantial
reductions in consumption, especially in China (see Figures 5.3 and 5.4).
Looking specifically at China as an example, it is evident that the
transport sector will account for progressively more of the country's
demand for oil (see Figure 5.5). Furthermore, alternative transport fuels
are likely to make much less impact on oil demand in China's transport
sector than will policies which seek to enhance the overall efficiency of
energy use in the sector (see Figure 5.6).

Figure 5.3

Projected World Demand for Oil to 2030

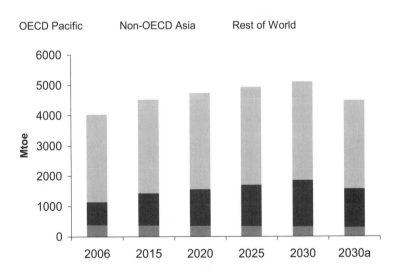

Note: (2030a) refers to the alternative policy scenario in which energy efficiency and clean
and renewable energy are successfully promoted.

Sources: International Energy Agency, *World Energy Outlook 2007* and *World Energy
Outlook 2008* (Paris: OECD).

Figure 5.4

Future Oil Demand in Asia to 2030

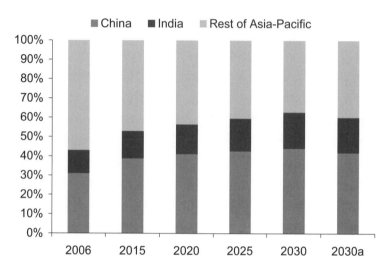

Note and sources: as for Figure 5.3.

Figure 5.5

Structure for Future Oil Demand in China to 2030

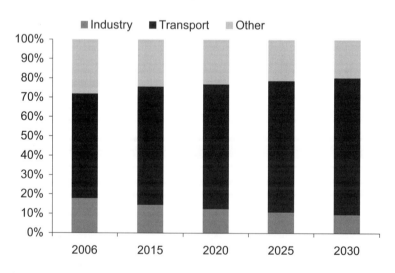

Note and sources: as for Figure 5.3.

Figure 5.6

Forecast Demand for Transport Fuels in China to 2030

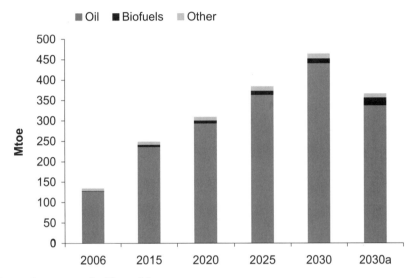

Note and sources: as for Figure 5.3.

Demand for Gas

Over the last twenty years, the Middle East has seen a much greater rate of growth in its exports of gas than for its exports of oil (see Figure 5.7). This is explained by the distance from suitable markets which might have been supplied by pipeline, the consequent reliance on LNG technology which took time to spread across Asia, and the relatively late take-up of natural gas as an important source of energy in South and East Asia—Japan being the notable exception. Although Asia receives between 78 and 80 percent of the Middle East's gas exports, this proportion has remained relatively static since 2004 in contrast to the steady relative growth of oil shipments to Asia (see Figure 5.1). This may be explained by the relative abundance of natural gas resources close to the Asian markets in South-east Asia and Australasia, in contrast to the declining capacity of the same region to export oil.

Looking to the future using the IEA's projections, world gas demand is set to grow over the next twenty years to 2030, but the non-OECD Asia-Pacific does not play as prominent role in this growth as was the case for oil (see Figure 5.8). Furthermore, the greatest savings in gas consumption in the alternative policy scenario are likely to be made outside Asia.

Within the Asia region, China and India will be the major sources of additional demand for gas. Of greater significance is that China's gas consumption in the alternative policy scenario for 2030 is *higher* than in the base-case scenario (see Figure 5.9). Such an increase would be driven by a switch from coal to natural gas, especially in the power sector (see Figure 5.10).

Figure 5.7
Natural Gas Exports from the Middle East to the West and to the East (1990–2008)

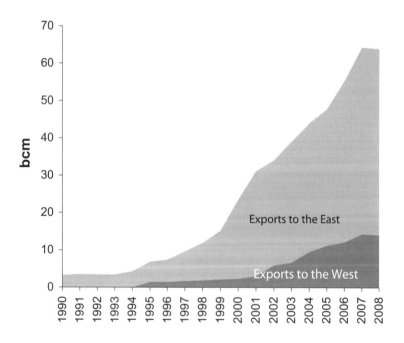

Source: *BP Statistical review of World Energy*, various years.

Figure 5.8

Projected World Demand for Gas to 2030

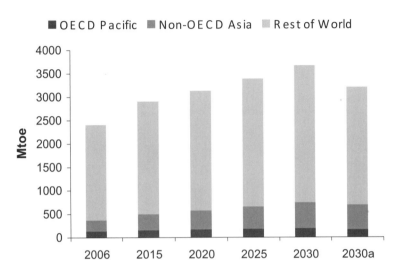

Note and sources: as for Figure 5.3.

Figure 5.9

Projected Gas Demand for Asia to 2030

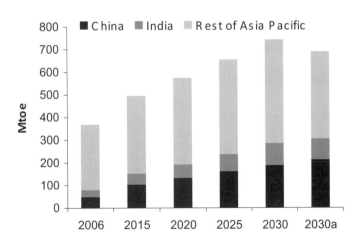

Note and sources: as for Figure 5.3.

Figure 5.10

Projected Fuel Mix in China's Power Sector to 2030 (excluding coal)

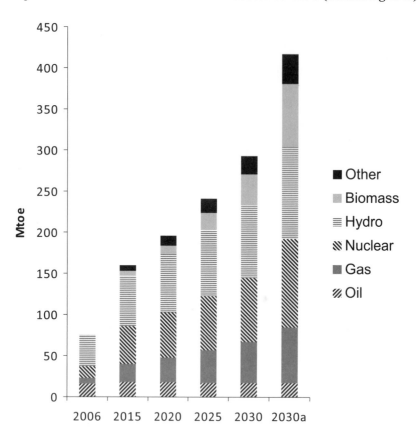

Note and sources: as for Figure 5.3.

Future Asian Oil and Gas Imports

The level of future imports of oil and gas to Asia depends not on just demand but on domestic production. Thus the estimate of imports to Asia is dependent on the difference between two parameters, both of which themselves carry a high degree of uncertainty. That being said, the forecasts of the IEA for China and India contain some important messages (see Table 5.1).

Future imports to these two countries will rise significantly over the period to 2030, for oil and to an even greater extent for gas. In the alternative policy scenario, the import requirement for oil will be less than in the base case scenario, whereas for gas it will be greater, on account of China's fuel switching.

Table 5.1

Projected Imports of Oil and Gas to China and India in 2030

	Oil mbpd			Gas bcm/yr		
	2008	2030 Reference scenario	2030 Alternative policy scenario	2008	2030 Reference scenario	2030 Alternative policy scenario
China	4.0	13.1	9.7	4.5	128	158
India	2.3	6.0	4.9	10.8	61	56
Total	6.3	19.1	14.6	15.3	189	214

Note and sources: as for Figure 5.3.

The Case of China

China is of critical importance to the future of Middle Eastern exports of oil and gas to Asia on account of its large size, rapid economic growth and limited domestic energy resources. Yet the future success of Middle Eastern states in capturing a large share of this growing market depends on many factors. The aim of this section is to highlight some of these considerations through examining, in turn, China's oil and gas strategies, the nature of energy relations between China and the states of the Middle East, and the variety of motivations behind China's international oil and gas strategies. It concludes by identifying some constraints on deepening energy relations between these two regions.

China's Oil and Gas Strategies

Oil and Liquid Fuels

China is the world's fifth largest producer of oil, after Saudi Arabia, Russia, the United States and Iran, and accounts for five percent of world production. Yet existing proven reserves will provide for barely more than ten years of present day consumption. Demand has been rising at an annual rate of 7–9 percent, despite government moves to restrict the use of oil in transport and petrochemicals,[4] whilst domestic production grows by just 1–2 percent per year. Already imports account for 50 percent of consumption (see Figure 5.11).

Figure 5.11
Oil Production, Consumption and Refinery Throughput in China, 1980–2008 (in millions of tons per year)

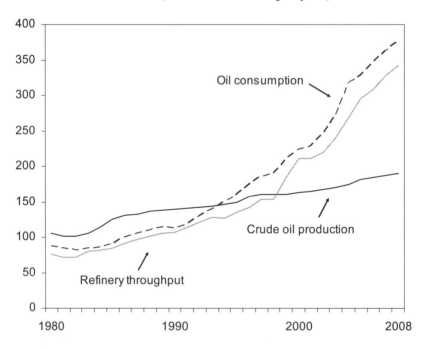

Source: *BP Statistical Review of World Energy*, 2009.

With the exception of a few offshore areas, China has been well-explored for oil over the past fifty years. Onshore exploration has been carried out almost entirely by the Chinese national oil companies. In the early 1980s China's government was keen to explore for domestic offshore oil and gas reserves. Realizing that its own companies lacked the necessary expertise, it invited foreign oil companies to participate, in collaboration with the state oil company China National Offshore Oil Corporation (CNOOC). In later years, onshore regions were progressively opened up to foreign companies. Although some discoveries were made offshore, overall the results have been disappointing, primarily for geological reasons, but also on account of administrative challenges onshore.[5]

Estimates of remaining reserves of oil range between 2.1 and 2.5 billion tons. Recent discoveries will certainly add to this figure—for example, the Nanpu oilfield in the shallow water areas of Bohai Bay.[6] Projections for future levels of crude oil production vary from a decline from 185 million tons in 2006 to levels as low as 150 million tons during the period 2015–2020 and even lower by 2030, to a modest rise to 210–220 million tons over the period 2020–2030.

In order to maximize its security of supply and the economic benefits derived from refining, China continues to invest heavily in upgrading and expanding its refining capacity. Upgrading is necessary to cope with sour crude oils imported from the Middle East, and expansion is required to keep pace with the rising level of demand for oil products.[7] Despite this construction, a gap still remains between oil consumption and refinery output (see Figure 5.11) and thus net imports of oil products remain at a high level (see Figure 5.12). The recent involvement of foreign companies – comprising both international companies and national oil companies from Saudi Arabia and Kuwait – should help accelerate the construction of new refineries, and the IEA has assumed that refining capacity will reach the level of demand by the year 2012. But the challenge will remain to match the demand in terms of product type and quality. In the past, China's refineries have produced too much gasoline and not enough diesel, and in recent years have struggled to raise the quality of output to meet ever rising technical specifications driven by environmental policies.[8]

Even the most optimistic projections for domestic crude oil production show that the trend of rising import dependence is set to continue unabated. As a consequence, and in light of its security of supply fears, the government has supported the development of two sources of alternative supply of liquid fuels for transportation and petrochemicals: biofuels and coal-to-liquids.

Figure 5.12

China's Imports and Exports of Crude Oil and Oil Products, 1990–2008 (in millions of tons)

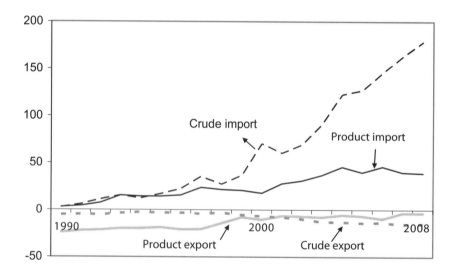

Source: *BP Statistical Review of World Energy*, various years.

Official documents have given targets as high as 20 million tons of annual biofuel output by 2020, although this level is likely to depend on the level of international oil prices, with higher prices leading to higher levels of biofuel production, as well as on China's ability to produce biofuels from non-edible crops.[9]

The government and the major coal companies have also invested large amounts of money in the development and initial commercialization of coal-to-liquids technology, in order to produce liquids which can be used for transport and petrochemicals. But enthusiasm for this technology waned during 2007 as the environmental costs became increasingly apparent.[10] Official targets and projections suggest that the production of liquids from this technology may reach 10 million tons by 2015 and more than 35 million tons by 2030.

Figure 5.13

Sources of Crude Oil Imports to China, 1994–2008

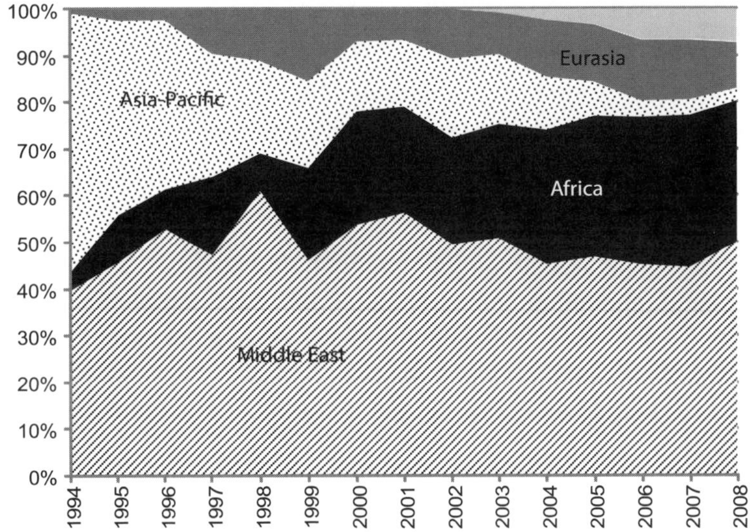

Source: see Figure 5.2.

These sources of liquid fuels may provide a useful supplement to China's domestic supply of crude oil. Yet net imports of oil remain set to rise from 184 million tons in 2007 to possibly more than 300 million tons by 2015, and to as much as 500 million tons by 2020. Import dependency could reach 70–80 percent by 2030, up from 50 percent in 2008.[11] As a result the government made the decision in 2003 to construct emergency oil storage facilities in order to enhance its ability to react to short term interruptions to supply or to price spikes. Although construction started in 2004, the high level of oil prices rendered the filling of the tanks unviable until international crude oil prices fell in the summer of 2008. China then took advantage of the low prices to fill its existing tanks, taking its reserve to 15 million tons or two weeks' supply.[12]

Natural Gas and Coal-bed-methane

The period since 1997 has seen a concerted attempt by the government and by state companies to raise the level of natural gas use. Two considerations have underpinned this policy: to introduce a cleaner fuel to replace coal and to diversify the energy supply mix.[13] Despite annual increases of 15–20 percent in the domestic production of natural gas that have allowed China to raise its domestic production from 19 billion cubic meters (bcm) in 1997 to 69 bcm in 2007, gas continues to provide less than 3 percent of the country's energy supply, up marginally from 2 percent ten years previously.

The long-term future of the domestic gas supply industry is quite uncertain, as systematic exploration for gas only began in the 1990s. Major new discoveries continue to be made, especially in the Ordos Basin of northern China, in the Tarim Basin of north-west China and in Sichuan Province, and these should allow gas consumption to grow rapidly over the coming years.[14] Exploration proceeds offshore, including in the East China Sea where China and Japan have overlapping claims.[15] Projections show domestic supply of natural gas rising to levels in the range 120–150 bcm in 2020.

The second strand of China's natural gas strategy relies on imported gas both through pipelines and on ships as liquefied natural gas (LNG).[16] Total imports of natural gas are projected to rise from 1 bcm in 2006 to 60 bcm or more in 2020 and to more than 100 bcm by 2030. Pipelines are seen as being more secure because the flow of gas is not open to interruption on the high seas. LNG is more cost-effective over very long distances and, as regional LNG markets develop, LNG can be more flexible because a buyer of gas can have a number of suppliers. The first imports of gas arrived in Guangdong in 2006 – as LNG – accounting for less than 2 percent of China's total gas consumption that year.

Price continues to be a concern for LNG imports.[17] By chance, China's first LNG plant in Guangdong was able to secure a very low price for a supply of gas from Australia in 2002. This was on account of a temporary excess of supply over demand in the global LNG market. Encouraged by this low price, China's oil companies announced a number of LNG terminals along the east coast of the country.[18] However, the low price achieved by the Guangdong project could not be replicated in the following years as demand for LNG grew throughout the world.[19] By late 2007 Chinese companies and the government had conceded that the high prices had to be paid. Current plans would add three more LNG terminals to the operational plants in Guangdong, Fujian and Shanghai, bringing a total of six plants on-stream by 2012 with a total capacity of about 25 bcm per year, and a further growth of import capacity to more than 40 bcm per year by 2020. The volume of LNG already contracted on a long-term basis by Chinese companies now exceeds 30 bcm from the year 2014.[20]

Central Asia and Russia both contain substantial proven and potential reserves of gas which could be imported through pipelines and make a major contribution to China's gas supply.[21] In 2006 China and Turkmenistan signed agreements which gave CNPC rights to explore for and produce gas in Turkmenistan and to construct an export pipeline to China with a planned capacity of 40 bcm per year. This pipeline was commissioned at the end of 2009. It connects to the new, second West-to-East gas pipeline within China which brings the gas to southern and eastern parts of the country.[22] In Russia, progress in developing gas resources and exporting them to China has been rather slow, despite planning and discussion since the late 1990s. Progress has been delayed by changes of gas policy priorities within Russia and a failure to agree a price acceptable to both parties.[23]

[153]

Despite these projections of rising domestic production and imports, it is clear that natural gas will only ever be able to provide a small proportion of the national energy supply, and that little of this gas will be cheap. As a result, the last ten years have seen significant efforts in China to identify and exploit an alternative domestic source of gas, coal-bed methane, and these are now starting to bear fruit. Ambitious plans to expand production to 10 bcm have not yet been achieved, partly owing to a shortage of pipelines to deliver the gas to the consumers. Annual production is set to rise to 1 bcm in 2010. This would add just 1 percent to domestic gas supply, but resources have been found which would allow coal-bed methane to make a much greater contribution to China's energy supply.[24]

China–Middle East Energy Relations

Energy relations between China and Middle Eastern states take a number of forms:

- Growing imports of oil, mainly crude oil, from the Middle East to China (See Figure 5.2);

- Long-term, inter-governmental agreements to supply oil or gas to China;

- Investments by Chinese companies in oil and gas assets in the Middle East, mainly upstream (see Table 5.2);

- Investments by Middle Eastern companies in oil assets in China, mainly downstream (see Table 5.3);

- The provision of oil-field and construction services by Chinese companies in the Middle East.

In the 1990s, Oman and Yemen dominated oil exports to China from the Middle East, as the crude oil from these countries had a low sulfur content—or in oil-field jargon, was "sweet." In contrast, most crude oil from the Middle East is rich in sulfur and is "sour." China's traditional refining capacity was constructed to process China's domestic crude oil which is "sweet."[25] As a result, China has been slowly upgrading its refineries and constructing new refineries able to process sour crude oils from the Middle East. By the end of 2008, China's capacity to process sour crude oil amounted to some 1.6 mbpd or 20 percent of the country's total capacity.

The proportion of oil from Saudi Arabia and Iran grew dramatically from the late 1990s, but China's ability to import the sour crude oils from Saudi Arabia, Iran and other Middle East exporters was for several years constrained by a shortage of suitable refining capacity. As a result China has put great effort into raising imports of sweet crude oil from Africa and Eurasia. A further reason constraining the level of imports from the Middle East has been the desire to limit, as far as possible, the country's dependence on the Middle East through diversifying sources of supply.

The years since 2000 have seen Chinese national oil companies (NOCs) take a number of steps to gain access to investment opportunities in the Middle East, mainly in exploration and production, but also in the construction of refineries (see Table 5.1). The target investments are of two types. The first type comprises a small number of large or very large oil and gas fields in the countries with major oil and gas reserves such as Iran and, to a lesser extent, Iraq, Saudi Arabia, Kuwait and the UAE. Before June 2009, only the Yadavaran oil field in Iran and the Al-Ahdab field in Iraq could be considered secure and substantial deals. The months of June and July 2009 saw Chinese oil companies securing three significant deals: the China National Petroleum Corporation (CNPC) concluded an agreement with the Iranian government to replace Total in the contract to develop Phase 11 of the South Pars gas field; Sinopec launched a friendly bid for the Swiss company, Addax, which is producing oil fields in the Kurdish region of Iraq; and CNPC and BP jointly won a bid to develop the giant South Rumaila oil field in southern Iraq.

The second type of investment involves a number of smaller or higher risk projects which may yield commercial profits for the Chinese NOCs, but are not of sufficient size to be of strategic importance either to the large NOCs or to China's government.

Chinese NOCs will certainly continue with their attempts to gain access to large and high quality reserves in the Middle East, but host governments may consider that they lack the technical and managerial skills for the largest and most complex projects. As a result China's NOCs may benefit from cooperating with major international oil companies, as they already do in other parts of the world. In this context, it is significant that in April 2009, Shell raised the possibility of working with Chinese NOCs in Iraq.

China and East Asia are potentially of as great importance to the Middle East oil and gas producers as the Middle East is to China and East Asia. Today some 68 percent of Middle Eastern oil exports flow to the Asia-Pacific region. Although only 8 percent reaches China, this proportion is set to rise. Furthermore, 75 percent of Middle Eastern LNG goes to East Asia—mainly Japan and South Korea. Until 2009, none of China's LNG imports came from the Middle East, but this changed with the first cargo arriving from Qatar in September 2009, and a further supply contract with Qatar was signed later that year. Iran has also committed to supply China with LNG at such time when supplies are available.

As a consequence, certain national oil companies in the Middle East have sought opportunities to invest in China. The first of these was Saudi Aramco which entered negotiations with Sinopec as early as 1993 to construct new refining capacity at Qingdao, in Shandong Province. This project only came on-stream in 2008 and without the participation of Saudi Aramco who, in late 2009, were still negotiating participation with Sinopec. Saudi Aramco's first cooperative refinery project with Sinopec, in Fujian Province, was commissioned in 2009. Another Saudi company, the Saudi Arabian Basic Industries Corporation (SABIC), plans to build a cracking plant in Tianjian, whilst the Kuwait Petroleum Corporation (KPC) and the Qatar Petroleum Company (QPC) also plan to build refineries and petrochemical plants (see Table 5.2). In addition, these companies plan to be involved in the construction of oil storage facilities as well as to participate in the retail of oil products.

Table 5.2

Summary of Exploration, Production and Refining Investments Made, Agreed or Proposed by Chinese NOCs in the Middle East

Country	Country reserves		Project name (O) = Oil (G) = Gas	Project type	Date signed	Company	Project status	Reserves/production	Investment
	Oil bn bbl	Gas tcm							
Saudi Arabia	264	7.2	Section B (G)	E & P	2004	Sinopec	Exploration	? 11 TCF	< US $2.2 bn
Iran	138	27.8	Block 3 (O)	E & P	2005	CNPC	Exploration		
Iran			Masjed-I-Suleiman (O)	Acquisition	2004	CNPC	Exploration		US $150 m
Iran			South Pars (G)	Development	2009	CNPC		50 million cubic meters per day	US $ 5 bn
Iran			Yadavaran (O)	E & P	2007	Sinopec	Development	1.5-3.0 bn bbl (payment in LNG)	US$ 2 bn
Iran			Zavareh-Kashan	E & P	2001	Sinopec	Failed exploration		US $160 m
Iran			North Pars (G)	E & P	2006	CNOOC	Development	20 mtpa of LNG	US $16 bn
Iran			Arak (O)	Refinery upgrade	2006	Sinopec	Construction	200 kbpd	
Iraq	115	3.2	Al-Ahdab (O)	Development	1997/2008	CNPC	Development	< 110 kbpd, 1 bn bbl	
Iraq			South Rumaila (O)	Development	2009	CNPC	Development	7.3 bn bbl	
Iraq			Addax assets (O)	E & P, refinery	To be finalized	Sinopec	Producing	42 mmb	
Kuwait	101	1.8	?	Development	2009	Sinopec	Development		US $350m
UAE	98	6.1	Uraq & Zora (G)	Acquisition	2003	Sinochem	Exploration		
Oman	5.6	0.7	Blocks 36 & 38	E & P	2004	Sinopec	Exploration		
Oman			Blocks 17 & 40	Acquisition	2003	Sinochem	Exploration		
Oman			Block 5 (O)	E & P		CNPC		1.5 mmb	
Yemen	2.8	0.5	Block S2		2001	Sinopec			
Yemen			Block 69 & 71	Development	2005	Sinopec			
Syria	2.5	0.3	Qubibe (O)	Development	2004	CNPC	Development		
Syria			Al Furat Petroleum Co (O)	Acquisition	2005	CNPC	Producing	58 kbpd, 24 mmb	US $ 570m
Syria			Two PSAs (O)		negotiation	Sinopec	Producing	6 kbpd, 185-660 mmb	US $2 bn
Syria			Al Zour (O)	Refinery	2008	CNPC			
Syria			Block 10 (O)	Acquisition	2008	Sinochem	Producing	6.7 kbpd	

Source: mostly from FACTS Global Energy, *An Update of China's Overseas Oil and Gas Investment*, China Energy Series, Oil Edition, December 2008.

In many respects the energy strategies China pursues in the Middle East resemble those it pursues in other parts of the world. The distinguishing features of China's energy relations and activities in the Middle East include:

- the large scale and long duration of the diplomatic effort expended by China in the Middle East;[26]

- the consistently large proportion of oil imports from the Middle East and the apparent importance of long-term supply agreements;

- the very small number of exploration and production contracts of substantial size which have been concluded by China's NOCs, and the patience displayed by China's NOCs in negotiating large exploration and production deals; and

- the growing size of inward investment from the Middle East to China's oil sector.

In addition, China's long-term dependence on Middle East oil has driven it to take steps to protect sea-lanes in South and East Asia[27] and also, more recently, in the seas off Northeast Africa. The decision to invite the participation of Iran as an observer to the Shanghai Cooperation Organization (SCO) further emphasizes China's interests in energy cooperation with that country.

Motivations for China's International Oil and Gas Strategies

The nature, scope and rate of development of China's international oil and gas strategies are remarkable even in today's economically-integrated world. In part they can be explained by the convergence of four sets of interests. In the context of the Middle East, these are the interests of China's government, of China's NOCs, of the Middle Eastern governments, and of their NOCs.

[158]

Table 5.3

Inward Investment by Middle Eastern NOCs into China

Company/ Country	Project	Capacity	Location	Partners	Date signed	Completion date
Saudi Aramco	Refinery	240 kbpd	Fujian	Sinopec ExxonMobil	2001	2009
Saudi Aramco	Refinery	< 400 kbpd	Qingdao	Sinopec	Under negotiation	2008
SABIC	Cracker	240 kbpd	Tianjin	Sinopec	2007	2009
Saudi Aramco	Oil storage		Hainan		2006	2009
Saudi Aramco	Retail stations	600 stations				
Kuwait Petroleum Corp	Refinery & petrochemicals	260 kbpd	Guangdong	Sinopec	2006	2011
Kuwait Petroleum Corp	Oil storage	1.9 mmb	Guangdong	CNAF	2007	2009
Qatar	Refinery & petrochemicals	—	—	PetroChina, Shell	MOU 2008	

Sources: press reports.

China's Government

China's government has a number of motivations for the scale and scope of the effort it is devoting to its international oil and gas strategy, although the primary motivation for this is to enhance the security of international supplies of oil and gas. In this respect China's government has specific concerns relating to price and physical interruptions of supply, triggered by its increasing reliance on imported oil and gas.[28]

As is the case for all importers of oil, China is subject to the vagaries of international market prices. However it regulates its domestic markets and however much oil it refines, an importing nation is obliged to pay the prevailing market price for imports of crude oil. The concerns of China's government relating to international oil markets are three-fold. First, it

[159]

dislikes the volatile and unpredictable nature of the market. Second, it distrusts what it perceives as the undue influence that a few countries – especially the United States – have on the market. Third, it resents the "premium" that China and other East Asian countries have to pay for every barrel of oil imported from the Middle East.

In the 1990s and early 2000's China's government appeared to be taking what was variously called a "strategic"[29] or "neo-mercantilist"[30] approach in addressing these security of supply challenges. A belief existed in government and its circle of advisers that security of supply could be enhanced by owning rights to oil and gas in the ground around the world, and by producing this oil and gas. The national oil companies would be instruments of this policy. Such resources would be secure, and the produced equity oil would be cheaper than oil bought on the open market. Given that the world's remaining oil and gas reserves appeared to be limited, it was vital for China to move quickly to gain its fair share of what was remaining.[31] The security of international oil and gas flows to China would be further enhanced by signing long-term supply agreements with major exporters, by building military capacity to protect sea-lanes and by constructing import pipelines where possible.

In addition to these objectives relating to security of supply, the government had other aims in its support for the overseas strategies of the oil companies. The most important of these relate to industrial and foreign policies.

Since the late 1990s the government has pursued an official policy to protect a small number of pillar industries which remained in state hands and to promote their development into major international players. The oil industry was one of these.[32] The restructuring and partial listing of the national oil companies in the late 1990s confirmed that the managers shared these ambitions. Indeed, as discussed above, the very survival of the companies depended on success abroad.

Allied to this was the desire on the part of both the government and the oil companies to promote opportunities for oilfield service companies to win business overseas. This would not only keep a greater proportion for the oil companies' revenues in Chinese hands, but would also provide employment for tens of thousands of oilfield workers and managers. Furthermore, as both oil companies and service companies expanded their businesses overseas they would provide more tax revenues and more foreign exchange to the government.[33]

Just as foreign policy can support energy policy, so can energy be used to support foreign policy. Indeed it has long been recognized that energy, or funds to invest in energy development, can be wielded in the international arena either as a carrot or as a stick. Given its status as an energy importer, China has chosen to use energy as a diplomatic carrot. It has used energy as a starting point for building new relations, as a catalyst to renew dormant relations, and to deepen existing relations. As described above, energy has been packaged together with other instruments to achieve both political and economic gains, and in some countries energy forms a critical component of China's diplomatic strategy.[34]

In the Middle East, the scale of the region's oil and gas resources, the potential scope for investment and services, and the international strategic importance of the region allow China's government to pursue a wide range of interests through its involvement in the oil and gas sector. As a consequence China's government has played a major role in supporting its oil companies in their efforts to gain access to commercial opportunities, especially in Iran, Iraq and Saudi Arabia which together hold the bulk of the region's oil and gas reserves. In all three countries the barriers to foreign investors in the oil and gas industry have been high for many years, and government support will have been critical to China's NOCs gaining a foothold ahead of other competitors.

China's National Oil Companies

Although the government may have been the main force behind the diversification of supplies and the securing of long-term supply arrangements, the prime movers behind the growth of overseas commercial activity by China's NOCs have been the companies themselves; not just the three main national oil companies, but also their subsidiary service companies, smaller oil companies and various provincial companies. For most of these players the driving forces for internationalization have been a combination of necessity and opportunity.[35]

This necessity has arisen from constraints and threats on their home ground, within China. China's onshore areas and, to a lesser extent, its offshore seas have been well explored. Although new discoveries continue to be made, NOCs are struggling to increase production within China. The possession of oil and gas reserves for future production is a fundamental requirement for the long-term success of an oil company. With limited opportunity at home, Chinese companies have been forced to go overseas in order to secure their long-term survival. As well as just surviving, the commercialization and overseas listing of the national oil companies in the late 1990s placed on them a clear obligation to seek growth in revenues, profits and value.

A second domestic threat arises from the manner in which oil and natural gas are priced. The government retains the right to control or set the prices of all energy products. Although producer prices for oil have risen along with international prices, producer prices for natural gas have not kept pace, and consumer prices for most forms of energy have been tightly controlled at a low level. As a result, companies which refine crude oil have been making massive financial losses, and those supplying gas have had their profits constrained. With tightly controlled energy markets at home, China's oil companies have evident incentives to invest abroad in such a way as to allow them to sell their products at international prices with no restrictions.

The opportunities for these companies are multiple. First, and most importantly, overseas expansion allows them to take the first steps towards becoming truly international corporations rather than just very large NOCs. This is the prime ambition of PetroChina, Sinopec and

CNOOC. To become major international players they will require capital, assets and skills. They have the capital, they are building their asset base around the world, and they are starting to develop their technical and managerial expertise to international levels, building on many decades of domestic experience. Within this context, overseas expansion allows these companies to expand their range of activities beyond their historic bases more rapidly than would be possible at home.

For Chinese NOCs, as for international oil companies, the Middle East is a region of key strategic importance for future investments as well as for service and construction contracts. Chinese companies have been able to leverage government support in order to a gain modest advantage over their rivals, but the scale of activity in countries such as Saudi Arabia, Iran, Iraq and Kuwait has been constrained by domestic political and legal constraints on foreign investment in natural resources.

Host Governments

Host governments play a key role in the internationalization of China's oil companies, for it is they – or their national oil companies – who agree the deals and award the contracts. Although many host governments treat Chinese companies in the same way as companies from other countries, a number of governments have their own specific objectives when seeking investment in their oil and gas sectors from China. These objectives range from the mainly economic to the largely political.[36]

Countries such as Iran, Sudan, Myanmar and Syria urgently require foreign investment in their energy sectors, and yet US and other Western governments forbid or discourage their companies from investing there. As a result, these governments have no choice but to seek investment from countries which do not pursue the same political agenda, such as China, India, Russia and Malaysia. Of these, China has the largest oil companies with the greatest ambitions for internationalization and the largest sources of finance, though Russia's Gazprom is taking its first steps to become a major international gas player.

[163]

There are those governments which are successful at attracting inward investment to their oil and gas sectors, but wish to reduce their dependence on certain outside parties. Countries such as Libya, Equatorial Guinea and Kazakhstan have clearly stated that they wish to diversify investment away from the Western oil companies, and Kazakhstan and Turkmenistan want to break their historic dependence on Russia.

In Africa, many countries are in great need of investment both in their petroleum sectors and general infrastructure to accelerate their economic development. The governments of Angola, Sudan, Nigeria and other African countries have been keen to accept such assistance from China in association with oil investments because this aid has been delivered in a very timely manner and comes with none of the conditions associated with aid programs from the West.[37]

The governments of the petroleum-rich countries of the Middle East have objectives which relate to their desire for security of demand and to the ambitions of their own NOCs. These governments know that Asia, rather than the West, will be their biggest customer in the future and therefore they must build better economic and political relations with governments in the region, and with China in particular. Thus they are keen to sign long-term supply agreements and appear to be willing to allow Chinese companies to invest in their domestic petroleum sectors.

From the perspective of foreign relations, certain governments appear to take advantage of China's interest in their resources in order to use China as a political and strategic counter-balance to the United States or to the West in general. This is likely to be the case for a number of Middle Eastern governments.

Host Country National Oil Companies

Whilst the objectives of host country NOCs are usually broadly consistent with those of their government, NOCs are likely to have a number of specific business goals. First, an NOC may be willing to use Chinese service and construction companies on account of their relatively cheap price and owing to the work ethic with usually results in timely completion of even the toughest projects. This has certainly been the case in the Middle East.

Second, a host NOC may lack the cash to implement its investment program and may be keen to have a cash-rich, joint venture Chinese partner, or indeed to receive cash loans from China's government or NOCs. For example, in February 2009, the Chinese government agreed to lend US$25 billion to two of Russia's state oil companies, Rosneft and Transneft, in return for a guaranteed supply of 300 kbpd for 20 years. That same week, The China Development Bank agreed to lend Brazil's NOC, Petrobras, $10 billion in return for supplying 60 to 100 kbpd of crude oil to Sinopec, China's main state-owned refiner, and between 40 and 60 kbpd to PetroChina.

Finally, the larger NOCs of those Middle Eastern countries which lack a large domestic market are keen to integrate vertically downstream in refining, petrochemicals and retailing in a large market such as that of China. This strategy mirrors, to a certain extent, that of the Chinese NOCs and may help them to develop into major, internationalized companies.

Constraints on Deepening Energy Relations

The future of energy relations between China and the Middle East depend on many factors. At the most fundamental level is the future scale of China's total requirement for oil and gas imports. This in turn depends on the rate of economic growth, the structure of the economy, energy policies which may encourage fuel efficiency and fuel substitution in the transport sector, and on a switch from coal to gas in the power sector. However, China, like other countries, still continues to have a wide choice of suppliers for oil and gas. Africa and the former Soviet Union are starting to match the Middle East as suppliers of oil to China, and the former Soviet Union, South-East Asia and Australia also have large reserves of natural gas with which they can supply China.

[165]

A further fundamental consideration in this apparently simple supply chain is the growth of demand for oil and gas in the Middle Eastern countries themselves. As the economies of the more populous countries develop, domestic demand for energy will grow, thus progressively less may be available for export. Estimates suggest that the period to 2030 is likely to see a decline in the volume of oil and gas available for export from the region, including from countries such as Saudi Arabia, Iran and Kuwait.[38]

The highly politicized nature of energy relations between China and the Middle East along with the global strategic importance of the Middle East will mean that the course of the development of energy relations between China and any particular Middle Eastern state will depend on a variety of factors and interests. These include, on the one hand, general global or regional trends and events, and, on the other, factors which relate directly to the specific interests of the four parties described above.

China's ability to deepen its energy relations with Middle Eastern states will be highly dependent on the political stability of the region, and on the policies and actions of other outside parties in the region. Any favorable or unfavorable trends in this respect may be ameliorated or exacerbated by relations between China and the West concerning the Middle East.

With respect to the interests of the four main parties, a number of potential sources of tension may be identified which could constrain the progress of energy relations and these can be viewed in a hierarchy starting with inter-governmental relations.

The relations between Middle Eastern governments themselves and the Chinese government have been critical to the development of energy relations, especially in the case of those countries with large petroleum resources, such as Iran, Saudi Arabia, Iraq and Kuwait. A change of government or of policy approach by the host government could constrain a deepening of energy relations, as could a sustained failure by either party to deliver on its commitments. Such failures might include a substantial decline in oil deliveries to China, a major delay or shortfall in promised investment by China into the Middle Eastern supplier, or vice versa, or by the erection or maintenance of barriers to investment by either party. One example of the latter is the constant complaint of Middle Eastern NOCs that China's domestic pricing policy for oil products undermines the commercial viability of their refinery projects in China.

Given the heavy involvement of the respective governments in building the activities of China's NOCs in some Middle Eastern states, relations between the host governments and the Chinese NOCs will be highly dependent on the cordiality of inter-government relations. In addition, the attitude of the host governments to Chinese NOCs may well be colored by other factors such as the technical performance of the Chinese NOCs, as well as their track record in addressing wider responsibilities relating to economic development, environmental protection and community relations. Furthermore, host governments may grow reluctant to become – or be seen to become – over-dependent on Chinese oil companies.

Conversely, the Chinese NOCs themselves may lose interest in certain countries, at least temporarily, if the security situation deteriorates significantly or if the ease of access to investment opportunities deteriorates or, in certain cases, fails to improve.

The cordiality of relations between the Middle Eastern NOCs and Chinese NOCs will to a great extent be dependent on higher-level relations, but will also depend on the specific commercial or strategic objectives of the respective companies. Such objectives may diverge or be in direct competition with each other. A case in point in the desire of both sets of NOCs to become major international producers of petrochemicals.

Finally, the relationship between the Chinese NOCs and the Chinese government itself is also of critical importance to the NOCs' ability to invest in the Middle East, or, indeed, anywhere else in the world. In particular, China's government is likely to be less generous in its support for the overseas activities of China's NOCs if they start to make substantial financial losses or if their behavior damages China's international reputation.

[167]

Conclusions

The future centers of demand for oil and, to a lesser extent, for gas lie in Asia rather than in Europe, America and Africa. The Middle East is well-placed to take advantage of this demand on account of its vast reserves of oil and gas and owing to its geographical location. Success in developing a growing flow of oil and exports from the Middle East to Asia will be critical to the economic development of the countries of the Middle East.

The extent to which Asia's import requirements for oil and gas grow and can be supplied by the Middle East depends on a wide range of factors over which Middle Eastern states have a varying degree of control. At one extreme, Middle Eastern states can take steps to ensure that production capacity in the region for both oil and gas grows ahead of global demand, thus assuring that they are able to supply Asia's demand. This of course runs the risk that prices fall to unacceptable levels. Related to this is the need for Middle Eastern states to continue to prove themselves to be reliable suppliers once agreements have been put in place. One dimension of this reliability is the extent to which the capacity of Middle Eastern states to export oil and gas will be constrained by their own domestic demand for energy as their economies grow over the coming decades.

In the middle ground, Middle Eastern states have a modest ability to influence international prices for oil and gas, either intentionally or unintentionally. Collectively they can work to enhance regional political stability and individually they can seek to strengthen bilateral relations with Asian importing states.

At the other extreme are a range of issues over which Middle Eastern states have little or no influence, at least not directly. These include the rate and nature of economic growth in Asia and the rest of the world, national policies in Asian countries relating to energy efficiency, and new and cleaner forms of energy. Furthermore, they can have little direct influence over investment in oil and gas production in other parts of the world, or over relations between Asian importers and other exporters.

That being said, Middle Eastern states do indeed have some indirect influence over these issues through their influence on international prices and their efforts to build good relations with Asian importers. The higher the prices, the greater the incentive for importers to save energy or develop other sources of energy, and the less reliable the Middle Eastern states are as suppliers, the greater the incentive for Asian importers to seek alternatives.

Setting aside the chance of a major crisis, political and economic links between the Middle East and Asia are set to strengthen further as trade and cross-investment in oil and gas grows. In certain Middle Eastern states, the involvement of Asian NOCs should assist development of domestic oil and gas industries. This deepening engagement will bring new strategic players into the Middle East who have in the past been bystanders to political events in the region, notably China and India

But questions remain concerning how long political and economic interests between Asian and Middle Eastern countries will continue to converge, as well as over which party needs the other most. It is also important to realize that future developments will vary greatly from country to country, for both exporters and importers.

6

The OPEC–Russia Relationship: Current Status and Future Outlook

Nodari A. Simoniya

The issue of energy security provision touches upon the vital interests of all countries of the world, to a greater or lesser degree. Today this security has acquired new aspects and is facing new challenges. It seems, however, that for a deeper comprehension of these changes, and owing to the very nature of the new challenges in this area, it is useful to briefly review the most important aspects of the development of world oil markets over the past half-century.

Up to 1973, relations between oil-producing and -exporting countries, and those importing and consuming oil were based on a concession system, characterized by the absolute dominance of the "seven sisters" over the posted price mechanism. Indeed, the establishment of OPEC in 1960 was provoked by an attempt to lower the posted price of oil. The struggle for the improvement of world oil trade conditions was now on, and an important breakthrough regarding the monopoly of the "seven sisters" was achieved with the conclusion by Indonesia of a number of agreements with independent oil companies from Delaware on a production-sharing basis, a model which was later to spread worldwide.

The decisive blow to the old system, however, was struck by OPEC countries in 1973. The result was to completely demolish the monopoly of the seven sisters over posted pricing. This transformed OPEC into the main governor of oil prices on world markets for the following decade.

The middle of the 1980s, however, was marked by another historic turn in relations between the principal oil market players. From 1983 oil was traded at the New York Mercantile Exchange (NYMEX) alongside potatoes, milk and meat. It is in this period that all of today's significant negative oil and gas processes are rooted. The exchange quickly became the main mechanism of a framework in which active players – hedge-funds, investment funds, dealers and brokers and even pension funds – began to influence pricing processes, while trade in oil and oil products itself began increasing, transforming from real trade (trade in physical volumes of commodities) into virtual trade (future trade in derivatives). Thus, the exchange transformed from a once useful instrument of the capitalist system into a negative, largely uncontrollable factor in production and international trade which generated price shocks.

Not so long ago, issues of energy security were associated exclusively with ensuring reliable supplies of hydrocarbons for consumers. However, producing countries have since become acutely aware of their dependence on guaranteed demand. In a world where most old oil and gas fields have passed their production peaks, and in which some major producing countries have entered a period of continued instability, producers are reluctant to invest the enormous amounts required by the development of new fields in the absence of long-term demand guarantees. This is why the Russian government decided to include all these issues in the agenda of the 2006 G-8 summit in St. Petersburg.

In the run-up to the summit, the hottest debate (which continued right up until the day before the summit was convened) concerned the interpretation of the concept of "energy security" itself. Most Western representatives proposed a unilateral interpretation – guaranteed supplies – which implied security only for consumers. Russia, however, insisted that supply guarantees should be supplemented by demand guarantees, and that consuming countries (their governments and businesses) should share the responsibilities and risks alongside producing states. The expert

[172]

community's efforts* made it possible to devise compromise formulas, and the St. Petersburg G-8 summit ultimately approved both the Joint Statement and Plan of Action for Ensuring Global Energy Security, which enshrined the concept of the mutual responsibility of producers and consumers for the stable and sustainable development of the global energy system.

However, a number of unresolved issues remained outside the framework of this compromise, which sparked off a new debate soon after the summit, even though the agreements reached at the summit remained on paper. It appeared that this was destined to happen, as the leaders of certain countries – primarily the US administration and the EU Commission – had not been sincere in their intention to give up their one-sided interpretation of energy security. To substantiate this statement I shall quote here some extracts from a lengthy interview given to the Russian *Kommersant GUIDE* by Energy Commissioner Andris Piebalgs following the EU summit, where he unambiguously expressed his interpretation of the interdependence of demand and supply within the framework of Russian–EU energy cooperation, which is typical of Brussels bureaucrats:

> I should offer a good forecast for Russian producers in what concerns development of the market, meaning the level of gas consumption in Europe. It is surely not a plan ... rather a precise forecast. What it means for Russia is that it may calmly decide [*sic*] whether it should invest in new production or not — domestic consumption in the European Union is based on market mechanisms, and it may always happen that a new technology may emerge, which will be so much more convenient and cheaper that it will sweep the market and change the situation in gas consumption. Besides, no one knows how oil and gas prices are going to change. In other words, if gas is very expensive, people will use more coal ... [so] Russia should decide for itself which arrangement it finds more convenient. We would prefer to have no interruption of supplies.[1]

---

* I and several scholars of the Russian Institute of World Economy and International Relations were involved in the process, under my guidance.

It is worth noting that Andris Piebalgs does not say a word in his long interview about guarantees for producers, or long-term contracts. The importance of his consumption forecast, on the basis of which Russia should "calmly" invest in new field development, is immediately reduced to naught as Piebalgs admits the possibility of a radical reduction in demand as a result of unpredictable technological or price changes on the market. Does the EU Commissioner seriously believe there may be even a marginally respectable financial institution to be found in the world that would grant multi-billion dollar credits against such an ephemeral and non-committal document as a "forecast" from a Brussels official, regardless of his position?

Considering the above statement, it seems obvious that owing to this asymmetric and – I would say – egoistic approach to the world energy security problem, OPEC and Russia, as two independent world oil and gas market participants, have an objective basis for close cooperation and coordination in the international arena. The aim of this cooperation should not be to cause damage consumers; the main goal should be to impel the leaders of these countries to realize the universal nature of the energy security problem and to assist in its resolution. On the other hand, however, it is prudent to expect that cooperation between OPEC and Russia is destined to be dialectically controversial. Being producers of such similar strategic commodities as oil and natural gas, OPEC and Russia inevitably compete with each other. It is important, however, that this competition, and the contradictions which it provokes from time to time, do not overshadow the main historic goal of such cooperation.

Differences in the Oil Industry Structures of the Russian Federation and OPEC

OPEC member states occasionally raise the question of Russia's participation in this organization. A few voices in support of this idea can sometimes be heard in Russia itself, but how real and productive is such a proposition?

In my view, such a proposition is not only practically impossible to accomplish (we shall explore this below), but may turn out to be harmful for the attainment of the main goals—joint work on a new system of world trade in oil and gas, stability of demand, and achieving balanced consumption. The quantitative build-up of forces on both sides of the barricades will only lead to further aggravation and growing confrontation between producing and consuming countries, without eliminating the main causes of recurrent oil and gas shocks. Today, in the aftermath of the global financial and economic crisis, there is a growing conviction that we should no longer "use old rails," but rather reassess our approach to this important issue. At the same time, however, there also are other important impediments to an organizational alliance between OPEC and Russia; first of all, the long-standing differences between the oil and gas industry structures of Russia and the OPEC states.

Main Structural Differences

Over the course of previous decades, as developing countries struggled for their sovereignty, OPEC members underwent a gradual strengthening of their national oil and gas companies, resulting in the complete control by the state over national resources, their development and export, as well as the strategy of these industries' further development. In the early 1980s OPEC began to develop the features of a cartel organization, a fact which manifested itself in attempts to control oil prices on world markets through a quotation mechanism. It is this combination of strict state control and a comprehensive quotation system that characterizes OPEC.

In Russia, development proceeded in the opposite direction. The strictly centralized system of oil and gas industry management in the USSR was built on the basis of the state's ownership not only of the subsoil but also all enterprise. This arrangement was eventually to fall to pieces, and the property itself was split during privatization (mainly through a corrupt system of mortgage auctions). As a result, in the course of the 1990s eleven large, vertically-integrated companies emerged in

Russia (with only Rosneft owned by the state), which have produced about 88 percent of the country's crude oil over the past decade. There were also two other types of oil company—dozens of small- and medium-sized independent producers, as well as joint ventures with the participation of foreign capital (numbering about 130), with each group accounting for 3 percent of Russia's overall production. By the year 2000, another one percent of crude oil was produced in the fields developed on a production-sharing basis with the participation of foreign majors such as Exxon, Shell, Total and some smaller Japanese companies.[2]

The changes that have taken place in this structure over the past 15–16 years are practically similar to what has been going on elsewhere in the world—on the one hand, there has been a growing process of merger and acquisition, and on the other hand, the state has been increasingly active, and national state corporations have been consolidating their positions in oil-producing (and also many importing) countries. For example, in Russia, TNK and YUKOS have been especially active in the realm of mergers and acquisitions, unlike companies such as LUKOIL or Surgutneftegas, which were headed not by oil industry professionals but by people who in the West might be described as 'speculative traders.' The top executives of those companies were concerned not so much with the development and modernization of production as with building up assets to raise their capitalization. They were actually engaged in what would be more accurately described as 'pre-sale preparation,' which was confirmed by developments in 2003, when TNK – which had previously taken over more than one of the large/mid-sized Russian oil companies – was itself sold to BP. This takeover was for several months enthusiastically and falsely touted among the Russian liberal media as a significant act of foreign direct investment (FDI). However, the main outcome of this deal was the unprecedented buildup of capital, income and profits for this foreign company, which lasted until the beginning of the current global financial crisis. As for YUKOS, its top executives in the same year forced a merger process with Sibneft and were only a step away from the final signing of appropriate documents while simultaneously conducting secret talks about selling up to 40 percent of the assets of the integrated company (YUKSI) to one of the US majors.

This situation served as the impetus for the beginning of the Russian government's interference in the oil business to introduce proper order (by fighting large-scale tax evasion, and correcting hardship clauses in agreements and contracts imposed on Russia in the times of severe crisis and rampant corruption during Yeltsin's rule, etc.). It is important to note, however, that these government actions do not at all imply nationalization or, even less so, confiscation. All asset transactions are carried out for compensation, and at adequate prices.

Even this brief description of the situation in Russia's oil industry demonstrates its fundamental difference from those of OPEC members. Under the given circumstances, even if any Russian government decides – as a result of tactical or other reasons – to formally join OPEC, nothing will come of it, as that government would have failed to keep in check the established heterogeneous structure of its oil industry. Furthermore all of the large oil and gas companies in Russia have learned how to lobby their corporate interests effectively and energetically (interests that do not always coincide with those of the state) in legislative and executive bodies.

Impact of the Financial Crisis on Relations between OPEC and Russia

The financial crisis has partly lifted the veil on relations between OPEC and Russia, which have proved to be more complicated than simple differences in their oil and gas business structures. The fact is that the Russian state faces substantial challenges, the solutions to which depend on the 40 percent of budget revenue that is provided by the oil and gas sector: these challenges include the need for selective restoration and simultaneous modernization of an economy wrecked during Yeltsin's rule, and a desire for IT structure formation—i.e., building the structures of a post-industrial economy. The problem is that Russia is still suffering from a widespread "brain drain" (directly in terms of emigration, and indirectly through outsourcing). Thus, the country generously facilitates innovational development in a large number of states – both highly developed and transitional ones – from the United States to South Korea. Russia requires indigenous expertise itself – in software production, for example – but retaining its human capital requires the creation of the appropriate conditions. Hence, it is obvious that having set itself such lofty goals the Russian government simply cannot afford to restrict its options in terms of official participation in OPEC. At the highest political level in Russia, owing to the present global crisis, there is likely a growing realization of the fact that the temporary tactical advantages and financial gains from the agreed reduction of oil supply to world markets may soon spawn another oil bubble with further prospects for price collapses. Moreover, anomalously high oil and gas prices (US$147 per barrel in July 2008) only serve to stimulate diversification of oil sources in importing countries, to the detriment of oil and gas exporters.

It is obvious that the "quota weapon" can not be used indefinitely. The recent crisis has demonstrated the fact that under the present circumstances this weapon is losing its effectiveness. Everyone remembers the situation when in the second half of 2008 OPEC toughened quotas for its members on several occasions; oil prices, however, continued to fall. Similarly, in 2009 when OPEC insisted on preserving its old quotas, oil prices rose steadily (and continue to do so). The crisis has taken everybody by surprise, but initially some failed to appreciate the seriousness, extent and size of the possible damage. Naturally, this also concerns many Russian decision-makers, especially in the Ministry of Finance, the Central Bank, etc., which at the height of the crisis in 2008 erred by making preposterous and ill-conceived public statements to the effect that Russia was an island of financial stability, that the banking crisis was practically over, etc. Perhaps reassured by such assessments, some leaders within the Russian fuel and energy complex (FEC) – upon witnessing the oil prices fall in the autumn of 2008 –

imprudently began to make oral overtures to the OPEC leadership regarding support for their measures to reduce supply.[3] Later, however, when the true extent of the damage caused by the crisis to the Russian economy was revealed, everyone conveniently forgot about export reductions; and when oil prices started to rise, Russian oil companies began to make up for the losses caused by the crises. In turn, some in OPEC also decided to attribute blame elsewhere.[4] This may go some way toward explaining the unprecedented public criticism of the Russian Federation which its prime minister voiced during the 154th meeting of OPEC on September 10, 2009, in Vienna. It is curious that – whilst practically condemning Russia for the seizure of 'somebody else's' oil markets – one of the speakers at the Vienna meeting also voiced accusations against Russia contained in *The New York Times* on the eve of that meeting's opening day, namely that instead of reducing production, "Russia is providing tax breaks for new fields in Siberia."[5] In reality, however, tax breaks were provided not for deposits in Siberia in general, but for those in East Siberia and the Russian Far East, oil from which is meant to supply the East Siberia–Pacific Ocean (ESPO) pipeline, construction of which began years ago. Before the crisis, Russia's government repeatedly declared that this project was a top priority, within the framework of its export routes diversification program, and that construction would proceed in spite of the crisis.

Naturally, the economic crisis caused serious damage to the majority of OPEC member states. According to OPEC, 35 out of 165 oil projects in OPEC countries have been postponed to 2013; and, according to the US Department of Energy (DoE), in 2009 oil incomes in OPEC countries would fall by 51 percent compared to the previous year. The International Energy Agency (IEA), in turn, forecast that incomes will fall to $476 billion, as a result of which investment programs will shrink by at least by 20 percent.[6] But these reductions will not be equally painful for all the OPEC states. For example, Kuwait, with its comparatively small population, made a decision in March 2009 to cancel the construction of a large oil-refining plant with a capacity of 630,000 barrels per day (bpd—amounting to around 31.5 million tons per year) and costing $15 billion, which will not affect the standard of living of its population. Nigeria, however, is a different story, thanks to its population of more than 120 million, the permanent tension associated with the division of oil incomes on the basis of clan or tribe, and the regular armed attacks on oil companies working both on land and at sea. The analytical service of the Russian *Neftegazovaya Vertikal* ("Oil and Gas Vertical") magazine featured the following table in the Summer of 2009:

Table 6:1

Per Capita Incomes from Oil Exports in OPEC Countries

Country	2008	January–July, 2009
Algeria	US$ 2,039	US$ 598
Angola	US$ 5,404	US$ 1,598
Ecuador	US$ 735	US$ 222
Iran	US$ 1,253	US$ 398
Iraq	US$ 2,143	US$ 667
Kuwait	US$ 30,952	US$ 9,006
Libya	US$ 9,228	US$ 2,748
Nigeria	US$ 505	US$ 153
Qatar	US$ 41,028	US$ 12,474
Saudi Arabia	US$ 10,139	US$ 2,636
UAE	US$ 14,304	US$ 5,488
Venezuela	US$ 2,247	US$ 596
OPEC on the average	US$ 2,680	US$ 768

Source: *Neftegazovaya Vertikal*, No. 18, August 2009, p. 26.

The crisis originated in the United States and quickly turned into a global disaster, so one should not publicly pour scorn on Russia. However, irrespective of the crisis – and long before it occurred – in a number of reports at international seminars, interviews with Russian and foreign mass media sources and in some publications, the author negatively assessed the unrestrained increase of Russian oil exports, based on the following:

Firstly, proven oil reserves in Russia at the end of 2008 amounted to 79 billion barrels (10.8 billion tons), which only accounts for 6.3 percent of proven world reserves. According to this indicator, Russia today is considerably behind not only the leader – Saudi Arabia, whose share in world reserves is 21 percent – but also OPEC countries such as Iran (10.9 percent), Iraq (9.1 percent), Kuwait (8.1 percent), Venezuela (7.9 percent) and the United Arab Emirates (7.8 percent).[7] Given this difference, Russia's nonsensical "competition" with Saudi Arabia in oil exports is tantamount to sacrificing long-term Russian national interests for the narrow pursuit of immediate momentary gain.

Secondly, thanks to increasing crude oil exports, oil companies are reluctant to make long-term investments in deep oil-processing and general modernization of their production infrastructure. Furthermore, the chronic "sore point" associated with production is the widespread wastage of another very precious raw material—associated petroleum gas. Thus, Russia is missing an opportunity to generate enormous profits.

Third, until very recently, oil and gas companies paid no serious attention to the pressing, ongoing problems associated with the development of a new oil and gas province in East Siberia, and the development of the Russian Arctic. Only following the construction of the main ESPO oil pipeline has the oil and gas business begun to move into this largely neglected region. Naturally, it will take a minimum of 10–12 years for commercial development of a new oil and gas province, but there are already signs that Russia could become a force to be reckoned with in the sphere of oil and gas deliveries to the dynamically developing countries of the Asia-Pacific. Oil deliveries to China, for example, have already begun, and at the end of 2009, when the first stage of the ESPO project and its branch to Daqing are completed, Rosneft will deliver 15 million tons of oil per year to China. Oil and gas deliveries to Japan are also increasing. A mere 2–3 years ago Russia did not appear in Japanese statistics as an oil import source, but by 2007 Russia's share of Japanese oil imports reached 3.5 percent.[8] It is obvious that after 2012, with completion of ESPO's second stage (including construction of a large oil-processing plant), oil exports to Japan, South Korea or Taiwan will increase considerably.

Prospects for Post-Crisis OPEC–Russia Relations

Every crisis comes to an end, and experts differ in opinion only on the question of when that end will come. However, there also are inveterate skeptics who in spite of the first signs of recovery predict a prolongation of the crisis up to the end of 2011. Be that as it may, it is important that those in the oil and gas business not give in to emotional decision-making but build upon their relations and actions with others in the world market, proceeding from a thorough analysis of post-crisis development, as is the practice among leading oil and gas majors as well as many other energy companies worldwide. Careful analysis of the statements and practical steps taken by these players suggests that they do not all intend to give up their planned realization of large contracts—the exception being small and marginal deposits which have been postponed. Some experts logically proceed from the fact that even in the hypothetic case that world consumption in 2020–2030 remains at today's levels, the necessity of developing new deposits to compensate production decline is clear. This will cause another round of price rises. (Indeed, signs of such expectations were already evident in December 2008, when five-year futures contracts were concluded at the price of $74 per barrel and nine-year futures at $80 per barrel.)[9]

Moreover, in their annual 2009 report *World Energy Outlook*, the IEA calculated that the productivity of oil deposits reduces by an average of 6.7 percent per year, and that it is therefore necessary to develop more oil fields than in the previous year to maintain the achieved level of output.

Based on production data from 800 world oil fields, these experts concluded that the rate of depletion clearly expressed an *acceleration tendency*, as a result of which by 2030 – *only due to this acceleration* – it will be necessary to put into operation new output capacity amounting to 64 mbpd in order to retain levels of development equivalent to 2007. At the same time, old fields require considerable additional investment to maintain well pressure, and therefore productivity. Most costly is the process of maintaining production at fields which have reached their peak output. The annual, average world depletion rate for such fields is nine percent. In this regard, IEA experts have concluded that without additional investment in such fields, their depletion will occur one-third faster.[10]

I believe that despite all the efforts being made in the areas of energy efficiency and alternative, renewable energy sources, all serious mid-term and long-term forecasts continue to proceed from growth in demand for world hydrocarbons, even in highly developed capitalist countries which are targeting a transition to post-industrial structures in their economies. (A lot has been said about the reduction of investments in the oil and gas sector, but in the meantime projects dealing with renewable energy sources have also witnessed falling investment, which promotes – indirectly – growth in oil prices. Hence, in March 2009, Shell officials declared the cancellation of a majority of their "green" projects.[11]) The same goes for large industrial and transitional countries experiencing fast economic growth, where the lion's share of this growth will be provided (as it is now) primarily at the expense of expansion in their industrial sectors, which also spells increases in hydrocarbon energy consumption.

Taking into consideration all the above-mentioned facts, it is no wonder that the leaders of oil and gas corporations base their decisions not so much on the current crisis situation, but from a mid-term (or indeed long-term) perspective. They are sure that the collapse in oil prices is a short-term phenomenon (recent months seem to confirm this assurance, although supply to world markets still slightly exceeds demand) and since the end of 2008–beginning of 2009 had begun to

[183]

prepare for post-crisis general economic recovery and the accompanying increases in demand for energy resources. By December 2008, the Shell leadership announced their plans to invest $31–32 billion over 2009 (while in 2008 the corporation's investments amounted to $30 billion). Chevron followed suit and declared an expansion of investments in 2009 to $22.8 billion. In turn, BP's Executive Director Tony Hayward said in December 2008 that investments in the oil and gas industry of countries such as China and India presented good opportunities even under crisis circumstances, which is why BP stated its intention to increase its investments in China several times over; as of today its accumulated investments in this country amount to $4.6 billion.[12] (Incidentally, BP's cooperation with China is not limited to China proper. In the middle of October 2009, BP and the China National Petroleum Corporation [CNPC] signed a contract for the development of the Rumeila oil field in Iraq, which was approved by the Iraqi government. The BP-led consortium is divided as follows: BP, 38 percent; CNPC, 37 percent; and the remaining 25 percent belonging to the Iraqi "State Oil Marketing Organization.")[13]

It is worth mentioning that such statements are not isolated or limited to the singular position of particular leaders of separate corporations. In fact, they form an integral part of a general strategic view from the West—where we can also easily discern the presence of a geo-economic anti-OPEC constituent, aimed at intensifying the development of deposits in non-OPEC countries. A clear example of this is the research carried out by Douglas-Westwood on deepwater market development. In "The World Deepwater Market Report 2009–2013," researchers came to the conclusion that in the next five years $162 billion is earmarked for the development of deepwater deposits. The authors also provide an interesting breakdown of this sum among four main regions:

- $60 billion on the shelf of Africa (mainly western coast – Nigeria, Equatorial Guinea, Angola);

- $29.3 billion on the shelf of North America (mainly in the US part of the Mexican Gulf);

- $29.0 billion on the shelf of Latin America (mainly Brazil); and

- $14.6 billion in Asia.

The researchers also point out the fact that the analysis proceeded from quite conservative, moderate estimations—i.e., from the expectation that mid-term oil prices will be within the region of $50–70 per barrel.[14] The realization of these plans might mean that OPEC (especially Middle East members) will face more serious problems in the mid-term, rather than from the long-term plans to develop alternative energy sources which the Western mass media loves so much to write about and which preoccupies a number of politicians in consuming countries.

Ultimately, however, it is impossible to discuss oil pricing processes at the global level with an emphasis on relations between OPEC and Russia without paying due attention to the seemingly obvious but often overlooked fact that it isn't Russia but the United States that is the main factor in world markets. The United States has the highest level of consumption of oil and associated products in the world—22.5 percent in 2008 (in pre-crisis 2007 it amounted to 23.9 percent). That same year the United States was the largest importer of hydrocarbon products—636.6 million tons or 23.6 percent of worldwide imports.[15] It was the previous administrations of the United States that were the first in the world to implement policies restricting their steadfastly increasing oil imports from OPEC countries. Many in the Bush administration hoped for a successful "democratic crusade" within the framework of the "Greater Middle East" project; indeed, expectations of a quick realization of this project amounted to gross miscalculations. In any case, the United States has become concerned with geographical diversification of this import, as we can clearly see from Table 6.2.

Table 6.2

Sources of US Oil Imports (mbpd)

Source	1992	May 2009
Algeria	2,010	272
Kuwait	1,600	930
Nigeria	675	600
Saudi Arabia	1,756	1,079
Venezuela	1,088	1,341
Other OPEC	279	581
Total OPEC	**4,015**	**4,471**
Angola[*]	332	505
Canada	1,059	2,206
Mexico	835	1,186
Norway	122	171
Great Britain	191	250
Virginia Islands	246	313
Other non-OPEC	981	2,999
Total non-OPEC	**3,766**	**7,125**
Total import	**7,781**	**11,596**

*In 2007 Angola joined OPEC and its data for May 2009 is included in the summary column "Total OPEC."

Sources: *Oil and Gas Journal*, December 27, 1993, p. 116; and September 28, 2009, p. 76.

In view of this data, it is obvious that with the steadfast and large-scale growth in US oil imports over the last 17 years, serious changes have taken place in their geographical distribution. While in 1992, US oil imports from OPEC countries outstripped those from non-OPEC countries, today the latter dominate imports having provided a considerable share of import growth. At the same time, were it not for Angola's membership of OPEC, the share of this organization would have remained roughly on the same level.

The new US administration is yet to clearly determine its energy strategy. During the pre-election heat of 2008, the Democrat majority in the US Congress justifiably condemned the Bush administration for making no effort to restrain speculative activity involving commodities. Thus, Democrats

[186]

compelled the Commodity Futures Trading Commission (CFTC) to increase control over speculative deals. After the election victory, however, this focus waned and oil prices rose too quickly—reaching $80 per barrel by the beginning of October 2009. This caused anxiety among the leaders of both OPEC and Russia. OPEC Secretary General Abdalla Salem El-Badri, in his speech on October 20 in London at the international conference "Oil and Money," declared that the $80 price was a result of the fall of the dollar and speculation at the exchange.[16] Similar anxiety has also been expressed by the Russian President, Dmitri Medvedev, in his recent speeches.

Bearing in mind the fact that the world has just recently begun to drag itself out of a financial crisis and that the recession is still young, these anxieties are quite justifiable. The price of $80–100 per barrel is fair only under the circumstances of a stable upward trend in world economic growth. Besides, as of today, the volume of oil and oil products in floating oil reservoirs exceeds 125 million tons, and supply is still exceeding demand.[17]

The second issue relating to US policy involves the interplay between further development of the oil and gas industry and excessive focus on the development of alternative sources of energy. It is impossible to stop scientific and technological progress, and we will in any case develop alternative energy sources, but why should this be done at the expense of traditional energy industries we shall have to rely on for many decades to come? In the realm of the oil and gas industry there are still vast opportunities for technological innovation that demand attention.

OPEC countries need not fear growth Russian competitiveness. The old oil and gas province in West Siberia, where the bulk of Russian oil exports come from, has long passed its production peak and entered a stage of accelerating depletion. The country's leadership has recently formulated a strategy involving the development of oil and gas provinces in East Siberia, the Russian Far East and the Arctic, with a focus on simultaneous construction of oil processing, petrochemical, gas chemical, and gas-liquefaction plants. These are grand plans, demanding equally grand investments and, most importantly, 10–15 years for their realization.

Conclusion

In conclusion I would like once again to reiterate the simple but often ignored view that oil (and nowadays natural gas) is not an ordinary commodity, but a strategic one, which since its appearance has been closely intertwined with politics at both the national and international levels. The world is divided into those who have reserves of this precious raw material and those who either do not have it or do not have enough of it. Thus far, attempts to solve the problems of relations between the 'haves' and the 'have-nots' at the international level have been built on confrontation between the OPEC countries and the IEA. This is where the root of today's seemingly impossible task of achieving normal cooperation lies.

Importers interpret energy security only from the point of view of supply, while exporters view it as a matter of demand. At the G-8 Summit in St. Petersburg, Russia proposed to consider energy security from both points of view. The West, however, was unable to accept the idea of an *equitable* and *mutually beneficial* solution for energy cooperation between exporters and importers. If we fail to devise a fair approach to this problem, to formulate and fix a mutually acceptable agreement at the international level with an international mechanism to control its implementation, the world will face an epoch of continued energy conflict. The current global financial crisis has convinced many of the necessity to reconstruct the existing world financial system; I would hope that at the same time it will encourage the realization of new global approaches to energy security in all its aspects. It is important to overcome the barrier between the haves and have-nots inherited from the twentieth century, and to come to an agreement on fair oil prices, after having released this commodity from the whims of uncontrolled speculation and having created an international regulating mechanism with strict controls and wide-ranging powers. Such an outcome would not only preserve energy security, but foster greater peace worldwide in general.

Section 3

GLOBAL DIMENSIONS OF ENERGY SECURITY

Dimensions of Energy Security: Competition, Interaction and Maximization

Anas F. Alhajji[*]

Although the concept of energy security has existed for several decades and despite the fact that our understanding of this concept has evolved over the years, it has nonetheless remained somewhat ill-defined and immeasurable. As a result, politicians are able to invoke 'energy security' whenever it suits their political interests, even if their actions lead eventually to a national energy crisis that in fact threatens global energy security. Without a clear definition and appropriate measures, nations are unable to maximize their energy security.

Energy security is difficult to measure with acceptable certainty, perhaps because 'security' is a psychological – and sometimes ideological – issue that is based on threat perception, regardless of evidence. Nevertheless, gauging energy security remains vital for all nations. The objective of this paper is to explore the various dimensions of energy security in order to define and measure it. A well-defined, measurable concept of energy security should reduce its politicization by preventing politicians from manipulating the concept to fit their agendas. In addition, it should enhance global energy security as a whole.

The first part of this paper stresses the fact that energy markets are global and interdependent, which makes 'reciprocal energy security' a

[*] The views expressed in this paper are those of the author and do not necessarily represent the views of NGP Energy Capital Management and its affiliates.

condition for national energy security; enhancing energy security in the oil producing countries will eventually enhance energy security in consuming countries, and vice versa. Solving the current power shortage crisis in some oil producing countries would, for example, free more oil for exports to consumer states.[1] Furthermore, preventing energy prices from inhibiting economic growth in consuming countries will ensure continued economic growth in energy-producing countries as their energy exports continue to grow.

The second part seeks to illustrate how our thinking about energy security has evolved in recent years from being limited to the politics of oil to full consideration of all of the factors that affect energy supply and demand. The third part of the paper explores six dimensions of energy security for both consuming and producing countries, while the fourth section illustrates how these different dimensions of energy security compete and interact, making them extremely difficult to balance. The paper then proceeds to introduce a graphic illustration of the various dimensions of energy security – in the form of the "Energy Security Star" – and seeks to present a new definition of energy security, whilst the final section offers a number of related conclusions.

Energy Security: It's not all about Politics

Historically, the objective of any energy security policy initiative has been to prevent the governments of oil-producing countries from taking political actions that disrupt the flow of oil to consuming nations.[2] However, our understanding of the concept of energy security has evolved in recent years to cover both producing and consuming countries, and includes factors other than politics, such as economic, natural and technological factors. Since the September 11 terrorist attacks, terrorism has also become a major threat to energy security.

A quick review of the energy security literature over the last 30 years, which will be explored later in this paper, points to striking differences between the various definitions of energy security. While these definitions cut along political and philosophical lines in the consuming countries – particularly in the United States – many common threads exist:

- Prior definitions were mostly limited to oil.[3] Only in recent years have natural gas, the security of energy facilities, safety (especially in terms of transportation of liquefied natural gas [LNG]), the failure of technology and the possibility of cyber attacks surfaced as concerns. Our understanding of energy security has thus evolved over time to match events on the ground. These include:

  o *Increased dependence on natural gas imports*: as Europe's dependence on natural gas imports from Russia increased, concerns about such dependence also rose.[4] However, it took a major cut-off of gas supplies to Europe during the frigid winter of 2009 to make politicians realize that energy security was not limited to oil.[5]

  o *Increased threat of terrorism*: since the terrorist attacks of September 11, experts have realized that energy facilities, especially nuclear power plants, are attractive targets for terrorists. As a result, nuclear power and energy infrastructure have become part of the energy security debate.[6]

  o *Increased imports of LNG*: as more LNG import terminals are built around the world, people in coastal areas near the terminals have become concerned that a terrorist attack on an LNG tanker or an accident might cause a catastrophe.

  o *Increased threats of technology failure and cyber terrorism*: energy industries depend heavily on technology and information technology. A technological failure or a cyber attack that curtails output could be as disruptive as any political event in a major oil producing country. The disruption stems from the fact that many production facilities and pipelines are electronically controlled. While technology was not an issue in the past, it has become a significant factor in the energy security debate.

- o *Continued – and in some cases, increased – dependence of energy-producing countries on energy exports has become a threat to global energy security and to the energy security of producers.* Their economies, and therefore income and employment, are a function of oil prices. If oil prices decline, incomes and employment decline, leading to social and political problems that might threaten oil supplies to the rest of the world. If oil prices increase, inflation and income gaps contribute to social and political instability, which might affect oil exports.

- o In short, energy security is no longer limited to the field of oil. Now it covers all energy sources and their fiscal and virtual infrastructures.

- Despite the addition of natural gas and energy infrastructure to the picture, energy security concerns remain largely limited to dependence on imports.[7] US politicians focus on the danger of dependence on oil imports from the Middle East, while European politicians have focused in recent years on the danger of dependence on natural gas imports from Russia. This restriction of energy security to cover only oil and gas imports explains the continuing connection that Western nations make between "energy independence" and "energy security."[8] The result has been a push by politicians to increase domestic energy supplies such as biofuels, solar, wind and nuclear, mostly through government subsidies, without regard to the optimal use of such resources.

- Unfortunately, those who advocate energy independence and limit energy security to preventing the dangers of dependence on imports, especially in the United States, miss an important point. All of the United States' major energy problems in the last decade have been domestic and have had nothing to do with imports except in a brief period in the Spring of 2002 when Venezuelan oil supplies were disrupted because of a labor strike and short-lived coup. Several factors have contributed to these problems, including policy choices that favor environmental protection over increasing domestic energy supplies or the objectives of foreign policy over those of energy policy. Other factors include the following:

o Despite the fact that hurricanes in the Gulf of Mexico are as old as the Gulf itself, the United States had not experienced their potential effect on energy markets until entrepreneurs ventured into its deep waters and planted hundreds of rigs and platforms in the path of hurricanes. We have witnessed several destructive hurricanes in the past few years, including Ivan, Katrina, Rita and Ike. They not only affected domestic oil supplies but also curtailed natural gas supplies, destroyed refineries and products pipelines, and reduced imports of foreign oil. Hurricanes Katrina and Rita destroyed 113 platforms and damaged another 52. Data indicates that 95 percent of oil production and 88 percent of natural gas production in the Gulf of Mexico was shut in after hurricane Katrina.[9]

o The California power crisis of 2000–01 was a domestic problem not related to oil or oil imports. Some of the main causes were price controls that kept electricity retail prices artificially low while wholesale power prices were deregulated and priced higher at market prices.[10]

o Shortages of natural gas supplies between 2003 and mid-2008 were not related to oil and gas imports but to various regulations that limited natural gas supply and increased its demand. President and CEO of the American Chemistry Council, Jack N. Gerard, summed up the problem in late September 2006: "The natural gas crisis is self-inflicted, caused by 25 year-old policies that drive up demand while restricting access to American energy supplies. We are the only industrialized nation that puts our energy supplies off-limits in this way."[11]

o Oil production in the United States has been declining since the early 1970s. Energy Information Administration (EIA) data shows that US oil production reached its peak in November 1970 at slightly more than 10 million barrels per day (mbpd). Production continued to decline to average about 5.3 mbpd in 2009.[12] Furthermore, various environmental laws prohibited oil and gas companies from drilling in oil rich areas in the lower 48 states and Alaska.

o US ethanol mandates led to higher gasoline prices and higher price volatility. The EIA reported in many of its studies and reports that the switch from methyl tertiary butyl ether (MTBE) blended gasoline to a reformulated gasoline that is blended with ethanol has caused disruptions and higher gasoline prices. In one of its reports, the EIA stated:

> California was one of the first States to ban the gasoline additive methyl tertiary butyl ether (MTBE) after it was detected in ground water. Ethanol, a non-petroleum product usually made from corn, is being used in place of MTBE. Gasoline without MTBE is more expensive to produce and requires refineries to change the way they produce and distribute gasoline. Some supply dislocations and price surges occurred in the summer of 2003 as the State moved away from MTBE. Similar problems have also occurred in past fuel transitions ... The supply and distribution system must undergo a number of changes to switch from MTBE-blended RFG to ethanol-blended RFG, including developing supply chains to move more ethanol into undersupplied areas, converting terminal tanks from petroleum to ethanol, and adding blending equipment at terminals. It is expected that reformulated gasoline areas on the East Coast, especially in the Mid-Atlantic, will experience the most trouble obtaining ethanol supplies in a timely fashion due to logistical challenges of getting ethanol to and from terminals further inland by rail car. The Dallas–Fort Worth and Houston areas may also experience some trouble getting ethanol to major terminals due to limited rail access.[13]

o No new refineries have been built in the United States in the last 30 years, as stringent environmental laws have made such projects uneconomical. As a result, US dependence on imported refined petroleum products has increased in recent years from 2 mbpd in 1990 to 3.2 mbpd in 2008.[14]

Dependence on energy imports is only a small part of a large problem. In order to improve energy security all the domestic issues mentioned above must be addressed.

Definitions of Energy Security

Differences between the various definitions of energy security reflect the private interests of the country, group or business responsible for creating them. Every definition of energy security is self-serving. In all cases, definitions of energy security have ignored global energy security as a whole; and in most cases, the definitions have not even reflected the collective interests of a consuming nation. For example, the coal industry views energy security from its own point of view, which ultimately means more reliance on coal.[15] The same applies to the biofuel, solar, wind and nuclear industries.

Domestic independent oil and gas producers call for more drilling, and they call on the government to limit foreign oil and gas imports. Others in the oil industry want less government intervention, which links energy security to free markets: "US energy security is best maintained by ensuring that the United States is, and is perceived to be, supportive of free trade and of the use of market forces on [a] global scale."[16] The International energy Agency (IEA) defines energy security from the industrialized countries' point of view: "the uninterrupted physical availability at a price which is affordable, while respecting environment concerns."[17] The Saudis, who until recently were the world's largest oil producer and exporter,[18] have also introduced a self-serving definition: "maintaining and enhancing access to where the oil exists in such obvious abundance."[19] The Bush administration's view was summed up in the title of its 2001 energy report, "Reliable, Affordable and Environmentally Sound."[20] Even the Ethanol industry defined energy security in a way that served its interest: "Do we mean national security? Well, sort of. Do we mean energy independence? Well, sort of that, too. Do we mean economic security? Yes, all of the above."[21]

All definitions have ignored the interaction and the contradictions among energy, environmental, economic, foreign and security policies. For example, contradictions between US foreign policy and its declared energy policy have led to results on the ground that contradict the objectives of the declared energy policy. Imposing sanctions on some oil-producing countries has limited the growth of world oil supplies and concentrated imports, while the declared energy policy calls for increased world supplies and diversity of oil imports.[22]

Most definitions have focused on oil-consuming countries, while global energy markets tell a different story. Any problems in the oil-producing countries – not just those of a political nature – can affect the energy security of consuming countries. While some politicians in consuming states think that low oil prices stimulate economic growth in their countries, they do not realize that such prices lower government revenues, economic growth and incomes in the oil-producing countries. As a result, these countries invest less in capacity expansion and may not be able to maintain existing production. The result is higher prices and greater price volatility, both of which threaten energy security in the consuming countries. In addition, low economic growth and low incomes in the oil-producing countries lead to higher unemployment, which in turn can cause political instability and threaten oil exports. The result is energy insecurity in the consuming nations. If the oil-producing countries do not procure new technologies for oil exploration, development, and production, global oil supply might not keep up with world demand. Shortages will result in higher oil prices that threaten economic growth in consuming countries. Even if a country is completely energy independent, it is not immune to higher energy prices and high price volatility. Its oil prices would increase if oil production in any major oil-producing country were halted for any reason, including technical problems or natural disasters. Oil-producing countries have emphasized in recent years the importance of "security of demand." They want consumers to guarantee a certain level of demand that is needed to plan for future capacity expansions and maintain investment in the industry.

Oil markets are fungible and global. When oil prices increase, they increase everywhere. Therefore, energy independence is a fantasy, especially for the United States, which cannot be the world's superpower and energy independent at the same time. History shows that the United States became dependent on foreign oil the moment it decided to be a major political player on the world stage. The power and reach of the US armed forces require access to nearby energy supplies, not domestic energy supplies at home on the other side of the globe.

If the revenues of oil-producing countries decline, these countries can end up becoming failed states. Is it in the interest of the United States and its allies to see the oil-producing countries fail? Therefore, energy *interdependence* will improve energy security in the consuming countries, while calls for energy independence might lead to energy insecurity, and perhaps worse effects.[23] Energy security is as important to producing nations as it is to consuming nations.

Also, environmental issues have been gaining ground in energy policies and in the energy security literature in recent years. One of the main contributions of this paper is to incorporate environmental issues as one of the dimensions of energy security.

Not just Politics

The development of the oil market in recent years shows that energy security is as much about economics and technology as politics, and probably more so. Conventional wisdom states that high oil prices lower economic growth, increase unemployment and inflation, and threaten the social fabric of oil-consuming countries. These were the very factors that raised concerns about energy security during major political upheavals in the oil-producing countries in 1973 during and after the October oil embargo, in 1979 during and after the Islamic revolution in Iran, and in 1990 when Iraq invaded Kuwait. However, record oil prices in 2008 were not related to a major political event. There were no embargos imposed by the oil-producing countries, no revolutions and no invasions.

Figure 7.1 plots oil prices and the various factors that have led to major spikes since 1973. The figure illustrates that major political events caused all major spikes except the last one. If policy makers are worried about the impact of high oil prices, then the factors that led to record oil prices in 2008 are as important as those that led to price spikes in 1973, 1979 and 1990. In fact, given the magnitude of this price increase – and the recession of 2009 – the factors that led to the 2008 spike should be more worrisome the previous ones.

New York Mercantile Exchange (NYMEX) crude oil prices increased from about $33 per barrel at the beginning of 2004 to an average monthly price of $127 in May 2008. What caused this four-fold increase? The answer is simple: market fundamentals, which comprise all the factors that affected supply and demand, including the declining dollar.[24] Oil supply remained virtually the same (Figure 7.2) while world oil demand continued to grow (Figure 7.3). The only way to meet the difference between stable oil supply and growing demand was to utilize OPEC spare capacity (Figure 7.4) and draw on commercial stocks in consuming countries (Figure 7.5). Once OPEC spare capacity vanished and commercial stocks declined to critical levels, oil prices increased drastically.[25] It took a major recession in 2009 to rein in world demand, change bullish expectations and lower oil prices by more than 50 percent.

The inability of OPEC and non-OPEC members to increase production during this period indicates that those who are interested in energy security should look beyond political factors and examine the economic, technological, legal and natural issues that prevented the industry from increasing supplies. They should also consider the monetary and fiscal policies of consuming nations that increased oil demand and prices and prevented rising oil prices from affecting economic growth between 2004 and early 2008. Neither a major energy policy shift nor a major energy security initiative produced the decline in oil prices in 2009—the recession caused the decline. Therefore, energy security is not limited to political events that affect the security of supplies, but all of the political, economic, technological, legal and natural factors that affect the flow of energy sources.

Figure 7.1
Oil Prices vs. Major Events (1970–2009)*

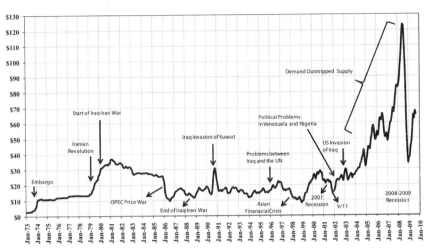

*Prices are the FOB cost of crude oil imports to the United States.

Sources: EIA, 2010 and NGP, 2010.[26]

Figure 7.2
Oil Production vs. Real Oil Prices ($2007)

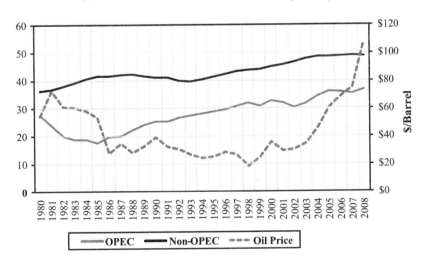

Sources: EIA, 2010 and NGP, 2010.

Figure 7.3
World Oil Demand (1995–June 2008)

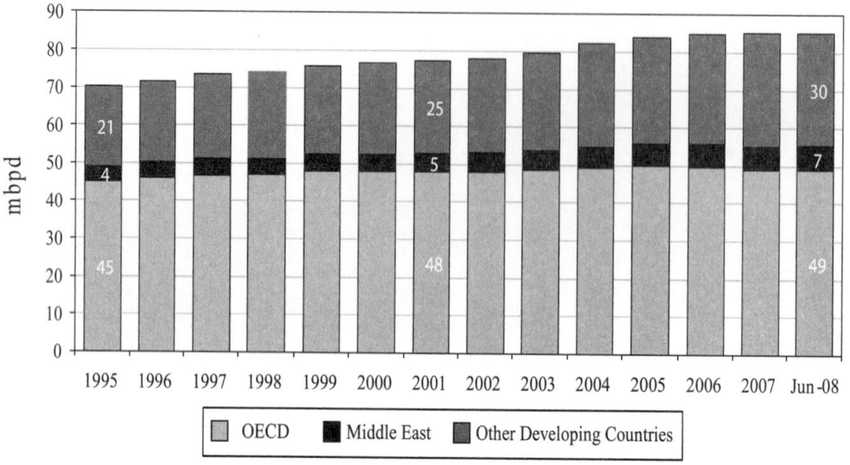

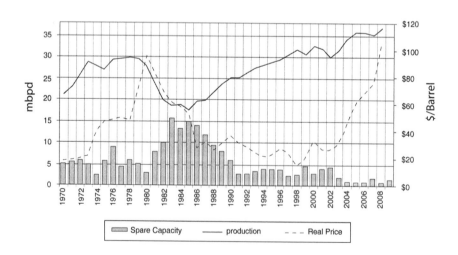

Source: BP Statistical Review of World Energy, 2009.

Figure 7.4
OPEC Spare Capacity and Production vs. Real Prices ($2007)[27]

Sources: EIA, 2010 and NGP, 2010.

Figure 7.5

Oil Price vs. Days of Stocks according to Consumption

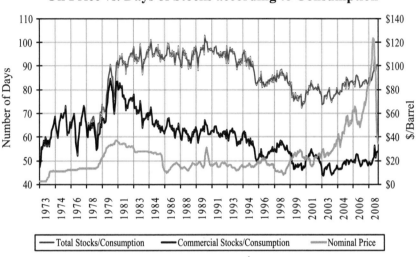

Source: EIA, 2010 and NGP, 2010.

The Six Dimensions of Energy Security

Energy security has six dimensions: economic, environmental, social, foreign policy, technological and national security.[28] These are competing and interactive dimensions, as we will see in the next section.

The Economic Dimension

The objective of the economic dimension of energy security in consuming nations is to ensure that scarcity or shortages of energy resources do not stall economic growth, increase inflation, raise unemployment, weaken the balance of payments or reduce the value of a county's currency. Unfortunately, major energy consuming nations design energy policies without regard to other policies, especially fiscal and monetary. However, this dimension indicates that the level of interaction among energy,

[203]

monetary and fiscal policies is significant. In fact, if the economic dimension of energy security is in danger, the solution is not to be found in energy policy but in monetary and fiscal policies. Expansionary fiscal and monetary policies in the oil-consuming countries, especially the United States, India and China, prevented the continuous increase in oil prices between 2004 and early 2008 from reducing economic growth.[29]

While expansionary monetary and fiscal policies can mitigate the effects of high energy prices, a reduction in energy intensity should improve energy security while contributing positively to other dimensions. Increased efficiency and reorganization of economic sectors would reduce energy intensity and thus reduce the amount of energy needed to produce one unit of GDP. Developing countries could improve the economic dimension of their energy security by expanding their service economies, which require substantially less energy per unit of GDP than other sectors. Such a move would break the link between GDP and energy and allow for economic growth with less growth in energy consumption.

The economic dimension of energy security in producing nations is the mirror image of that in consuming nations. The objective of producers is to ensure steady revenues from energy exports, which can translate into economic growth and development that creates jobs for their young populations.

Neither high energy prices nor low energy prices maximize the economic dimension of energy security in the producing countries. Only prices that sustain the industry in the long run will enhance energy security. However, energy markets are imperfect and volatile. As a result, energy producers can maximize the economic dimension of their energy security, not by cutting production and increasing prices, but by diversifying their sources of income and lowering their dependence on energy exports.

However, improvements in energy efficiency will help producing as well as consuming countries. First, energy efficiency will enable those countries to lower their domestic energy bill and the amount they spend on energy subsidies. Second, energy efficiency will free some energy sources for exports without the cost of major upstream investment. Third, improved energy efficiency would decrease animosity toward certain energy sources and ensure a longer market life for them. While improved energy efficiency might not lead necessarily to lower demand, it does improve the welfare of society.[30]

The competitive and interactive nature of this dimension means that the policies that shape it in consuming countries affect the economic situation in the producing countries and vice versa. For example, high energy prices threaten the economic dimension of the energy security of consuming countries. Their economic growth would decline, and with it their demand for energy. Energy prices would in turn decline, which would reduce the export revenues of the producing nations. As a result, the economic growth of producing nations would decline, most of their development projects would be delayed or canceled, and unemployment would increase.

While low energy prices might help the economic dimension of energy security in the consuming countries in the short term, they would not be beneficial in the long run, as revenues of the energy producing countries decline. In this case, producers would spend less on capacity expansion and maintenance, which would soon result in sharp increases in energy prices that threaten the economic growth in consuming countries. In fact, one of the explanations of the increase in oil prices in the 2000s is their sharp price decline in 1998 and the first quarter of 1999. Thus, the economic dimensions of the energy security of both consuming and producing countries are interdependent, especially in the long term.

The Environmental Dimension

The objective of the environmental dimension of energy security is to reduce, or to eliminate if possible, the negative environmental impact of exploration, production, transportation, processing and use of energy sources. The environmental dimension is not limited to consuming countries. Exploration and production do take place in producing countries, but transportation and processing often take place in other countries. Use, of course, takes place in consuming countries, but at times energy producers are also transporters, processors and major consumers. Combating global warming requires efforts by all involved—producers, processors, transporters and consumers. Only interdependence can maximize this dimension in both consuming and producing countries.

To improve the environmental dimension while avoiding deterioration in other dimensions, all parties must increase energy efficiency and reduce the carbon footprint of energy production, processing and transportation. Reduction in energy use will improve the environment, but it will also reduce economic growth and affect the economic dimension of energy security in both consuming and producing countries. Only improvements in the efficiency of cars, equipment and machines can reduce emissions and still ensure economic growth. While some environmentalists might claim that such an approach is not sufficient to counter the forthcoming global warming crisis, they should realize the interactive nature of various policies. People will behave based on their priorities and when faced with lower incomes, job losses, and future environmental problems, people will most likely choose to solve the immediate income and employment problems and do what they do best to solve future environmental issues: adapt.

Maximizing the environmental dimension without minimizing other dimensions of energy security requires a price range for petroleum products that is neither too low nor too high. Low prices might help the economic dimension of the consuming nations, but at the expense of the environmental dimension for both consumers and producers. Therefore, enhancing the environmental dimension requires reduction or elimination of fuel subsidies. Some policy makers, experts, and newspaper opinion writers believe that high energy prices, brought about by deep production cuts or increased taxes on petroleum products, will help the environment. The opposite is true, especially in heavily populated developing countries. Low-income families, which constitute the largest population segment in

[206]

the developing world, will not be able to afford heavily-taxed or higher-priced fuel. Instead they will burn wood, hard coal and animal dung, which will lead inevitably to deforestation and increased pollution. Therefore, taxation and higher energy prices do not necessarily enhance global energy security, or that of most countries—especially developing nations.

The Social Dimension

The objective of the social dimension of energy security is to minimize the energy gap between the energy-rich and the energy-poor, not only in consuming countries, but also in producing and transit countries. The social dimension of energy security is not directly related to the availability of energy resources, but rather to the ability of the poor to acquire these resources. The larger the energy gap, the more insecure a country becomes; the larger the proportion of the poor who are not able to obtain energy resources, the more energy insecurity a country experiences. The result of such an 'energy gap' could well be political unrest, which would reduce economic growth. Governments might resort to price controls and energy subsidies to reduce income and energy inequalities and thereby attempt to reduce social tension. Unfortunately such policies, especially price controls and across-the-board subsides, often worsen the environmental dimension and lead to energy shortages. In fact, lowering energy prices through price controls or subsides would help the rich, who own several cars and several homes, while the poor would benefit little. Energy price controls also benefit smugglers and gangs if energy prices in neighboring countries are high relative to the country in question. Such smuggling reduces energy supplies and makes it extremely difficult for the poor to obtain energy sources. A government can enhance the social dimension by adopting fiscal policies that reduce the income gap between the poor and the rich but should do so without subsidizing energy prices, even for the poor. Efforts to affect energy prices for society as a whole or for certain groups invariably distort energy markets, create black markets and threaten energy security. While efforts to subsidize cleaner energy for the poor might make energy more accessible, policy makers should be wary of the fact that such policies might create a social wedge by identifying certain energy sources with particular social classes. Such a wedge will not only reduce the social dimension of energy security, but would also make the middle classes and the rich shun the cleaner energy sources used by the poor, despite their environmental benefits.

For producing countries, revenues from energy exports are essential for economic growth, job creation and economic development. They can improve the social dimension of energy security by using a large proportion of oil revenues for direct income transfer programs and subsides for staple items and basic services. While such programs definitely reduce the economic dimension of energy security, some argue that they are a necessary evil to prevent conflict that would halt oil exports to the rest of the world. Nevertheless, proper use of oil revenues, reducing corruption, and the use of the right combinations of fiscal and monetary policies to achieve sustainable economic development would reduce the energy gap between rich and poor.

While turmoil in the oil-producing countries threatens the energy security of consuming countries, social problems that lead to turmoil in consuming countries also threaten the energy security of the producing countries by reducing the demand for oil. Therefore, even the social dimensions of the energy security of producing, consuming and transit countries are interdependent.

The Foreign Policy Dimension

The objective of this dimension is to prevent countries that are dependent on energy imports or exports from making counterproductive foreign policy decisions to please the countries upon which they rely. In this paper, I consider foreign policy decisions under this dimension to be limited to diplomatic and trade relations—they do not include threats and wars, which are covered under the national security dimension.

The need for oil or gas might force some consuming countries, with or without pressure from producers, to make foreign policy decisions that would compromise them on other important issues or principles such as human rights, environmental protection, copyrights, and free markets. In addition, the need for oil and gas might force some consuming countries to limit their foreign policy options, which could be viewed as a threat to national security. For example, the United States may have five foreign policy options to deal with a certain oil-producing country. It would view dependence on foreign oil imports as a threat if, as a result of that dependence, its policy options decline from five options to, say, three options. The Council on Foreign Relations' (CFR) report "National Security Consequences of US Oil Dependence," released in 2006, stresses this point. The report states:

> All consuming countries, including the United States, are more constrained in dealing with producing states when oil markets are tight. To cite one current example, concern about losing Iran's 2.5 million barrels per day of world oil exports will cause importing states to be reluctant to take action against Iran's nuclear program.[31]

A consuming country can maximize the foreign policy dimension of its energy security simply by diversifying its energy sources and imports. A more complex but feasible approach involves building an energy portfolio that maximizes the foreign policy dimension of its energy security. For example, experts in an oil consuming country can build a portfolio of imports from 20 countries. They can give a larger weight to imports from countries in which imports will enhance the foreign policy dimension significantly. For example, the United States might increase oil imports from a certain country if the corresponding improvement in relations can improve human rights in that country or bolsters US trade with that country. Experts can give lesser weight to imports that can enhance this dimension slightly. Imports from countries that will affect the foreign policy dimension negatively would be stopped.

On the other side, the dependence of energy-producing countries on energy exports might limit their foreign policy options if their exports – or the transit of their exports – are concentrated in certain countries. Producing countries can maximize the foreign policy dimension of their energy security by diversifying their sources of income, exports clients and the routes of these exports. However, if consuming countries feel that they have to compromise their foreign policy to import oil, their instinctive reaction would be to work toward lowering imports, and probably the demand for that energy source. As a result, energy-producing countries will suffer. Likewise, if energy-producing countries feel that they have to compromise their foreign policy to export oil to certain countries, they might reduce production and upstream investment. The result is lower supplies and higher prices in consuming countries.

Since we do not live in a perfect world and treaties are a function of ever-changing politics, global energy security would be maximized if all countries diversified their energy imports and exports and their transportation routes. Thus, even the foreign policy dimensions of producers and consumers are interdependent.

The Technological Dimension

The objective of this dimension is to ensure that low prices for a certain energy resource – such as oil – and government regulations do not choke new technologies that improve energy efficiency, increase energy productivity, lower production costs, lower emissions, and bring new energy sources to the market place. In addition, it guarantees that certain technologies are readily available to producers and consumers around the world and that government support of certain energy technologies does not inadvertently minimize other dimensions of energy security.

For example, any new technology that improves energy efficiency should be made available for use by consumers worldwide without any political or economic barriers, as long as the marketplace supports the technology.[32] Any new technology that increases the productivity of oil and gas wells should be available to all oil producers worldwide. The expansion of new clean coal technology would greatly improve global energy security. The use of biomass energy in electricity generation in countries such as India has proven to be very successful, especially in high oil price environments.

Government support of certain new energy technologies that are not supported by market forces could increase energy prices and volatility, which in turn would affect the economic and social dimensions of energy security. Future energy technology should be determined by competition in the market place, not by governments. Government choices of technology might result in several adverse effects on energy security. For example, in their quest for energy independence, governments might support certain technologies that facilitate the production of certain energy resources, which may actually lead to energy insecurity; as a case in point, a country might become hostage to spare parts that come from other countries. Fuel cell technology requires the use of palladium, which only Russia and South Africa export. Several countries, including the United States, might view dependence on palladium imports from these countries as a threat to the foreign policy or national security dimensions of energy security. Another example: government support of certain energy resources that are not supported by markets might lead to energy insecurity if the country needs to import the skilled labor to operate that technology. In addition, government support of certain energy sources might reduce the benefits from such a source if market forces support small scale projects, while governments insist on mega projects. Or, in some cases, governments might impose a certain energy source on a specific economic sector while this energy source would be better-suited to another sector. For example, small-scale solar projects might be more efficient than large-scale projects. While governments' efforts to impose the fuel cell/hydrogen technology on the transportation sector failed, the private sector succeeded in commercializing stationary fuel cells for hospitals, large buildings, and isolated communities.

National Security Dimension

While the foreign policy dimension focuses on diplomatic and trade relations, the objective of the national security dimension of energy security is to protect energy infrastructure and installations from enemy attacks, terrorist attacks, human errors, natural disasters and technical malfunctions. In addition, its objective is to ensure the availability of energy resources for the nation's military and police forces, especially during wars, domestic violence or national disasters. While an oil embargo or any other political event is a direct threat to the foreign policy dimension of energy security, it might end up a threat to national security if energy supplies are limited to the extent that it affects the mobility of the army and the police. Similarly, a natural disaster that curtails energy supplies might threaten the national security dimension if the army and the National Guard do not have access to fuel for rescue operations. Such threats give credence to strategic reserves, especially since the need for fuel is immediate and transient. While the possession of strategic reserves is a controversial issue, the benefits from such reserves depend on the objective and the policies that determine their management and use. Government-held strategic petroleum reserves would enhance the national security dimension of energy security only if a buildup of such reserves does not lead to a decline in commercial reserves.

Besides protecting energy facilities and infrastructure and building strategic fuel reserves, a country can enhance the national security dimension of energy security by dispersing domestic energy resources and installations. Knowledge of the geographic location of energy resources and installations relative to the location of the market, the locations of various religious, ethnic and political groups in the nation, and the location relative to natural disaster prone areas, is vital for improving the national security dimension.

Dimensions of Energy Security are Competitive and Interactive

Creating an energy policy that incorporates these dimensions is the easy part. Balancing them over time, however, is an extremely difficult task. These are competing dimensions. Maximizing one dimension might well come at the expense of another. While these six dimensions are universal and apply to global energy security as well as to the energy security of any nation, policy makers should realize the following:

- The weight of each dimension of energy security differs from country to country. It differs from time to time even within the same country. For example, some countries might assign the environmental dimension a significantly greater weight than the economic dimension, while others might assign most of the weight to foreign policy and national security. A country might also assign the foreign policy and national security dimensions greater weight during times of war than during periods of peace.

- These are competing dimensions. Balancing this competition among dimensions is an extremely difficult task. For example, emphasizing the economic dimension might come at the expense of the environmental dimension; and emphasizing the foreign policy dimension might come at the expense of the economic dimension. Declining energy supplies and rising energy prices can easily lead to lower economic growth, especially when governments adopt contradictory fiscal and monetary policies.

- These are interactive dimensions. A change in one dimension affects all other dimensions at differing rates, which makes balancing them even more difficult. While the result of the "competition" mentioned above is the growth of one dimension at the expense of others, "interaction" might result in growth in one dimension in a way that leads to growth in other dimensions, probably with some multiplier effect. For example, a major technological breakthrough would not

[213]

only increase energy supplies, but would also lower prices and price volatility, change world trade patterns and provide cleaner energy to countries with high greenhouse gas emissions. Lower prices would stimulate economic growth and reduce the energy gap between the rich and the poor, thus enhancing the social dimension of energy security. Meanwhile, lower prices guarantee demand growth for energy producers.[33] As mentioned in the introduction, solving the power shortage crisis in the oil producing countries would enhance their energy security by providing enough power for economic growth while increasing oil exports, thereby enhancing the energy security of consuming countries. If the power shortage problem is resolved by using natural gas, for example, the environmental dimension of energy security for the producing country and for the rest of the world is improved.

Measurement, the 'Energy Security Star' and the 'Energy Security Index'

Each dimension can be measured for each country with available data on several measurable components. Once the measures are calculated, an index for each dimension can be calculated which allows the construction of an "Energy Security Star" for each country with an associated overall "Energy Security Index." The objective of each country is to maximize the area of the star. Countries can improve their energy security over time by increasing the area of the star. A decline in the area of the star equates to a deterioration in energy security. It is outside the scope of this paper to list these measures (about 90 of them), the method of calculations and the calculated indices.[34] However, in Figure 7.6 are four hypothetical radar chart examples that show different shapes of the Energy Security Star with its six dimensions. They represent either four different countries at one point in time, or one country that is changing its priorities over time.

Figure 7.6
Energy Security Star

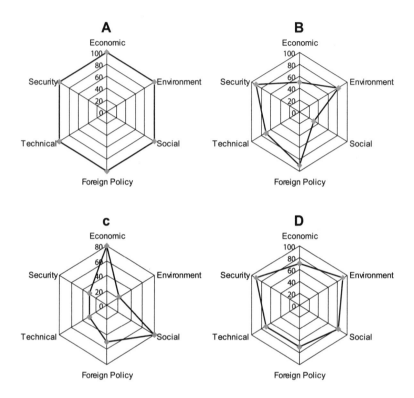

Star A depicts optimal energy security. This model is imaginary and will not occur in reality for many known reasons. For example, emissions will remain with us no matter what we do; therefore, the environmental dimension cannot stand at 100. Star B is more realistic; it represents a country that favors foreign policy, national security and the environment over other dimensions. In such a country, a huge energy gap exists between the rich and the poor. This country can improve its energy security by reducing this gap and rebalancing its priorities. Star C depicts a country that cares less about the environment, but emphasizes the economic and social dimensions of energy security. Star D depicts a country with relatively balanced priorities. It is clear from the area of the three realistic stars – B, C and D – that country D is more energy secure than countries B and C.

Stars B, C and D, might also represent one country at three different times with three different sets of priorities, or a country struggling to maximize its energy security. If star D reflects the energy security in the most recent year, we can say that energy security has improved relative to previous years. It is also worth noting that the sides of the Star can be a weighted index instead of an absolute index. This allows experts to compare energy security among countries despite different priorities.

Definition of Energy Security

The following definition encompasses all six dimensions of energy security and other issues related to interdependence: *The steady availability of energy supplies that ensures economic growth in both producing and consuming countries with the lowest social cost and the lowest price volatility.*

While the economic dimension is clear in the language, other dimensions are embedded in 'economic growth,' 'social cost' and 'price volatility.' For example, the social cost includes the social, environmental, foreign policy, and national security dimensions. In addition, 'price volatility' encompasses various dimensions, including technological, economic, and foreign policy dimensions for both producing and consuming countries.

Conclusions

Energy interdependence, not energy independence, is the key to energy security for any nation. While energy independence might improve some aspects of energy security, it does not shield a country from energy shocks. The petroleum market is fungible and global, and a shortage in any part of the world will increase petroleum prices worldwide. The same applies to coal, gas and LNG, although they are not as global as the oil market. Hence, consuming countries can only enhance their energy security through "reciprocal energy security." Energy security, in all of its dimensions, is as important for producing countries as it is for consuming countries. Interdependence and reciprocal energy security will result in global energy security. Any national efforts to enhance national energy security at the expense of global energy security will backfire.

Energy security has six competitive and interactive dimensions: economic, environmental, social, foreign policy, technological and national security. These dimensions are measurable and can provide a clear view of the energy security of the country in question. This paper illustrates that interdependence extends to every dimension of energy security. Improving the economic dimension of energy security in the oil producing countries would enhance the economic dimension of energy security in the consuming countries and vice versa.

Two important words for energy security in both consuming and producing countries are 'diversification' and 'maximization.' Since the objective of any country is to maximize energy security, it should try to maximize all dimensions—although this is extremely difficult to do, given the competitive nature of these dimensions. As indicated by the Energy Security Star, energy security is enhanced by maximizing the area of the Star. The easiest and fastest way to maximize the Energy Security Star for any country is diversification of energy sources, imports and exports. For energy producing countries, income diversification and lower dependence on energy exports enhance their energy security.

As shown above, the Energy Security Star and the Energy Security Index are data-intensive. They can benefit policy makers and researchers only if up-to-date data is available, which might add another dimension to energy security that has not been included in the Energy Security Star: data availability. Without measurement and assessment, decision makers cannot make the correct policy recommendations to avoid an energy crisis.

To improve its energy security, a country must collect relevant, up-to-date data, measure the various dimensions mentioned above, and continually assess its energy security. Only then can policy makers make informed decisions and protect their country – and consequently the world – from future energy crises. Keep in mind that even a correct policy will not be effective if it contradicts another policy response. Policy responses must be integrated in a way that maximizes energy security, along with other security concerns.

8

The Producer–Consumer Gap:
Experience and Prospects

Vincent Lauerman

The gap between oil producers and consumers was considerable for most of the twentieth century, being characterized by mistrust, resentment and monologue. However, a formal dialogue began shortly after the 1990–91 Gulf War that gradually increased trust and understanding between producers and consumers, culminating in the two sides recognizing their common interest in oil price stability at reasonable levels.

Since the major international oil companies (IOCs) lost control of prices and production levels in the early 1970s, the world oil market has failed in its primary function—price discovery. This fact has become increasingly apparent in recent years, with New York Mercantile Exchange (NYMEX) West Texas Intermediate (WTI) surging from US\$20 per barrel in 2002 to \$147 in July 2008, collapsing to about \$33 in less than six months time, and rebounding to over \$80 per barrel by the fourth quarter of 2009.

The extreme oil price movements of recent years and the decline of 'market fundamentalism' owing to the global financial crisis and recession are opening the door for an option that has only recently been discussed in political circles—a formal price band mechanism administered by both oil producers and consumers.

In the first section of this paper, past relations between producers and consumers are discussed, including the convergence of interests

[219]

regarding stable prices at reasonable levels. The decline of American hegemony and market fundamentalism, and a plausible oil price band mechanism are discussed in the second and third sections, respectively. In the fourth and final section, the likelihood of producer–consumer relations developing into a price band mechanism is discussed in the context of scenario analysis.

Producer–Consumer Convergence on the Oil Price Issue

The basis of oil producer mistrust and resentment towards consumers during the colonial and post-colonial eras was the concession system. In the colonial era, the major IOCs – instruments of the Western powers – tended to impose contracts on oil producers and dictate terms. Through a small number of concession agreements, seven American and Western European companies, dubbed the "Seven Sisters" – Exxon, Royal Dutch Shell, BP, Mobil, Chevron, Texaco and Gulf Corporation based on their modern names – locked up the bulk of the oil resources in Southeast Asia and Latin America by the 1910s and in the Middle East by the 1930s.[1]

The original concession agreements paid the producing countries a pittance compared to oil company profits and home government taxes, and were of extraordinary longevity and size—up to ninety-nine years in length and covering up to one half the size of countries as large as Iran. Oil producers had no formal rights to renegotiate the terms of their concessions, barring outright nationalization, which governments could only achieve at the risk of their own survival.[2] Owing to the quasi-extraterritorial rights granted to the Western oil companies, producing countries had no recourse to their own courts in disputes with IOCs, and had no right to take part in oil-related decisions on pricing, taxation and production levels.[3]

In addition, the Seven Sisters, often with the support of their home governments, cynically played producer against producer to squeeze the best possible deal for themselves. For example, after developing the

Mexican oil industry early in the twentieth century, the IOCs shifted future investments to Venezuela, a more financially appealing Latin American country.[4]

As the colonial system crumbled following the Second World War and the neo-colonial era emerged, the financial terms for concessions and the dialogue between oil producers and Western oil companies improved somewhat, but producers remained mistrustful and resentful.

The struggle for control of the international oil industry between producers and consumers began in earnest in the 1970–1973 period. In 1971, the Texas Railroad Commission, the *de facto* arbiter of US crude oil production, approved the production of all available oil capacity in the country—definitive evidence that the world oil market was tightening, and shifting from a buyer's to a seller's market.[5]

The Tripoli and Tehran agreements in September 1970 and February 1971, respectively, granting Libya and Iran a 55 percent share of oil companies' pre-tax profits instead of 50 percent (the norm since the early 1950s) signaled the beginning of a long retreat by Western oil companies relative to the producing countries. Demands by members of the Organization of the Petroleum Exporting Countries (OPEC) for additional price and contractual revisions became the norm, causing a leapfrogging in price and contract terms.[6] At the extreme, Algeria nationalized its oil industry in March 1971, Iraq in June 1972, and Libya in mid-1973.[7]

Francisco Parra has suggested that a major reason for the lack of intervention by Western governments on behalf of their oil companies to thwart these nationalizations – as they did in Iran in the early 1950s – was their fear that it would cause a major oil price spike and damage the global economy as a result of the tight supply situation in the early 1970s.[8]

Despite their best efforts to placate OPEC members in the early 1970s, the fourth Arab–Israeli conflict – during the Jewish festivity of Yom Kippur in October 1973 – precipitated the oil price shock the Western governments had been trying to avoid. In reaction to the United States re-arming Israel during the war, on October 16, 1973 the six Gulf members of OPEC unilaterally increased the official price of Arabian Light from \$2.90 to \$5.11 per barrel—the first time OPEC members had dictated pricing terms to the IOCs, and a clear sign of things to come.[9]

The next day, members of the Organization of Arab Petroleum Exporting Countries (OAPEC) announced a "selective" oil embargo against Israel's supporters. Despite the embargo being porous, oil prices shot higher. At its December 1973 meeting, OPEC raised the official price for Arabian Light to \$11.65 per barrel—a fourfold increase in less than four months and an almost tenfold increase from 1970s levels.[10]

Thus, the tables had turned by the end of 1973. OPEC was dictating the price of crude oil to the major oil companies, rather than the other way around. In addition, OPEC members had gained control of other important aspects of their oil industries, including production levels and investment decisions, either by nationalization, so-called 'participation,' or the simple abrogation of some of the companies' key contractual rights.[11] As a result, the monologue continued, but with OPEC now dictating terms to the IOCs.

The first oil shock, its negative impact on the global economy, and the shift in oil power had the same impact on oil consuming countries as did the concession system on oil producers—it bred mistrust and resentment.

In an attempt to promote dialogue between oil producing and consuming countries in particular, and resource producing and consuming countries in general, the Conference on International Economic Cooperation (CIEC) was convened in Paris in December 1975. This conference was an unmitigated failure, and as Robert Mabro wrote, "killed for a long time the concept of formal multilateral negotiations between governments on the energy issue."[12]

Of course, the second oil shock – caused by the Islamic revolution in Iran and the Iran–Iraq war – the Iran hostage crisis, and nationalizations spreading to all OPEC members did not help matters. In late 1980, the spot price for Arabian Light reached \$42 per barrel, and the global economy again fell into major recession.[13]

However, the OPEC era proved to be shorter and more dramatic than the reign of the Seven Sisters. In an attempt to defend prices in the face of declining oil demand and rising non-OPEC supply, OPEC was forced to become a formal cartel and impose a production ceiling on its members at its March 1982 meeting. In order to strengthen the new system, Saudi Arabia offered to act as "swing producer."[14]

Thanks partly to a lack of discipline by other OPEC members, Saudi Arabia was forced to slash its crude oil production to 2.2 million barrels per day (mbpd) by August 1985, compared to 10.5 mbpd in 1980. In order to win back market share, the Saudis adopted 'netback' pricing in the autumn of 1985, a system that guaranteed refiners a fixed profit margin per barrel. At its December 1985 meeting, all OPEC members adopted the netback pricing mechanism. Oil prices collapsed, with WTI and Brent falling below $10 per barrel, and Dubai hitting $7 in the spring of 1986.[15]

Despite adopting an official price of $18 per barrel for a basket of seven OPEC crude oils at its December 1986 meeting, and all members besides Iraq agreeing to new production quotas, it was the beginning of the end for OPEC dominance.[16] In September 1987, under threat from its main customers in the Aramco group, the Saudis secretly stopped charging the official price, replacing it with market-related pricing based on benchmark spot prices for different markets instead. The arrangement was openly confirmed in January 1988, and the OPEC fixed price system permanently collapsed by the end of the first quarter.[17]

The OPEC era was over. OPEC had been humbled by the oil market, just as the Western oil companies had been humbled by the market in the early 1970s – although for opposite reasons – and the market had become the new master. As Leonardo Maugeri wrote in his book *The Age of Oil*:

> All of a sudden, the free market had displaced oligopolies, and oil seemed to have lost its status as a vital resource, the tight control of which was key to global power and national security. The credo was supported by free-market orthodoxy, by then the dominant religion of the United States and Great Britain under the leadership of Ronald Reagan and Margaret Thatcher.[18]

[223]

The Gulf crisis at the beginning of the 1990s was a turning point in relations between oil producers and consumers. It underscored the close relationship between oil and political power, the mutual interdependence between producers and consumers, and the rising role of the oil market.[19] More importantly, it proved that producers were willing to act in the interests of consumers when OPEC members quickly mobilized 4.5 mbpd of spare capacity to make up for lost Iraqi and Kuwaiti crude oil exports.[20]

Seizing the opportunity, Presidents François Mitterrand of France and Carlos Perez of Venezuela took the initiative to convene a 'Ministerial Seminar' among oil producing and consuming countries in Paris in July 1991 to break the political ice.[21]

Prior to the first formal dialogue between the ministers, Robert Mabro wrote an extremely insightful and prophetic paper, "A Dialogue between Oil Producers and Consumers: The Why and the How." In this paper, Mabro argued that the price level should be the central issue for the dialogue because sharp shifts in oil prices are often very damaging to producer and consumer countries. Oil price spikes tend to cause global recessions, while sudden increases or declines in oil income can destabilize oil producing countries.[22]

Mabro went on to argue that extreme price movements are the norm for the world oil market for two reasons. First, oil prices do not receive much guidance from economics because of a very low cost floor for crude oil production and a very high ceiling set by substitutes in the transportation sector.[23] Second, oil industry projects tend to have long lead times compared to other industries, primarily because of very long delays in the pre-investment stage owing to regulatory hurdles and complex negotiations between companies and governments.[24]

Oil prices tend to be inherently unstable in the shorter term owing to the first reason, and inherently unstable in the longer term as a result of a combination of the first and the second. Since most oil companies tend to overreact to short-term price signals, high prices encourage excessive investment in oil related infrastructure, while low prices affect investment behavior in the opposite manner. As a result, the oil industry is prone to either being overloaded with surplus capacity or finding itself short in the longer term.[25]

To tame inherently unstable short-run oil prices, Mabro recommended a better flow of information to improve investment decisions and a system to anchor oil prices around their best long-run level—while still allowing prices to fluctuate up and down in response to short-term economic forces.[26]

The goal of Mabro's recommendations was to moderate oil price and investment spending swings in an attempt to avoid the boom-bust cycles that had plagued the international oil industry since the Seven Sisters lost control of the market in the early 1970s.

However, it was simply impossible for the ministers from the producer and consumer countries to discuss the price issue in Paris in July 1991, partly owing to their history of mistrust and resentment, and partly as a result of American anti-trust laws and the spread of market fundamentalism. Mabro prophetically mused, "The energy problem has become entangled with that of the US political hegemony. Change Washington's mind and everything else will change."[27]

Ever since the Paris seminar, ministers and energy experts from producer and consumer countries have met in alternate years in different locations around the world. The main purpose of the dialogue at the International Energy Forum (IEF), as it came to be known, was to build trust and understanding between producers and consumers, and to focus on subjects in which the two groups have common interests.[28] As a rule, the IEF has intentionally avoided sensitive or controversial issues in an attempt to accomplish these goals.

By the end of the twentieth century, the confrontational attitude that had persisted between producers and consumers for much of the century had dissipated, a degree of trust had been built, and the awareness of long-term common interests increased.[29] The 1998–99 oil price crash and the surge in oil prices in 2000 focused the attention of both producers and consumers on the importance of maintaining stable prices at reasonable levels, and on oil security issues—security of demand and supply, respectively. However, discussions about oil prices were tentative and constrained by American anti-trust laws and market fundamentalism.

The role of 'missing barrels' in the 1998–99 oil price crash put the quest for better oil market data and information at the forefront of the producer–consumer dialogue in the first half of the decade. The common belief was that better data and information would lead to more efficient oil markets and greater price stability. In 2005, the IEF Secretariat in Riyadh was made responsible for the Joint Oil Data Exercise, making it the flagship activity of the organization.[30]

The price of oil taking off in the middle of the last decade increased concern about stable prices at reasonable levels and energy security among producers and consumers. Energy security was the main theme of the 10th IEF Ministerial in Doha and the Group of Eight (G-8) Summit in St. Petersburg in April and July 2006, respectively. In Doha, ministers from producer and consumer countries confirmed their shared interest in reduced market volatility and prices at reasonable levels.[31] However, the dialogue about oil prices continued to be constrained by market fundamentalism. The St. Petersburg Principles on Global Energy Security read: "Free, competitive and open markets are essential to the efficient functioning of the global energy system."[32]

The extreme price movements in recent years, despite improving data and information flows, have raised concerns about the role of non-fundamental factors in price determination. According to Noe van Hulst, ministers at the 11th IEF Ministerial in Rome in April 2008 expressed concerns about the level of oil prices and the unprecedented level of oil price volatility, noting "an increasing connection between oil and financial markets."[33]

The G-8 summit in L'Aquila, Italy in July 2009, called on the IEF to take up the case of the first pillar of the St. Petersburg action plan – increasing transparency, predictability and stability of energy markets – through an *ad hoc* high-level steering group.[34] The communiqué from the

Pittsburgh Group of Twenty (G-20) Summit in September 2009 read: "We will promote energy market transparency and market stability as part of our broader effort to avoid excessive volatility [because] [i]nefficient markets and excessive volatility negatively affect both producers and consumers."[35] Importantly, the Pittsburgh communiqué failed to provide explicit support for free, competitive and open markets in its discussion about the oil market.[36]

Hence, two issues were identified as priorities for the 12th IEF Ministerial to be held in Cancun, Mexico on March 29–31, 2010: the first to develop an enhanced IEF architecture to allow it to better achieve the objectives of the producer–consumer dialogue; the second to gain a deeper understanding of the functioning of energy markets and to consider ways and means that could improve their performance.[37]

An Opportunity for a Price Band Mechanism

The global financial crisis and recession have humbled the American hegemon and pushed market fundamentalism off its pedestal, providing an opportunity for the adoption of an oil price band mechanism administered by producers and consumers.

Although the US became the sole superpower on the planet with the collapse of the Soviet Union in 1991, it was not until the late 1990s that concerns about American power began to spread. President Bill Clinton's signing of the National Missile Defense Act of 1999 seriously harmed major power relations, with the Chinese and Russians warning it would have grave consequences for global strategic stability. During this period, Russian Prime Minister Yevgeny Primakov advocated a 'strategic triangle' between Russia, China and India to counterbalance the United States (the Primakov doctrine).[38]

The 9/11 terrorist attacks on New York and Washington, DC provided the George W. Bush administration with a green light from Congress and the American public to implement a more robust defense and foreign policy, eviscerating the international political order. The National Security Strategy of the United States of America, released in September 2002, formalized what American historian John Lewis Gaddis described as "the most sweeping redesign of US grand strategy since the presidency of Franklin D. Roosevelt."[39]

The primary goal of the new strategy was to retain America's role as the sole superpower into the indefinite future by maintaining its military superiority. The secondary goal, known as the Bush doctrine, was to move the goalpost for preemptive war to protect the United States from the nexus between rogue states, global terrorist networks and the proliferation of weapons of mass destruction—a doctrine that was used to "justify" the ill-fated Iraq war.[40]

However, what few people realized was that American power had been financed by domestic and foreign debt over the past three decades, and this debt is the basis for the recent financial and economic crisis.

The global economy has long been wracked by irregular bouts of extreme volatility owing to the credit cycles at the heart of the capitalist system. Some financial mistakes we make every generation, and the more serious ones every second or third. The last time the global debt pyramid came tumbling down was during the Great Depression of the 1930s.

The present pyramid did not begin to build in earnest until the early 1980s, when US President Ronald Reagan joined UK Prime Minister Margaret Thatcher in power. It was during this time that deregulation of banks and financial markets started to gather momentum, lending standards became increasingly lax, and private sector debt began to balloon. America's deregulation process culminated in President Clinton signing the Financial Services Modernization Act in November 1999.[41]

Between 1980 and 2007, US private sector debt more than doubled from 124 percent of Gross Domestic Product (GDP) to 288 percent. Public sector debt also increased by 13 percentage points to 52 percent of GDP over this period, contributing to a rise in total American domestic debt from 163 percent of GDP to 340 percent.

Since investment did not decline as much as savings in the United States, the country has been running large current account deficits and experiencing increasing levels of foreign indebtedness over this period. America's net international investment position shifted from positive 13 percent of GDP at the end of 1980 to negative 18 percent at the end of 2007.[42]

Financial deregulation culminated in the proliferation of US sub-prime mortgages in the middle of the past decade. As the name of these loans imply, sub-prime borrowers were not eligible for prime mortgage rates thanks to limited income or poor credit histories. Sub-prime loans increased from 8 percent of US home loans issued in 2002 to 28 percent in 2006, at which point 14 percent of outstanding home loans in the United States were sub-prime.[43]

In the 2004–2006 period, over 90 percent of the sub-prime mortgages issued had a feature whereby borrowers paid a low fixed rate for the first few years of the mortgage and substantially higher adjustable rates thereafter. A quarter of the 7.2 million outstanding sub-prime mortgages had an interest rate reset in 2007 and 2008, with typical monthly loan payments increasing between 30 percent to 50 percent. These higher loan payments led to a surge in sub-prime mortgage defaults, and the American debt pyramid began tumbling down.[44]

The primary reason why the sub-prime financial crisis went global, besides the United States being the epicenter of global capitalism, is that sub-prime mortgages were packaged by investment bankers into securities and sold to financial institutions around the world, especially European ones. Globalization, financial derivatives and the diversification of risk came together to morph the sub-prime crisis into the global financial crisis in September 2008.[45] According to Piergiorgio Alessandri and Andrew Haldane of the Bank of England, the total gross value of government interventions to support financial institutions around the world has been $14 trillion.[46]

[229]

Ironically, President Bush was forced to reverse his unilateral ways near the end of his second administration and call upon the G-20 to help save the global and US financial systems and economies from collapse. At the first G-20 summit in Washington, DC in November 2008, the leaders from the largest advanced and emerging economies agreed to adopt the 'necessary' monetary and fiscal policies to shore up the global economy, avoid new barriers to trade and investment, and move quickly on global financial reform. To encourage their cooperation, the advanced economies agreed in principle to increase the voting rights of the emerging economies in the International Monetary Fund (IMF), and increase their membership in key standards-setting bodies, including the Financial Stability Forum.[47]

President Barack Obama has continued the process of transferring economic power to the G-20 in exchange for economic cooperation to deal with the crisis. At the third G-20 summit in Pittsburgh in September 2009, the leaders pledged a new era of global economic cooperation. The summit communiqué read: "We designated the G-20 to be the premier forum for international economic cooperation."[48] Hence, the global economy has a new financial architecture, with the G-20 at the centre of international economic policy making, instead of the American-dominated G-8.

Since regulation cycles have gone hand in hand with debt cycles in modern times, the United States has suddenly emerged as the champion of financial market regulation, rather than deregulation. In June 2009, President Obama proposed a new US regulatory structure that he justifiably called the, "most ambitious overhaul of the financial system since the Great Depression," according to *Financial Times* columnist Martin Wolf.[49]

The proposed US regulatory reforms include: establishing a formal mechanism to allow for the orderly resolution of any financial holding company whose failure may threaten the stability of the financial system; raising capital and liquidity requirements for all financial institutions, with more stringent requirements for the largest and most interconnected firms;

harmonizing the regulation of futures and securities and strong oversight of 'over-the-counter' derivatives; robust reporting standards on asset-backed securities and a requirement that the originator of a securitization retain a financial interest in its performance; and greater protection to consumers and investors through regulatory agencies.[50]

In January 2010, the Obama administration put forth the 'Volcker rule' to de-risk banks and the 'Obama levy' to tax them according to their size. The Volcker rule, named after former Federal Reserve Chairman Paul Volcker, would ban banks from trading for their own accounts and from "owning, investing in or sponsoring" hedge funds and private equity groups if passed into law.[51] The Obama levy is a potential 0.15 percent tax on bank balance sheets over $50 billion.[52]

Although not as strict or comprehensive as those proposed in the United States, the G-20 proposed similar regulatory reforms for its members at the Pittsburgh summit, besides the Volcker rule and the Obama levy.

A number of regulatory reforms have also been proposed by the United States and the G-20 to curb speculation on oil markets, with the American ones again stricter and more comprehensive. The US reforms include: the supervision and regulation of energy markets being transferred from NYMEX to the Commodity Futures Trading Commission (CFTC); the withdrawal of position limit and margin exemptions for investment banks; greater market oversight as it relates to the reporting of non-commercial activity; and increasing cooperation between the CFTC and non-US exchanges. Although these reforms have the potential to moderate oil price instability, prices would remain inherently unstable for the reasons discussed in the previous section.

Of course, the global financial industry is fighting back. The financial industry's main line of defense, as argued by Barclays Chairman Marcus Agius, is the risk of "regulatory arbitrage."[53] For example, British banks would be damaged if regulators were too rigorous compared to other jurisdictions, leading to a shift in financial business from countries with stricter regulations to ones with weaker regulations. Given the power of the financial industry, especially in America, we should expect proposed regulatory reforms to be diluted.

In an interview with *The Huffington Post* during the heart of the global financial meltdown in September 2008, Nobel Prize winning economist Joseph Stiglitz said:

> [T]he fall of Wall Street is for market fundamentalism what the fall of the Berlin Wall was for communism – it tells the world that this way of economic organization turns out not to be sustainable. In the end, everyone says, that model doesn't work. This moment is a marker that the claims of financial market liberalization were bogus.[54]

It is important to remember that market fundamentalism cycles in capitalist countries and the latest period of free market supremacy have been relatively short – from the early 1980s until autumn 2008 – and even shorter for the world oil market. In addition, even in the heyday of oil market fundamentalism, OPEC still adjusted production levels in the hope of affecting prices, and US presidents still sent emissaries – Vice President Bush in April 1986 and Secretary of Energy Richardson in February 1999 – to Saudi Arabia when low oil prices threatened America's domestic industry and energy security.

The extreme oil price movements in recent years and the fall of market fundamentalism and its primary sponsor have potentially opened the door for an oil price band mechanism administered by both producers and consumers, especially since no other country has the inclination or the power to take up America's former free market mantle.

A Plausible Price Band Mechanism

The first political call for an oil price band mechanism administered by producers and consumers was from Indian Finance Minister Palaniappan Chidambaram at the Energy Minister's meeting in Jeddah, Saudi Arabia in June 2008.[55] French President Nicolas Sarkozy and British Prime Minister Gordon Brown since hinted at a price band mechanism in a joint article in *The Wall Street Journal* in July 2009, where they wrote: "Producers and consumers are closer now than at any time in the past 30 years to recognizing the huge common interest in giving clear and stable signals to long-term investment."[56] They went on to suggest that the Expert Group of the IEF should, "consider any measures that could be put in place to reduce volatility."[57]

The ideal basis for the price band mechanism would be a treaty between members of OPEC, the International Energy Agency (IEA) and the G-20 to create a so-called "Global Oil Agency" with a governing structure similar to the IEA—i.e., governing board, management committee, steering groups, and secretariat. The more formal and rule-bound the price band mechanism, the more likely it is to be taken seriously by market players, and hence, the more likely it is to be effective.

US anti-trust laws would certainly have stood in the way of American involvement in such a scheme in the past, but this may no longer be the case with the new anti-financial market spirit in Washington, DC. Due to the importance of stable oil prices to the global and US economies, ingenious lawmakers may be able to frame the price band mechanism in the same context as public utilities.

On the other side of the institutional spectrum, Bassam Fattouh and Christopher Allsopp recently argued in an Oxford Energy Comment that a logical first step towards a price band mechanism (of which they are skeptical) would be "focal points" or informal targets agreed upon by producers and consumers.[58] However, their suggested first step was basically tried and failed during the recent oil price boom. As crude oil prices rose above $80 per barrel in autumn 2007, representatives from OPEC and the IEA frequently stated that oil prices were too high, but prices still increased to almost twice this level by mid-2008.

Assuming a more institutionalized framework, a steering group of producer and consumer countries would need to be formed, and would have to identify a potentially sustainable price band. A good starting point would be Ali Aissaoui's work in the area (see Chapter 4). His target range is based on IEA estimates of the investment cost to develop frontier petroleum projects (such as Canada's oil sands) and the fiscal value of recoverable oil reserves in producing countries. Based on Aissaoui's methodology and assumptions, the range should be set at $60 to $80 per barrel.[59]

The same group would need to convene follow-up meetings to either rubberstamp the current price band or change it if it is no longer considered a sustainable range. Fortunately, relatively stable prices at a reasonable level would contribute to relatively stable investment flows and capacity additions all along the supply chain, including spare OPEC production capacity to help protect against supply shocks.

When Chidambaram recommended the adoption of the price band mechanism at Jeddah, he also suggested a system to police it. In particular, he recommended that OPEC protect the upper end of the price band and consumers protect the lower band. Unfortunately, Chidambaram's approach plays into the central criticism of a producer–consumer administered price band mechanism as long argued by numerous analysts and most recently by Fattouh and Allsopp:

> [A] fundamental weakness in policing such an oil price band is that it has to be managed by parties with very divergent interests. In a rising market, OPEC loses the interest in policing the upper bound and, when prices fall, importing governments lose interest in policing the lower bound. In other words, the attempt to create any oil price band in the current situation would not be credible.[60]

Of course, Fattouh and Allsopp are correct, unless you take the opposite approach to the price band mechanism: OPEC is responsible for protecting the bottom end of the band through cuts to individual quotas and its overall ceiling; major consuming countries are responsible for protecting the upper end of the band through coordinated releases of crude oil from their strategic reserves.

In addition, OPEC would continue to have the option to increase its quotas and production ceiling when prices are within and above the price band; and major consumers would have the option to add to their strategic reserves when prices are within and below the price band.

Our suggested price band mechanism has several more positive attributes. First, consumers would normally have the right type of crude oil (read: light sweet crude) in their strategic reserves to keep prices from rising above the top end of the band. In 2004 and 2005, OPEC flooded the market with heavy, sour crude oil in an attempt to keep oil prices from rising, but blew out quality differentials instead. Between the second quarter of 2004 and the fourth quarter of 2005, the OPEC-10 production ceiling was increased by 4.5 mbpd to 28 mbpd, but the price of WTI still increased by 57 percent to $60.01 per barrel, while the WTI–Maya differential almost doubled to $16.66 per barrel.[61]

Second, our price band mechanism is a potential revenue generator for major consuming countries, since they would be buying crude oil low and selling it high from their strategic reserves—unless, of course, the price band mechanism were to break down. This attribute should be especially attractive to financially-constrained countries such as Ireland, Spain, and the United States.

Third, if the American Congress is unable to pass a treaty to formally join a global energy agency, the United States could still be informally involved in the system since releases from its Strategic Petroleum Reserve (SPR) are made at the discretion of the President. In August 2008, while he was on the campaign trail, Obama supported a 70 million barrel release from the SPR to quell oil prices.[62]

Finally, the financial industry in the United States and elsewhere would probably expend less money and energy lobbying against a price band mechanism than oil market reform because the industry could still make money within the band and even test it, assuming they want to take a chance.

Would a formal price band mechanism administered by oil producers and consumers keep prices relatively stable and at reasonable levels? Generally speaking, it should be able to do so, but it would not be perfect, just as a fixed exchange rate regime is never perfect. Oil prices should normally stay within the band, but sharp and prolonged supply and demand shocks would still have the potential to push prices above or below the target range.

The potential Achilles' heel of our producer–consumer administered price band mechanism – or any producer–consumer mechanism for that matter – is how to maintain high levels of quota compliance among OPEC members. The mechanism would appear to open the door to free-riders within the organization, since the Saudis lose their big stick—the threat of another oil price war to discipline hardcore quota-busters. However, rampant cheating on OPEC quotas would force the ratcheting down of the price band over time, and the members most prone to cheating tend to be those requiring relatively high prices to balance their budgets. For example, the four worst quota-busters as of January 2010 were Angola, Iran, Nigeria and Venezuela.[63] Angola and Nigeria have the lowest per capita incomes among OPEC members, while Iran and Venezuela require relatively high revenue to support social spending to maintain the backing of their people.

Likelihood of a Price Band Mechanism

The likelihood of a producer–consumer administered price band mechanism being adopted is highly dependent on whether the world of the future is a 'realist' or a 'liberal' one.

Realists believe national interest drives state behavior within the anarchical international system. The primary interest of states is survival; when that is ensured, interest shifts to power and wealth. To ensure survival, and possibly freedom of action, states tend to form coalitions to balance the power of a threatening alliance or hegemon—including global and regional ones.

Russia's drift away from America and the West towards China and a number of other authoritarian states in recent years supports the realist school of thought. In February 2007, President Putin vehemently denounced American hegemony at the Munich Conference on Security Policy;[64] and in August 2007, he announced that the Russian Air force would resume long-range strategic bomber patrols following a 15-year hiatus.[65]

In 2001, China and Russia signed a strategic treaty (Treaty of Good-Neighborliness and Friendly Cooperation) and founded the Shanghai Cooperation Organization (SCO) along with four Central Asian countries, while the two countries resolved their outstanding border disputes in 2005. In September 2007, the *China Daily* reported President Putin telling his Chinese counterpart, President Hu Jintao: "We have achieved a peak in Russian–Chinese relations in recent times." The same article claimed, "[T]he momentum of the Sino-Russian strategic partnership … never looked better."[66]

Liberals, on the other hand, recognize the international system has been dominated by power politics in the past, but believe it is being tamed through the gradual spread of liberal economic and political thought (liberal democracy or democratic capitalism). According to liberals, the liberal democratic mentality promotes cooperation between states, rather than conflict. The high degree of economic and financial cooperation among the major powers to keep the global recession from becoming a global depression supports the liberal worldview.

The future response of the major powers to the economic and financial crisis may be the pivotal factor determining whether the international political system plays a realist or liberal tune in the coming years. If the major powers adopt aggressive and concerted policies to minimize the economic damage of the global financial crisis and rebalance spending from net-debtor to net-creditor countries, and the Western powers cede substantial power in international organizations to the rising powers, a liberal world is the more likely result.[67]

[237]

On the other hand, if economic nationalism again rears its head, China and Russia may decide it is time for the authoritarian capitalist bloc to challenge the dominance of the democratic capitalist bloc, just as the Axis powers (Germany, Italy and Japan) emerged from the depths of the Great Depression to challenge the world order of the 1930s.[68]

In the liberal 'Love Thy Neighbor' scenario economic and environmental cooperation among the major powers dominates. The major countries continue to cooperate and adopt the necessary financial, economic and structural policies to keep the current recession relatively short and ensure strong economic growth thereafter.[69]

The main reason China and Russia agree to play along with the democratic capitalist countries, despite their recent moves to form an authoritarian bloc, is the fact that President Dmitri Medvedev (and Prime Minister Putin) and President Hu do not want to make the same mistake that Germany and Japan made in the 1930s and challenge the democratic capitalist bloc before they have sufficient economic and technological power to do so.

In addition, President Hu recognizes a prolonged global recession caused by a breakdown in economic cooperation would seriously impede China's export-led growth in the coming years, hampering his country's economic, political and military rise. President Medvedev recognizes a prolonged global economic slowdown would cause severe downward pressure on commodity prices, including oil and gas, hampering Russia's resurgence.

The widespread cooperation required to save the global economy from a prolonged slump, including the redistribution of power within major international organizations, and rising economic prosperity serve to gradually mellow the Chinese dragon and the Russian bear.

In 'Beggar Thy Neighbor,' a realist scenario, geopolitical competition among the major powers dominates instead. A breakdown in major power cooperation prolongs the global recession and leads an authoritarian capitalistic bloc led by China and Russia to challenge the Western powers for dominance. The global recession is both longer and deeper, with a second dip in 2010, and sustainable growth is subsequently far slower than the recent past.[70]

The green shoots of economic revival in the second half of 2009 are trampled by rising trade friction between the Group of Two (G-2) – China and the United States. In the first half of 2010, the perception spreads among the US public and Congress that China is not stepping up to the economic plate to take over from the heavily indebted and credit squeezed American consumer. Chinese economic growth returns to pre-crisis levels by the end of 2009, while the American economy remains in the doldrums with unemployment around 10 percent. During this period, China fails to adopt significant structural policies to bolster consumer spending or allow the value of the renminbi to rise substantially.

The talk of a G-2 trade war and a new round of financial turmoil cause consumer and business confidence around the world to again crater, and the second dip of the global recession to begin.

China and Russia, leaders of the rising authoritarian capitalist bloc, decide it is no longer in their interest to cooperate with the democratic capitalist countries and time instead to start asserting their own political and economic model onto the international scene. China and Russia do not want to be fully co-opted into the Western structure of international standards and norms, but to replace the democratic capitalist-based system with their own set of standards and norms.

In 'Love Thy Neighbor,' the adoption of a producer–consumer administered price band mechanism is a solid possibility because cooperation among the G-20 plays a prominent role in this scenario, and this group includes the two superpowers (the United States and China) and two energy superpowers (Saudi Arabia and Russia). In contrast, the price band mechanism is a non-starter in 'Beggar Thy Neighbor,' because of rising geopolitical competition and a general lack of international cooperation.

The Politicization of Markets:
Implications for Conflict and Cooperation

Amy Myers Jaffe and *Ronald Soligo*

Politics and markets have always been intertwined. Governments are motivated to intervene in markets to protect national economic interests, to solve problems of public commons and redress externalities and in some cases, to redistribute wealth within society according to political imperatives. On the international stage, governments often interfere in global markets to achieve foreign policy objectives or to manipulate the terms of exchange with other countries either to advance their own ability to accumulate wealth or to guard against undue advantages being reaped by other nations. Sometimes, governments intervene in the market out of anxiety regarding the intentions of other countries.

Geopolitical interference in global markets has been especially pronounced in the case of oil, as it is a vital input to modern economic activity as well as the dominant fuel for warfare. Moreover, the oil and gas industry generates large economic returns. For many oil-producing countries, the costs of finding, developing and producing oil is significantly lower than current market prices, generating substantial windfalls or "economic rents." Competition for a share or control of those rents has generated geopolitical conflict since oil's inception as a major fuel.[1] Given these realities, oil markets often become politicized.

While few – if any – nations have gone to war solely for oil, the modern history of global trade has witnessed numerous disruptions to the flow of oil, often connected to conflicts unrelated to the resource, but occasionally as a function of a struggle to divide the "rents" from oil. Conflict has arisen both between neighboring countries over control of resources that span a geographical area as well as between oil producing countries and major oil consuming countries which depend on this resource to fuel economic prosperity. Low oil prices benefit consuming countries while high prices shift the terms of trade in favor of producers. Protecting access to oil to promote economic well-being is often described in consumer nations as 'energy security,' while protecting the value of oil and the control of resource rents by producing nations is often referred to 'resource nationalism.'

Oil has also been used as a 'weapon' by both producer and consumer countries. In the case of the West, unilateral and multilateral economic sanctions have been used to pressure oil producing countries to change their foreign policies. On the other hand, some oil producers or groups of oil producers have threatened supply cutoffs to influence the policies of oil consuming countries, as was the case in 1973 during the Arab-Israeli war.

Competition between oil producing and consuming countries to ensure that their individual national interests take precedence in managing the price of oil has led to wild swings in oil prices in the post-World War II period, culminating in the recent increase in oil prices to unprecedented levels in 2008. However, as this paper will discuss, these volatile prices have benefited neither producers nor consumers in the long run. Ultimately, despite periods of high oil prices and large capital flows to resource-rich countries, sustained per capita incomes in oil producing countries have not risen to the same extent as those in countries with less natural resources such as Japan, China and South Korea. By the same token, volatile oil prices have contributed to recessions and financial crises, damaging economic wellbeing in consuming countries as well, even if they temporarily benefited from the periods of lower oil prices that such volatility produced.

High prices generate vast shifts in the flow of funds. When prices move too much, too quickly, the rapidly rising capital inflows into countries with limited capacity to absorb them can lead to local asset bubbles and an inefficient use of that bounty—investments that can subsequently result in large losses. Volatile energy prices are also a concern for all countries because they increase uncertainty and are linked to economic recessions, slower growth and global financial instability.

As the dominant power of the post-WWII world, the United States has promoted a liberal world order where international treaties and organizations constrain the ability of countries to act opportunistically. Such a world reduces the power of states to supplant the market and use political means to alter the distribution of gains from trade and commerce. It also reduces uncertainty about the potential actions of others and channels conflict away from military confrontation.

Unfortunately, the globalization project has proceeded in an uneven fashion and is incomplete. The liberalization of trade and capital movements has proceeded without commensurate change in the institutions that regulate these flows. While the World Trade Organization (WTO) deals with trade barriers such as tariffs and subsidies, there are many other areas that affect competition such as policies regarding product, labor and environmental standards that have yet to be addressed. In the energy arena, the European Energy Charter was an attempt to provide a forum and basic law to deal with issues such as transit rights and protection for foreign investments, but that effort failed to inspire participation from Russia, a major energy producer that could have joined that effort. Other efforts such as the Extractive Industries Transparency Initiative (EITI), the IMF's Code of Good Practice on Fiscal Transparency and Chatham House's Document on Good Governance of the National Petroleum Sector are also helping to educate policy makers and setting admirable goals for the oil industry but have yet to take sufficient universal hold to make a significant difference in reducing conflict over rents or trade and investment rules and best practices.[2]

In the area of global monetary matters, the huge scale of global financial flows is straining the capacities of nationally-based central banks to provide prudential regulation. Recent meetings of the G-20 have seen attempts to address these problems but, so far, new institutions for regulation of derivatives and other complex financial instruments have yet to emerge, and little has been done to institutionally address the issue of volatility in global energy markets.

The emergence of a new multi-polar world will challenge this system further and could undermine support for the rules of the existing international order. In the United States and other developed countries, uncertainty about the aspirations and intentions of emerging economies and dissatisfaction with the distribution of costs and benefits from globalization threaten to undermine support for the system. For emerging economies, the distribution of power within existing institutions such as the IMF, World Bank and United Nations is being challenged and will need to be changed to maintain their support.

In this context, questions have arisen as to whether access to oil supplies or sharing of 'rents' could increasingly drive military conflicts over resources, even at a time when international conflict is diminishing. As Michael Ross notes, while the world has become more peaceful now than it was 15 years ago – with the number of major civil wars dropping dramatically – there has been no similar drop in the number of conflicts in countries that produce oil where the proportion of the world's internal conflicts have increased from one fifth in 1992 to over a third.[3]

As new countries become oil producers in the coming years such as Congo, Chad, Mauritania, Namibia, Cambodia, East Timor, and Vietnam, the prospects of managing a sudden influx of oil wealth looks dim, given the weak governance structures in many of these nations. Oil wealth often helps to support localized insurgencies by giving rebels the opportunity to steal and smuggle oil or to extort money from foreign oil companies operating in regions distant from the seat of central government. It can also invite separatism from localized groups who feel secession would leave them in control of the oil (and the related economic rents) under the ground where they live. Such conflicts have been seen in Bolivia, Indonesia (such as in Acheh), Iraq (in the Kurdish regions), Nigeria and Sudan.

In this paper, we examine several areas where politics interface with international energy markets. We discuss whether conflict over access to resources or over the division of oil rents could escalate to military action, whether the use of oil as a "weapon" in international economic discourse will continue to cause dislocations in the global economy, and what effect continued oil price volatility will have on the stability of the world economy. In a final conclusion, we consider some possible areas for cooperation and coordination between producing and consuming countries that might ameliorate some of the problems and issues discussed.

Militarization of Energy: Are Resource Wars Likely?

The concept that oil – or access to it – leads to war and conflict finds its roots in energy security literature. A major theme of the well-known history of oil, *The Prize*, is that control of oil comprises the spoils of modern warfare. Author Daniel Yergin notes in his forward to the book:

> ... Churchill, on the eve of World War I, had captured a fundamental truth (i.e. that mastery of oil was the "price of the venture") and one applicable not only to the conflagration that followed, but to the many decades ahead. For oil has meant mastery throughout the twentieth century. And that quest for mastery is what this book is about.[4]

Yergin argues that World War I and World War II established petroleum as an "element of national power" and that in the post-war period, the battle for control of oil between international companies and developing countries was "part of the great drama of decolonization" that eventually marked the demise of old "European imperial power."

The idea that mastery of oil still has strategic importance is echoed in the halls of the US Pentagon and among the People's Liberation Army (PLA) of China, and continues to be a vibrant part of the energy security literature. Daniel Moran and James A. Russell of the US Naval Post Graduate School in Monterey, California, note that:

> In a security environment that presents increasingly strong incentives to shift force-structure and doctrine toward irregular warfare, counter-terrorism, constabulary operations, and so on, the possibility of war to seize or defend energy resources provides a much-needed rationale for preserving the heavy conventional forces that still consume the lion's share of defense spending around the world. This is especially true of naval building programs, whose ostensible purpose is always presumed to include securing the sea-lines of communication that connect the producers and consumers of oil.[5]

There are two major lines of argument to the 'militarization of oil' literature. The most prominent is that oil is about to become a scarce commodity and, as such, will increasingly invite great powers into conflict for mastery of access to what few supplies are left. This scarcity could be generated by a natural peaking of existing finite geological resources or through geopolitical means as producers limit supplies to enhance their global power either individually or as a group. Indeed, much of the Western energy security literature focuses on the possibility that a major oil or gas producer would reduce output either to increase its leverage in influencing policies in consuming countries or simply to increase prices, as OPEC has in recent years.

The idea that ever dwindling oil supplies will lead to global conflict is articulately advocated by Michael Klare in his book *Resource Wars*, which theorizes that "diminishing supplies of vital materials" will raise the risk of conflict across the globe and "introduce new stresses into the international system."[6] Klare notes in his book: "No highly industrialized society can survive at present without substantial supplies of oil, and so any significant threat to the continued availability of this resource will prove a cause of crisis, and, in extreme cases, provoke the use of military force."[7]

Nader Elhefnawy takes the argument a step farther, asserting that since the US economy is the most oil dependent among world powers, "the United States could ultimately lose its position as a world power ... just as the UK's position declined along with the age of coal and steam that it pioneered."[8] Moran and Russell suggest that:

> ... militarization of energy security needs to be envisioned as occurring within a context of strategic anxiety and severe economic stress, in which economic productivity is far below what people are used to, and in which the perennial peacetime trade-offs between guns and butter had become correspondingly more contentious.[9]

They argue that such conditions have arisen before – in the 1930s – and that "developing states that are consumers of oil" have the "least leverage in market terms" that could make them "more willing to choose the military option in moments of desperation."[10]

The second line of argument is that in weak or ungovernable states, the presence of oil revenue exacerbates existing internal conflicts and fuels violence by networks of state and non-state actors. This position has been articulated by Mary Kaldor, Terry Lynn Karl and Yahia Said who try to define the mechanism for how oil scarcity might lead to conflict in the volume *Oil Wars*. They ask the question: "To what extent does oil cause, exacerbate or mitigate conflict, and what are the specific mechanisms through which this occurs?"[11] Kaldor and her co-editors contend that the nature of war has changed, and with it the nature of conflicts over oil. Referring to the two World Wars and the Cold War, the authors note: "In these wars, oil was considered a key strategic commodity and security of oil supplies could be achieved only through the direct military control of territory or the exercise of influence over the generally authoritarian rulers of exporting countries."[12] They suggest that new wars are "associated with weak and sometimes ungovernable states" where "the monopoly of organized violence is being eroded" and the "massive rents from petroleum are used in myriad ways to finance violence."

New wars are fought by networks of state and non-state actors and violence is directed against civilians or symbols of order rather than in battles between state-controlled armed forces over territory. The presumption is that these 'new wars' may have a debilitating impact on world oil supply, as sub-national groups compete for control of oil rents, disrupting oil production and transport facilities in the process. Examples of such violence spilling over to curtail oil production abound, from insurgents attacking Iraqi oil facilities in the early days of the US invasion of 2003, to political activists rioting in the Niger Delta and blocking oil production there in recent years.

In each of the cases of 'resource wars' described by various authors, the question of causation seems cloudy at best and in the many cases of violence cited, none actually involves an oil-thirsty industrial country attacking a weak oil producing country to solve a looming problem of resource scarcity. Vietnam and China did not go to war over a disputed border field in the South China Sea (a field, it might be added, that has yet to yield major oil and gas resources); and even Iraq's invasion of Kuwait was more complex in its roots. Iraq did not 'need' Kuwait's oil because supplies were scarce. The oil market was oversupplied at the time, and Iraq was angry with Kuwait for overproducing and thereby causing oil markets to weaken. But Baghdad was also concerned about its regional power and the fact that its Gulf Arab neighbors had refused to forgive its financial arrears from the eight-year Iraq–Iran war, arrears seen as 'loans' in the Gulf, but as a gift in exchange for protection by Iraq. It is unclear whether Saddam Hussein was interested in controlling Kuwait's oil or whether he had an equal or larger concern to teach Kuwait a lesson about who was more powerful.

As David Victor notes, "To be sure, resource money can magnify and prolong some conflicts, but the root causes of those hostilities usually lie elsewhere ... When conflicts do arise, the weak link isn't a dearth in resources but a dearth in governance."[13]

To analyze the kind of resource war that might threaten the global system in the future, it is important first to define the kinds of conflicts that are being used as examples of 'resource wars' and then to conceive which, if any, could threaten the global system, and what other alternative avenues countries would have to solve the same problems without recourse to war. Much of the literature on resource wars jumps from various examples of conflict regions in which oil happens to exist, ignoring differences in the driving forces to those conflicts and oil's role in them.

The competition for resources in the Caspian Basin is a much cited example of a hot spot that could lead to conflict over resources. In this case, 'resource war' theory would argue that large, powerful consuming countries like the United States and China would become increasingly concerned about access to oil supplies, vie for resources in the same geographical area and, through this competition, end up in military conflicts with each other.[14] This is the 'ultimate' resource war that would emerge from supply scarcity. But, so far, while such diplomatic and commercial jockeying in the Caspian and other regions has taken place between the United States and China – in some cases accompanied by military assistance or troop build-up by some party in a geographic oil-rich area – these events have yet to produce big power confrontation. China has not challenged the buildup of US troops in the Caspian region, which arguably has more to do with the 'war on terror' and failed states than any purposeful policy to control oil supply in the region. China's response to the increased US military presence has been diplomatic (through its sponsorship of the Shanghai Cooperation Organization [SCO] meetings) and economic (through Chinese investment in domestic energy infrastructure in the region). China has not responded to the US military presence by building up its own forces on the ground in or around the Caspian.

In Africa, in the aftermath of its increased involvement in Sudan's oil industry, China has built a quasi-military presence in Sudan, and Chinese assistance to the Sudanese government has made it difficult to resolve the violent conflict in Darfur. But again, the United States has not responded to these issues militarily; instead, it has sought a solution through diplomacy, seeking United Nations involvement to send peacekeeping troops to Darfur and pressing China through quiet diplomacy to cooperate.

Thus, while it is impossible to rule out that if supplies of oil tighten over time, competition for oil among large, powerful consuming countries might intensify and lead to conflict, in the immediate term, there is no geopolitical behavior on the horizon that signals a start to this pattern of international conflict. Moreover, for larger industrializing countries which are net energy importers (e.g., India and China), an aggressive resource strategy would be less likely because of their integration into the world trading system. The potential of trade sanctions serves as an effective deterrent as these countries need access to Western markets for their exports of services and manufactured goods.

Another category of resource war that is predicted to emerge owing to the impending scarcity of supply is an act of war by a large consuming country against a smaller, weaker, oil-rich country to take over its resources. The US invasion of Iraq is frequently referred to as an example of this kind of 'resource war.' In fact, the US invasion had a larger and more complex set of motivations. The United States has neither in practice nor intention 'taken over control' of Iraq's oil. If anything, the Bush administration bent over backwards to say that the Iraqi government was in charge of all administration related to oil, and the constitution drafted by Iraqi politicians and backed by the United States specifically states that oil is the property of the Iraqi people for the benefit of the whole country. The only invasions of oil-rich areas by another country in recent history have involved countries that had their own oil, again driven by more complex issues not related to grabbing resource supplies *per se*, such as the Iraq–Iran War and the Iraq–Kuwait conflict. Furthermore, Russian actions in Chechnya and Dagestan are cases where a nation used military force against an oil-rich region within the country itself.

While historical examples of a country invading another to gain access to its oil do exist from World War I and World War II, it is unclear whether international relations would return to a situation where such extreme events were likely to occur. Instead, we have argued that the concept of resource war is outdated in contemporary times where there is a world order that promotes open and free markets.[15] Today, competition for resources takes place within the context of a marketplace where oil and gas flow to the buyer who is willing to offer the best terms. Even if countries compete to secure access to a particular resource in a particular country through investment, it is unlikely under the current global economic regime that they will have access on a basis that is very different from that offered to other firms from other countries. The reality is that short of the breakdown of the international order, there is no reason to fight for access to resources.

The lessons of the 1970s oil crises were not that desperate oil-consuming nations will go to war over resources. While the costs of those oil shocks were huge – estimated at $1.2 trillion in lost economic growth for the seven largest industrial countries[16] – the experience of the 1970s was that "markets can and do adjust without recourse to state violence."[17] Instead of resorting to warfare, industrialized oil-importing countries undertook various domestic, bilateral and multilateral efforts, including oil sharing and stockpiling agreements as well as energy efficiency and diversification strategies. Today, presumably, the same responses would be easier to accomplish, given the existence of transparent, global oil futures exchanges that broaden the opportunities to adjust to sudden changes in prices. Furthermore, many consuming countries already have robust programs to shift to a wider range of emerging technologies in alternative fuel and energy efficiency.[18]

In a recent book, Clifford Singer takes a historical perspective on conflicts over resources, and points out the large number of different resources that have provoked wars in the past, suggesting that one day we will view oil as just another commodity.[19] He questions the typical assumption that oil is a critical input in modern economies and provokingly asks: "Oil, is it a strategic commodity? Or is it just one of many useful materials whose prices fluctuate?"[20] He goes on to assert that "… oil is not in fact a strategic commodity for industrialized countries in this century, either from a military or economic perspective," pointing out that oil use by the military accounts for 1.8 percent of US consumption while fossil fuels account for less than 3 percent of US national defense expenditures.[21] War over oil is unlikely because:

> … countries and alliances that have the industrial capacity to launch foreign military interventions, notably NATO, also have the greatest potential for fielding the alternative energy production and efficiency measures that will be adopted during the shift away from oil as a dominant industrial energy source.[22]

Although he does not mention it, Germany during the Second World War and South Africa when it was under international sanctions both demonstrated that it was possible to operate successful economies without unlimited access to oil by developing a coal-to-liquids industry.

Finally, Singer argues that energy use will shift in the future to gas and nuclear, fuels which are less likely to lead to conflict or war because gas supplies are more widely distributed and nuclear production will be produced domestically—albeit in some cases with imported fuel.

Also, it is worth noting that warfare has become increasing destructive in the modern age, where countries have the capacity to wipe out enemies' capital stock and human population at relatively low cost. So, war has become less appealing as a solution to conflict. The experience of the Second World War was a sobering one for the nations in Europe as well as the Soviet Union, which had huge cities destroyed along with the industrial and commercial capacity of the nation. Human deaths were staggering. With so many other alternative routes available to confront a shortage of oil – especially in terms of 'peak oil,' which would unfold over a long period of time and therefore could be planned for – wars over access are very unlikely. The United States' experience in adjusting to the 1970s price increases is instructive. Less than 15 percent of Americans heat their homes with oil today, versus over 30 percent in the 1970s, and oil has been virtually removed as a fuel for electricity production in the United States in favor of other sources such as coal, natural gas, hydroelectric, nuclear, wind, biomass and solar energy. This diversity of fuels lends itself to both a resilient system and 'supplier temperance,' and opens the door to introduce electricity as a means to power automobiles without recourse to oil-based fuel.[23]

Monopoly Power and Profits

Another form of resource war is a situation where a major oil supplier either alone or in concert with other suppliers tries to influence policies in consuming countries by withholding, or threatening to withhold oil supplies. The possibility that such a strategy might succeed increases in tight oil markets where there is little excess capacity and where several producers with a significant share of world oil output participate in the effort. Such an event would be a challenge for the international system and could lead to overt conflict and war.

However, it is instructive to note that when OPEC cut off oil supplies in 1973, consuming countries did not respond with military force. Although, to be sure, the OPEC embargo occurred during the Cold War and when the United States was bogged down in Vietnam—factors that may have constrained a more forceful response. Times have changed and the reaction of consuming countries to an embargo today might be different; but again, consumer countries have other means to respond either diplomatically through trade sanctions, the coordinated sharing of alternative fuel supplies or through domestic rationing and other programs to limit oil use at home. In short, consumers might opt for less burdensome pathways than invading oil fields in foreign lands.

The threat of an oil or energy weapon has emerged in international discourse in recent years, though no prolonged cutoff has ensued as of yet. Two oil producers, Venezuela and Iran, have specifically made public statements threatening to cut off oil supplies as a matter of state policy as a defensive and retaliatory response to political or commercial conflicts. In the case of Venezuela, President Hugo Chavez in February 2008 threatened to cut off oil exports to the United States if ExxonMobil pursued its legal battle to attach Venezuelan assets in the West as collateral payment for the upstream oil field stake nationalized in Venezuela by Caracas last year.[24] Similarly, Iran said it would cut its oil exports to the West if a US-led coalition imposed sanctions on it in response to its alleged plans to develop nuclear weapons.

Threats to cut off oil supplies to a particular market such as to the West or the United States are meaningless in a world of global oil markets. The threat makes sense only if the producing country shuts off all exports. But that would inflict severe damage on the producer in terms of lost export revenues while spreading the pain in the form of higher oil prices over all consumer countries. However, Iranian Supreme Leader Ayatollah Ali Khamenei in June 2006 warned the United States that Washington "should know that the slightest misbehavior on your part would endanger the entire region's energy security ... You are not capable of guaranteeing energy security in the region."[25] Saudi Arabia responded to this rhetoric by increasing its investments in upstream oil production capability to be able to replace any lost Iranian exports.[26] More importantly, if the threat was to stop all oil from transiting the Arabian Gulf, an action that would cut off supplies from other producers in the region as well, the United States and its allies would undoubtedly intervene militarily as it did during the Iraq–Iran war in the 1980s when Iran attempted to prevent exports from Iraq.

It has been the specter of Russia wielding an energy weapon, however, that has prompted a re-evaluation of energy strategies in Europe. While Russia has not actually threatened such a scenario, its policies towards neighboring states who had previously received subsidized energy supplies has opened debate about Russia's foreign policy goals and whether it might use an energy supply lever to achieve political ends and enhance its regional or global power.

Prior to the breakup of the Soviet Union, energy trade was used by Moscow to achieve political acquiescence in the Warsaw Pact. "The Soviet energy grid is a tangible manifestation of Soviet energy diplomacy, which found its roots in the Brezhnev doctrine of restricted sovereignty," writes Dr. Kevin Rosner.[27] Eastern and Central European states were highly dependent on subsidized Soviet energy supplies under the central control of Moscow, linking their economies in a manner difficult to alter. After the collapse of the Soviet Union, economic reform in Eastern and Central Europe opened the way for more competition in the energy sphere. But while privatizations and other reforms were characteristic of the Russian oil sector in the 1990s, President Vladimir Putin, in his second term, initiated a retrenchment towards greater state control and centralization of investment and export policy in Russia's energy sector.

Coincident with what some would regard as strong-armed methods used against Russian and foreign businesses, Russia initiated several cut-offs of gas exports to neighboring countries (Georgia, Ukraine and Belarus) in disputes that were ostensibly over pricing, but which have been viewed in the West as efforts to reassert Russian influence in these parts of the former Soviet Union and a reaction to the eastward push of NATO and the so-called 'colored' revolutions in Georgia and Ukraine. The policy of reducing natural gas deliveries had the unfortunate side effect of reducing natural gas deliveries to Western Europe and raised the issue of energy supply security for parts of Europe.

Concern over the share of Russian gas in the European market has prompted some countries to propose different gas pipelines that would bypass Russian territory. The first such pipeline – the BTC line from Baku to Ceyhan in Turkey – was completed in 2005 and actually predates much of the more recent concerns but was designed to provide an alternative to

Russia as a means of exporting Azeri oil and gas resources. At the time the project was justified more in terms of capacity limitations on the Bosporus as an export route but it was clearly an attempt to break the monopoly held by Transneft, the Russian state-owned pipeline company, on transmission of all oil produced in the former Soviet states. After the oil pipeline was built a gas line was added. There have been discussions of linking both pipelines to Kazakhstan by means of trans-Caspian pipelines but so far these proposals have not advanced.

Europe can reduce potential Russian leverage by diversifying its gas supplies. As the authors have pointed out,[28] there are many sources of natural gas that are now economically available—given the technological changes in the liquefied natural gas (LNG) industry that have significantly lowered transport costs. More recently some Europeans are pushing the Nabucco gas pipeline that links Europe to Central Asian resources by way of Turkey; Russia has countered with its South Stream proposal that would serve to preserve its dominance over deliveries of Central Asian gas to Europe.

In an effort to provide for a multilateral framework for resolving disputes over energy and to promote energy security, European countries proposed an Energy Charter shortly after the collapse of the Soviet Union. The Charter's aim was to secure transit rules for Russian and Central Asian gas and to promote western investment in Russian resources by ensuring that Russia would grant them non-discriminatory treatment. At a time of low energy prices and a faltering economy the prospect of large foreign investments in the energy sector was attractive for Russia.

The Energy Charter eventually evolved into the Energy Charter Treaty, which became effective in April 1998. It has so far garnered some 51 signatories, although Russia announced in June 2009 that it would not sign. There is a great deal of speculation about Russia's motives but two factors seem plausible. First, there may be a concern that the treaty might require that Russia open its pipeline system to Central Asian producers without having those countries market their natural gas through Gazprom.

[256]

Second, former Yukos shareholders are suing the Russian government for damages arising from the forced liquidation of Yukos. Their case rests on a provision of the Energy Charter that protects foreign investors by prohibiting discrimination and arbitrary legal procedures. Russia claims that although it signed the original charter it did not ratify it and hence is not bound by its provisions. More recently, Russia has proposed an alternative treaty that eliminates the offending provision.

The Russian case opens the possibility of non-military conflict between a major energy supplier and consuming nations with non-economic goals in mind; but it remains unclear how successful Russia will be in the long-run using oil and natural gas as a political lever. In the case of countries where an imbalance of power already exists (with small neighboring countries in Eastern Europe or the Caucasus), Russia's politicization of energy may be secondary to the threat of Russia's military power in light of its 2008 invasion of Georgia. For other stronger or more distant countries in Europe, Russia's politicization of energy could cost Moscow precious market share to other competing suppliers or alternative fuels.[29]

To date, the Russian example of politicization of energy supply by a producing country has been relatively limited. Elsewhere, the goal of OPEC and its members is to capture a larger share of the rents from their oil, rather than seeking other foreign policy-related objectives. In this endeavor, the producer group has had mixed success over the years, but it has clearly held prices higher than they would have been without its existence. OPEC has seen its market power grow in recent years as its share in total world supply has increased. That power may grow in the future if, as some predict, world oil production becomes ever more concentrated within OPEC.

However, as in the case with Russia, OPEC's market power is constrained by the fact that high prices can create the unintended consequence of reducing the world's dependence on its resources in the longer run. At very high prices, demand for oil will grow more slowly and even decline as high prices reduce economic growth in some countries, induce further non-OPEC production, spur efficiency improvements and speed up the development of new, alternate fuels. Over time these trends will have a negative effect on oil prices and output and hence on the wellbeing of oil producers themselves. From the consuming countries' perspective, keeping prices stable at levels that are high by historical standards serves recently popular objectives of promoting energy efficiency and developing new technologies as well as rendering environmental policy related to climate change easier to adopt.

But higher prices do not necessarily mean increased rents for producers. The distribution of rents is a distinct issue from the level of prices. European countries, Japan and South Korea have been quite successful in sharing in these rents by imposing steep taxes on automobile fuels. So far, the United States and China have not been willing to follow suit but that might change over time as global climate policy and other national security considerations enter the mix. The United States has preferred the use of mileage standards as an alternative to higher prices. These can be quite effective. For example, the new corporate average fuel efficiency standard of 35 mpg will reduce US demand for oil by 2.3 million barrels per day (mbpd) by 2020.[30] But using taxes rather than mandates is a better solution, as taxes allow manufacturers and consumers to find the lowest cost means for achieving conservation and environmental goals. The US Congress is considering legislation to 'price' carbon emissions which effectively would serve as a tax on oil, which is high in carbon content.

While the level of energy taxes in oil-importing countries is a contentious one, exporting countries must realize that support for higher prices in consuming countries cannot be sustained unless those rents are shared.

With its very high rate of growth and rapidly expanding vehicle fleets, China is becoming increasingly dependent on imported oil. A large proportion of that oil will come from the Middle East—subject to the chokepoints of Hormuz and Malacca, not to mention increasing piracy. China has sought to diversify its supply sources by supporting or proposing oil and gas pipelines from Central Asia, potentially competing with Russia, which had until recently virtually stranded those supplies for its own use by blocking the development of new pipeline routes from the region.

It has been suggested by Klare[31] and others[32] that China's increasing need for oil might bring it into conflict with other oil consuming nations. But China is less likely to pursue an aggressive resource strategy because of its integration into the world trading system. The potential of trade sanctions serves as an effective deterrent for any country that relies on access to Western markets for their exports. Furthermore, as Moran and Russell note, "A state that chose a militarized energy strategy would of course need to consider that other states might gang up against it, and that it might risk being excluded from other markets in which it might have preferred to continue to participate."[33] Like the United States and Europe, China is already implementing new policies to restrain growth in oil demand, including implementing mileage standards for automobiles, developing renewable and alternative energies and mandating that state-run industries lower the energy intensity of their operations. As China's economy continues to face negative impacts from volatile oil pricing, the country is likely to pursue additional domestic policies in line with other industrialized nations.

Energy Prices and Financial Flows

Another aspect of the politicization of markets lies in the sphere of macroeconomics and financial markets. Hamilton[34] has observed a relationship between oil prices and GDP, arguing that spikes in prices cause recessions. Six of the last eight recessions in the United States (including the current one) have been preceded by oil price spikes. Both of the major run-ups in prices – in the 1970s and recently – have been followed by painful recessions across most of the world.

[259]

To the extent that oil prices are a factor in economic crises, they interact with the global economy in two ways. The first is that discussed by Hamilton—a direct link from a price shock to real GDP. The second mechanism is through the financial system, where large increases in petrodollar flows have fueled asset bubbles and financed investments that turn out to be uneconomic.

The direct link between oil prices and GDP is counterintuitive. Oil accounts for less than 2 percent of GDP and two thirds is used in the transportation sector, only a part of which is linked to the production of other goods and services. However, the literature has enumerated a number of channels by which this direct effect is transmitted.[35] For example, an immediate demand side channel is through the balance of payments; a large increase in the price of imported oil will result in an increase in the current account deficit in the balance of payments, creating an effect similar to that of a large tax increase, i.e., it will lower disposable income and reduce aggregate demand. This reduction could be offset if oil-exporting countries, which are accumulating current account surpluses, increased their imports from those countries experiencing the deficits. But this does not always happen. In particular, increases in imports from the United States by oil-exporting countries tend not to increase proportionately with revenues earned from oil exports to the United States.

Other channels linking oil prices with the real economy relate to the complementarities of capital and energy and the costs of reallocating capital between sectors in response to changes in relative prices. Large changes in energy prices – by altering the relative prices of energy, capital and labor – can render past investments obsolete and cause firms to reduce or cease output. If the price changes are temporary, output will be restored when prices return to normal levels. But if the price changes are permanent, the decline in output will persist until the economy has had time to adjust and investors have been able to reallocate capital in accordance to the new set of relative prices.

Finally, increases in the volatility of energy prices can impact GDP by their effect on investment. Dealing with price volatility entails a cost, and investors will demand a higher rate of return on their investments if volatility increases. Uncertainty about future levels of oil prices and volatility can delay investment and prolong recessions.

The idea that oil price shocks 'cause' recessions has been challenged. For example Barsky and Kilian argue that the causality may run in the opposite direction: macroeconomic events that increase the demand for oil can generate rises in oil prices.[36] By generating counterfactual production levels for producing countries affected by a event that leads to a supply disruption, Kilian finds that "the effects of exogenous oil supply shocks on US real GDP growth and CPI inflation were comparatively small on average..." He also finds that these exogenous events explain relatively few of the oil price increases, suggesting that the source of price increases lies in shifts in oil demand or changes in expectations about future oil supplies.[37]

While the issue remains unsettled, the importance of energy prices, and oil prices in particular, is declining in the developed countries as the energy intensity of their economies declines. Also, oil use in these countries has shifted more and more towards the transport sector, a large part of which is for personal transport, which has relatively few feedback or linkage effects.

The second mechanism by which oil prices can impact the economy is through the financial system. In a recent book Mahmoud El Gamal and Amy Myers Jaffe argued that oil prices and GDP are inexorably linked in a cycle that produces sequential asset bubbles and economic recessions.[38] Their model overlays an oil investment cycle onto a general cycle of swings between prudential government regulation and conservative financial management on the one hand, and over-optimism and regulatory laxity on the other that characterizes capitalist economies. This cycle of over-optimism and restraint has been observed by many but was popularized by Hyman Minsky[39] who argued that after a bubble investors are cautious and new regulations are introduced to prevent the excess that characterized the preceding euphoria and collapse. However, over time, without renewed crises, investors take on increasing risk and clamor for regulatory reform that weakens the constraints on their behavior. Initial success in higher risk investment strategies leads to even more risk taking, often through a process of financial innovation, creating new types of financial instruments that combine higher leverage with opaqueness. Higher profits generate still more optimism as individuals bid up the prices of assets on the assumption that they will be able to sell them at still higher prices. Ultimately, the process is unsustainable and the bubble is pricked. Asset prices crash, bringing down the whole economy with them.

The logic of the El Gamal–Jaffe model is that there is a similar cycle in oil markets which interacts with the Minsky cycle, amplifying both the booms and the crashes. Investment in oil production capacity stagnates when oil prices are low for a variety of reasons. In many producing countries, governments have made commitments to provide a level of public services – including fuel subsidies – that are difficult to reduce, leaving few resources available to finance investment. For private companies, the commitment is to shareholders (to maintain dividend payouts). Since many of these firms finance investments from retained earnings, resources available for investment decline with lower oil prices. Those firms that rely on sales of shares to finance new investment will similarly have difficulty raising significant amounts because share prices will reflect oil prices. When oil prices are low, investments in additional capacity seem uneconomic.

During the upswing part of the Minsky cycle, incomes are rising and the consumption of oil increases, gradually absorbing any excess production capacity that accumulated in the past. With little or no new investment, excess capacity continues to shrink with the result that further increases in demand drive oil prices upward. Although investment in additional capacity now becomes attractive, there is a lag between the time investments are planned and installed, and when additional production occurs. In the meantime, demand and oil prices continue to climb, generating an enormous inflow of capital to oil-exporting countries. Unless this inflow is sterilized, money supply in those countries increases, interest rates fall and an economic boom and an asset bubble ensue. Given the limited absorptive capacity of these countries, oil profits are also cycled to other countries, lowering interest rates, stimulating spending and inflating asset prices in those countries as well.

The devastating outcomes occur with the confluence of these two cycles. The sudden end to the asset bubble produces a serious recession – often world-wide – which in turn reduces demand for oil and hence, oil prices. Investment in additional oil production capacity occurs during the period of high oil prices but late in the cycle—only to exacerbate the downward pressure on oil prices; this completes the cycle.

El Gamal and Jaffe point out that the collapse of financial markets and the subsequent recessions hurt both oil producers and consumers, suggesting that it is in the interest of both sets of countries to find solutions to price volatility and dollar recycling.

The idea that oil price spikes are the *cause* of the subsequent economic setbacks is not without controversy. In both the 1970s and in recent years, the United States was at war and following loose monetary and fiscal policies. Indeed it was these policies that in part stoked the increase in demand for primary commodities, including oil, which began the process of price increases. This point of view focuses on the failure of the US Federal Reserve to pursue correct monetary policies as the source of the crises—with oil price rises partially a consequence of those failed policies. William McChesney Martin, who was Chairman of the Federal Reserve from 1951 to 1970, once joked that an important function of financial regulation is "to take away the punch bowl just as the party gets going." Critics would argue that the Fed allowed the "party" to go on for far too long and that it finally led to excess.

[263]

The Way Forward

As we have discussed throughout this paper, the politicization of oil has tended to be detrimental to both oil consuming and oil producing countries alike. We have discussed the roots of militarization over oil resources and shown how consuming countries have found better, more market-related solutions to scarcity or supply cutoffs. In more localized resource-war settings, we have discussed how conflicts over oil rents can cause supply disruptions that do not benefit – and most often harm – the well being of local populations. We have similarly pointed out that oil exporters do not benefit in the long run from high prices that result in significant long-term losses in market share and from sharp, rapid price increases that contribute to global financial imbalances which can lead to recessions and financial market crises.

The peaceful way to deal with conflict and macroeconomic crises is through dialogue and negotiation. International institutions play the role of providing a forum for this dialogue and over time a set of rules emerges that eventually becomes recognized as 'international law.' The institutions set up after WWII – the United Nations (UN), International Monetary Fund (IMF) and World Bank – were designed to deal with the issues that produced the great depression as well as the Second World War (naturally looking backward to prevent a reoccurrence of those catastrophes). But the world has changed in the sixty-five years since the war and member nations have not adequately addressed the need for reform of existing institutions or for the creation of new bodies to deal with new problems.

In the wake of the oil crisis in the 1970s, consuming countries did create the International Energy Agency (IEA), partially as a counterweight to OPEC but also to coordinate the collection and dissemination of data on energy demand and supply and to mandate that oil inventories be accumulated in the event of another oil embargo. The IEA has rules to govern how these inventories will be allocated in the event of a supply interruption. But energy markets have changed since the 1970s. Supply interruptions aimed at one or a few countries would not be effective in a world of globally traded oil where producers cannot dictate where oil will eventually end up. Furthermore, gas use and production has increased, displacing many of the former uses of oil. As noted above, the problems today faced by consuming countries are price volatility and dealing with the absorption of vast petrodollar flows—issues that are beyond the original scope of the IEA.

Creation of Multilateral Organizations to Deal with Energy Issues

One approach to dealing with the problems of price instability in energy markets is better coordination between energy exporters and importers. The Energy Charter Treaty is one model that might be useful, although treaties do not permit the flexibility of decision-making that is necessary in the uncertain world of energy markets. The G-20 is another model, and has recently been used to address a broader range of issues intersecting the interests of oil consumer and producer countries. But the G-20 is an informal structure designed more as a means to exchange views and to make commitments only on an *ad hoc* basis. A specialized multilateral organization which focuses on both the trade and monetary issues arising from the energy trade is an idea that seems to be worth looking at. It would have the advantage of providing some rules that structure the obligations and response of countries to various contingencies that affect energy markets and the financial flows that arise from them, and would also provide a context for discussions of ongoing concerns by member countries. Such organizations with broad powers are difficult to set up, since countries will be concerned about infringements to their sovereignty. For example, to the extent that US monetary policies have aggravated the effects of oil price spikes and contributed to asset bubbles, there may be little that oil producers can do to modify those policies. However, they can exercise some leverage by threatening to abandon the pricing of oil in dollars and reducing their purchases and holdings of Treasury Bills. Producing countries can also undertake some initiatives directly that would ameliorate and hopefully dampen the amplitude of price swings. In particular, oil producers could engage in counter-cyclical rather than pro-cyclical investments in oil production capacity.

Commodity Buffers

Another approach to dealing with price volatility is to create a buffer stock program. There was serious discussion in the United States and elsewhere about the possibility of using such programs to reduce price volatility after the commodity booms of the 1970s. The idea has surfaced again in response to the current run up in oil prices.

However, the history of buffer stock programs has not been encouraging. Managing the price of a commodity, knowing when to intervene and by how much is a difficult task. Many buffer stock programs failed because they did not focus solely on price fluctuations and instead tried to fix a price, usually a price floor, with the result of an accumulation of excess inventories. But even focusing on volatility is difficult because it is not always possible to distinguish between short-term price fluctuations and longer term changes in market fundamentals. Nonetheless, while a tightly monitored program dealing with very short-term fluctuations may be impractical, a program to respond to exceptionally large swings in prices, especially increases, could, at a minimum, serve to dampen the severity and rapidity of price changes, giving more time for economies to adjust and, therefore, reducing the costs of adjustment.

For example, the United States and other consuming countries could have tempered the speculative excess in oil markets that drove prices to almost $150 per barrel in 2008 by releasing strategic reserves. As Ed Morse[40] has argued, the announcement by US administration officials that the government would not use the strategic petroleum reserve (SPR) to constrain price movements essentially reduced the lower end of the distribution of (negative) returns to oil traders, increasing the expected payoff of betting on price increases and lowering the probability that they would incur losses. While the SPR was not set up to be used as a price buffer, US policy was driven by a mixture of *laissez faire* ideology and pressure from financial markets and oil companies. Clearly the United States and other IEA countries need to re-think the purpose of their stockpiles and modify their policies to accommodate the changes that have occurred in energy markets.

While a price stabilization program requires an inventory of oil, the buffer stock could also take the form of excess production capacity such as that maintained by Saudi Aramco in the past. Saudi Arabia has borne the cost of maintaining excess capacity in the past but investing and maintaining excess capacity is costly. While it makes more sense to have excess capacity in the Gulf region – where investment and production costs are relatively low compared to more mature regions or in the newer offshore deposits where investment costs are very high – that choice should be independent of the question of who should bear the cost of the excess capacity. While IEA countries are shouldering the cost of maintaining oil stockpiles, they as well as the rest of the world have been free-riding on Aramco's willingness to maintain excess capacity. Aramco's decision not to invest in additional capacity in the late 1990s and early 2000s eliminated its ability to tame the steep price increases of recent years. While Aramco has recently added capacity, a case can be made that all countries should contribute to the cost of maintaining that excess capacity and, in return, have some role in how it is managed.[41]

Money Flows

High oil prices in both the 1970s and in recent years have generated huge inflows of capital into countries with limited absorptive capacity. In a well-functioning global financial system these flows would not be a problem. There is a long history of countries with current account surpluses exporting capital to countries with good investment opportunities. Countries with high savings rates but relatively low rates of return on investments have financed investments in countries where investment returns are higher and where savings rates are not sufficient to finance all available opportunities. This process occurs in very much the same way that high savings regions within a country finance investments in areas where savings rates are insufficient to satisfy the demands for capital.

In the 1970s, petrodollars were cycled through banks in the United States and Europe, much of it going to Latin American countries. The result was a disaster for both the Latin American borrowers and the oil-exporting countries which also lost a great deal of their capital. The principle behind the recycling and lending was correct. Oil exporters had a lot of cash that they could not invest at home while Latin America had many worthy investment targets with limited investment resources to finance them. To be sure, in the exuberance brought on by plentiful, cheap money, some investments were not sound. The genesis of the subsequent crisis was the fact that Latin American governments, who did most of the borrowing, agreed to loans with a floating interest rate, based on the London Inter-bank Offered Rate (LIBOR). The proximate cause of the subsequent crash was US monetary policy which engineered a rapid escalation of interest rates to stamp out domestic inflation. High interest rates generated a recession in the United States and elsewhere, and that recession combined with escalating interest costs meant that Latin American countries defaulted on foreign debts, plunging the region into what has been called the 'lost decade,' in which per capita income fell almost 10 percent between 1980 and 1983 and did not return to the 1980 level until the early 1990s.

The problem in the 1970s, as well as in current crises, is that the influx of cash into oil exporting countries is too rapid to be invested in a prudent manner. Banks acted as if countries could never fail and lent billions to Latin American governments with little apparent due diligence. Similarly, the present episode of high oil prices resulted in a channeling of oil surpluses into mortgage-backed securities in the United States and other countries; but again, the inflow was too large and too fast. The housing bubble began independently of the oil price rise (due to Federal Reserve policy to maintain low interest rates) but the inflow of foreign capital added additional fuel to what was already and overheated real estate market. Again, the resultant crash has generated a great deal of pain for all parties—lenders as well as borrowers.

Reducing the volatility of oil prices will reduce the swings in export earnings and dampen the surges in petrodollars that cannot be invested prudently in the short run. The Gulf states need to develop more diversified economies, not only to provide employment to their burgeoning labor force but also to provide more productive investment opportunities for their oil revenues. In addition, the current crisis points out the need – in a globalized capital market with few impediments to capital flows – for better coordination of policies dealing with international capital flows, interest rates and foreign exchange rates.

Conclusions

We have argued that while consuming countries may compete for access to resources and producers and consumers will struggle over the distribution of oil rents, these conflicts can be handled within the context of the current global economic system. The costs to a country from defecting from the implicit as well as explicit contracts on which the system is built are high in terms of sanctions or war. Countries that are willing to pay the prevailing price for oil are able to get what they want and despite some turbulent history, 'negotiations' between producers and consumers over price and the distribution of oil rents have not resulted in open conflict. Countries have, and will probably continue to use oil as a means for pressuring others to alter policies that they do not like; but again, actions are constrained by the existence of a global market for oil and substitutes for oil.

We have highlighted oil price volatility and the problems that stem from it as areas where we think there is need for reform. Reducing oil price volatility benefits both producers and consumers. In our opinion, creating a framework for consultations between exporters and importers of oil and gas to deal with price volatility and financial flows is the minimum that is required. This can be done within the context of existing institutions (G-20, IEA, Energy Charter) or in a new, more specialized institution that would develop rules and procedures to prevent energy related crises in the future or to deal effectively with them when they occur. Creating a new institution is obviously a major project and would require a great deal more study than is within the scope of this paper.

There is a need for a mechanism to coordinate the use of strategic inventories held by consuming countries and excess capacity held primarily by some producers to deal with unusual price spikes. Since all countries benefit from price stability, all should participate in the cost of maintaining these buffers. The exception should be countries with very low per capita income. Oil producing countries need to be encouraged to counter-cyclically invest in oil fields so that spare capacity is always available.

Agreement to reduce volatility will not end competition for shares in oil rents. That competition will continue but can do so within the context of a more stable price environment. Competition from other energy sources (fuel types as well as geographical supplies of oil) and new, more energy efficient technologies will constrain competition for rents.

There is a need for both lending and borrowing countries to coordinate policies dealing with petrodollar flows. Reducing price volatility will go a long way toward reducing these problems by slowing the rate of change in petrodollar flows. To the extent that flows do increase rapidly, oil exporters need to resist the temptation to increase domestic spending or lending in a pro-cyclical fashion. Sovereign wealth funds need to be managed more prudently. Oil consuming countries need to monitor investment flows and institute counter-cyclical monetary policies and financial market regulations to limit speculative excesses.

Over the longer run all countries should work to slow the growth in the demand for oil – by encouraging efficiency and new automobile technologies – so as to keep the share of oil coming from the Middle East at 'reasonable levels.' The United States should impose a tax on oil (and other fossil fuels) both to capture some of the rents that now accrue to producers and to deal with GHG emissions. Finally, oil producers should eliminate fuel subsidies to lower their own oil demand growth.

ENERGY SECURITY AND SUSTAINABILITY

10

A Sustainable Energy Mix: Options and Consequences for the Gulf

Leila Benali

Every change in energy use has been intimately linked to a corresponding change in living standards. That has been the case for thousands of years. In the 21st century, a major evolution is deeply affecting emerging economies. This evolution is similar in significance to the utilization of steam power, the spread of the internal combustion engine, and the large scale electricity-generation achieved over the past two centuries. Living standards and energy use have changed significantly in the Gulf region; as we evaluate the sustainability of the present energy mix, however, profound questions about energy use will be an unavoidable consequence.

Sustainability is a broad and complex concept, as it encompasses economic, social and environmental aspects. However, as the Gulf region faces new challenges and opportunities, there is an urgent need for an assessment of the region's energy mix options and the implications of these options.

The first section of this paper will examine challenges and opportunities for the Gulf relating to the future energy mix in the region. It will then focus on the electricity fuel mix, as this is the only sector which presents major prospects for fuel switching, considering the foreseeable state of technologies. Oil and gas should continue to play a leading role, but the region is also introducing alternatives for various reasons. Even if their share of the energy mix is limited, the development of green initiatives – including renewables – and nuclear power is dependant on strategic considerations which could have important implications. The central issue of fuel pricing is also analyzed, as is fuel competition for power generation with unchanged fuel prices, and the implications of evolving fuel prices.

Finally, the sustainability of the energy mix will be assessed against the sustainability of the economic development path of the GCC countries. Most Middle East and North Africa (MENA) countries failed to make genuine investments in the 1970s and 1980s during periods of high oil revenue. Today, however, this seems to be changing. The guiding hypothesis is that natural resources depletion should be offset by manufactured and human capital increases. Emerging conclusions show that, under specific conditions, major hydrocarbons exporters with energy-intensive industrial orientations could be building genuine wealth over time, even with below-market rates for domestic fuel.

Challenges and Opportunities for the Future Gulf Energy Mix

What would be the ideal energy mix for the GCC countries? There is no one-size-fits-all solution for all GCC countries. The answer will depend on the particulars of the decisions made by each GCC country; in other words, it will primarily depend on a set of policy decisions and orientations that might be, arbitrarily or otherwise, chosen by governments. As Jeroen Van der Veer, former CEO of Royal Dutch Shell, stated at the 10th International Oil Summit in April 2009: "Energy companies do not determine the energy mix, governments do, through granting permits, imposing or lifting taxes and providing subsidies. The energy mix is a government decision."

In all countries of the world, the choice of energy – or more specifically electricity – fuel mix has been a critical aspect in shaping energy policies. Indeed, the behavior of governments and the nature of their policy decisions are completely different when their fuel mix is dominated by nuclear (France), coal (South Africa), or oil or gas (most MENA countries). Another layer of differentiation lies in the question of whether fuel resources are endogenous or imported. But even in the case of energy exporters like the GCC states, access to fuel (in terms of volume and cost) is a major issue for governments since international markets are becoming more liquid and fuel export netback prices (opportunity costs) are increasingly viewed as the correct benchmark for energy pricing.

Owing to strategic, liability and geopolitical considerations, nuclear decisions are often seen as a prerogative of the state. Hydrocarbons and coal are more 'commoditized,' so for hydrocarbon exporters, oil – and increasingly gas – utilization in the electricity sector must be aligned with the country's overall export policy. In the region, most countries are revisiting their attitudes toward an electricity fuel mix dominated by hydrocarbons, sometimes arguing the need to free up more hydrocarbons for exports; but the core issues related to the fuel mix usually lie elsewhere—in the need to limit the use of valuable distillates (during summer electricity demand peaks) and the rising competition for increasingly expensive natural gas. As some states become occasional fuel importers, the need to ensure some level of security of supply is also relevant.

In the specific case of the members of the Organization of the Petroleum Exporting Countries (OPEC), there is a need to maintain a proper balance between oil exports and domestic consumption. The power sector is then used as an outlet for discounted crudes, particularly when the countries lack complex refining capabilities. However, this may change in the future as major refining projects eventually come onstream.

The policy decisions mentioned earlier must address a series of new challenges, issues and opportunities faced by the region:

- The diversification of the fuel mix is rising higher on government agendas for a number of reasons, such as strained fuel supplies, environmental concerns and geopolitics, to cite a few. This also poses the important question of fuel pricing and, potentially, of changes in consumer tariffs.

- Countries are increasingly concerned about the need to achieve 'sustainable' development growth, while maximizing/optimizing the use of their natural resources.

- There are growing interconnections and interdependencies between countries (in terms of electricity and gas). Therefore, it is all the more relevant that the different parts of the energy chain become more integrated. For example, it is becoming increasingly difficult to plan for the power sector in complete isolation to the upstream sector, when the two sectors are increasingly interdependent.

- There are several new players involved in the energy sector. Some of them, historically active in the exploration and production (E&P) business, are now integrated companies with power businesses. Others which were originally absent from the power sector in the region, such as Asian companies, have now found their way in.[1] Finally, local state-owned entities (separate to national utilities), banks, funds, and private companies are increasingly investing in energy assets both inside and outside the region.[2]

Options and Consequences of Sustainability and Diversification in the Gulf Energy Mix

Hydrocarbons (steam oil plants and gas turbine plants) dominate the electricity fuel mix in the GCC, even if fuel resources vary from one country to another, with natural gas playing an increasingly important role.

In the future, natural gas will likely remain the fuel of choice, except in some large projects that will be oil-fired mainly because of lack of availability of gas or for strategic reasons.[3] In countries like Saudi Arabia, Kuwait, Oman and Bahrain, where more than half of the gas resources are associated with oil, gas availability for power generation has been problematic. In these cases, it is a significant challenge to account for and then monetize associated gas—flared, recycled or at best reinjected into oilfields. Some of these countries have begun to tackle this question and consider how best to use the gas before pursuing gas-gathering projects. Others have implemented – relatively early on – policies to manage associated gas 'in spite of' the country's oil-oriented policies. However, most have to face regulatory or technological issues. Given the increasing maturity of some oil-producing areas, the greater use of gas for *in situ* power generation and reservoir management (reinjection) means it is increasingly important to estimate how much gas is required. Therefore, even the upstream oil sector is beginning to compete with the electricity sector for gas supplies.

To be fair, very competitive fuel offerings (long-term fuel supply agreements coupled with long-term power purchasing agreements, at below-market prices, usually backed by sovereign guarantees) largely contributed to the attractiveness of industrial projects and Independent Power Producer (IPP) schemes in the region. However, energy demand in absolute terms and per capita has increased to unsustainable levels. In such an increasingly strained environment – particularly for gas supplies – the authorities in the region are (a) considering ways to encourage fuel pricing to evolve, and (b) thinking about 'alternatives' to hydrocarbons, in a general drive to enhance security of supply (including indigenous supply).

In theory, the main alternatives to hydrocarbons considered in the region are coal, renewables and (long term) nuclear power—although there are some practical considerations to take into account first.

Finally, let's not forget another alternative source of supply: 'hidden generation,' i.e., the additional MW that could be saved by using demand management techniques. For example, converting open cycle power plants to combined cycle plants is a low-cost option that should be pursued in most countries, although it does require re-negotiation of existing contracts. Demand side management (DSM) and energy conservation are also low-cost options, but with institutional challenges arising from the large number of entities involved (distribution companies, municipalities, customs departments, etc). The cost of DSM is often less than that of new generation, but implementation takes time and results require patience.

Can Natural Gas-Fired Generation Remain Dominant?

Barring a few exceptions, most countries with an established gas potential shifted from oil to gas in the 1980s. This followed an international trend in which gas turbines (simple or combined cycle) were considered the technology of choice for new power plants. More than 90 percent of installed capacity in greenfield independent power investments worldwide was gas-fired. Lower capital costs, higher fuel efficiency, lower emissions, and shorter lead times were among the reasons behind the success of gas-fired generation[4]. The introduction of competition in generation supported its growth while capital-intensive coal and nuclear were favored by vertically integrated monopolies.

In the region, the less gas-rich neighbors preferred to keep a more diversified fuel mix, while securing preferential gas pipeline deals. Today, more than half of electricity generation in MENA is gas-fired.

We have already discussed the impact of oil-driven energy policies on the fuel mix. For other countries, gas-fired generation does not really need a facilitator to impose itself at this stage. In MENA, natural gas accounts for 67 percent of the installed capacity and more than half of announced projects. However, most countries in the region today face the dilemma of marginal energy costs exceeding long-term contractual supply prices in fuel supply agreements to IPPs and integrated water and power plants (IWPPs). Moreover, the pace of deliverability of gas supplies might not be sufficient to comfortably cover all power generation needs in the region, despite their important gas endowments.

Table 10.1

MENA Countries with Proven Gas Reserves

of more than 280 bcm (10 tcf)

	Reserves P1 (bcm)	Mostly associated	Mostly non-associated	Annual Production (bcm)	Annual exports (bcm)
Iran	29,610	—	—	116.3	4.2
Qatar	25,466		•	76.9	56.7
Saudi Arabia	7,570	2/3		80.4	0
UAE	6,091		•	50.2	7.5
Iraq	3,170	•		1.8	0
Egypt	1,890		•	50	—
Kuwait	1,784	60%		12.7	0
Oman	978	•		23	11
Yemen	475		•	20 (95% reinjected)	—

Sources: OPEC Statistical Bulletin 2009; EIA for non-OPEC, data for 2008.

Table 10.1 examines countries with gas reserves of more than 280 billion cubic meters (or 10 trillion cubic feet) of gas. The total of their reserves constitutes more than 90 percent of proven reserves in the whole of the MENA region. 280 bcm is equivalent to the amount of reserves needed for two LNG trains – of 7.8 million tons (mt) per year capacity each – over 20 years, or for nearly five power plants – of 1.2 gigawatt (GW) capacity each – running at 85 percent of their capacity factor over 30 years.

If one assumes that 100 GW are needed to be installed between 2006 and 2015 in the region, and if the 100 GW were entirely gas-fired, a 30 year production lifetime at 85 percent capacity factor would require around 5,000 bcm of cumulative gas consumption (and more if part of this gas-fired capacity is open-cycle). That is around a third of the amount produced over 30 years, assuming flat production levels. In other words, the MENA region will need to increase its gas supplies (either

[279]

endogenous or imports) by more than a third and direct all of that output to power generation should it want to make all new projects gas-fired. In fact, however, approximately 40 percent of new gas production in the region has been directed to LNG exports since 2000.

For various strategic and technical reasons it may be difficult to increase production by a third by 2015 in order to fuel 100 GW of additional capacity. Moreover, some countries have already committed to long-term fuel supply agreements with industries and contracted LNG exports. Therefore, other solutions would be needed to complement the fuel mix.

Coal: Practical and Reputation Considerations

First, the introduction of coal requires the development of a coal port, with relevant facilities that can be shared with other coal-consuming industries. The additional costs of such a project will have to be taken into account. Moreover, in addition to the reputation-related aspects linked to CO_2 issues, oil and gas exporting countries will need to be careful about the message they would be sending to their consuming markets should they decide to introduce coal. For the others, coal is still considered as a viable option within a framework of tight oil and gas markets.[5]

There is no obvious reason to support the introduction of coal, aside from the fact that it is the only fuel apart from oil and gas which can add substantial generation capacity in a relatively short period of time (4–5 years) if pursued on a large scale, and with no big institutional 'hassle.' On a pure cost basis, coal will have to compete with thermal generation. Based on a US$1–1.5 per million British thermal units (mBtu) gas price, imported coal ($55 per megawatt hour [MWh]) obviously cannot compete with gas–fired combined cycle gas turbines (CCGTs—$20 per MWh), but starts to become competitive if fuel prices are aligned with their international market value (heavy fuel oil [HFO] as an example)[6].

What about Oil?

Burning distillates (usually diesel) to generate electricity is a high-cost option but also one of the most flexible, since most recent power plants in the region are dual-fuelled and can burn distillates. This is now a widely used practice in the Gulf region during the summer peak period. If pursued on a large scale or long-term basis, logistical, contractual and environmental issues would need to be taken into consideration. In terms of supply security, it is generally recommended that all new gas turbine (GT) and combined cycle (CC) plants be dual-fired (gas and diesel) and that storage of diesel be provided at each gas-fired station. In countries with a gas-oriented fuel mix, steam power plants burning HFO or crude could improve fuel security in the event of unavailability of gas supplies, but this option is usually weighted against its higher capital cost and lower efficiency. Limited global experience exists of operating dual-fired plants based on natural gas and HFO, mainly because of the reduced availability of HFO and the relatively high maintenance costs when operating on HFO.

Nuclear and Renewables: Costly, but May Bring Other Benefits

Nuclear and renewables are also more expensive than gas-fired CCGTs, but they bear other strategic benefits and could act as a hedge against uncertain gas supplies or to raise possible CO_2 'opportunity costs' (in case of additional development of the Carbon Development Mechanism [CDM] and carbon trading schemes).

The potential for renewable is being constantly assessed, but the two technologies with some natural and technical potential in the region – namely solar and wind – still have several intrinsic technological challenges to face. They bring some benefits for distributed generation but they need a strong and clear subsidization policy. Renewables would be of low potential and would not make up a substantial share of the generation fuel mix unless pursued with an aggressive subsidization policy which allows them to compete with thermal generation. Renewables require strong governmental will and backing, as well as various concrete commitments from the highest authorities—as we are now seeing in some Gulf countries. Certainly, despite large but dispersed solar or wind initiatives, the contribution by renewable energy sources to the energy mix will remain limited. However, they could play an important role in policy.

Green Initiatives: From Oil Exports to Energy Exports?

In particular, countries with more limited resource endowments in the region have launched a number of renewable electricity projects, focusing for the most part on wind and solar. In general, however, there has been no major clean energy policy apart from some ambitious targets in the energy mix. The use of the Kyoto Clean Development Mechanism's (CDM) Certified Emissions Reductions (CERs) has only recently been pursued in the wider MENA region. Mediterranean countries have been the most active in this regard, sometimes spurred on by European Union support and the Barcelona Process. The lessons learnt from regional experiences show that the definition of realistic targets is important. Government support (and subsidies) is central, but in this process external financing and loans have been key as well.

As far as hydrocarbon producers are concerned, they used to be of the opinion that the emphasis on clean technologies and CO_2 emissions caps could only end up harming long-term demand for the hydrocarbons they export. At best, energy efficiency featured in some governments' agendas to limit skyrocketing energy demand growth. Today, however, the discourse has changed. The initiatives in various countries are not merely driven by surging domestic energy demand, external political support/pressure or commercial incentives, as it is too often conventionally stated. First, given their modest size – and in the absence of a major technological or cost change – renewables can only be one part of a more comprehensive solution to the domestic demand growth issue.

Second, various examples have demonstrated that external political support is not sufficient, but in any case is not really relevant for most GCC countries. Third, commercial incentives have actually been very limited in the region. By February 2009, 79 CDM projects were on the horizon in the MENA region, accounting for only 1.3 percent of take-up in the developing world.[7] These three factors could be important contributing elements, but are not the main drivers behind the change in discourse towards clean energy in general. Rather, some of the major producers have decided to be proactive instead of undergoing the consequences of a future they could not control. The scale of regional investment in renewables and clean energy ventures is estimated at around $33 billion between 2009 and 2013.[8]

Driven by economic and strategic factors, Saudi Arabia, Abu Dhabi and Oman, for example, have developed various business models. Some initiatives might be delayed or shelved, but others will survive. That will at least have an impact on the electricity fuel mix, but also on the energy policies of these countries. After reviewing the options, GCC countries appear to have identified solar and carbon capture and storage (CCS) as the main focus areas of their involvement in the clean energy scene.

As far as solar is concerned, solar photovoltaic (PV) is potentially the lowest cost option in terms of kWh produced, provided it is on an adequate scale. Solar thermal – more mature than solar PV in terms of deployment – is less demanding in capital costs, but production costs could be higher because of the steam turbine process. Abu Dhabi's $15 billion Masdar initiative can be used as an example of government drivers transcending economic and commercial incentives.[9] This is important, particularly in periods of economic downturn, tight finances, and low oil prices, which discourage research and development (R&D) in alternatives to oil globally and which generally divert oil-producing countries' attention.[10] Based on January 2009 prices and costs, according to the Global Wind Energy Council, the internal rate of return (IRR) for renewables is 6–15 percent compared with 20–35 percent for conventional oil projects.

An important question for hydrocarbon-producers relates to CCS eligibility for CDM credits. Also, the value of such credits remains in doubt, as the future of the CDM is unclear.[11] CCS projects are not yet permitted under the CDM framework. This may change in the post-Kyoto period, although that change still requires extensive lobbying from interested parties.[12] Some countries already have ministries of environment or related government bodies, while others don't. Therefore, governments would need to establish an appropriate regulatory structure. However, with or without the creation of a dedicated agency, the upstream sector could play a major role in helping to introduce some of the mechanisms needed to launch these initiatives without direct government involvement.

The first mechanism would be relevant in the case of distributed generation (solar for example), which could help cover the electricity and energy needs of upstream operations. The second mechanism would relate to the development of CCS from various carbon emitters (power plants and industries) and inject the CO_2 into oilfields to boost oil production and, in some cases, free up the gas used for reinjection. Enhanced oil recovery (EOR) projects are not currently recognized under the CDM, nor are any projects that employ geological storage of CO_2 emissions. The local authorities and the upstream sector (even NOCs) could play a role in supporting that political dialogue.

Beyond specific technologies, institutional feasibility appears important for the development of green initiatives, whichever form these initiatives take. Feasibility is reinforced by strong government backing, particularly when funds are available and when a certain part of the private sector is willing to share or facilitate technology sharing. In this regard, centralized policy planning (and not price-driven planning) should act as an enabler, with the private sector allowed to play an important role.

A 'Second Chance' for Nuclear
despite Proliferation Concerns

The potential for nuclear power in the region is debatable. Its implementation would take 15–20 years at least; it would have limited impact on oil and gas supplies; and there is still much to do in terms of establishing institutions, regulatory frameworks and education provision. Nuclear is generally viewed as an exclusive prerogative of the state, for strategic, security and geopolitical reasons.

Since the beginning of the decade, most MENA governments have expressed interest in acquiring nuclear technology for civilian purposes, partly spurred by the debate on the Iranian nuclear program.[13] Today, countries in the region are announcing their intention to revive dormant programs or to develop new civilian nuclear programs, as in the GCC. This time, the coordination with the IAEA is stronger than in the past and all declared programs are in the realm of civilian applications, including power generation and much-needed water desalination.

First, it is important to stress the fact that the introduction of nuclear power would not affect oil supply and demand fundamentals. Although the ongoing debate may have an indirect effect on the 'psychological' factor driving oil prices, the displaced hydrocarbons would be minimal relative to the global market. For example, a 1 GW nuclear reactor could, in theory, displace a 1 GW crude-fired power plant that consumes around 50,000 barrels per day (bpd) of crude or HFO.

In countries that have established nuclear infrastructure and institutions, nuclear power generation costs have recently been in the range of $55–75 per megawatt hour (MWh). With today's domestic fuel prices, nuclear power generation will not be able to compete on a pure cost-basis with thermal power generation. However, including nuclear power in a broader power generation diversification effort could bring other benefits. If handled carefully, the ongoing discussions with the international community may lead to the demystification of nuclear power for peaceful purposes. The discussions may help facilitate debate on other regional geopolitical issues that often fuel the 'psychological premium' on oil prices.

All GCC countries are experiencing high electricity demand growth rates but the desire for nuclear power is generally driven by strategic and geopolitical considerations, transcending pure economics. For nuclear power generation to succeed, continuous international and regional cooperation will be critical. Even if nuclear programs are not new to the region, current discussions around the introduction of nuclear power have grown in complexity, as they come amid the global debate on Iran's nuclear program and more generally on the application and credibility of the Non-Proliferation Treaty (NPT).

Introducing nuclear power for electricity generation in the region will not be an easy task. There is a long history of mutual suspicion surrounding nuclear programs. In addition to a comprehensive nuclear legal framework, an ongoing political and economic dialogue with the International Atomic Energy Agency (IAEA) and technology and fuel suppliers will be required, covering access to enriched fuel as well as the safeguards implementation and verification process.

Multilateralism is Attractive for Political, Technological and Economic Reasons[14]

Individual initiatives would benefit from the flexibility of bilateral discussions but lack the political 'warranty' of a regional organization. There have already been a few initiatives proposed by Russia, Germany and the United States for international fuel cycle services in order to guarantee fuel supply. Some of these initiatives are difficult to accept by some countries, as they are conditional on the abandonment of the right to indigenous enrichment.

In the case of a shared reactor, each GCC country would benefit from economies of scale, assuming smaller units could be developed in the future. Such an arrangement would mean sharing not only the output, but also the risks and costs of a reactor. A reactor's overnight capital costs could be assumed at around \$2,500–3,000 per kilowatt (kW), or a total of \$2.5–3 billion for a 1GW reactor. Further costs to be shared include site costs, transmission, and financing. Having a shared nuclear plant would obviate the need to target the baseload power of one specific country.

Regional programs, like the GCC energy plan, are more likely to come to fruition after a further 20 years (at least 4–5 years to go through the administrative process with the IAEA and to agree on cost-sharing mechanisms, location of the plant, capacity allocations, and other legal agreements, two or three years to issue the license to build the nuclear reactor and another 8–10 years to build the plant). In such a monitored framework, it appears more difficult to divert fissile fuel or to produce highly enriched uranium (HEU) for military purposes—at least, more difficult than if each individual country pursued its own nuclear program.

'Going it Alone': Faster, but still Difficult

Any individual country can pursue a nuclear program on its own, as has historically been the case with almost all nuclear states. However, this 'go-it-alone' strategy will be difficult for new candidates unless some issues are properly dealt with:

First, a 'go-it-alone' strategy requires that an individual government bear the entire capital cost of a nuclear power plant – approaching \$3 billion for a 1 GW reactor – in addition to the costs of fuel and spent fuel management. The government would also need to address all of the standard administrative processes, including IAEA safeguards.

Second, the country will have to find a reliable fuel supply source, since it is highly unlikely that investment in uranium processing and enrichment would either be allowed by the international community or economically justifiable for a single country. Spent fuel recycling, and waste treatment for disposal would need to be conducted in a nuclear country such as Russia or the United States.

Finally, the option of direct bilateral talks with the IAEA may allow flexibility on the size of a nuclear power plant, but there are still very limited commercial options for small nuclear reactors. Small reactors will not be ready for commercial orders for another 15 to 20 years. Although mid-size reactors – with a capacity of 600 megawatts (MW) – may be ready before then, they will be relatively expensive on a per kW basis. Moreover, the commercial worth of small-scale reactors is yet to be demonstrated.[15]

Challenges of the Road Ahead

Access to uranium reserves and securing supply agreements will be critical for any nuclear program. Clarifications will be needed of the impact of non-proliferation policies on nuclear programs, the level of enrichment permitted – if any – and more importantly on the access to enriched fuel. IAEA safeguards implementation and any further verification processes will take into account geopolitical considerations. Thorough verifications will include close monitoring of spent fuel recycling and waste treatment and disposal, and a deal for treatment and disposal with an established nuclear power country will be required. Other important aspects are linked to the necessary institutional infrastructure to support a nuclear power program (licensing and regulation frameworks, legal entities, and trained personnel to work in these entities and operate the facilities). A comprehensive nuclear legal framework would need to include safety and security aspects, safeguards, and liabilities. Financing for the construction, maintenance and safety of the plant, as well as its decommissioning and radioactive waste management would have to be secured. A nuclear power program in the region would take at least a decade to materialize. That assumes the planning and discussions begin now and proceed without interruption, with diplomatic efforts sustained throughout the process. Abu Dhabi is heading in that direction. Several arguments lean in favor of shared regional programs wherever possible. Such regional programs might also benefit from that unifying effort. Just as the European Union emerged from the European Coal and Steel Community created in 1951, it is possible that a stronger regional union could benefit more from a unified nuclear energy agenda than from coordinated macroeconomic and monetary convergence efforts.

In the long term, and with the exception of coal, strong and continuous state support (direct or indirect) will be needed in order to allow other generation technologies such as renewables and nuclear to materialize.

Evolving Fuel Prices

Attractive fuel prices have been helpful in securing investment in the power and industrial sectors, and in supporting LNG industries. However, marginal fuel production costs are increasingly higher than fuel prices agreed under several fuel supply agreements (FSAs) in the region. This is all the more relevant as fuel supplies are becoming more costly to develop and produce. Reasons for this include the maturity of upstream assets, higher energy intensity of upstream production, increases in engineering, procurement and construction (EPC) costs owing to tight service sector markets, remaining undeveloped resources in increasingly more complex structures, tight reservoirs and impurities such as sour gas.[16]

Some countries have already begun to review their fuel pricing structure. This reconsideration is spurred by upstream players or by scarcity of supply, or both. One main assumption is that while some governments are reviewing fuel pricing structures, a testing period of adaptation would be required during which generators will be asked to deliver competitive wholesale electricity prices under different fuel pricing schemes.

Unchanged gas prices would lead to a growing subsidy relative to market price and to cost of energy. This sizeable increase in subsidy alone should drive a reconsideration of gas pricing policy, particularly given that there is a need to drive consistent commercial decision-making in the marginal usage or substitution of gas. In any case, this can be partially accomplished with higher price assumptions for planning of future investments in order to impact operational usage as well; but would actual prices need to change?

Ideally, the first step would be to establish a process to make all energy subsidies more explicit, to enable them to be managed with a clear view on their actual size, purpose and future evolution. More focused subsidy support can then be offered to key user sectors via grants and tax breaks and/or via structured compensation arrangements, in return for agreed gas price changes.

Then, it would be possible to review and implement the most appropriate approaches to set gas prices. It is possible to achieve a transition from a mix of prices to a new universal price set to reflect the balance of pressures to make subsidies more explicit and ensure they are not applied via energy prices. This may drive efficiency in energy usage, encourage industrial and LNG users to seek alternative fuels or feedstock, force consistent and efficient choices in new energy-related investments and respond to real marginal market values.

Finally, it will be important to institute a process to continuously review the pricing approach as the balance of these needs change, or as supply and demand fundamentals can be seen to respond primarily to a particular external price driver (i.e., a regional market price—should it materialize).

However, we need to bear in mind that re-pricing gas would make the marginal costs of industrial and LNG production directly comparable with those from other sources and may result in displacing some local production. While a change in gas price would spur some limited, efficiency improvements, particularly in countries with very recent projects, it would also force a 'natural selection' between future projects, which in turn would affect Gross Domestic Product (GDP).

Most countries in the region face the dilemma of marginal energy costs exceeding long-term contractual supply prices. Countries might address this situation in a variety of ways: some would apply marginal costs to new off-takers only—this is possible if the supply and demand balance continues to be positive; others would review long term contracts where possible, using review clauses when they exist in contracts. Finally, the extreme approach would be a widespread, complete renegotiation, or imposed transition of end-user energy prices to new levels. This last approach may involve breaching long-term supply agreements, and would entail a heavy institutional burden.

New fuel pricing can be applied selectively to discriminate between end-use sectors or to distinguish between core and marginal uses. Some countries differentiate between domestic and export industries in pricing (Egypt) or between power and industrial usage. Unification of pricing (and use of alternative support mechanisms or subsidies for specific industries) allows for the elimination of any distortion of project efficiency and subsequent production decisions.

Options for setting gas prices include cost-related, oil price-linked or linked to freely-traded market prices. Some countries have linked gas prices to electricity, coal or other commodity price references. The ultimate decision will depend on the relative emphasis needed on driving efficiency of use or on investing in alternative energy sources.

Such emphases usually shift over time. Therefore, countries which introduce these mechanisms could adopt a progressive or evolutionary managed approach to re-pricing, i.e., setting prices that are sufficient to drive short-term substitution/efficiency economics without necessarily forcing long term investment solutions which may incur major costs. It is generally better to take it in steps. This transition mechanism is meant to accompany a country as it transforms from a fuel exporter into a fuel 'monetizer' before becoming a mature economy.

Revising fuel supply agreements will necessarily raise the question of renegotiating power purchasing agreement terms. More generally, any material revision of pricing or mechanisms will give rise to claims from contractual gas off-takers.

Introducing new fuels and new technologies will require the state to step in, either directly or indirectly, through the upstream sector or investment arms. In both cases, regulation will play a critical role in ensuring that electricity cost structures and system efficiency are maintained or enhanced, and that the right investment signals are sent at the right time. Changes in fuel offerings (fuel type, pricing, contract terms, etc.) will require a delicate balancing act.

How Robust in View of Sustainable Development Needs?

The electricity sector is a vehicle for development and a backbone of economic activity. The sustainability of its fuel mix cannot be evaluated in isolation from macro-economic policies and needs. In order to test the sustainability of the fuel mix and fuel pricing in the framework of governments' general macro-economic policies, we will call upon a major branch of the economy: the neo-Walrasian general equilibrium theory and welfare economics.

As per Ken Arrow's definition, the capital assets of a specific country or society include manufactured capital, human capital, knowledge base and natural capital. Institutions and capital assets constitute the Productive Base of a country, at any specific time. The potential exists to substitute one category of capital asset for another, but it is difficult to quantify in the absence of comprehensive and transparent data—the benefits/losses of consuming natural capital, for instance. Institutions guide the allocation of capital assets. A 'sustainable' growth path would assume that 'genuine wealth' at constant accounting prices does not decline over time.[17] The work of Arrow, Dasgupta, Ler and others emphasizes the need to use other metrics such as Net National Product, rather than GDP or GDP per capita, in order to evaluate economic policies and authorities' choices in terms of capital asset allocation.

Genuine Wealth Creation and Sustainable Growth

We assume that the global quantity of capital assets is limited and finite; therefore, genuine wealth increases in some countries should normally be balanced by a genuine wealth decrease in others. Thus, countries' growth paths are not independent from one another.

Measuring countries' performance is not a straightforward exercise.[18] Forecasting performance in order to decide on the best way to allocate resources is even trickier. There is an increasingly wide array of theoretical and empirical literature on the concept of sustainable development and the accumulation of wealth and the ways to measure them. These concepts are becoming gradually more comprehensive and measurable. In general, valuation methods for human and natural capital are still imperfect. Existing economic research falls short of quantifying the losses of natural capital, particularly for hydrocarbon-producing countries.

However, even these imperfect calculations show that most countries in the MENA region failed to make genuine investments in the 1970s and the 1980s when their windfall oil incomes could have been used to build up their long-term economic potential. These conclusions, although based on imperfect valuations, caused enough serious concerns among policymakers to spur them to rethink their resource monetization policy. The concept of Dutch Disease has been widely used to analyze more broadly the inability of resource holders to economically perform in real terms.[19] The empirical research of the low economic performance of hydrocarbon resource holders was developed during the 1990s. In general, there are two main mechanisms by which the curse would strike: economic distortions linked to Dutch Disease and/or deficits in governance. Some MENA countries attempted to address these two mechanisms by expanding the non-oil sector of the economy and by rethinking their institutions. The results are mixed, and some countries have performed better then others. Our underlying goal is to revisit the general assumption of low economic performance associated with oil producing countries, in light of global and regional developments. We will use the progress made by the aforementioned body of research on measuring countries' performance in order to achieve that.

In theory, the decrease in natural capital should be offset by the increase in produced or manufactured capital and human capital. Genuine wealth (or a comprehensive measure of wealth) at constant prices should not decline over time to ensure that a specific country is following a sustainable development path, and that it is becoming genuinely wealthier.

This analysis benefited from the methods developed by Hamilton and the World Bank team in recent years in order to try and propose comprehensive wealth accounting. The World Bank (2006) provides an assessment of changes in comprehensive wealth in almost every nation of the world. However, a number of Middle Eastern countries are missing. There is no data for Qatar, and the assessment of Saudi Arabia is incomplete. The work of Arrow et al. (2004, 2008) complements the theoretical framework developed by the World Bank by incorporating technological change and population growth. More importantly, Arrow et al. (2008) offer a theoretical approach to valuing natural resources. Other aspects developed include the utilization of educational attainment instead of simple education expenditure to assess growth in human capital, and an improved method to assess environmental damage associated with economic and human activity applying to specific countries.

The general rationale of the method is simple, but its application is very much dependant on data availability over a sufficiently long period of time and a deep knowledge of each country's conditions and policies in order to apply the right metric (particularly for accounting prices). Let V be the productive base and K_t the vector of stocks of all capital assets at date t. V is a function of K_t and if we make the simplifying assumption that t does not directly influence V (which might not be always true in the case of some natural capital), then $V_t=V(K_t)$.

Let K_{it} denote the stock of capital (i) which is good at date (t), and using the chain rule of differentiation:

(1) $\quad dV/dt = \Sigma\ (\partial V/\partial K_{it})\ (\partial K_{it}/\partial t)$

Arrow defines the right-hand side of (1) (*genuine investment or the change in genuine wealth*) as the accounting value of the changes in the stocks of all society's capital assets at t (in other words, the sum of the changes in capital assets' stocks, times an accounting price of that capital asset). For example, investment in non renewable natural resources is necessarily negative. Sustainability requires that real (at constant prices) and comprehensive (including all stocks of capital) wealth is increasing:

(2) $dV/dt > 0$

While capital stock changes are relatively easy to quantify, the notion of accounting price is more subtle, as it is not typically equal to the market price of the asset. The problem is that genuine wealth would be highly vulnerable to the accounting price that we choose to apply. Arrow, et al. (2008), propose to evaluate the accounting price using the notion of 'shadow price.' The shadow prices would be "the prices that would prevail if all commodities were traded in commodities' markets and if there were perfect foresight." If we were to apply this definition to hydrocarbon-producing countries, we would face two hurdles. The first condition is true for part of the oil (which is exported) but not true for most of the gas exported (LNG, long-term contracts). By definition, the second condition does not seem applicable in empirical analysis, partly because hydrocarbon-producers can influence future prices, and partly because they are not the only ones who can have that influence. Having said that, shadow prices are – by nature – theoretical prices. For a non-renewable resource like oil, the shadow price would be the discounted value of future use, or the price at which the owner of the well would be indifferent between selling the oil/gas immediately and holding it for future sale (rental value), or the difference between the sale price of the oil and its extraction cost or the price paid for the scarcity of the resource.

At the same time, when considering a specific country over a long period of time, we somehow need to factor in the rise in the rental value of the non-renewable resource, owing to its assumed increased scarcity (depletion premium). Resource stock owners should expect to receive capital gains and consumers should expect to pay higher prices (or the subsidies bill of the government to increase if subsidies are maintained).

[295]

In our analysis, we will consider a CO_2 price as a proxy for environmental damage in the country and as an opportunity cost of these emissions, supposing they were to be monetized. For the valuation of human capital, in our application to the empirical cases of Qatar and Saudi Arabia, we will use investment in education as a proxy, recognizing the limits of this approximation (mismatch between curricula and job market needs, access to education, relevance for higher education, etc).

Finally, we will need to factor in the international assets (and liabilities) held by a specific country. With the rise of sovereign wealth funds (SWFs) in oil-producing countries, this part of capital cannot be neglected.

Arrow, et al. (2003), calculated Genuine Investment rates for all regions in the world, and concluded that MENA countries were not building wealth (-7.1 percent over 1975–2001). In 2008, the same team offered a more nuanced approach, explaining that they could have understated the sustainability of Middle Eastern development growth. We offer a more refined approach that we apply to the first years of this century. For the time being, preliminary estimates for some Gulf countries point to the fact that this balance is improving. However, a refinement of the calculation will be needed in order to develop a more comprehensive view. In any case, it is far from certain that the development growth path undertaken by Gulf countries today is optimal, but it appears more sustainable than economic policies followed in past periods of high oil prices. The central question is whether their hydrocarbon resources are *properly valued* to ensure genuine wealth creation and sustainable growth.

Monetizing Resources: Empirical Cases of Saudi Arabia and Qatar

Opting for the examples of Saudi Arabia and Qatar as case studies for the multifaceted subject of resource monetization is not accidental. These two states are major Gulf oil or gas exporters who have prudently reformed their electricity sectors. Both have embarked on ambitious industrial programs based on subsidized fuel supplies. Yet, their development growth path appears very different. In 2008, Saudi Arabia's GDP per capita was $19,405 while Qatar's was $106,000.[20] The geographical and demographic size of each country should be playing a role, but this simplistic assumption looks insufficient.[21]

The 2009 Saudi budget points to a -4.6 percent of GDP deficit, its first deficit since 2001, mainly because the country decides to run on an expansionary budget, despite the relative fall in oil prices.[22] But the government has much more fiscal room in which to maneuver. The 2009 budget is instructive as the increase in capital expenditures is in marked contrast with previous periods of decreasing oil prices. Capital spending in the 1998 budget, when oil revenue dropped by 50 percent, declined by 15 percent. The industrial and infrastructure expansion in Saudi Arabia began effectively in 2003. In addition to the impressive increases in public spending, supported by increasing oil prices, the energized and liquid private sector has been channeling investments into several economic sectors, including hydrocarbons and utilities. Latest official estimates put joblessness among nationals at 12 percent (and higher among young people—probably 25 percent for the 25–29 age group). The authorities have invested heavily in vocational training, and have tried to address the mismatch between school curricula and job market needs (more technical and scientific orientations than religious, for example). As far as natural capital is concerned, we mainly focused on hydrocarbons. Saudi Aramco has been conducting a major investment program to increase productive capacity to 12.5 mbpd. Gas exploration is becoming a major part of the company's program as it plans to raise gas reserves by 20 percent over the next five years. As far as foreign assets are concerned, their value depends on the behavior of international markets. For example, Saudi Arabia's investments in foreign securities and foreign banks plunged by a third between December 2008 and June 2009. This was coupled with a massive withdrawal of funds from international markets, because of the expansionary budget of the country and lower oil prices.[23] In parallel, the country's public debt had decreased to 13 percent of GDP at the end of 2008, from more than 100 percent in 1999.

[297]

Qatar registers the second highest GDP per capita in the world ($106,000 in 2008), but the Qatari authorities are increasingly conscious that this criterion is far from being sufficient to ensure accumulation of wealth, genuine investments and the best use of natural resources for current and future generations. In other words, the question is how to ensure that Qatar's genuine wealth per capita at constant accounting prices does not decline. The country was able to build a strong economic presence in the region and internationally. The 'healthy deficit' (2 percent of GDP) earmarked in the 2009–2010 budget is a signal that the authorities will continue to stimulate the economy (by maintaining a high level of state spending) and to maintain high growth rates, despite the global economic downturn and the fall in hydrocarbon revenue. LNG exports help offset flat or declining oil revenue. The high GDP growth rate of more than 10 percent registered in recent years, in real terms, would decline to a still strong position: 7–9 percent in the foreseeable future. The external debt is maintained at 60–70 percent of GDP, and the fiscal balance is in constant surplus. Official reserves had increased to $15 billion in May 2009, up from $9.8 billion in 2008 and less than $2 billion in 2002.[24] This positive outlook, however, is highly vulnerable to the timing of LNG output increases. Qatar's sovereign wealth fund – the Qatar Investment Authority (QIA) set up in 2005 – held $60 billion in assets in 2008. The global recession hit some hydrocarbons and petrochemicals projects, in addition to tourism, real estate and retail, but the country is well perceived and still able to tap the bond markets. Inflation moderated to 1.3 percent in the first quarter of 2009, down from its 17 percent peak reached in the first half of 2008.

Given the low extraction costs, we decided to use export oil prices for each of the main crudes exported by the two countries. As far as gas is concerned, we used the average export netback price of QatarGas IV as a proxy for gas price valuation. As a reminder, the shadow prices would be "the prices that would prevail if all commodities were traded in commodities' markets and if there were perfect foresight." Therefore, the export netback value would be used even in the case of Saudi Arabia, which does not export gas and only uses it domestically. It is important to note that natural gas produced but used for reinjection would be considered mostly recoverable, barring a loss of 5–10 percent.

In order to assess whether Saudi Arabia and Qatar are becoming genuinely wealthier, we applied formula 1. Tables 10.2 and 10.3 summarize the results for the two countries. There are several caveats in this calculation, however:

- Data limits: data generally differs between various official sources, including ministries, and bears many inconsistencies. The least probable data is highlighted.

- CO_2 was priced at \$20 per ton, considered as the opportunity cost of these emissions.

- Our assessment of assets in foreign countries is based on publicly available information and is therefore limited. The financial investments and the role of the increasingly sophisticated SWFs and other investment vehicles are only partly taken into account.

- The population in Qatar has doubled since 2004. This artificial increase is due to the intense economic activity and the immigration of expatriates, usually for short-term periods. Therefore, for this calculation, we retained the 'natural' growth of the pre-2002 population in Qatar.

- Education expenditures are limited to governments' direct expenditures in fundamental education. They do not include professional training or human development and do not capture inappropriate curricula (lack of scientific or engineering orientations for example).

Table 10.2
Genuine Wealth Creation in Saudi Arabia

SAUDI ARABIA	2000	2001	2002	2003	2004	2005	2006	2007	2008	2000–2008
GDP ($ millions)	188,440	186,240	188,530	211,200	212,000	270,000	353,000	378,000	481,000	2,468,410
Population (millions)	20	21	21	22	23	23	24	24	25	
Foreign assets ($ millions)										59,000
Domestic Net Investment ($ millions)**	4,897	8,435	8,000	8,925	10,014	16,614	18,910	31,773	40,000	147,567
Education expenditure ($ millions)	13,200	14,200	14,500	15,300	17,000	18,000	20,000	25,000	28,000	165,200
Damage from CO_2 emissions ($ millions)*	-5,160	-5,300	-5,500	-5,780	-6,080	-6,480	-6,740	-6,942	-7,150	-55,133
Energy Depletion ($ millions)	-3,674	-3,764	-3,345	-4,585	-5,978	-12,602	-12,024	-12,591	-26,497	-85,061
Genuine Investment rate (%)										9.4
CO_2 emissions (Mt of CO_2)***	258	265	275	289	304	324	337	347	358	
Crude Oil Production (mbpd)	8.00	7.80	7.09	8.40	8.90	9.35	9.20	8.80	9.2	
Gas Production (bcm)	49.8	53.7	57.3	60.1	65.7	71.2	73.5	74.4	80.4	

Sources: IMF, Ministry of Finance, OPEC, IEA.
Shaded: forecasts, estimates, budgets and author's assumptions.
* CO_2 cost assumed at $20 per ton.
** Does not take into account financial investments.
*** IEA and author's own estimates after 1999.

Table 10.3
Genuine Wealth Creation in Qatar

QATAR	2000	2001	2002	2003	2004	2005	2006	2007	2008	2000–2008
GDP ($ millions)	16,000	19,000	20,000	25,000	35,000	43,000	57,000	71,000	91,000	377,000
Population (millions)	0.61	0.64	0.68	0.72	0.76	0.79	0.82	0.84	0.86	
Foreign assets ($ millions)										16,500
Domestic Net Investment ($ millions)**	500	772	1,302	1,230	1,764	2,920	3,441	5,756	5,786	23,471
Education expenditure ($ millions)	40	86	145	217	387	2,029	1,338	3,528	5,341	13,111
Damage from CO_2 emissions ($ millions)*	-520	-540	-560	-600	-660	-700	-780	-800	-800	-5,960
Energy Depletion ($ millions)	-878	-3,198	-3,418	-3,861	-4,304	-5,057	-5,602	-6,980	-8,497	-41,795
Genuine Investment rate (%)										1.4
CO_2 emissions (Mt of CO_2)***	26	27	28	30	33	35	39	40	40	
Crude Oil Production (in kbpd)	648	632	568	676	755	765	802	845	843	
Gas Production (in bcm)	25	29	31	35	39	45.8	50.7	63.2	76.9	

Sources: IMF, Ministry of Finance, OPEC, IEA.
Shaded: forecasts, estimates, budgets and author's assumptions.
* CO_2 cost assumed at $20 per ton.
** Does not take into account financial investments.
*** IEA and author's own estimates after 1999.

It is possible to draw the conclusion that for these two countries the balance offsetting natural resources decline with human and manufactured capital is improving. For all the uncertainties mentioned above, it appears that the two countries are improving the way they manage their economies. With the assumption that the structural price of hydrocarbons will increase in the future, the energy depletion element will become more important—and should be offset with more investments in human capital, in industries and infrastructure.

Suggestions for future research include ways to *genuinely* include financial investments, first by finding the relevant data and second by thinking about the best way to handle them, particularly given their volatile and exogenous nature. A better understanding of investments in human capital in these countries would be helpful. Finally, it could be misleading to judge the performance of a country over a period of nine years. Ideally this calculation would be performed over three decades in order to assess the impact on at least one generation. This method could be also used to forecast future genuine wealth creation and support decision making (concerning allocation of resources and capital).

The second major conclusion relates to the pricing of natural resources. Assuming these calculations were not imperfect, it would imply that Saudi Arabia, for instance, would be following the right approach in terms of resource valuation by exporting its light crude, consuming internally its heavy crude and discounted products (for the electricity sector), and by selling its gas domestically—mainly to industries at $0.75 per mBtu. Fuel subsidies are meant to support a certain level of economic growth, while exhausting resources at discounted prices without a substantial creation of other forms of capital would be self-destructive.

Science and Technology: Prerequisites for Energy Security in the GCC

Riyad Y. Hamzah

This paper will discuss the strategies being planned and implemented to achieve both short- and long-term energy security in the GCC states, and the necessity for combining the development of new technologies with innovative government policies in cooperation with universities and research institutes.

In a region that possesses more than two-fifths of global oil reserves and represents as much as one fifth of total global production, past investment in the development of science and technology has not been proportional to their significance in the economy. However, numerous initiatives have been launched recently to strengthen the role of universities and research centers and to overcome the obstacles to technology transfer in areas relevant to short-term energy security – including research on petroleum, natural gas, nuclear power, and renewable energies such as biofuels, bioelectricity, solar energy, and wind power – and to long-term energy security—such as reducing dependence on any one source of energy, increasing the number of suppliers, efficiently exploiting native fossil fuels or renewable energies, and energy conservation.

In spite of all the calls for economic diversity over the past two decades, today – more than 80 years after the discovery of oil in Bahrain in 1932 – oil and gas remain the main sources of revenue for the countries of the GCC, and their economies are still predominantly oil and gas-based. Although it contains around 40 percent of the world's oil reserves and 23.6 percent of global gas reserves, the new technologies required for this industry continue to be developed outside the GCC region. The GCC countries therefore continue to have no alternative but to import these technologies to aid production.

Owing to its dependence on oil – a depleting natural resource – it is essential that the GCC seek out alternative energies to ensure energy security for the future—particularly in Bahrain and Oman, where oil reserves are more limited than in the other GCC states and have been largely depleted. Political awareness of the necessity of finding alternative energies has already begun to materialize. This stage of awareness and promotion must now be transformed into concrete action plans and shortcuts to implementation.

Aside from demand management through initiatives such as educational campaigns on environmental awareness, conservation to prolong the life of existing natural resources, and more efficient energy usage, solutions to finding alternative energies can be brought about through the application of science and technology. In order to achieve this, it is essential that previously existing and newly established research centers, in conjunction with universities, take an active stake in this process.

The development of science and technology has never been a significant source of revenue in the GCC, thus the investment made in their development is not proportional to their significance to the economy. Private higher education in the region is still in its early stages of development and has not embraced science and technology specializations as research is more expensive to fund in these areas. It therefore remains the responsibility of national universities, supported by GCC governments, to strengthen their research role in these areas.

This paper will discuss the need to combine the development of new technologies with innovative government policy in cooperation with universities and research institutes to develop strategic plans for ensuring energy security in the GCC.

Regional and International Issues Facing the GCC

The GCC faces a number of regional and international issues with which it must contend, including: the current economic crisis, the depletion of natural resources and non-renewable reserves of fossil fuels; higher standards of – and calls for – environmental protection; population increases with subsequent increases in electricity demand; fluctuation of oil prices; and political tension in the area.

Climate change and global warming are of particular interest in the GCC countries, as a recent study has shown that:

> At the nation level, the United Arab Emirates (UAE), Qatar and Bahrain will witness the highest SLR [sea level rise] effect in terms of the percentage of population at risk from the total country population. Here, we project that more than 50% of the population of each country will be impacted by 5m SLR … The current analysis indicates that Bahrain and Qatar would experience a significant reduction of about 13.4% and 6.9%, respectively, of their land as a result of the 5m SLR scenario.[1]

Rising energy costs, questions of national energy security, environmental and related societal threats, and fears of economic slow-down contribute to the need to seek methods for bolstering the energy security of the GCC countries. Such methods include seeking to further develop alternative energies such as wind, solar, and nuclear energy, and the development of a comprehensive, knowledge-based, green economy with the potential to eventually develop even more environmentally-friendly energy technologies and products in the coming years.

This would mean a transformation to an economy that makes more efficient and sustainable use of its limited natural resources. Furthermore, and considering its percentage of global fossil fuel reserves stated above, the GCC would benefit from being involved in efforts to both improve the quality of its fossil fuels and seek alternative energies.

[305]

Development of GCC Education and Scientific Research through Decades of Oil Production

At the beginning of the 20th century, the people of the GCC were living in harsh conditions in primarily desert and arid lands. Trade, pearl diving, fishing, and ship building were the major sources of income.

The lack of formal education and health services contributed to the harshness of life and low standards of living. This lack of formal education is demonstrated by the fact that the first public schools to be established in the GCC countries were in 1919 for boys and in 1928 for girls, both in Bahrain.

The economic fortunes of the GCC began to change with the discovery of oil in the 1930s in many of the GCC countries. The income from oil production contributed to increased standards of living and the establishment of primary, intermediate, secondary, technical, and commercial education. This was accompanied by the investment of GCC countries in electricity services, transportation, health services and infrastructure. Economic prosperity gradually led to the establishment of universities in Saudi Arabia in 1956, Kuwait in 1966, the UAE in 1976, Qatar in 1977, and Bahrain and Oman in 1986.

Thus, as late as the 1970's, the countries of the GCC were still fighting to eliminate illiteracy, as illustrated in Table 11.1.

By the 1980s, the GCC countries had established a number of universities, including Kuwait University, King Faisal University, King Fahd University for Petroleum and Minerals, King Saud University, Imam Muhammad bin Saud Islamic University, King Abdul Aziz University, the Islamic University in Saudi Arabia, Qatar University, and the UAE University, in addition to two colleges, Bahrain University College and Gulf Polytechnic, which were later united to form Bahrain University in 1986.

Table 11.1

Illiteracy Rates in the GCC States (%)[2]

Year	Bahrain	Kuwait	Oman	Qatar	Saudi Arabia	UAE
1970	49.1	42.4	81.5	41.8	66.7	47.8
1975	37.1	38.2	72.4	36.6	58.3	40.4
1980	28.8	32.2	63.8	30.2	49.2	34.6
1985	23.3	27.9	54.5	25.6	40.8	31.2
1990	17.9	23.3	45.3	23.0	33.8	29.0
1995	14.8	21.0	36.3	20.8	28.7	26.6
2000	12.5	18.1	28.3	18.8	23.8	23.8
2005	10	15.6	21.7	16.5	19.6	21.2
2010	8.1	13.8	16.6	14.6	16	19

The only university in the Gulf dedicated to the study of petroleum and minerals was King Fahd University. The remaining universities, for years since their establishment, remained primarily educational universities without facilities for advanced scientific research. Graduate programs only began to emerge in the late 1980s when the GCC countries recognized their significance and that of advanced research in issues that were of concern to the region. This led to the establishment of the Arabian Gulf University (AGU) in Bahrain, one of the first 'regional' universities in the world, established to encourage cooperation within the GCC in tackling significant issues relating to the environment, biotechnology, energy, technology management, and space sciences, among others. The university also had an ambitious scholarship program whereby students were sent for their Master's and Ph.D. studies to prominent universities in the West, designed to prepare future professors to return as members of the AGU teaching staff. This project, by the late 1980s, suffered significant shortages in financing, however, which led to reductions in its scope, mandate, and ambitions. The

1980s were also marred by wars and the decline in oil prices that negatively affected the economies of the Arabian Gulf.

By the late 1990s and early 21st century, the GCC, like the rest of the Arab World, was confronted by a growing demand for university enrollment owing to rapid increases in population. At the same time, study outside the Arab World became more difficult for GCC students, particularly following the September 11th attacks in 2001 which resulted in tighter controls on study visas for Arab students.

This increased difficulty in studying abroad led to the emergence of private universities, which flourished as a result of the increased demand for enrollment within the GCC rather than abroad. By the end of 2009, in addition to government-run universities, there were approximately seventy private universities and colleges located throughout the GCC. Most of these private universities, however, have avoided the establishment of high-cost specialties, i.e., sciences and engineering. This has coincided with low enrollment in the previous few years in specialties such as biology, chemistry and physics. There are only a handful of universities that offer Ph.D. programs in the sciences, as shown in Table 11.2, which demonstrates the scarcity of graduate programs offering advanced scientific degrees in the GCC.

Aside from in Bahrain, public universities in the GCC do not charge fees, which contributes to budget limitations since the main source of income for public universities remains direct government funding. With a few exceptions, oil companies have not contributed significantly to funding research, possibly because of the lack of research infrastructure in the GCC, and maybe a lack of confidence in local universities. Until recently, the percentage of expenditure on research in GCC universities, as in the rest of the Arab World, has remained lower than the world average, in spite of their gross national incomes. Table 11.3 demonstrates the typical annual percentage of expenditure on scientific research compared to gross domestic product (GDP) during the first decade of the 21st century, as reported in 2004.

Table 11.2

GCC Countries Offering Degrees in Energy Studies

COUNTRY	INSTITUTION	DEGREES OFFERED	WEBSITE
Saudi Arabia	King Fahd University of Petroleum and Minerals	Petroleum Engineering Program	http://www.kfupm.edu.sa/pet/
		Applied Petroleum Engineering Program	http://www.kfupm.edu.sa/pet/
		Master of Science Program	http://www.kfupm.edu.sa/pet/
		Ph.D Program	http://www.kfupm.edu.sa/pet/
	King Saud University - College of Engineering	B.Sc. in Petroleum and Natural Gas Engineering	http://colleges.ksu.edu.sa/Engineering/PetroleumNaturalGas(2)/Pages/AcademicPrograms.aspx
		Master of Science in Petroleum and Natural Gas Engineering	http://colleges.ksu.edu.sa/Engineering/PetroleumNaturalGas(2)/Pages/AcademicPrograms.aspx
Kuwait	Kuwait University - College of Engineering & Petroleum	Petroleum Engineering Program	http://www.eng.kuniv.edu/petroleum/
Bahrain	Arabian Gulf University	Diploma and Masters in Petroleum Biotechnology	http://www.agu.edu.bh
UAE	The Petroleum Institute, Engineering, Education and Research	Graduate - Petroleum Engineering Program	http://www.pi.ac.ae/PI_ACA/pe/undergraduate/welcome.php
		Master of Engineering in Petroleum Engineering	http://www.pi.ac.ae/PI_ACA/pe/post_graduate/objectives.php
Oman	Sultan Qaboos University	B. Eng. in Petroleum and Natural Gas Engineering	http://www.squ.edu.om/tabid/7126/language/en-US/Default.aspx
		Masters program in Petroleum Engineering	http://www.squ.edu.om/tabid/7128/language/en-US/Default.aspx
Qatar	Texas A&M University	Undergraduate – Petroleum Engineering Program	http://www.pe.tamu.edu/academics/Undergraduate.shtml
		Master of Science (M.S) Engineering Program	http://www.pe.tamu.edu/academics/DegreeInfo.shtml#ME
		Master of Engineering (M.Eng.)	http://www.pe.tamu.edu/academics/DegreeInfo.shtml#ME
		PhD (Petroleum Engineering	http://www.pe.tamu.edu/academics/DegreeInfo.shtml#ME

[309]

Table 11.3
Research Funding as a Percentage of GDP[3]

Country	Percentage of GDP
Bahrain	0.1
Kuwait	0.4
Oman	0.1
Qatar	0.1
Saudi Arabia	0.2
United Arab Emirates	0.1

According to the 2008 Report of the Arab Forum for Environment and Development:

> Inputs can generally be divided into the number of researchers and the rate of expenditure on scientific research, both in relative and absolute terms. While the number of researchers in the Arab world stands close to that in the rest of the world, and has been growing by 6–7 percent annually between 1994 and 1998, double the population growth rate, the rate of expenditure on scientific research as a percentage of GDP is abysmally low in the Arab region, at around 0.2%. The world average is 1.4%, with the rate being 4% in Japan. The Arab region's rate is the lowest regional rate in the entire world.[4]

Naturally, the number of published scientific works from the GCC in indexed scientific journals – as in the rest of the Arab World – does not reflect the wealth of these countries, as is illustrated in Table 11.4.[5]

In 2006, the journal *Nature* published an article entitled "Oil Rich, Science Poor," in reference to the minimal contribution to science of the GCC countries, stating:

> The annual output of scientific papers from Saudi Arabia, which generates almost as many papers as the other monarchies combined, was static between 2000 and 2005. Even in desalination technology, investment has been limited. The Middle East Desalination Research Center in Muscat, Oman, set up in 1996 to encourage research cooperation in the region, is currently limping along with a budget of just US$2 million a year.[6]

Figure 11.1
Scientific Publications in the MENA Region

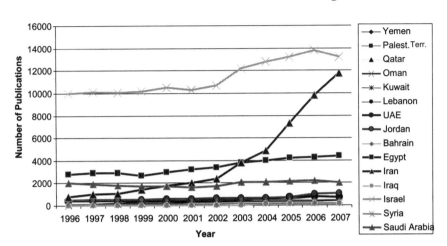

However, all the GCC countries have developed major projects in the years 2006–2010 which have now begun to change this status by establishing a culture of scientific research and pursuit of excellence in education, as discussed later in this paper.

Published statistical reports indicate that the contributions of Arab countries in the fields of scientific research and development are very modest. Scientific publications and patents are minimal,[7] as demonstrated in Table 11.5.

Table 11.4
Patents Granted by the GCC Patent Office[8]

Year	1998	1999	2000	2001	2002	2003	2004	2005	2006	2007	Total
Filed Applications	57	417	635	687	622	722	1037	1465	1900	1852	9394
Granted Patents	0	0	0	0	30	0	62	78	158	155	483

Furthermore, Arab universities' rankings among their international counterparts are far from flattering, as shown in Table 11.6.

[311]

Table 11.5

Ranking of the Top 10 Universities in the GCC States[9]

GCC Ranking	University	Country	World Ranking
1	King Saud University	KSA	199
2	King Fahd University of Petroleum & Minerals	KSA	404
3	King Abdulaziz University	KSA	496
4	Imam Muhammad bin Saud University	KSA	835
5	Umm Al-Qura University	KSA	1,050
6	King Faisal University	KSA	1,527
7	Kuwait University	KUWAIT	1,691
8	United Arab Emirates University	UAE	1,736
9	King Khalid University	KSA	2,227
10	Sultan Qaboos University	OMAN	2,407

The contributions of scientific communities to their national economies in terms of stimulating industrial growth are also marginal. As scientific research and development is now advancing at ever-increasing rates in developed countries, the gap between the Arab countries and the developed countries continues to widen.[10] This situation has been so severe that it can almost be labeled a crisis.

With so little funding being channeled to all fields of scientific research, it is alarming to consider how small a percentage of these funds is actually earmarked specifically for energy security, whether for increasing the efficiency of fossil fuels or for the development of renewable or nuclear energy. For a region whose source of economic prosperity has been fossil fuels since the 1930s, little work has been done to produce scientific advancement aimed at better utilization of this precious source of income for the region. Universities and research centers in this region should devise more significant goals and objectives in the realm of advancing energy security based upon scientific research.

[312]

This may serve to reduce the gap between expenditures in this area in the GCC in comparison with the rest of the world, and to reduce the region's dependence on imported technologies and innovations. The need for participation in the advancement of such technologies is demonstrated by the fluctuation of the global political climate. Dependence on foreign technologies can leave states vulnerable to the negative effects of political changes on energy security within the GCC, an example of which is the use of oil sanctions as a means of punishing nations.

For decades now, we have witnessed a paradox, with universities putting the blame for this increasing gap between indigenous and imported technologies on the lack of sponsorship and contributions from the private sector, while the private sector places the blame on universities for not developing new ideas and projects for sponsorship that would make a beneficial contribution to their fields or industries and thereby be worthy of sponsorship. This impasse is the combined result of Gulf private sectors not grasping the significance of scientific research, and research institutions not understanding the central role which marketability plays in the realm of funding. The contributions of the private sector to the scientific community therefore remain mainly cosmetic, comprising small amounts donated primarily for the purpose of PR.

Government support remained marginal as universities continued to face heavier intakes.[11] Increases in admissions without corresponding increases in government spending thus contributed to the weakening of university standards. This unpromising situation needed to be addressed with a new vision and new strategies in the Arab countries wherein science could play a significant role in their economies.

In a world where advancements in science are market-driven, scientific research is expanding.[12] In the developed countries, companies in the private sector – such as Dow Chemicals[13] and Eli Lilly[14] – make major contributions to scientific research in view of the potential profits generated from advances in fields such as biotechnology, health services, agriculture, computer sciences, information technology, pharmaceuticals, and tackling environmental issues such as biodegradation and bioremediation of wastes.

Research and development can make a major contribution to achieving economic growth, but new approaches must be adopted wherein the private sector and the scientific community come together in joint business ventures, with research being conducted in areas that will benefit the industrial and economic sectors. In the absence of fundamental research, science must adopt a business mentality, with the results of the research making a contribution that is beneficial to the private sector. Searches for sponsorship should also not be limited locally, as approaches for grants and sponsorship should also be made to international firms and organizations, and the significance of contributions from the petroleum industry and the private sector for funding research should not be overlooked.

Cooperation in the Fields of Science and Technology

The GCC countries have recognized the necessity of exploring alternative and renewable energies, and that the development of science and technology plays a crucial role in permanent and sustainable development. As such, the advancement of scientific and technological research is increasingly coming to the forefront of national and regional priorities.

> An understanding of the potential involved in the development of scientific research and technology has been an essential aspect of cooperation between the Gulf countries since the initial organization and founding of the GCC. The GCC Charter states that the basic objectives are to effect coordination, integration and inter-connection between Member States in all fields, strengthening ties between their peoples, formulating similar regulations in various fields such as economy, finance, trade, customs, tourism, legislation, administration, as well as fostering scientific and technical progress in industry, mining, agriculture, water and animal resources, establishing scientific research centres, setting up joint ventures, and encouraging cooperation of the private sector.[15]

The Economic Agreement of 1981 further stressed these efforts to foster cooperation in scientific research, as did the Economic Agreement of 2001. Chapter V, "Education," Article Fifteen, of the Economic Agreement of 2001 focused on the need for the GCC countries:

> ... to develop programs and curricula of public, higher, and technical education, to ensure high levels of scientific content and compatibility with [their] development needs ... to achieve integration between GCC universities in all fields ... [and to] adopt appropriate policies and mechanisms to ensure compatibility between the outputs of higher education and scientific and technical research on the one hand, and the needs of the labor market and economic development, on the other.[16]

As stated in Chapter VI, "Scientific and Technical Research," Article Eighteen, of the Economic Agreement of 2001:

> Member States shall adopt, as basic priorities for development, policies to support joint scientific and technical research, and develop their own joint scientific, technical, and information technology databases, including the adoption of the following policies:
>
> 1. Increase the funds allocated to scientific and technical research. Encourage and provide the necessary incentives to the private sector to contribute to the funding of specialized scientific and technical research.
>
> 2. Ensure that international companies operating in the GCC States sponsor specialized programs for scientific and technical research in the Member States.
>
> 3. Establish a native scientific, technical, and information technology base that fully utilizes the expertise of international and regional organizations.
>
> 4. Integrate scientific research institutions in the GCC States in order to develop and activate the scientific, technical, and information technology base referred to in this Economic Agreement and work jointly to set up common research centers.[17]

[315]

Article Nineteen of the Economic Agreement, "Utilization of the Scientific, Technical, and Information Technology Base," further states:

> For the purposes of developing and fully utilizing their scientific, technical, and information technology base, Member States shall take the following measures, as a minimum:
>
> 1. Develop mechanisms for achieving optimal utilization of scientific and technical research in both public and private sectors, and continued coordination between the executive bodies on the one hand and the outputs of the scientific, technical, and information technology base, on the other.
>
> 2. Make the outputs of the scientific, technical, and information technology base available to specialists, researchers, businessmen, and investors through simplified procedures.
>
> 3. Support and develop technical information networks, systems and centers in member states, and adopt programs to facilitate information dissemination and exchange among the institutions of scientific and technical research in the GCC States.[18]

In order to assist in meeting these objectives, a committee was formed to coordinate and promote cooperation between the GCC countries in the various fields of scientific and technical research, to develop policies and programs of scientific and technical research, and to propose areas where scientific and technological collaboration can be achieved.

Universities and research institutes should play a primary role in fostering comprehensive and sustainable development in the GCC. The committee's goal is to establish and enhance partnerships and cooperation between scientific research institutions and industry.

An initiative that is gaining popularity is the possible development of a peaceful, civil nuclear program in the GCC. Some of the countries of the GCC have signed bilateral agreements with the United States on nuclear energy cooperation and the enhancement of the use of nuclear technology for peaceful purposes, providing a new avenue for the development of renewable energy policies.

In addition to energy traditionally supplied by the oil and gas industry, nuclear energy would provide a further source of power, thus supporting the pursuit of economic sustainability and energy security. More diversified sources of energy can contribute to a reduction in the rate of depletion of oil and natural gas reserves, thereby prolonging their production periods and helping to preserve these non-renewable resources for future generations.

The possibility of utilizing nuclear energy for such tasks as electrical power generation and water desalination has many advantages. One such incentive is its utility in helping to reduce emissions of carbon dioxide (CO_2), one of the gases that contributes to the greenhouse effect and the phenomenon of global warming. Although there have been accidents involving nuclear reactors in the past, leading to high levels of public awareness and concerns over safety issues, the extremely high standards of modern safety measures and performance in the nuclear energy field have gone a long way towards abating public concern about the construction and maintenance of nuclear reactors. Moreover, it is the capital costs of the construction of nuclear reactors that constitute the primary costs of utilizing nuclear energy; this means that nuclear energy is to some extent protected from the constant price fluctuations that characterize the oil and gas industries.

In 2006, the Supreme Council of the GCC, taking its first steps towards the realization of a nuclear program, agreed a proposal for a preliminary feasibility study of the various uses of nuclear energy for peaceful purposes in line with international standards, to be conducted by the International Atomic Energy Agency (IAEA) and focusing on the use of nuclear energy for power generation and water desalination. This would be followed up by a more detailed study and implementation work program.

The preliminary feasibility study concluded that the use of nuclear energy for power generation and water desalination in the GCC would be one of the most cost-effective options available. The study further included general directives on the methods, steps and procedures for developing a joint nuclear energy program, including the legal and legislative aspects, the institutional infrastructures, security controls, and nuclear and radioactive safety controls.

In 2007, motivated primarily by the increase in oil demand and soaring oil prices, the GCC countries began to invest heavily in expansion projects in the petroleum-based industries, increasing their refining capacities, developing large-scale expansion projects, and announcing their intention to invest as much as $500 billion in these projects in the 2007–2012 period. Following the economic crisis of 2008, more than 30 percent of these projects have been put on hold.[19]

Universities Offering Energy Programs

The GCC hosts a number of universities and institutes that specialize in programs designed to serve energy security by promoting advances in petroleum production through increased efficiency to prolong the life of petroleum reserves.

A prominent example is the Kuwait Institute for Scientific Research (KISR). KISR's Petroleum Resources Program focuses on research and development to improve cost-effectiveness and efficiency within the field of petroleum production, providing technical support for the production of clean fuels, examining environment-related issues in petroleum refining such as disposal of spent catalysts, and developing novel technologies such as nanotechnology and using petroleum derivatives for fuel cells.

Another example is the King Fahd University of Petroleum and Minerals (KFUPM) in Saudi Arabia, which emphasizes research on petroleum production engineering and reservoir engineering, aimed at preparing contingencies for potential future problems resulting from situations such as lack of pressure in reservoirs and extraction from reservoirs in their secondary, enhanced, or tertiary oil recovery stages.

Also in Saudi Arabia, Aramco has recently established a Biotechnology Research Department dedicated to studying ways to upgrade the quality of fossil fuels, with emphasis on the processes of biodesulfurization.

In the United Arab Emirates, the Petroleum Institute is conducting research projects to develop improvements in the efficiency of the petroleum production industry, and in Oman the Sultan Qaboos University is conducting research aimed at providing solutions to industrial problems faced by the petrochemical industry, with specializations including petroleum and natural gas engineering, chemical and process engineering, and mining and mineral economics. A further, prominent example of the efforts being made to promote energy efficiency is the research being conducted by the Biotechnology Department at the Arabian Gulf University in Bahrain, where environmental biotechnology has focused on issues such as biodesulfurization, biodenitrogenation, biodegradation and bioremediation of fossil fuels and their derivatives.

Exemplary Initiatives in the GCC

Although renewable energy currently constitutes only a very small proportion of the total energy resources of the GCC, a recognition of the need for renewable energy and energy security has recently led to a series of long-term strategies throughout the GCC countries aimed at increasing production while becoming 'greener.'

There are a few examples of exemplary initiatives that have already been taken in the GCC in its attempts to deal with the issues of energy security. One of the most ambitious and significant is the Masdar initiative launched by the Abu Dhabi Future Energy Company (ADFEC) in the United Arab Emirates to serve as an open platform for global discussions on issues such as energy security, renewable energy, sustainable development, and climate change. This initiative consists of a number of projects designed to encourage energy efficiency and innovation, and seeks to establish the UAE as a technology innovator rather than predominantly an importer of technology. Such projects will add to economic diversity by establishing a new economic sector revolving around new knowledge-based industries.

A major component of this initiative is the development of Masdar City, which aims to become the "first carbon-neutral city in the world ... characterized by emission free energy supplies, mainly from solar power, modern ecological architecture with a good passive energy balance and high energy-efficiency, extensive recycling of waste and a modern system of public transport,"[20] designed to reduce carbon footprints while, at the same time, meeting increasing energy needs. This is a significant step forward as all the GCC countries are listed among the top 25 countries with the highest CO_2 emissions per capita, and energy conservation can be said to be one of the most significant energy issues. An additional goal is an 80 percent reduction in the consumption of desalinated water through re-purification techniques and irrigation projects which use wastewater.

The stated target of Masdar City is to provide housing for 50,000 inhabitants in close proximity to their educational institutions and workplaces. This project is expected to be completed by 2013, with people moving into the city as early as 2010.

Another primary component of this initiative is the Masdar Institute of Science and Technology (MIST), a higher education institute established in alliance with the Massachusetts Institute of Technology (MIT). The goal of this institute is to provide an environment for innovation and the development of renewable energy technologies, thereby transforming the UAE into a developer and producer of new technologies. Finally, Masdar is also developing the Shams 1 Plant, a solar power plant designed to harness the energy of the sun.

Also in the United Arab Emirates, the Gulf Research Center (GRC), in association with the Institute of Communications and Computer Systems of the National Technical University of Athens (ICCS-NTUA), is set to begin work on establishing the EU–GCC Clean Energy Network, aimed at creating a permanent network to develop and coordinate cooperation between the European Union and the GCC countries to promote clean energy. This network will bring together universities and research institutions, as well as governments and the private sector, to work on issues promoting clean energy.[21]

Further examples are the research programs developed at the King Abdullah University of Science and Technology (KAUST) in Saudi Arabia, with close ties to the global research community. Its areas of focus for research include: resources, energy, environment, biosciences, and bioengineering. Adopting methods that include interdisciplinary and problem-driven research in its postgraduate programs, KAUST provides research opportunities in energy sources, systems and uses, water and coastal zone resources, and environmental quality and improvement.

KAUST has also established a number of different research centers that focus on specific fields in its search for alternative energies, renewables, and energy security. These include the Solar and Alternative Energy Science and Engineering Research Center, the Clean Combustion Research Center, the Catalysis Research Center, and the Water Desalination Research Center.

The focus of its Solar and Alternative Energy Science and Engineering Research Center is on innovation and making concrete contributions to the development of new technologies in the fields of renewable energy sciences and engineering. Its mission includes spreading community awareness of the benefits of alternative energies, and it runs an outreach plan aimed at contributing to student education through programs providing entrepreneurship and hands-on training in the field of renewable energies.

Its research areas focus primarily on the development of solar energy technologies and developing efficient and cost effective solar cells, and will incorporate areas such as wind energy, energy storage, and geothermal energy.

Table 11.6
Energy Research Centers in the GCC

COUNTRY	RESEARCH CENTERS	WEBSITE
Saudi Arabia	King Fahd University of Petroleum and Minerals Research Institute	(http://www.kfupm.edu.sa/RI/cpm/petroleum.html)
	King Abdullah University of Science and Technology (KAUST) - Solar and Alternative Energy Science and Engineering Research Center	(http://www.kaust.edu.sa/research/centers/solar.html)
Kuwait	KISR - Petroleum Research & Studies Center	(http://www1.kisr.edu.kw/divisions_petro_mission.asp)
UAE	The Petroleum Institute, Engineering, Education and Research	(http://www.pi.ac.ae/PI_ACA/pe/research/res_projects.php)
	Gulf Research Center	(http://www.grc.ae/index.php?CAT_ID=11&Cat_Title=Gulf+Energy+Program&frm_module=&override=Gulf+Energy+Program%20Research%20Program&sec=Research+Programs&sec_type=h&set_lang=en)
Oman	Petroleum Development Oman	(http://www.oilandgasdirectory.com/ogd/pages/cps/ads/petroleumdev.html)
	Sultan Qaboos University - Oil and Gas Research Center	(http://squ.edu.om/Default.aspx?alias=squ.edu.om/ogrc)
	Department of Petroleum and Chemical Engineering – Sultan Qaboos University	(http://www.squ.edu.om/tabid/2651/language/en-US/Default.aspx)

A further example is the Qatar Foundation, which will organize its research goals around its core platforms of medicine, biotechnology, environmental sciences, information and communication technologies, molecular sciences, and nanotechnology.

Other initiatives in the region include Saudi plans for the development of waste-to-energy plants designed to convert hazardous wastes into electricity, a Dubai Electricity and Water Authority study on the possibility of creating a $1 billion wind farm capable of supplying 10 percent of Dubai's electricity demand,[22] the Mediterranean Solar Plan focusing on investment in renewable energies and green technology,[23] the World Trade Center in Bahrain incorporating three built-in wind turbines designed to produce 15 percent of its own energy requirements, and the Lighthouse Tower in the Dubai International Financial Center (DIFC) which is designed to cut its own conventional energy consumption by 65 percent through the use of wind and solar energy. Finally, the development of a 750 megawatt wind farm and a large-scale solar plant are being considered as possible projects in the Sultanate of Oman.

Science Parks and Entrepreneurship

As previously stated, the universities in the GCC face a number of challenges and problems, some chronic and endemic to universities all over the world, and some influenced by events in the global arena. Globalization, competitiveness, changing economies, privatization of higher education, high rates of unemployment, limited resources and funding, and the inevitable market pressures of supply and demand of skilled graduates are just some of the forces presenting new challenges to higher education.

In the current global arena, science and technology are emerging as the keys to economic growth, creating significant contributions to national competitiveness. In terms of its contribution, the Arab world was bypassed by the Industrial Revolution, and missed out again in contributing to the emergence of economies based upon information technology. It is on the edge of missing the third major global economic revolution, the wave of advancements in biological sciences and the combination of biological sciences with technological innovation and information technology.

[323]

One of the mechanisms through which the GCC countries could contribute to the knowledge-based economic revolution is through the development of science parks and science incubators dedicated to energy, which can serve as links between universities, research centers, oil and gas companies, and industries. Science parks and science incubators are proving to be some of the most effective means of promoting scientific and technological innovation, accelerating university/industry synergies and promoting the commercialization of innovation in numerous developed countries. Combining scientific research with economic development, science parks not only promote research and development through the involvement of financing from private companies, but also facilitate the methods through which universities and their faculties and staff expedite economic development by means of their intellectual property.

Science parks and science incubators, and the universities associated with them, provide a comprehensive approach to the commercialization of energy technology, with the core groups of technology transfer, innovation and entrepreneurship, business incubation, corporate business development, and venture capital investments, all working together.

Furthermore, as universities strive to position themselves nationally, regionally, and globally, it is becoming necessary to be part of a network with other universities, research centers, or research and development departments of industries to create alliances (national, regional, and international) of excellence and strengthen the position and reach of participating institutes.

Science parks have become a means through which efforts are being made to bring together industry, universities, and the governments of the GCC with a desire to take a leading role in the development of new technologies.

The Qatar Petroleum Research and Technology Center in the Qatar Science and Technology Park, a research center supported by Qatar Petroleum, represents a step towards collaborative research among industry, research institutes, international organizations and the government, and aims to develop and apply cutting-edge technologies in the fields of oil and gas production whilst also finding innovative solutions to environmental and operational problems. Its focus will include environmental issues such as environmental protection regulations, conservation of natural resources, sustainable development, energy efficiency and management, and optimization of oil and gas reserves.[24]

The newly opened King Abdulla City for Science and Technology in Saudi Arabia is another prime example. This $10 billion project is set to lead science and technology research in the Arab world. The development of advanced sciences and technologies in the fields of energy and the environment is one of its primary aims. It has recruited scientists with considerable expertise from all over the world to constitute its work force, and offers scholarships to students for scientific research. This city will set new benchmarks for the development of science and technology in the Arab world.

Financing Scientific Research in the GCC

In 2004, the Kuwait Petroleum Corporation (KPC) pledged $100 million to fund research on the environmentally-friendly use of fossil fuels through the use of fuel cell technology, carbon sequestration, and oil gasification. In 2007, the GCC pledged $750 million to fund research on clean energy technologies, focusing on carbon capture and storage (CCS) in its efforts to fight global warming.

In its various projects within the Masdar initiative, the UAE has earmarked billions of dollars for investment. This includes a $22 billion investment in the development of Masdar City, although part of this investment will constitute real estate and construction investment—albeit with energy-efficient designs and architecture aimed at carbon reduction and management. Another $1.5 million will be given annually in the form of the Zayed Future Energy Prize, an annual international prize to be awarded as encouragement for development and innovation in the areas of sustainable development and clean energy. A budget of a further $15 billion has been established for various projects promoting renewable energy. The development of a $500 million solar power plant is also under consideration, as is the possibility of building a $100 million hydrogen-fueled power plant.

The Masdar initiative thereby constitutes an investment of $37 billion, with the possibility of another $600 million if the power plant projects should become a reality, in addition to the annual $1.5 million for the Zayed Future Energy Prize.[25]

The Qatar Petroleum Research and Technology Center represents a $75 million investment over its first five years of operation.[26]

Statistics from the Emirates Energy Award state that it is expected that between $160–200 billion will be invested in the GCC over the coming years to support the development of renewable energy resources, including projects focusing on wind, solar, and hydrogen technology.

New Trends in Scientific Research on Fossil Fuels

Extensive world consumption of fossil fuels has led to long-lasting and profound impacts on the environment and human health, the most prominent of which are global warming, air pollution from hazardous emissions, and soil and water contamination with petroleum hydrocarbons released into the environment through accidental oil spills and from refineries. Moreover, the increased dependence of modern societies on fossil fuels has lead to the depletion of light crude oil reserves and the accumulation of heavy crude petroleum resources which contain more impurities and hazardous hydrocarbons. Consequently, the inevitable use of transportation fuels (diesel and gasoline) derived from heavy oils will burden the environment with even more pollutants. Environmental pollution has become so worrisome that international governmental and environmental authorities have mandated stringent regulations that limit the amounts of certain impurities, such as sulfur, in transportation fuels. Unfortunately, the conventional scenarios employed for environmental remediation and petroleum upgrading are costly, not completely efficient, and are polluting. Therefore, there has been growing interest in novel sustainable technologies that can be used to clean up the environment, and which can be applied in the production of alternative clean energy to minimize dependence on fossil fuels.

Biotechnology provides promising approaches towards environmental reclamation and production of bioenergy from renewable resources. In contrast to conventional techniques, bioprocesses are environmentally friendly, more efficient, and cost effective. Bioprocesses are carbon-neutral, i.e., they produce no CO_2 emissions. An integrated biotechnology-based approach can tackle environmental pollution issues via three different channels: (1) bioremediation of polluted environments using microorganisms as biocatalysts; (2) use of waste and environmental pollutants, as well as biomass, for the production of green bioenergy by dedicated microorganisms— bioenergy can be in the form of biofuel (bioethanol, biohydrogen, biodiesel) and bioelectricity; and (3) development of biorefining technology for upgrading crude oil, which should replace or complement conventional upgrading strategy to reduce the level of some undesirable components of crude oil such as sulfur, nitrogen, metals and asphaltenes.[27]

Scientific endeavors in energy should involve various fields, including petroleum biotechnology such as biological upgrading (biorefining) of crude oils, biocatalysis of petroleum products, biocorrosion problems, as well as bioremediation of crude oil-contaminated environments. The overall aim is to develop efficient biocatalysts that can be applied in environmental clean-ups as well as the removal of sulfur, nitrogen and metals from crude oil and transportation fuels such as diesel and gasoline. Such endeavors are essential for the production of ultra-low sulfur fossil fuel that complies with governmental and environmental regulations. They can also tackle the issue of upgrading heavy crude oils and the transformation of low-value oils and refinery residues into high-value fuels and petrochemicals; and can incorporate research in the area of production of bio-energy from renewable resources, namely bio-energy using microorganisms. This line of research will target the development of a wastewater treatment approach coupled with bio-energy production.

Concerns about fossil fuel reserves, the impact of industry on the environment, increasing domestic demands for energy consumption, and favorable conditions for the production of energy alternatives such as wind and solar power are all factors supporting the development of renewable and alternative energy resources in the GCC. The development of such resources will also help to expand the life of oil and gas reserves in the GCC. The search for renewable and alternative resources is therefore not a luxury, but a necessity for the GCC. Although this necessity has yet to be manifested in a succinct policy strategy for energy efficiency across the GCC, there have been numerous individual projects that offer great promise and potential. These, in turn, may provide the basis leading to the development of legislation for long-term energy security, such as the green building code adopted in Dubai.

Numerous efforts can still be made to further the development of energy security in the GCC. These include initiating postgraduate programs and research dedicated to issues of energy, legislation, sources, financing new scientific research to increase the efficiency of fossil fuels, use of renewable energies, biofuels, solar energy, wind technology, and nuclear for peaceful purposes, and universities and research centers should have entrepreneurship arrangements and infrastructure for initiating scientific breakthroughs.

Ultimately, only a combination of all these various methods for establishing energy security – whatever the options and scenarios – including the development of new technologies within the GCC rather than purchasing technology, can lead to long-lasting energy security.

Conclusion

In an area that collectively possesses more than two-fifths of global oil reserves and constitutes as much as one-fifth of total global production, the past investments made in the development of science and technology have not been proportional to their significance to the economy. However, numerous initiatives have been launched recently to strengthen the role of universities and research centers, and to overcome the obstacles to technology transfer in the areas of short-term energy security, including research on petroleum, natural gas, nuclear power, renewable energies such as biofuels, bioelectricity, solar energy, and wind power, and on long-term energy security, including reducing dependence on any one source, increasing the number of suppliers, better exploiting native fossil fuels or renewable energies, and energy conservation via a reduction in overall demand.

The essence of this paper has been to review the progress of science and technology – prerequisites for energy security in the GCC – alongside the development of universities and research centers offering dedicated energy-related programs and specializations. It is evident that the region needs more graduate programs focused on the different aspects of energy, particularly in terms of capacity-building and scientific advancement. The region has been depending on the purchase of technologies that are vital to its survival, which has made it dependent upon others for the security of its primary source of income.

The GCC should devise strategies for the future that involve diversification of income and confront dependence on fossil fuels, as GCC governments have been realizing through their various initiatives.

[329]

These strategies should be planned and carried out to ensure both short-term and long-term energy security, and the development of new technologies should be combined with innovative government policies, in cooperation with universities and research institutes in the region, to incorporate this strategic planning in an effort to ensure energy security in the GCC.

These strategies should link the industries themselves with research centers and institutes of higher education in order to economically harvest scientific achievements from the energy sector. The initiatives that GCC governments have implemented in recent years in terms of the establishment of highly-reputable universities and research centers dedicated to energy are very promising and constitute a turning point in the region's contribution to its energy security.

Clean Energy Perspectives in the Gulf: The Role of Carbon Capture and Storage (CCS)

Sa'ad Al Jandal

Fossil fuels currently dominate most aspects of social and economic activity, and will continue to account for about 85 percent of the world's energy supply. Most techno-economical outlooks imply that fossil fuels will continue to be the prime source of energy and shall remain critical to meeting energy security needs well into the 21st century. World demand projections indicate that fossil fuels will supply about 81 percent of energy needs by 2030 and 64 percent by 2050. In absolute terms, these projections are driven by increases in power generation and end-use consumption.

However, the combustion of fossil fuels produces greenhouse gas (GHG) emissions, widely acknowledged as the main cause of climate change. The reduction of adverse environmental impacts requires mitigating the contribution of fossil fuel carbon emissions – to a large extent carbon dioxide (CO_2) – to global warming. The combustion of fossil fuels accounts for about 60–90 percent of current net anthropogenic emissions of CO_2.[1]

It is noted that the only realistic long-term approach for reducing GHG emissions, assuming that energy use will continue to grow, is to separate energy use and CO_2 release. This can be done by moving to cleaner and low carbon-energy sources such as renewables, hydro, geothermal and nuclear energy. However, currently available low carbon-energy sources and technologies do not comprise a full substitute to fossil fuels, particularly given the abundant ways in which such fuels are made available and used, and the current economic framework for energy.

The result is that fossil fuel-dependent energy infrastructure is currently being planned that will continue to increase atmospheric CO_2 levels for many years to come. It has been estimated that the lifetime emissions from power plants projected to be built for the next 25 years are equivalent to all emissions for the last 250 years.[2]

There is a variety of methods with which to reduce carbon emissions, ranging from the enhancement of energy efficiency processes, switching to low carbon fuel mixtures and the replacement of fossil-based energy production by zero-carbon technologies.

An alternative possibility, however, is that fossil fuels can continue to form the basis of energy infrastructure, but that CO_2 can be eliminated by 'capture' from the emission point sources and stored away from the atmosphere for very long periods, or transported and then used in certain other applications. The atmosphere has been a convenient repository for such waste, but there is no justifiable technical reason why this should continue. Other parts of the Earth – namely geological formations and vast oceans – can be used to deposit CO_2 and many industries such as oil exploration can make use of it for enhancing production.[3]

The hypothetical approach is to capture and remove ambient air CO_2 from large point sources, such as industrial processes and power generation plants. On a broad scale, capturing CO_2 is indirectly performed in nature by photosynthesis and the formation of mineral carbonates, but the rates of CO_2 capture by natural processes are currently exceeded by the rates at which biomass and fossil fuels are producing CO_2, resulting in a net increase in the CO_2 concentration in the atmosphere. Industrial processes on a large-scale are required to supplement natural processes for capturing CO_2 from the atmosphere if the global carbon cycle is to be brought back into balance.[4]

Kyoto and subsequent agreements are attracting much attention. Kyoto in itself is not significant as regards the actual impact on global warming or even on the future course of oil demand. Subsequent meetings culminating with Marrakech have turned Kyoto from a principle into actual commitments. The target for 2012, however, was brought down from a 5.2 percent reduction of emissions from 1990s levels to a 1.7 percent reduction. Furthermore, attempts to persuade the United States to ratify have failed, while the European countries have made commitments to lower CO_2 emissions by up to 8 percent because they realize the hazard posed by global warming.

Reducing anthropogenic CO_2 emissions is still a necessity. There are several options that may contribute partially and progressively to this aim:

- Energy saving by collective and individual efforts means a major change in our actual way of living and acting. Housing, transport and industry hide large energy saving potential. Ecological conception of products may contribute to those savings.

- Switching to less carbon intensive energy sources is already advancing (natural gas, for instance, reduces CO_2 emissions by 40 percent compared to coal). Only nuclear energy is CO_2 free—but it is a controversial technique. Other renewable energy sources – wind, solar, hydro and biomass – may be used more intensively in the future, but are not yet 'operational' and competitive. The United States and the European Union (EU) are pursuing the objective of producing roughly 20 percent of their energy from 'clean' sources by 2010.

- In the realm of transport, 'clean' or bio-fuel (vegetable oils, wheat … etc.) and less energy-consuming engines will contribute; several programs to develop and reinforce these techniques exist in Europe and around the world. In 1997, a car emitted about 190 grams of CO_2 per kilometer. The European automobile constructors will attempt to reduce this quantity to 120 grams per kilometer by 2012. The development and the potential industrial deployment of the hydrogen fuel cell is another option.

Still, this may not be enough to meet the United Nations Framework Convention on Climate Change (UNFCCC) and the Kyoto Protocol objectives and satisfy the growing demand for energy. Energy production in power plants is one of the most important CO_2-producing human activities (contributing about 40 percent, i.e. over 7 billion tons of CO_2 per year). It seems impossible to reach the objective of 'zero CO_2 emissions,' as fossil fuels are still needed. Therefore, action must be taken to deal with the CO_2 released. One option which can contribute to this is reforestation: forests constitute a natural CO_2 sink; however, it is impossible to reforest to the extent that would lead to the absorption of all the surplus CO_2 released into the atmosphere. Another, supplementary option is CO_2 capture, already widely used in certain industrial processes (use of natural gas, agricultural industry, petrol industry). The captured CO_2 could be compressed and stored, and will therefore not contribute to climate degradation.

Carbon Capture Technologies and Applications

The development of technology for the capture and storage of CO_2 could make a significant contribution towards the reduction of anthropogenic GHG emissions within a relatively short period. The general concept of Carbon Capture and Storage (CCS) comprises three main elements (see Figure 12.1).

Power plants are the largest point sources of CO_2 emissions and hence CO_2 capture from power plants can have a substantial impact on emissions reduction. CO_2 emissions from power production account for around 30 percent of all emissions. Large amounts of CO_2 are emitted in diluted streams of flue gases at atmospheric pressure, as the fuel is usually burned in air. Other major single point sources of diluted CO_2 are furnaces, industrial boilers and cement production plants. The emitted CO_2 is captured at the source. In order to simplify the ensuing steps of transport and storage a near pure CO_2 product at an absolute pressure of 100 bar needs to be produced by the capture process. Therefore, a compression process is also needed to achieve the right transport/storage conditions.

Figure 12.1
CO$_2$ Capture Process

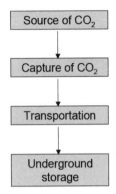

There are three basic methods for capturing CO$_2$ from such emission streams: pre-combustion; post-combustion; and oxy-fuel combustion.

- Pre-combustion reacts a primary fuel with air or oxygen and steam to produce hydrogen and carbon monoxide (CO) which can be further treated to produce more hydrogen (H$_2$) and CO$_2$ (15–60 percent by volume), which can then be separated. As indicated in Figure 12.2, the H$_2$ (synthesis gas) can be used for energy production, with water as a by-product; the CO$_2$ – at relatively high pressure and concentrations – is more amenable to be captured than would have been the case if the fuel were combusted as it is. This type of technology is used in Canada in four coal-fired integrated gasification combined cycle (IGCC) plants, although none captures the CO$_2$. The production of synthesis gas is relatively old technology but has been used in combination with pre-combustion capture only in specific circumstances. This capture option needs special installations and does not fit existing installations. Pre-combustion capture can be deployed today at full scale, giving large-scale operating plant by 2015.[5]

[335]

Figure 12.2
Pre-Combustion CO$_2$ Capture Process

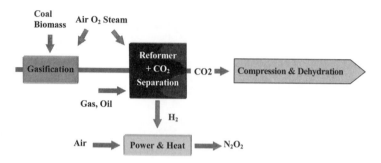

- Post-combustion processes, shown in Figure 12.3, generally use a recyclable solvent to trap CO$_2$ in the emission stream, though some projects are attempting to demonstrate biogenic capture through photosynthetic algae. Post-combustion capture has been used only in specific circumstances and has been proven on rigs of 0.25 up to 2 MW$_{th}$.[6] It is possible to use this option in existing plants without modifying the installation. CO$_2$ is captured by using a solvent or membrane, and then separated and compressed (ready for storage) and the solvent reinserted.

Figure 12.3
Post-Combustion CO$_2$ Capture Process

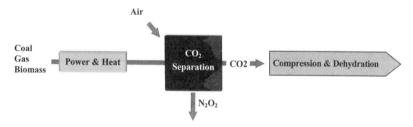

- Oxy-fuel combustion burns the primary fuel in almost pure oxygen to produce a very pure CO$_2$ stream which can then be compressed for storage purposes. This is not a true CO$_2$ capture technique, because the CO$_2$ is separated before the combustion. As indicated in Figure 12.4, this process requires an elaborate mechanism to purify the oxygen. In fact, using pure oxygen in the combustion process gives a 90 percent CO_2 concentration in smoke that is then retreated. Oxy-fuel technology is in the demonstration phase and has been proven to scale on rigs of 0.5 up to 1 MW_{th}.[7] In other cases, such as fertilizer production (ammonia), CO_2 is separated as part of the chemical process of producing the product. These latter types of operations already operate in a mature market, though once again not in combination with storage. This option is used in industry already (production of glass). It is particularly suited to retrofitting existing installations, but the separation process is highly energy consuming and expensive.

Figure 12.4

Oxy-fuel CO_2 Capture Process

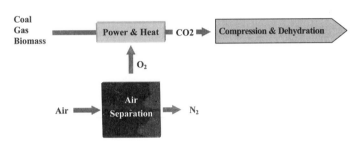

The Intergovernmental Panel on Climate Change (IPCC) has estimated that the increase in energy required to capture the CO_2 is between 10 percent and 40 percent, depending on the technology; the natural gas combined cycle requires the least and pulverized coal requires the most. Capturing CO_2 is the most energy-intensive phase (and therefore the largest contributor to CO_2 releases and costs of energy production)[8] in a complete CCS mechanism.

It should also be noted that since biofuels such as ethanol and biodiesel are derived from plant material that uses atmospheric CO_2, the capture and storage of CO_2 from the combustion of these fuels would actually remove CO_2 from the atmosphere.

Transportation of CO_2

Many point sources of captured CO_2 would not be close to geological or oceanic storage facilities. Therefore, a transport system is needed to link the CO_2 sources to the CO_2 storage sites. Because of the magnitude of the volumes of CO_2 produced by power plants, transport of the CO_2 is most likely to be by pipeline, apart from those routes where ships may be used. Feasibility studies have indicated that it is possible to adapt current tankers to carry significant volumes of CO_2. However, the implications of ship transport need to be considered both in terms of terminal storage and at the delivery site to determine compression needs. Trains and trucks are thought to be too small for projects of this size.

The transportation of natural gas and hydrocarbon liquids by pipeline relies on globally well-established technology which is widely used within countries' natural gas networks. Large scale movement of CO_2 by pipeline dates from the 1970s, when the potential for replacing the use of natural gas with CO_2 from natural CO_2 reservoirs in Enhanced Oil Recovery (EOR) applications was first recognized. However, pipelines would require a new regulatory regime to ensure that proper materials are used (CO_2 combined with water, for instance, is highly corrosive to some pipeline materials), all equipment is monitored for leaks, and health and safety measures are adequate. However, these are all technically possible, and pipelines in general currently operate in a mature market.

Storage of CO_2

Once processed, captured and compressed, CO_2 may be stored. Storage of CO_2 should be such that it remains isolated from the atmosphere for a suitably long period. Geological storage options combine a number of engineering processes after CO_2 capture, i.e., compression, transportation via pipelines or ships and injection into underground formations via wells. The storage of gases is a well-established oil industry process, with a history stretching back nearly a century. The increased interest in CCS in recent years has triggered a plethora of trials and demonstration projects of these options in a range of countries around the world. A variety of options exists for the storage of CO_2 in geologic formations. Of these, depleted oil and gas fields have been used for natural gas storage since the early 1900s, and are now widely used for this purpose globally. Other options range from using injected CO_2 for increasing underground pressure in oil fields to recover additional oil, i.e., EOR or enhanced gas recovery (EGR), to simply storing large volumes of CO_2 in depleted hydrocarbon fields.

Several storage options are available; most are geological storage options (alternative emerging solutions like mineralogical storage or storage via bacteria and micro-algae treatment are explored, but are far from being operational). Geological storage means injecting CO_2 in spaces offered by permeable and porous rocks deep under the ground. CO_2 must be injected deeper than 800 meters in order to reach the conditions of its supercritical state (above 31 degrees and 74 bar), where it is less dense and needs less space.

- The first geological storage option is deep saline aquifers. Deep saline aquifers exist all over the world, and could absorb the entire quantity of anthropogenic CO_2 emissions for centuries. The cost would be about $2.5–3.5 per ton (more expensive offshore). The Sleipner installation in the North Sea is an experimental pilot site which has operated since 1996.

- A second possibility is CO_2 injection into depleted gas or petroleum reservoirs. Industry has made use of CO_2 injection for EOR since the late 1950s. Well known research sites are Weyburn (Canada), or the K12B gas field in the North Sea (Holland). The injected CO_2 maintains the pressure in the reservoir, liquefies the oil and facilitates oil recovery. Depleted reservoirs could be used for CO_2 storage, allowing storage of about 1,000 billion tons of CO_2.

- Finally, CO_2 could be injected into non-exploited deep coal veins. There are several points which favor this option: the geographical repartition of those veins (all over the world, near to CO_2 emitting sites), and economical advantages by exploiting the by-product methane (as an energy source). There are disadvantages, too: coal is hardly permeable and does not permit rapid injection of CO_2, and the quantity of CO_2 potentially to be stored in coal veins is only in the region of 40 billion tons of CO_2. Other sites and experimental pilots do exist (Allison, New Mexico).

Table 12.1

Sites where CO_2 Storage is Implemented, in Progress or Planned

Project Name	Location Country	Injection Start (year)	Approximate Average Daily Injection Rate (tCO_2 day-1)	Total (planned) Storage (tCO_2)	Storage Reservoir Type
Weyburn	Canada	2000	3,000-5,000	20,000,000	EOR
In Salah	Algeria	2004	3,000-4,000	17,000,000	Gas field
Sleipner	Norway	1996	3,000	20,000,000	Saline formation
K12B	Netherlands	2004	100	8,000,000	EGR
Frio	U.S.A	2004	177	1600	Saline formation
Fenn Big Valley	Canada 1	1998	50	200	ECBM
Basin	China	2003	30	150	ECBM
Yubari	Japan	2004	10	200	ECBM
Recopol	Poland	2003	1	10	ECBM
Gorgon (planned)	Australia	~2009	10,000	unknown	Saline formation
Snøhvit (planned)	Norway	2006	2,000	unknown	Saline formation

Source: B. Metz, et al.; (IPCC, 2005).

Geological storage of CO_2 is ongoing in three industrial scale projects (projects in the order of 1 million tons of CO_2 [$MtCO_2$] per year or more): the Sleipner project in the North Sea, the Weyburn project in Canada and the In Salah project in Algeria. About 3–4 $MtCO_2$ that would, otherwise be released into the atmosphere is captured and stored annually in geological formations. Additional projects are listed in Table 12.1.

In addition to the CCS projects currently in place, 30 $MtCO_2$ is injected annually for EOR, mostly in Texas, where EOR commenced in the early 1970s. Most of this CO_2 is obtained from natural CO_2 reservoirs found in western regions of the United States, with some coming from anthropogenic sources such as natural gas processing. Much of the CO_2 injected for EOR is produced with the oil, from which it is separated and then re-injected. After use in oil recovery, the CO_2 can be retained for the purpose of climate change mitigation, rather than vented to the atmosphere. This is planned for the Weyburn project in Canada.

Storage sites will presumably be designed to confine all injected CO_2 for long time scales. Nevertheless, experience with engineered systems suggests a small fraction of operational storage sites may form leaks. Gradual release of CO_2 merely returns some of the greenhouse gas to the air. Rapid escape of large amounts, on the other hand, could have more severe consequences than not storing it at all. Although CO_2 is usually harmless, a large, rapid release of the gas is worrisome because high concentrations can kill.

Such an occurrence would likely involve CO_2 contact with drinking water aquifers. Depending on the mineral composition of the rock matrix within the groundwater aquifer zone, the reaction of CO_2 with the rock matrix could release contaminants. A leakage could be caused by the following:

- Through openings in the cap rock or fractures from abandoned wells caused by material and cement degradation or other faults.

- Through anthropomorphic pathways, such as poorly completed and/or abandoned pre-existing wells.

- Through the pore system in low-permeability cap rocks such as shales, if the capillary injection entry pressure at which CO_2 may enter the cap rock is exceeded.

No existing studies systematically estimate the probability and magnitude of release across a sample of credible geological storage systems. However, some risk-assessment and -management geological studies suggest that CO_2 storage and leakage problems are key technical barriers to the adoption of CCS technology and could still defeat the climate goals of sequestration and storage.

Carbon Dioxide (CO_2) Capture Technology and Options for Fossil Fuel Power Plants

CO_2 capture technology already exists for all of the referenced capturing processes, although in most cases it has not been developed specifically for that purpose. Furthermore, the application of CO_2 capture systems will not be limited to new plants. For instance, the vast majority of present-day coal-fired capacity is based on existing pulverized fuel (PF)-fired stations. As these existing power stations become old, decisions must be reached on whether there is sufficient incentive to retrofit such plants with CO_2 capture systems, or to upgrade or replace them with newer forms of technology. In all cases, the flue gas stream being treated from a fossil fuel-fired plant comprises diluted CO_2 of various concentrations depending on the particular technology (see Table 12.2). In order to capture it, the CO_2 must therefore be separated from the flue gas.

[342]

Table 12.2
CO_2 Content in Flue Gas

Power Plant Technology	Typical CO_2 Content (vol. % dry)
Pulverized fuel-fired stations (PF) (with SO_2 cleanup)	14
Integrated gasification combined cycle (IGCC) plants	7
Natural gas combined cycle (NGCC)	4
Oil-fired (OF) plants	12

Source: Estimates from IEA GHG R&D Program published by IEA working party on fossil fuels CO_2 "Capture at Power Stations and other Major Point Sources: Zero Emissions Technologies for Fossil Fuels," (2003), p. 8.

In PF power stations (already including flue gas desulphurization [FGD] technology), adding or retrofitting a CO_2 capture technology system would be relatively expensive. According to the IEA Greenhouse Gas R&D Program,[9] with circulating fluidized bed combustion (CFBC) technology, capture systems in the form of amine-based scrubbers are presently being used successfully in several relatively low-capacity plants in the United States (e.g. at the 320 MWe Shady Point and the 180 MWe Warrior Run plants). Likewise, at least one gas-fired plant in the United States of similar capacity (at the 320 MWe Bellingham Cogeneration Facility) is also using an amine scrubber to capture CO_2 produced. If natural gas combined cycles are involved, retrofitting of a suitable system would also be expensive.

Thus far, there are only a small number of coal-fired IGCC plants in commercial operation, even though this form of technology is acknowledged as the most efficient and cleanest coal-based power generation technology. Up to now, estimated costs are comparatively low for the addition of a suitable carbon capture system, especially where the gasifier is oxygen-blown. Where air-blowing is used, costs for CO_2 capture would be greater.

CO_2 capture options are employed in fossil fuel-fired power plants that produce a variety of pollutants that need to be controlled and

[343]

minimized (see Table 12.3). These include SO_2, often controlled through the application of a variety of commercially available FGD systems. The nitrogen oxides (NOx) produced can be controlled through fuel and air staging, the use of special low-NOx burners, or through downstream control measures such as selective catalytic reduction (SCR) or selective non-catalytic reduction (SNCR). The presence of gaseous substances such as these, and their concentration compared with CO_2, have an impact on the viability of the CO_2 capture process in question. For instance, the presence of both SO_2 and/or NOx in the flue gas can have damaging effects on some chemical scrubber-based systems. Careful consideration of such issues is therefore required when the application of a particular system is being considered.

Table 12.3
Emissions from a Typical PF-fired Power Plant

Species	Amount emitted (kg/MWh)	Examples of control technology applied
CO_2	830	Amine scrubbers
SO_2	0.6	Staging, low-NO_x burners, SCR, SNCR
$NO + NO_x$	2.16	Wet and dry FGD processes
Particulates	0.1	Electrostatic precipitators, bag filters, cyclones, hot gas cleanup systems

Source: Estimates from IEA GHG R&D Program, op. cit., 2003, p. 8.

Potentially, a variety of approaches could be applied to flue gas from fossil fuel-fired power plants. CO_2 capture systems that are possible candidates are described below.

Scrubbing Systems

These are well established and are usually based on the use of amines (often monoethanolamine [MEA]), scrubbing systems use a solvent for removing CO_2 from exhaust gases. Typically, prior to the CO_2 removal stage, the flue gas is cooled, treated to reduce the levels of particulates and other impurities present, then passed into an absorption tower where it is brought into contact with the absorption solution. The amine solvent selectively absorbs the CO_2 by chemically reacting with it to form a loosely bound compound. The CO_2-rich absorbent is then pumped into a desorber (stripper tower) where the pressure is reduced and/or the temperature increased to roughly 120°C in order to release the CO_2. As the released CO_2 is compressed, the regenerated absorbent is recycled to the stripper in a fully continuous process.

Systems of this type were typically developed originally for the chemical and oil industries and can achieve a CO_2 recovery rate of up to 98 percent, with a purity of more than 99 percent. At present, only a small number of coal and gas-fired power plants in operation use amine scrubbers for CO_2 capture. Recently, more advanced amines have been developed and are starting to be applied. These are claimed to reduce solvent loss and degradation and to reduce plant operating costs.

However, scrubber-based systems require substantial capital and equipment; in addition, overall plant efficiency suffers. Where more concentrated CO_2 streams are encountered and/or higher process operating pressures are in use (as with IGCC systems and some industrial activities), scrubbing systems based on a number of proprietary physical solvent-based technologies can be applied. These include the Selexol, Rectisol and Fluor solvent processes. Solvents used include methanol, polyethylene glycol dimethylether and propylene carbonate.

Membranes

Membranes can be deployed to separate gases by exploiting differences in physical or chemical interactions between gases and the membrane material. The differences allow one component to pass more quickly through the membrane. A variety of separation membranes are in use or being developed. In general, only a modest degree of separation can be achieved, while systems are likely to be relatively complex and energy consumption may be more insensitive.

[345]

Cryogenics

CO_2 can be separated from other gaseous compounds through cooling and condensation. The main application of this method is the purification of gas streams that contain a high percentage of CO_2 (over some 90 percent), and the technology is not at present applied to more dilute CO_2 streams such as those encountered with a typical power generation plant. One drawback is that the process requires a significant amount of energy, as well as the elimination of water from the gas stream.

Adsorption

CO_2 can be separated from gas mixtures using some solids. These include certain zeolites and activated carbon. Pressure and temperature swing adsorption (PTSA) is among the most common techniques used in this operation, although it is not yet considered to be attractive for power plant application because the capacity and CO_2 selectivity of adsorbents is generally low.

In practice, the most widely adopted form of technology presently used for CO_2 capture from power generation plants and other industrial processing is the scrubber based system.

Carbon Dioxide (CO_2) for Enhanced Hydrocarbon Recovery Process

Enhanced hydrocarbon recovery (EHR) is a generic term used to describe a range of techniques that allow more oil or gas to be recovered from a reservoir than would otherwise be possible. Enhanced oil recovery (EOR) can be regarded as established in the United States, but less so in the EU. It is generally more effective than enhanced gas recovery (EGR). Another option is enhanced coal bed methane recovery, an option under active consideration in Belgium and Poland. In order to focus on the key issues using a straightforward case, however, the remainder of this paper addresses EOR.

CO_2 is one of a number of injection substances that is used for EOR but is generally held to be the most effective. As shown in Figure 12.5, when CO_2 is injected into an oil-saturated geological reservoir formation (an operational or abandoned oil field) during EOR, some of it remains permanently trapped in the reservoir and some of it associates with the oil or gas and is recovered to the surface facilities as part of the petroleum production process. The recovered CO_2 is separated from the petroleum in enclosed conditions in a pressure vessel and is normally recompressed and returned to the oil reservoir. The quantity of CO_2 used is typically substantially larger in terms of mass than the increment in oil produced.

Figure 12.5
Enhanced Hydrocarbon Recovery (EHR) with CO_2

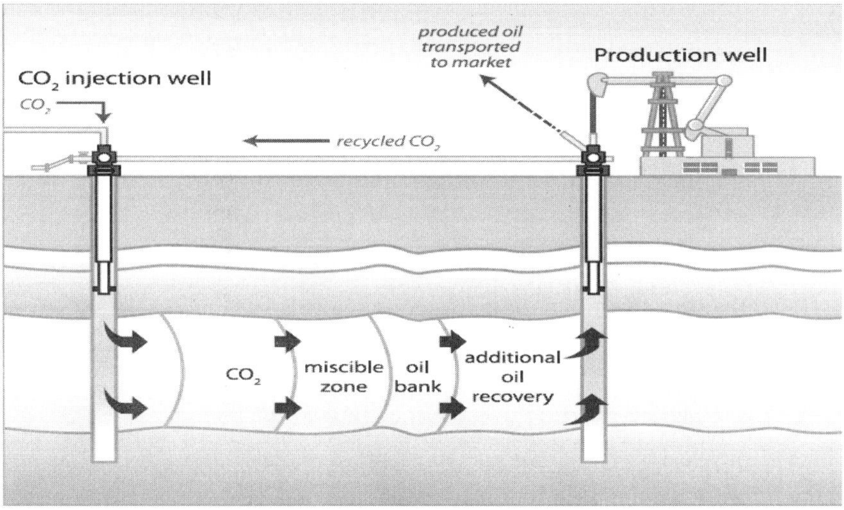

Source: B. Metz, et al., op. cit.

This process would accomplish permanent storage of CO_2 provided that the site and reservoir in question are selected on the basis of suitability for permanent CO_2 storage, and if the appropriate regulatory framework for permanent storage is fully complied with. Most oil field reservoirs by their very nature provide appropriate conditions for such permanent sequestration

[347]

of CO_2. Provided that the CCS directive conditions described by the EU apply, the storage of carbon dioxide through EHR is as permanent as that of an exclusive storage activity.

The Economics of CCS Combined with EHR

CCS is not currently economically viable even when stored CO_2 is counted as abated. Current industry estimates range from US\$30/ton to \$65/ton of CO_2 abated among the different technologies and are very dependent on the assumptions made about the prevailing fuel costs. With the price of CO_2 around \$20 under some European Directives, there is currently no incentive for emitting installations to capture their CO_2. Furthermore, taking into account the cost of transport and storage leads many experts believe that the CO_2 price is unlikely to be high enough before 2020 to warrant CCS projects without public funding.[10]

CO_2-EOR is also not currently economically viable in Europe. This is in part because there are no natural sources of CO_2 in northern Europe that are large enough to enable EOR to take place on a commercial scale offshore. This means that no offshore oilfields in the EU that might have implemented CO_2-EOR have done so, because they do not have a sufficiently large accumulation of geologically sourced CO_2 nearby that can economically be accessed. In addition, CO_2-EOR can require retrofit of the injection and extraction facilities at an oilfield to cope with the corrosive nature of the mixture of CO_2 and formation water which is recycled.

If combined CO_2 storage and EHR were permitted, the income from the EHR would provide an additional revenue stream that would be available to offset the costs of CCS. These are primarily the costs of the storage itself: although the EHR income will decline to zero over the course of the project, and there may be a post-EHR period where only storage is conducted, the initial revenue can be used to offset the costs of the storage over time.

In some exceptional cases, it may even be the case that the EHR would not only offset the costs of storage, but also make a profit. In such cases, the market will dictate a price being placed on CO_2 for use in EHR, which could partially offset a CO_2 emitter's cost of capture and transportation. That is, there will always be a net cost of capture, transport and storage that the emitters would have to bear, but it would be reduced to some extent by the revenue stream coming from the EHR scheme.

If the EOR scheme is not allowed to obtain a CO_2 storage permit under the CCS Directive, the entire net cost would ultimately have to be borne by the electricity market (the customer). In some circumstances there is no incentive for the emitter to make any investment in capture and storage installations, since from an economic standpoint, the emitter would be better off continuing to directly emit CO_2 to the atmosphere.

Furthermore, availability of storage is expected to be a key constraint on the deployment of CCS, although the additional revenue generated from EOR is expected to considerably accelerate the construction of storage sites. It should also be noted that the transport infrastructure requirement for a large-scale EOR project would also reduce investment barriers to the development of the transport networks required for the large number of storage projects. This would be required in the longer-term (either by reuse of CO_2 transport facilities when the EHR project is finished, or by securing economies of scale for transport by aggregation of storage and EOR projects).

Recent studies show that the application of CCS in the power generation sector could lead to higher production costs. These costs could be as high as \$0.01–0.05 per kilowatt-hour of electricity, depending on the type of fuel and generation technology used. It is expected that with the use of CO_2-EOR, the unit cost of electricity generation would drop drastically to about one-half of the predicted costs without EOR.

[349]

Table 12.4

Comparative Analysis of Power Generation

with and without CCS

Power Generation Station	Combined Gas Cycle System (US$/kWh)	Combined Coal Cycle System (US$/kWh)
Without CCS (Compared Station)	0.03 – 0.05	0.04 – 0.06
With CCS (Geological)	0.04 – 0.08	0.05 – 0.09
With CCS and EOR	0.04 – 0.07	0.04 – 0.07

Notes: Assuming gas cost ranges between US $2.8 and $4.4/gigajoule (GJ), and coal between $1.0 and $1.5/GJ.

Source: Estimates published by UN ESCWA publication 09-0370, 2009; see Rubin, E.S., 2006.

Table 12.4 gives a comparative economic cost analysis of CCS for different types of electricity generation technologies depending on the source of CO_2 and the technology used for separation and storage. Based on these basic economic cost analyses the following can be summarized:

- The real benefits of the CCS–EOR process depends on the price of oil and on the costs met during exploration. Some analysis indicates that every ton of CO_2 injected will yield a $10–16/ton gain, assuming a cost of $15–20 per barrel. This could be increased to $30–50/ton if the cost of oil is $50–70 per barrel.

- CCS systems require intensive amounts of energy to operate—a constraint that adversely affects the overall efficiency of the power plant and the cost per kilowatt-hour of power produced, owing to additional fuel consumption. Increased fuel consumption leads to further emissions release for every kilowatt-hour of electricity produced, as compared to a new power production facility without CCS.

[350]

- With a re-design of existing natural gas pipeline networks to transport and store CO_2, the option of using CCS technology becomes a viable prospect in the Gulf region. This will also enhance the role of these countries as leaders in implementation of these technologies globally, and in terms of reducing global warming.

- It is recognized that the overall cost of the CCS–EOR process depends on the increases in the depth of the oil well, the quality and amount of CO_2, the relevant recyclable quantity ratios and the length of the transporting pipeline, all of which collectively increase the final cost. These aspects also influence the rate of oil production, and oil price changes can have major impacts on the cost of storage.

Prospects for Clean Technologies in the GCC Region

GCC countries face numerous environmental challenges and will have to resolve the many conflicting priorities of domestic energy demand, water supply, supply demand security, economic diversification, environmental protection and conservation, and limiting the hazardous impacts of global warming.

The GCC, after a history of intensive energy subsidies and price controls, is one of the highest energy consuming regions of the world, a situation accentuated by the climate-induced heavy reliance on air conditioning and water desalination. Moreover, many of the region's economic diversification ventures have built heavily on its abundant hydrocarbon reserves—logically enough, given their position as one of the key competitive advantages of the Gulf. Low-priced natural gas has brought about high energy-intensive industries such as petrochemicals, aluminum, cement and steel. Rising economic prosperity and populations have ensured sharp growth in electricity demand while inexpensive oil encourages the use of cars on a broad scale, including large models with high fuel consumption.

[351]

Climatic conditions in the Gulf have played a major role in increasing demand for energy in the region. Air-conditioning is a necessity in the hot desert climate and its use has grown rapidly with economic development, urbanization and population growth. The electricity and water production sector consumes up to 58 percent of total primary energy (oil and gas) supplies and the petroleum sector consumes more than 27 percent. Annual capital expenditure exceeds $10 billion and annual fuel exceeds $15 billion. In some GCC countries, fuel costs exceed 20 percent of the national budget. The residential, commercial and industrial building sectors are typically the major consumers of electrical energy, with a share of over 75 percent (Figure 12.6). Over the years 2001–2006, overall electricity consumption has risen considerably. As much as 65 percent is used for air-conditioning and on average the demand of peak power increases at 8.6 percent per year, with annual electricity use increasing at 7.1 percent.

The growing housing sector and retail property developments have raised the demand for water supply facilities, thereby increasing energy demand. Owing to the limited supply of underground water, the region has become increasingly dependent on seawater desalination through energy intensive thermal plant processes. Governments and municipalities in many instances have struggled to ensure adequate supply of key utilities to rapidly expanding residential and commercial developments.

Efforts to develop alternative energy sources and the technology to apply them on a mass scale offer an important means for the GCC countries to improve their 'green' credentials. The region has the unpleasant tag of being among the biggest per-capita emitters of CO_2 in the world. This is not surprising, given the high-energy intensity of the region, with almost all the energy being provided by hydrocarbon-based fuels—primarily oil and natural gas.

Figure 12.6

GCC Countries' Typical Electrical Consumption by Sector[11]

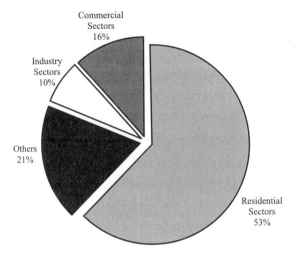

Source: GCC–CIGRE Data Records and Ministry of Electricity & Water (MEW) Kuwait Annual Statistical Book 2004–2005, (2006).

The Gulf region's contribution to global (CO_2) emissions (Figure 12.7) seems small at approximately 2.4 percent, which is far lower than the share of the top two—the United States (22.2 percent) and China (18.4 percent). In per capita terms, however, the situation is altogether different.

As shown in Figure 12.8, Qatar's annual per capita CO_2 emissions of 69.2 metric tons compare to an average of 'only' 20.4 metric-tons for the world's leading emitter, the United States, which ranks tenth globally in per capita terms. Following Qatar are Kuwait and the United Arab Emirates (UAE) in second and third place, respectively. Saudi Arabia and Oman are the only Gulf countries that do not feature among the top ten; nevertheless, even they are high emitters with world rankings of 18th and 22nd, respectively. 'Green and Clean' technology and fuel are likely to be an essential precondition for substantially altering this situation.

[353]

Figure 12.7

CO$_2$ Emissions: The GCC vs. the Rest of the World (2004)

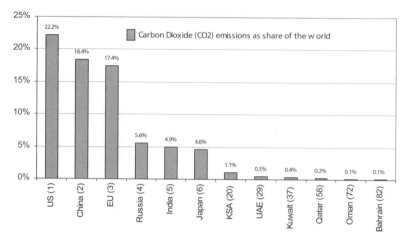

Source: Carbon Dioxide Information Analysis Center, 2009, p. 22.

Figure 12.8

**Per Capita Average CO$_2$ Emissions in Metric Tons:
GCC vs. the Rest of the World (2004)**

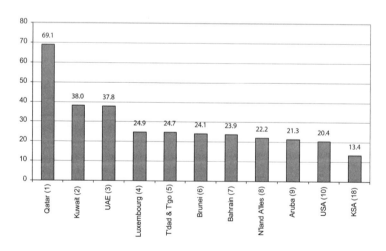

Source: Kotilaine, J.T., 2009.

Governments across the Gulf region seem to have recognized this. In the UAE, the Abu Dhabi government is pursuing the Masdar project's environmental and renewable energy technology initiatives, despite the current downturn. The emirate has set various programs to produce 15 percent of its total energy needs from renewable energy sources by 2020. The move to a carbon-free city alone could reduce CO_2 emissions by about 2.4 million tons per year.

The Masdar institute and HydrogenEnergy10 have launched the only CCS project planned in the Arabian peninsula, called Hydrogen Power Abu Dhabi (HPAD), which was originally planned to be in commercial operation in 2013. This project could be the first industrial-scale installation of an integrated 420MW hydrogen power and CCS system. It is expected that 1.7 million tons of CO_2 captured and stored per year will be injected, at Khalifa Port and Industrial Zone (KPIZ) in Taweelah. It will take natural gas from the grid and convert it to hydrogen and CO_2 using pre-combustion separation technology. The project requires a total capital investment (excluding CO_2 transportation and storage) of about $2 billion. This project, however, seems to have been delayed owing to financial complications.

In Saudi Arabia, the King Abdullah University of Science and Technology (KAUST) is planning to invest funds in research into CCS. The largest Saudi heavy industry and refining operations are managed by Saudi Arabian Basic Industries Corporation (SABIC) and ARAMCO and are located in specific industrial enclaves (some of which are managed by the Royal Commission for Jubail and Yanbu, another separate regulator with a good track record). This set-up could facilitate, among other things, future industrial CCS projects.

In addition, the KAUST Global Research Partnership (GRP) has announced a partnership with Cornell University which will focus on applications and fundamental studies of novel organic–inorganic hybrid nano-materials as new platforms for CCS. With a $25 million budget, the joint partnership effort on Energy and Sustainability will focus on the potential of these new materials, named NIMS (nano-particle ionic materials), for other applications, such as desalination of water, production of gas and oil, and solar energy conversion.

Qatar has negotiated a partnership with London's Imperial College that involves Qatar Petroleum, the Qatar Sciences and Technology Park and Shell in a 10-year, $70 million research project on new CO_2 storage technologies that can be applied in Qatar. In November 2007, Gulf OPEC members collectively pledged $750 million to fund research on clean technologies, focusing especially on CCS in order to fight global warming. Qatar Petroleum registered the first Gulf-based clean development mechanism (CDM) project, an oilfield gas recovery and utilization venture operated by Maersk Qatar Oil, that will prevent flaring of natural gas at the Al-Shaheen field. Qatar has also been considering setting up a carbon credit exchange.

Finally, the pan-GCC railway network currently under development is yet another effort to couple cheaper movement of people and freight across the region in a more energy-efficient manner. To reduce vehicle emissions, the GCC region has started focusing more on investing in public transport systems in general. Dubai government, for example, launched its metro rail network in the summer of 2009. Other regional governments, including Abu Dhabi, Kuwait and Oman are also planning similar systems.

The Role of Carbon Capture and Storage (CCS) in the GCC Region

Several studies have indicated that a 60–80 percent reduction of GHG emissions in 2050 is required for the EU and United States to limit the risks from climate change. The main technical options to reduce emissions of CO_2 include achieving higher energy efficiency, and moving towards low carbon technologies such as natural gas, renewables, nuclear and CO_2-CCS.

It is increasingly evident that there are huge opportunities for GCC oil-producing countries to exploit CCS technologies in order to enhance their oil production and at the same time greatly contribute to the mitigation of climate change. A number of studies and international reports have confirmed the potential and prospects of storage areas in the GGC region. They note that the Gulf states are very favorably positioned to make substantial investments in using CCS, because of the industrial concentration of carbon emission sources in the region (power generation, petrochemicals, oil refineries, cement and steel plants) and the potential for storage/sequestration in oil and gas fields using CO_2 injection as an EOR method.

Among the best-reported evidence is that of the maps published in the special report of the International Panel on Climate Change (IPCC) in 2005[12] and the IEA data[13] on CO_2 emissions from fuel combustion and the per capita production of CO_2 per ton of activity which show the highest emitting regions of the world. As indicated in Figure 12.9, these reports credit the Arabian Peninsula and the Middle East as a whole as containing a large number of appropriate geological formations suitable for CO_2 deposits. These geological formations can be used to directly store CO_2 at suitable depths of less than 300 km. This makes almost the entire region suitable for carbon capture application projects, regardless of current EOR efforts. However, there is a need to conduct appropriate economic feasibility studies for specific sites near CO_2 sources and to develop the necessary technical data to facilitate storage applications. Such studies will smooth the progress of understanding the cost of capture and transport, as well as storage volumes, and facilitate the decision-making process on large-scale application of CCS technologies in the Gulf region. These studies can provide the private sector with a great deal of flexibility, and will give an insight as to the profitability of ventures involving CCS projects.

As a more effective strategy, it is essential that the Gulf countries follow a research and development path to support the implementation and support of pilot projects by providing financial investments. These efforts are required in order to build expertise in developing their own techniques, and to bolster their capacity to apply these techniques in other parts of the region. In contrast, the developed countries bear the historic responsibility to contribute to the transfer of these technologies to the region. It appears that the support of the EU countries for carbon separation and CO_2 capture will be through a partnership with the private sector. These European companies have been building their technical capacities since 1996. This is evidenced by the financial support provided by certain European governments through the implementation of the necessary policies and laws, such as a 'Carbon Tax' (the Norwegian government has imposed such a tax of $40 per ton of CO_2 released into the atmosphere). If the Gulf states were to adopt such techniques as a methodology in the framework of the CDM, regional oil companies will be at the forefront of implementing projects, gaining the technical expertise to produce positive results on a global level.

Figure 12.9
High Prospective Opportunities for CO_2 Storage

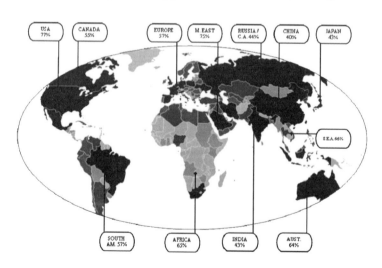

Source: IPCC, "IPCC Special Report on Carbon Dioxide Capture and Storage (CCS)," 2005, p. 96.

It is worth noting here the importance for the countries of the Arabian Gulf of examining the use of existing natural gas pipeline networks for transportation and storage of CO_2. Of course, this would entail investments in re-designing these pipelines in order to collect the CO_2 produced from multiple sources and move it to the geological formations where it can be stored as required.

Key Challenges to the Implementation of CCS

Some of the key challenges related to the implementation of CCS include:

- the technology challenges of CO_2 separation;

- the economics of CCS; and

- the need for a longer-term policy environment.

Technology Potential

CCS can be a significant, competitive option to simultaneously slow the growth of CO_2 emissions while promoting economic development and energy security in many countries for decades to come. On the assumption that CCS would reach its full potential in the next 30 to 50 years, CCS could curb energy-related global CO_2 emissions and concentrations by up to one third by 2050 compared with current levels.[14] If utilized together with improved combustion and higher plant efficiencies, CCS would have an even greater mitigation effect, estimated in the case of coal-based power generation at 50 percent and more by 2050. Indications are that through 2100, CCS could economically reduce CO_2 emissions by 220–2,200 billion tons ($GtCO_2$), which corresponds to 15–55 percent of the required worldwide cumulative mitigation effort. Whatever the numbers, CCS could serve as a bridge to a future sustainable energy economy.

Economic Cost

The economics of CCS suggest that it will cost \$50–80/ton to successfully sequester large quantities of CO_2.[15] This cost may be mitigated by the sale of CO_2 to EOR projects, but will provide a limited CO_2 market. The balance of the CO_2 will have to be sent to direct reservoir or cavern storage with no financial return. Removing CO_2 from the atmosphere represents a societal cost; a collective solution to the economics of CCS is needed. CCS projects are site-specific, driven by local conditions and business opportunities, and are hence unlikely to be replicable in all locations. In transportation, the (likely) mismatch between the location of the emitter and the geological sink may be a limiting factor for small volumes over long distances. The cost prospects of CCS are also determined by the permanence of storing billions of tons of CO_2 for centuries. Failure to prevent or control leakage (and re-assure the general public on this issue) would severely reduce the prospects of CCS applications.

Long-Term Policy Environment

Significant as it may be, CCS is not a universal remedy. CCS deployment would slow the growth of, and ultimately control, CO_2 emissions; however, under present assumptions, emissions would remain above present levels unless special measures were applied worldwide. The stringency of carbon constraints and related competition from alternative mitigation options would still need to be determined, as it would obviously affect the market penetration of CCS. A longer-term well-defined policy environment is needed given the capital costs involved in implementing CCS. A comprehensive CCS network in the GCC region to capture and store significant GHG emissions would involve billions of dollars in investment. Policies related to any fiscal incentives, pipeline access, and storage liabilities need to be developed with involvement by all key stakeholders.

[360]

Action

Successful deployment of CCS depends on the following:

- Predictable and positive climate control and non-discriminatory energy policies to attract investors;

- the integration of the CCS option into national energy policies, scenarios and emission trading processes, as part of a country portfolio of mitigation measures;

- enabling CCS laws and regulations on licensing, decommissioning, safety codes, and liabilities;

- international agreements on cross-border transportation;

- international cooperation and acceleration of CCS research, development and demonstration (RD&D), in particular on the permanence of storage, and leak and contamination prevention processes;

- the building of several cost-effective medium- to large-scale demonstration plants; and

- given their growing role as industrial emitters, the integration of countries into CCS piping networks, emission trading and carbon storage.

Implications and Conclusions

As is evident from this paper, the deployment of CCS is increasingly seen as an attractive option within a portfolio to mitigate climate change. It therefore moves from the outer edge to the center of international climate policy and related discussions regarding innovation. This examination has shown that there is no final answer to the question of whether CCS is beneficial to a sustainable transformation of the energy production sectors in the GCC countries and beyond. On the one hand, there are various

[361]

reasons why CCS could be seen as a bridging technology that allows for a smooth transition away from the current carbon focus of industrial-level electricity generation and others towards a more environmentally sustainable future.

Furthermore, CCS can be seen as more compatible with prevailing electricity system structures than other mitigation strategies. First, it allows governments to postpone or reconsider radical changes in these system structures and serves the vested interests of existing players. Second, it allows continuing exploitation of other resources in the GCC countries and thus fits well into considerations of energy security and sustainability. Third, national deployment of CCS allows GCC countries' oil companies and power establishments to pioneer regional pilot and demonstration projects and may lead to forefront expertise advantages. CCS may thus open up space for the concept of fossil fuels as 'transitional' fuels. On the other hand, it may prolong the dominance of the current fossil fuel-to-electricity 'business-as-usual' scenario for many years to come.

The combination of CO_2 storage with EHR would not pose any additional environmental risks to pure CO_2 storage, because all the requirements of the proposal for a directive on geological storage would have to be met by any combined project. If CO_2–EHR is commercially implemented in the GCC region on a large scale, this could be regarded as a 'win-win' strategy, whereby the captured CO_2 would be a source for EHR to produce further volumes of crude oil while international climate change obligations are met.

As carbon separation is only viable for high emission points, the current structure of centralized fossil fuel power plants would be largely conserved. Not all technology investment is likely to flow into such plants; rather, a mix of technology options based on different fuels is likely to result. Such a route seems reasonable as long as it is compatible with climate protection and other sustainability demands and as long as the transition period is used to develop alternatives to the fossil fuel system that may ultimately result in a low-carbon future electricity generation system.

The most important precondition for any further engagement in CCS is thus to create a reliable and stringent regulatory and climate policy framework, considering all relevant aspects of security and liability.

A responsible future technology and climate policy must consider all the different mitigation options. CCS is relevant not only for the GCC countries; it will be the focus of prominent discussion in post-2012 processes, particularly if it is viewed as an easy way forward in reducing industrial emissions without having to make major structural changes to existing energy and petrochemical infrastructure. This 'advantage' may also encourage and attract major emitting countries like the United States to join an international climate protection regime. Whether CCS will take off in emerging developing economies ultimately depends on the development of international climate change regimes, as well as advances in clean energy technology.

HISHAM KHATIB is an ex-Chairman of the Jordan Electricity Regulatory Commission, and Honorary Vice Chairman of the World Energy Council (WEC). He is an engineer and economist focusing on energy technology and security, as well as local and global environmental issues related to energy and development.

Dr. Khatib was a Minister in the Government of Jordan holding a number of portfolios covering planning, water and energy. He is one of the few engineers to be admitted to the fellowships of both the Institution of Engineering and Technology (IET-UK) and the Institution of Electrical and Electronics Engineers (IEEE-USA).

He is mentioned in all quality biographical references, including *American Men and Women of Science*. In 1998 he was awarded the Medal of Achievement of the Institution of Electrical Engineers in the UK. In the World Energy Congress in Rome, 2007, Dr. Khatib was awarded the highly prestigious Global Energy Award by the World Energy Council. Dr. Khatib has also been decorated in Jordan, Italy, Sweden, Indonesia, Austria and the Vatican.

RAAD ALKADIRI is Partner and Head of Global Risk at PFC Energy, the Washington-based strategic advisory firm. A country risk specialist, Dr. Alkadiri focuses on the political, economic and sectoral factors that influence decision-making in oil and gas producing states, particularly those in the Middle East and Africa. He also leads PFC Energy's Iraq Advisory practice, providing in-depth analysis of Iraq's ongoing political and oil and gas developments, and engagement strategies for companies interested in investing in the country's hydrocarbon sector.

In 2003–2004, Raad Alkadiri was seconded to the UK Foreign and Commonwealth Office (FCO) as the Policy Advisor and Assistant Private Secretary to the UK Special Representatives to Iraq, and in 2006–2007 was Senior Policy Advisor to Her Majesty's Ambassador in Baghdad. He has extensive policy-making experience, having been involved in, amongst other things, negotiations over the 2004 Transitional Administrative Law and the 2005 Constitution. He has also advised the FCO on the Hydrocarbon Law. In 2004, Dr. Alkadiri was made an Officer of the Order of the British Empire (OBE) for his work in Iraq.

Prior to joining PFC Energy in 1998, Dr. Alkadiri was Middle East Analyst and Deputy Managing Editor at the UK-based consultancy Oxford Analytica, where he focused in particular on political and economic developments in the northern Arabian Gulf States and the Israel–Palestine conflict. From 1990 to 1991, he was a teaching fellow of Politics at the University of St. Andrews, and from 2000 to 2001 he was an Associate Professor at the School of Advanced International Studies (SAIS), Johns Hopkins University.

Dr. Alkadiri holds a D.Phil. in International Relations from St. Antony's College, Oxford University, and an M.Phil. and MA from the University of St. Andrews. He was a Member of the Economy and Reconstruction Expert Working Group for the Baker/Hamilton Commission and a member of the Council on Foreign Relations/James A. Baker III Institute for Public Policy (Rice University) Independent Working Group on Guiding Principles for US Post-Conflict Policy in Iraq. He is also a founder member of the Arab Energy Club.

MOHAMMED A. AL-SAHLAWI is Professor of Economics in the Department of Finance and Economics at the College of Industrial Management, King Fahd University of Petroleum and Minerals (KFUPM), and previously was Dean of the College of Industrial Management. He holds a Ph.D in Economics from the University of Wisconsin and a BS in Chemical Engineering and MBA from KFUPM.

Dr. Al-Sahlawi was the Director of the OPEC Information Department and OPEC News Agency from 1991 to 1996, and was a member of the advisory board of the Saudi Arabian Supreme Economic Council from

1999 to 2002. He also established and was the Director of the Human Resources Development Fund from 2001 to 2006.

Dr. Al-Sahlawi serves on the editorial boards of several international journals focusing on energy economics and economic development/human resources management. He has advised both private and public sector corporations on economic, managerial and industrial issues, and was elected president of the Saudi Association for Energy Economics. His articles have appeared in *Energy Economics*, *The Energy Journal*, *The Journal of Energy and Development* and the *OPEC Review*, among others.

ALI AISSAOUI serves as Senior Consultant to the Arab Petroleum Investments Corporation (APICORP) where he previously held the position of Head of Economics & Research. Prior to joining APICORP, he was Senior Research Fellow at the Oxford Institute for Energy Studies (OIES). He was formerly a government advisor on energy policy issues and member/chairman of the OPEC Board of Governors.

When in Oxford, he acted occasionally as a consultant to leading oil and gas companies and producers' governments either directly or through reputable consulting firms. At APICORP he has set up and heads an economics and research department in charge of scanning the Corporation's environment, framing its business strategy and assessing and monitoring country and petroleum industry risks.

Ali Aissaoui is the author and co-author of three books and numerous comment pieces, analyses and critical reviews on oil markets and prices, energy investments and financing and, more generally, on the political economy of the major petroleum-exporting countries of the Middle East and North Africa. He is a member of several professional associations including the Oxford Energy Policy Club, the Paris Oil and Gas Club and the Arab Energy Club.

His most recent publications include the following Op-Ed analyses, which have been concurrently published in APICORP's monthly *Economic Commentary*, which he started in 2006: "The Oil Price

Dimension of the Producer-Consumer Dialogue: A Non-market Perspective," Op-Ed, MEES, September 28, 2009; "The Challenges of Diversifying Petroleum-dependent Economies: Algeria in the Context of the Middle East and North Africa," Op-Ed, MEES, June 1, 2009; "MENA Energy Investment Outlook Reassessed: Cost Uncertainties and Funding Challenges," Oxford Energy Forum, May 2009 (published under the title "Ali Aissaoui assesses the shrinking MENA energy investment outlook"); "What is a Fair Price for Oil and What Makes $75 a Barrel Seem Fair?" Op-Ed, MEES, April 6, 2009; and "Bringing Water into the Energy Equation: A Critical Review of the WEF-CERA Report and Discussion of the Missing MENA Dimension," Op-Ed, MEES, March 16, 2009.

PHILIP ANDREWS-SPEED is Professor of Energy Policy at the Centre for Energy, Petroleum and Mineral Law and Policy at the University of Dundee. He spent fourteen years as a geologist in the international mining and petroleum industries before coming to the Centre in 1994, gaining an LLM in Energy Law and Policy, and joining the academic staff. He leads the Centre's China Program. The focus of his research is on energy policy, regulation and reform, and on the interface between energy policy and international relations. His publications include: *The Strategic Implications of China's Energy Needs* (Adelphi Paper 346, 2002), *Energy Policy and Regulation in the People's Republic of China* (Kluwer Law International, 2004), and *International Competition for Resources: the Role of Law, the State and of Markets* (April 2008).

He is currently working with Roland Dannreuther on a book entitled *China, Oil and Global Politics*, and has recently begun to examine global challenges relating to energy and mineral resources and to the process of policy-making in these sectors. From January 2010 he has led a major European Union Framework 7 Program project with a world-wide remit on "Competition and Collaboration in Access to Oil, Gas and Mineral Resources."

[368]

NODARI A. SIMONIYA is Professor of Energy Policy at the Moscow State Institute of International Relations and Director of the Centre for Energy Studies at the Russian Academy of Sciences (RAS). He spent 30 years in the Institute of Oriental Studies, RAS, and 22 years in the Institute of World Economy and International Relations, RAS, as a Deputy-Director and Director.

He has published 17 books and more than 250 articles and chapters, including recent chapters in *Energy Security in the Globalizing World and Russia* (IMEMO, 2008) and *World Oil Industry: Problems and Perspectives* (IMEMO, 2009). He is currently working with members of his Center on his next book, *The World Gas Industry* (with special emphasis on LNG and innovations).

He is also a member of the Scientific Council at the Russian Ministry of Foreign Affairs, which advises the Ministry on Russian foreign policy.

ANAS F. ALHAJJI is chief economist at NGP Energy Capital Management, Irving, TX. He is a noted author and a regular contributor to national and international publications and academic journals with more than 500 papers, articles, and columns to his credit focusing on various energy issues. His articles have appeared in numerous countries and in more than 10 languages. He served as a professor of economics at Ohio Northern University where he held the George Patton Chair of Business and Economics. Before joining Ohio Northern, Dr. Alhajji worked at two universities that are strongly affiliated with the energy industry, the University of Oklahoma and the Colorado School of Mines. Dr. Alhajji is also a contributing editor for one of the industry's premier publications, *World Oil* magazine, and serves on the editorial board of several energy publications.

Dr. Alhajji holds an MA (1992) and a Ph.D (1995) in Economics, with specialization in energy economics from the University of Oklahoma. He has received many awards including the Teaching Excellence Award and the Outstanding Mentor Award. He is an Honorary

Associate at the Center for Energy, Petroleum and Mineral Law at the University of Dundee, Scotland, and a member of the Honor Society for International Scholars. He is also the Moderator of the Oil, Gas, and Energy Law Forum (OGEL).

VINCENT LAUERMAN is President of Geopolitics Central, a Calgary-based consultancy, and the former Editor-in-Chief of the journal *Geopolitics of Energy*. He regularly gives presentations on geopolitical and oil market developments, and comments and writes on these same issues in the media. Mr. Lauerman recently completed a joint study of Canada's oil sands with the Center for Global Energy Studies.

Mr. Lauerman has released two rounds of global energy scenarios over the past decade, the first of which was favorably reviewed in the December 2002 issue of the *Journal of Energy Literature*.

Prior to becoming President of Geopolitics Central, Mr. Lauerman worked for the Canadian Energy Research Institute (CERI), Energy ERA and the Alberta Petroleum Marketing Commission (APMC). During his time with CERI, he participated in the US Department of State's International Visitor Leadership Program.

Mr. Lauerman holds a Masters degree in economics, and is a triple major at undergraduate level (economics, political science and sociology). His recent publications include: *Canada's Oil Sands* (Center for Global Energy Studies and Geopolitics Central, November 2009); "Is Iraq on a Collision Course with OPEC?" (*National Post*, May 14, 2009); "Bravo OPEC, Take a Bow" (*National Post*, December 17, 2008); "Storm Brewing" (*Alberta Oil*, May 29, 2008); "The Fear Premium in the World Oil Market" (*Geopolitics of Energy*, July 2005); and "Saudi Arabia: In Search of a New Geopolitical Partner?" (*Geopolitics of Energy*, June–July 2004).

RONALD SOLIGO is a Professor of Economics at Rice University and a Rice Scholar at the James A. Baker III Institute for Public Policy. He holds a Ph.D from Yale University and a BA from the University of

British Columbia, Canada. His research focuses on economic growth and development and energy economics. He was awarded the 2001 Best Paper Prize from the International Association for Energy Economics for his co-authored paper with Kenneth B. Medlock III, "Economic Development and End-Use Energy Demand" (*Energy Journal*, April, 2001). Other recently published and forthcoming works include: "State-Backed Financing in Oil and Gas Projects," with Amy Myers Jaffe, in Andreas Goldthau and Jan Martin Witte (eds), *Global Energy Governance: The New Rules of the Game* (Brookings Press, 2010); "The United States, Cuba Sanctions and the Potential for Energy Trade," with Amy Myers Jaffe, in *9 Ways To Talk To Cuba & For Cuba To Talk To US* (Center for Democracy in the Americas, 2009); "The Militarization of Energy—The Russian Connection," with Amy Myers Jaffe, in Daniel Moran and James Russell (eds), *Energy Security and Global Politics: The Militarization of Resource Management* (Routledge, 2008); and "Market Structure in the New Gas Economy: Is Cartelization Possible?" with Amy Myers Jaffe, in *Natural Gas and Geopolitics: From 1970 to 2040* (Oxford University Press, 2006).

Dr. Soligo's next project is on the implications for oil demand and greenhouse gas emissions of the rapid growth in automobile stocks in China.

AMY MYERS JAFFE is the Wallace S. Wilson Fellow in Energy Studies and director of the Energy Forum at the James A. Baker III Institute for Public Policy, Rice University. Her research focuses on oil and gas geopolitics, strategic energy policy, and energy economics.

Amy Myers Jaffe was formerly senior editor and Middle East analyst for *Petroleum Intelligence Weekly*. She is widely published and served as co-editor of *Energy in the Caspian Region: Present and Future* (Palgrave, 2002) and *Natural Gas and Geopolitics: From 1970 to 2040* (Cambridge University Press, 2006), and as co-author, with Mahmoud El-Gamal, of *Oil, Dollars, Debt and Crises: The Global Curse of Black Gold* (Cambridge University Press, January 2010).

[371]

Amy Myers Jaffe has served as a member of the reconstruction and economy working group of the Baker/Hamilton Iraq Study Group, as project director for the Baker Institute/Council on Foreign Relations Task Force on Strategic Energy Policy, and as a principal adviser to USAID's project on Options for Developing a Long Term Sustainable Iraqi Oil Industry. She is currently chair of the working group on nuclear power in the Middle East for the US Institute for Peace–Stinson Center strategic task force on Iran and is a member of the Council on Foreign Relations.

LEILA BENALI, IHS CERA Director, focuses on the energy policies (oil, gas, and power) of Middle Eastern and African countries. Her expertise includes various projects for governments and international companies, advising them on energy strategies. This involves direct discussions and presentations to senior government officials and private sector senior management. For example, as a core member of IHS CERA's contribution to developing a National Economic Strategy in Libya, Mrs. Benali focused on the economics and issues to be addressed at the policy level in the gas and power sectors. Her recent research included several papers and analyses of the political, economic, and energy situations in most OPEC countries (Iran, Iraq, Libya, Saudi Arabia, the United Arab Emirates, Algeria, and others) as well as Oman, Sudan, and Mauritania. She also focuses on horizontal themes within the region such as gas developments and nuclear power. Prior to joining IHS CERA, Mrs. Benali conducted field research on the liberalization of the UAE power sector. She also worked on assessments of the political and social climate in Lebanon and Syria and as an industrial engineer at Schlumberger. Mrs. Benali is a member of the Executive Committee of the Arab Energy Club and a member of the International Association of Energy Economists. She holds an MS from l'Ecole Mohammadia d'Ingenieurs, Rabat, Morocco; an MS from l'Ecole Centrale Paris; and a Master of Political Science from l'Institut d'Etudes Politiques de Paris, where she is finishing her Ph.D in economics.

RIYAD Y. HAMZAH is a Professor of Biotechnology at the Arabian Gulf University in the Kingdom of Bahrain. He holds a Ph.D in Biochemistry (enzymology and protein chemistry, 1984) from the University of Houston, Texas. His research focus is the biochemistry and molecular biology of biodegradation of toxicants and pollutants by microorganisms, with special interests in biodegradation and bioremediation of crude oil and hazardous waste contamination, in addition to the environmental applications of genetic engineering. His work has been published in various international scientific journals and he has supervised a number of M.Sc and Ph.D students in various aspects of biotechnology.

Professor Hamzah has served on the boards of a number of scientific organizations and journals, and is one of the prominent pioneers of the Arabian Gulf University, where he has served as the Vice-President (1994–2005) and is currently the Editor-in-Chief of the *Arab Gulf Journal of Scientific Research.*

SA'AD AL JANDAL is a Research Scientist at the Building and Energy Technologies Department at the Kuwait Institute for Scientific Research (KISR). He joined KISR's Solar Energy Department in early 1982. Dr. Al Jandal graduated with a Bachelor of Science (BSc) degree from North Carolina University in Mechanical Engineering–Thermal, earned his Master of Philosophy (M.Phil) degree in thermal storage energy from the University of Wales, Cardiff, UK, and received a Doctor of Philosophy (Ph.D) for his work in design and analysis of solar thermal energy systems with latent storage from the University of Reading, UK. He also received an executive MBA on energy management from the Institut Français du Pétrole (IFP), France. Dr. Al Jandal's professional training and research work is diverse but focused on energy and environmental issues and technology implementations, including energy conservation, thermal efficiency analysis, and renewable and energy storage systems. His earlier project involvements include testing various solar thermal and electrical systems, and integration of solar cooling and heating with storage in buildings. His current lead projects cover sustainability issues, demand-side-management investigations, assessments of global energy technology and mitigation policies using various modeling techniques and developing national database systems.

Dr. Al Jandal's executive management responsibilities include renewable energy projects director at the Euro-Arab Environment Organization (EAEO) based in Germany and the Arab world. He is also an active member of a number of national and international professional bodies and national committees, and participates in numerous consultation and technical presentations. Dr. Al Jandal is a keen technical reviewer of number of journals and conferences, and has long been a member of steering committees for the World Renewable Energy Congress (WREC) and the International Solar Energy Society & Conferences of Arab Section (AISES). He is one of the founders of the Gulf Green Building Society (GGBS), founder of the Kuwait Clean Energy Society (CES) and of the Kuwait Research Scientists Society (KRSS), and is a member of the Emirates Green Building Council (EGBC). Dr. Al Jandal was awarded the prestigious Emirates Energy Award 2008 in the Education and Research category for his work in the field of energy conservation concepts and strategic building operations at KISR. He also wrote and compiled the booklets: "Glossary of Energy Related Terms" and "Solar Energy Program in Kuwait 1975–1985" (English & Arabic), and the book *Alternative Energy Resources and Technologies*.

Chapter 1

1. UNDP, UNDESA and World Energy Council (WEC), "World Energy Assessment" (2000) provides a comprehensive survey of all aspects pertaining to global energy issues.

2. Daniel Yergin, "It's Still the One," *Foreign Policy*, September 2009, gives an assessment of the present and future role of oil and emphasizes that it is irreplaceable in the foreseeable future.

3. *BP Statistical Review of World Energy*, June 2009.

4. Most figures and tables in this paper, such as Figure 1.1 below, will rely on the following sources: the estimates and data of the US Department of Energy (DOE) Energy Information Administration (EIA), whose *International Energy Outlook* (Washington, DC: 2009) is the world's leading reference on energy statistics; and the International Energy Agency's (IEA) *World Energy Outlook* (Paris: 2008). These two sources will be referred to as "IEO 2009" and "WEO 2008" respectively.

5. Ibid.

6. The Middle East Economic Survey (MEES) contains up-to-date valuable information on oil and other energy forms mostly relevant to the Middle East.

7. This refers to the US Geological Survey (USGS), *World Petroleum Assessment* (Washington, DC: USGS, 2000).

8. See IEO 2009 and WEO 2008.

9. The BP Statistical Review estimates this as 718 Mtoe against only 620 Mtoe for nuclear energy.

10. World Energy Council (WEC), "Survey of Energy Resources" (London: 2007). The WEC produces a survey every three years; the latest is the 2007 edition.

11. M.K. Hubbert, "Techniques of Production as Applied to Production of Oil," US Department of Commerce, May 1982.

12. Peter Jackson, "The Future of Global Oil Supply: Understanding the Building Blocks," Cambridge Energy Research Associates (CERA), presented at World Federation of Scientists Meeting at Erice, Sicily, August 2009.

13. Alan Petzet, "SEG: Saleri says Oil, Gas Key in New Energy Era," *Oil & Gas Journal*, October 29, 2009.

14. See: Paul Segal, "Why Do Oil Price Shocks No Longer Shock?" Oxford Institute for Energy Studies (OIES), WPM 35, October 2007.

15. International Panel on Climatic Change (IPCC), report 2007.

16. Hisham Khatib, "Financial and Economic Evaluation of Projects in the Electricity Supply Industry," The Institution of Engineering and Technology (London: 2003).

17. See: Mickinsey & Co., "Reducing US Greenhouse Gas Emission: How Much at What Cost?" December 2007.

18. See: Rice University publications, James Baker III Institute for Public Policy, particularly "Sustainable US Policy Options to Address Climate Change," June 2009.

19. International Energy Agency (IEA), "Energy Technology Perspective 2008" (Paris: IEA-OECD, 2008).

20. Giorgio Simbolotti, "Beyond Emerging Low-Carbon Technologies to Face Climate Change," World Federation of Scientists 42nd Seminar, Erice, Sicily, August 2008.

21. These three international organizations have already been defined in this paper. The International Energy Agency (IEA) in Paris publishes the annual *World Energy Outlook* (WEO), and the US Department of Energy's Energy Information Administration (DOE–EIA) publishes an annual *International Energy Outlook* (IEO). The World Energy Council (WEC) has a Scenarios Committee that periodically publishes its energy predictions to 2050.

22. The WEC's latest "Energy Scenarios" study dates back to March 2006. It is, however, now being updated.

23. IEO, 2009. Renewables other than hydro-electricity production in 2030 are estimated at 1.9 trillion kWh. In terms of global energy use this is only around two percent.

24. Prospects for future oil prices were discussed in detail in the previous section.

25. See International Monetary Fund (IMF) and World Bank future predictions for the world economy issued at the Istanbul meeting in September 2009, particularly "World Development Report 2010."

26. Middle East Economic Survey (MEES), August 31, 2009.

27. See: Thomas Shanker, "Despite Slump, US Role as Top Arms Supplier Grows," *New York Times*, September 7, 2009.

28. See: James Kanter, "In Finland, Nuclear Renaissance Runs into Trouble," *New York Times*, May 29, 2009.

29. See the method of calculating the cost of electricity production in: Hisham Khatib, "Economic Evaluation of Projects in the Electricity Supply Industry," The Institution of Engineering and Technology, (London: 2003).

30. Latest available figures in September 2009 cites a UAE population of around six million, of which around one million are indigenous the rest are mainly from South Asia.

31. Michael Jefferson, "Win-Win Strategies for Tackling Oil and Natural Gas Constraints, While Expanding Renewable Energy Use," in F. Barbir and S. Ulgiati (eds), *Sustainable Energy Production and Consumption* (Springer, 2008).

32. See: WEO 2008.

Chapter 2

1. For a good history of the development of oil in the twentieth century, see Daniel Yergin, *The Prize: The Epic Quest for Oil, Money & Power* (New York, NY: The Free Press, 1993).

2. Kristin Smith Diwan and Fareed Mohamedi, "The Gulf Comes Down to Earth," *Middle East Report* Vol. 252 (Fall 2009), pp. 12–16.

3. Figures based on PFC Energy internal estimates.

4. See PFC Energy, "Non-OPEC Decline Rates Accelerate," *Global Liquids Supply Forecast*, February 10, 2009.

5. PFC Energy, "Global Crude Oil Supply Forecast: Non-OPEC; Historical Summary and Outlook to 2030," *Global Liquids Supply Forecast*, March 2009.

6. PFC Energy, "Outlook for Fundamentals, Politics and Prices, Q4 2009," *Market Intelligence Service*, October 8, 2009.

7. For details, see International Monetary Fund (IMF), "Sustaining the Recovery," *World Economic Outlook*, October 2009 (http://www.imf.org/external/pubs/ft/weo/2009/02/index.htm).

8. See PFC Energy, "Saudi Arabia: Rising Capacity," *Market Intelligence Service*, July 16, 2008.

9. "Text of Bush's State of the Union Speech," CNN.com, February 1, 2006 (http://www.cnn.com/2006/POLITICS/01/31/sotu.transcript/).

10. See, for example, "Obama Aims for Oil Independence," *BBC News*, January 26, 2009 (http://news.bbc.co.uk/2/hi/7851038.stm); "President Obama Calls Energy Bill Passage Critical to Stronger American Economy," The White House, June 27, 2009 (http://www.whitehouse.gov/the_press_office/UPDATED-and-FINAL-WEEKLY-ADDRESS-President-Obama-Calls-Energy-Bill-Passage-Critical-to-Stronger-American-Economy/); "Barack Obama's Acceptance Speech," *NPR*, August 28, 2008 (http://www.npr.org/templates/story/story.php?storyId=94087570; and http://www.whitehouse.gov/issues/energy-and-environment). Indeed, in the first days of his administration, the Energy and Environment page on the White House website made cutting US imports by 2 mbpd an explicit goal, emphasizing that this was the volume of oil currently imported by the United States from Saudi Arabia and Venezuela. This reference has since been removed.

11. Bill Murray, "Obama's First Year brings Big Changes in US Energy Policy," *International Oil Daily*, December 30, 2009 (http://www.energyintel.com/DocumentDetail.asp?document_id=652346).

12. The White House, Office of the Press Secretary, "President Obama Announces National Fuel Efficiency Policy," May 18, 2009 (http://www.whitehouse.gov/the_press_office/President-Obama-Announces-National-Fuel-Efficiency-Policy/).

13. Spencer Swartz, "Is China's Oil and Coal Binge Coming to an End?" *Wall Street Journal Blogs*, December 2, 2009 (http://blogs.wsj.com/environmentalcapital/2009/12/02/is-chinas-oil-and-coal-binge-coming-to-an-end/).

14. Securing America's Future Energy, "China: New Home of the Hummer?" *Intelligence Report*, Vol. 2, Issue 10, June 16, 2009 (http://www.secureenergy.org/files/files/1052_SAFEIntelligenceReport2102 0090616.pdf).

15. For a discussion of the potential for leap-frogging in China, see Iain Carson and Vijay V. Vaitheeswaran, *Zoom: The Global Race to Fuel the Car of the Future* (New York, NY: Twelve, 2007), pp. 214–223.

16. For a discussion about the link between policy and technology in China, see Evan Osnos, "Green Giant: Beijing's Crash Program for Clean Energy," *The New Yorker*, December 21, 2009 (http://www. newyorker.com/reporting/2009/12/21/091221fa_fact_osnos).

17. For a study of alternative energy options, see Al Gore, *Our Choice: A Plan to Solve the Climate Crisis* (Emmaus, PA: Rodale Press, 2009).

18. Christopher Steiner, "The Road to $20 a Gallon," *Forbes.com*, July 16, 2009 (http://www.forbes.com/2009/07/14/road-to-20-dollar-gallon-business-energy-oil.html).

19. PFC Energy, "Interest in Unconventional Gas Growing Globally," *Upstream Competition Service*, September 21, 2009.

20. Kenneth B. Medlock III and Amy Myers Jaffe, "US Energy Policy and Transportation," James A Baker III Institute for Public Policy, The Global Energy Market: Comprehensive Strategies to Meet Geopolitical and Financial Risk Working Paper Series, May 2008, pp. 17–21.

21. PFC Energy, "New Fuel Efficiency Standards: Ambitious but Attainable," *Downstream Monitoring Service North America*, June 10, 2009.

22. PFC Energy, "Global Crude Oil Supply Forecast: Non-OPEC: Historical Summary and Outlook to 2030," op. cit.

Chapter 3

1. An overview of the security situation in the Gulf region is provided in: Bauer M. and C.P. Hanelt, "Security Situation in the Gulf Region involving Iran, Iraq and Saudi Arabia as Regional Powers: Policy Recommendations for the European Union and the International

Community," Discussion Paper, *Center for Applied Policy Research and Bertelsmann Stiftung,* September 2008.

2. J. Reppy, "Report on the Workshop on Energy Security: Arabian Gulf Oil, International Security, and American Strategy," *Cornell University* (January 2007).

3. J. Taylor and P. Van Doran, "The Energy Security Obsession," *The Georgetown Journal of Law and Public Policy*, vol. 6, no. 2 (Summer 2008).

4. Balamin B. Cosku, "The EU's Quest for Energy Security and Persian Gulf," 4th Pan-European Conference on EU Politics, University of Latvia, Riga, Latvia, September 25–27, 2008.

5. A.M. Jaffe and W. Wilson, "Energy Security: Oil—Geopolitical and Strategic Implications for China and the United States," The James A. Baker III Institute for Public Policy, Rice University, July 2005.

6. M. Al-Sahlawi, "GCC Energy Demand Outlook to 2000," *Energy Economics*, vol. 10, no. 1 (January 1988).

7. M. Al-Sahlawi, and M. Elbek, "An Alternative Oil Pricing Currency to Improve OPEC's Balance of Trade," *The Journal of Energy and Development*, vol. 22, no. 2 (Spring 1997), pp. 187–197.

Chapter 4

1. Press Release by the World Economic Forum (WEF), Geneva, May 19, 2007, announcing the publication of their report: *GCC Countries and the World: Scenarios to 2025* (Geneva: WEF, 2007).

2. For an informed, balanced and reasoned discussion of energy security see: Robin M. Mills, *The Myth of the Oil Crisis: Overcoming the Challenges of Depletion, Geopolitics, and Global Warming* (Westport, CT: Praeger, 2008), pp. 195–204.

3. Excerpts from the International Energy Agency's (IEA) "Progress Report on the implementation of the St Petersburg Plan of Action for Global Energy Security," as submitted to the G8 Summit in L'Aquila, July 8–10, 2009, p. 4.

4. This was particularly the case for American delegates who used to invoke the old US anti-trust law (the Sherman Act of 1890) to distance themselves from any tentative debate on oil prices.

5. Paul Segal, "Why Do Oil Price Shocks No Longer Shock?" Oxford Institute for Energy Studies, Working Paper 35, October 2007, p. 2. Segal's argument was updated in a *Financial Time*s comment piece: "Searching in Vain for the Oil Shock Effect," FT.com, September 1, 2009 (http://blogs.ft.com/energy-source/2009/09/01/comment-searching-in-vain-for-the-oil-shock-effect/).

6. In an exchange with the author, Bernard Mommer, who pre-reviewed this paper, expressed a different opinion than this predominant OPEC one. In his words, "oil 'revenues' in the importing countries are taxes, and nothing else; in the exporting countries, the 'taxes' on exports actually represents a real revenue, an international ground rent to be precise." For more on this see Bernard Mommer, *Global Oil and the Nation State* (New York, NY: Oxford University Press, 2002).

7. First reported in the online edition of the Saudi English-language daily *Arab News,* November 30, 2008.

8. World Economic Forum (WEF), Session "Energy Outlook 2009," session summary and trade press reports of the event, Davos, January 29–30, 2009.

9. Gordon Brown and Nicolas Sarkozy, "Oil Prices Need Government Supervision", Opinion, *Wall Street Journal*, July 8, 2009. This opinion was re-posted online under the title: "We Must Address Oil-Market Volatility."

10. There is a large body of literature on the formation of, and changes in, crude oil prices. For the working of the current oil price regime, see: Bassam Fattouh, "The Origins and Evolution of the Current International Oil Pricing System: A Critical Assessment," in Robert Mabro (ed.), *Oil in the 21st Century: Issues, Challenges, and Opportunities* (New York, NY: Oxford University Press, 2006), pp. 41–100. For a more formal reading of the factors responsible for price changes, see: James D. Hamilton, "Understanding Crude Oil Prices" (Mimeo, San Diego, CA: University of California, December 2008).

11. Cited by Llewellyn H. Rockwell Jr. in a talk to the "Birthplace of Economic Theory" conference, Salamanca, Spain, October 21–24, 2009.

12. Direct communication by John V. Mitchell, Associate Research Fellow in the Energy, Environment and Resource Management Programme at Chatham House.

13. Philip H. Abelson, "What Is a Fair Price for Oil," *Science*, vol. 171, Issue 3972, p. 633.

14. This view has been supported by Bernard Mommer in "Oil Prices and Fiscal Regimes," OIES Working Paper 24 (Oxford: Oxford Institute for Energy Studies, May 1999).

15. Delphi is a forecasting method, whose original objective was to obtain a consensus of opinion of a group of experts through a series of questions and opinion feedback. The method has evolved into a more sophisticated process of structuring a group communication to deal with complex problems.

16. International Energy Agency (IEA), *Word Energy Outlook* (Paris: IEA/OECD, 2008), pp. 217–219.

17. The major currencies index is defined by the US Federal Reserve as the weighted average of the foreign exchange values of the US dollar against a set of currencies that circulate widely outside the country of issue.

18. "Ali Aissaoui assesses the shrinking MENA energy investment outlook", *Oxford Energy Forum,* May 2009, pp. 7–9.

19. Deutsche Bank (DB), "The Cost of Producing Oil," February 2009, pp. 19–25.

20. Ibid., p. 4.

21. The economic literature on the use of the PIH framework is extensive, but dominated by the IMF's empirical case studies. For a recent analytical, generic paper on PIH-related models and their extension, see Wojciech Maliszewski, "Fiscal Policy Rules for Oil Producing Countries: A Welfare-Based Assessment," International Monetary Fund (IMF), WP/09/126 (Washington, DC: IMF, June 2009).

22. Similar simulations were originally conducted by the author in: Ali Aissaoui, *Algeria: The Political Economy of Oil and Gas* (New York, NY: Oxford University Press, 2001), pp. 278–282. Despite the weakness of the fiscal policy framework used at that time, the assumptions were more realistic than subsequent IMF studies, which tend to rely on simple-step production profiles based on constant R/P ratios (see next footnote). More likely production profiles have recently been worked out for a number of oil-producing countries, including Saudi Arabia and Kuwait, in Chatham House's Resource Depletion, Dependence and Development project: John V Mitchell and Paul Stevens, "Ending Dependence: Hard Choices for Oil-Exporting States" (London: Chatham House, 2008); (see also their associated working papers at: www.chathamhouse.org.uk).

23. For a thorough discussion on depletion policy (objectives, instruments, and preferences) see Paul Stevens and John V. Mitchell, "Resource Depletion, Dependence and Development: Can Theory Help?" (London: Chatham House, June 2008), pp. 8–18.

24. The R/P ratio should be interpreted with caution. It is a static indicator of the life of proven reserves. It would only remain constant if no reserves were added or if production remained constant, which are both unlikely.

25. This method has been adapted from Ali Aissaoui, op. cit., pp. 232–234.

26. Organization of the Petroleum Exporting Countries (OPEC), *World Oil Outlook* (Vienna: OPEC, 2009), pp. 59–64.

27. Stevens and Mitchell, op. cit., p. 15.

28. Exchange with John V Mitchell.

29. This is based on OPEC price adjustment methodology, which uses weighted average consumer price indices for inflation and weighted average index of currency exchange rates against a basket of currencies for the appreciation/depreciation of the US dollar; both factors are of the so-called Geneva I countries.

30. For a brief historical record of managing resource revenues in "oil rich countries', including Saudi Arabia, see Paul Collier et al., "Managing Resource Revenues in Developing Economies", OxCarre Research Paper 15, Oxford Centre for the Analysis of Resource Rich Economies, May 2009 (Revised), pp. 4–8.

31. See for instance: Jeffrey M. Davis, et al. (ed.), *Fiscal Policy Formulation and Implementation in Oil-Producing Countries* (Washington, DC: IMF, 2003), pp. 383–481; and for the case of the domestic pricing of natural gas, Hossein Razavi, "Natural Gas Pricing in Countries of the Middle East and North Africa," *The Energy Journal*, vol. 30, no. 3 (2009), pp. 1–22.

Chapter 5

1. BP, *Statistical Review of World Energy 2009* (London: BP, 2009).

2. BP, *Statistical Review of World Energy* (London: BP, various years).

3. The projections of the International Energy Agency's *World Energy Outlook* for 2007 and 2008 are used because they cover the full range

of relevant energy sources for the countries and region studied, and because they include alternative future scenarios relevant to this paper.

4. National Development and Reform Commission, *China's Medium and Long Term Energy Conservation Plan* (Beijing: NDRC, 2007).

5. Philip Andrews-Speed, *Energy Policy and Regulation in the People's Republic of China* (London: Kluwer Law, 2004), pp. 297–319.

6. "China Looks to Energy Independence," Xinhua News Agency, Beijing, October 26, 2007; International Energy Agency, *World Energy Outlook 2007*, p. 320.

7. Paul Horsnell, *Oil in Asia. Markets, Trading, Refining and Deregulation* (Oxford: Oxford University Press, 1997); Philip Andrews-Speed, Xuanli Liao and Roland Dannreuther *The Strategic Impact of China's Energy Needs,* International Institute for Strategic Studies, Adelphi Paper No. 346 (2002); Bernard D. Cole, *"Oil for the Lamps of China"– Beijing's 21st-Century Search for Energy*, McNair Paper 67 (Washington, DC: Institute for National Strategic Studies, 2003).

8. International Energy Agency, *World Energy Outlook 2007* (Paris: OECD/IEA, 2007), pp. 323–325.

9. US Energy Information Administration (EIA), *Projections of International Liquids Production to 2030*; available at: (http://www.eia.doe.gov/oiaf/ieo/pdf/ieopol.pdf), accessed November 12, 2007; International Energy Agency, *World Energy Outlook 2007* (Paris: OECD/IEA, 2007), p. 357; Noureddine Berrah, Fei Feng, Roland Priddle and Leiping Wang, *Sustainable Energy in China: The Closing Window of Opportunity* (Washington, DC: World Bank, 2007), p. 189.

10. International Energy Agency, *World Energy Outlook 2007* (Paris: OECD/IEA, 2007).

11. International Energy Agency, *World Energy Outlook 2007*; U.S. Energy Information Administration (EIA), *International Statistics 2007.*

12. Chen Aizhu, "China to Add 1.8 mln bbls African Crude to Reserves," Reuters, March 23, 2009.

13. International Energy Agency, *Developing China's Natural Gas Market: The Energy Policy Challenges* (Paris: OECD/IEA, 2002).

14. International Energy Agency, *World Energy Outlook 2007* (Paris: OECD/IEA, 2007).

15. Janet Xuanli Liao, *The Politics of Oil Behind Sino-Japanese Relations: Beyond Energy Cooperation* (Stockholm: Institute for Security and Development Policy, 2008).

16. Dan Girdis, Startos Tavoulareas and Ray Tomkins, *Liquefied Natural Gas in China. Options for Markets, Institutions and Finance* (Washington, DC: World Bank, 2000).

17. Dan Girdis, Startos Tavoulareas and Ray Tomkins, *Liquefied Natural Gas in China. Options for Markets, Institutions and Finance* (Washington, DC: World Bank, 2000); Akira Miyamoto and Chikako Ishiguro, *Pricing and Demand for LNG in China: Consistency between LNG and Pipeline Gas in a Fast Growing Market*, Oxford Institute for Energy Studies, Report NG 9 (2006).

18. Philip Andrews-Speed, *Energy Policy and Regulation in the People's Republic of China* (London: Kluwer Law, 2004).

19. Akira Miyamoto and Chikako Ishiguro, *Pricing and Demand for LNG in China: Consistency between LNG and Pipeline Gas in a Fast Growing Market*, Oxford Institute for Energy Studies, Report NG 9 (2006).

20. International Energy Agency, *World Energy Outlook 2007* (Paris: OECD/IEA, 2007), p.333; Nobuyuki Higashi, *Natural Gas in China. Market Evolution and Strategy* (Paris: OECD/IEA, 2009), p. 17.

21. Erica Strecker Downs, *China's Quest for Energy Security*, RAND Report MR-1244-AF, 2000; International Energy Agency, *China's Worldwide Quest for Energy*, (Paris: OECD/IEA, 2000); Philip Andrews-Speed, Xuanli Liao and Roland Dannreuther, *The Strategic Impact of China's Energy Needs*, International Institute for Strategic Studies, Adelphi Paper No. 346 (2002); Janet Xuanli Liao, "A Silk Road for Oil: Sino-Kazakh Energy Diplomacy," *Brown Journal of World Affairs* 12 (2006), pp. 39–51; Kevin Sheives, "China Turns West: Beijing's Contemporary Strategy Towards Central Asia," *Pacific Affairs* 79 (2006), pp. 205–224.

22. "CNPC Awarded Licenses for Sino-Turkmenistan Natural Gas Project," Interfax China Energy Report, vol. VI, issue 32, September 5, 2007, p. 16.

23. Leonty Eder, Philip Andrews-Speed and Andrey Korzhubaev, "Russia's Evolving Energy Policy for its Eastern Regions, and Implications for Oil and Gas Cooperation between Russia and China," *Journal of World Energy Law and Policy*, vol. 2, no. 3 (2009), pp. 219–241.

24. "CB Boom," *China Business Weekly*, October 22–28, 2007, p. 3; "China to Produce 500m cu m of Coal-Bed Methane this Year," Xinhua News Agency, Beijing, November 9, 2007; "China's Coal-Bed Methane Industry holds Promise," *Interfax China Energy Report Weekly*, November 6, 2007; Dongkun Luo and Youjin Dai, "Economic Evaluation of Coalbed Methane Production in China," *Energy Policy* vol. 37 (2009), pp. 3883–3889.

25. Paul Horsnell, *Oil in Asia: Markets, Trading, Refining and Deregulation* (Oxford: Oxford University Press, 1997).

26. See, for example, John Keefer Douglas, Matthew B. Nelson and Kevin Schwartz, *Fueling the Dragon's Flame. How China's Energy Demands Affect its relationships in the Middle East*, presented to US–China Economic and Security Review Commission, 14th September 2006, available at: (http://www.uscc.gov/researchpapers/2006/China_ME_FINAL.pdf); Daojiong Zha, "China's Energy Security: Domestic and International Issues," *Survival*, vol. 48, no. 1 (2006), pp. 179–190.

27. See, for example: Ian Storey, "Securing Southeast Asia's Sea Lanes: A Work in Progress," *Asia Policy* no. 6 (2008), pp. 95–127; Liselotte Odgaard, *Maritime Security between China and Southeast Asia* (Aldershot: Ashgate, 2002).

28. Philip Andrews-Speed, Xuanli Liao and Roland Dannreuther, *The Strategic Impact of China's Energy Needs*, International Institute for Strategic Studies, Adelphi Paper No. 346 (2002); Amy M. Jaffe and Steven W. Lewis, "Beijing's Oil Diplomacy," *Survival*, vol. 44, no. 1 (2002), pp. 115–134; Erica Downs, "The Chinese Energy Security Debate," *The China Quarterly*, no. 177 (March 2004), pp. 21–41; Kenneth Lieberthal and Mikkal Herberg, "China's Search for Energy Security: Implications for US Policy," *NBR Analysis*, vol. 17, no. 1 (2006), pp. 5–42; John Mitchell and Glada Lahn, *Oil for Asia* (London: Chatham House, 2007).

29. Philip Andrews-Speed, Xuanli Liao and Roland Dannreuther, *The Strategic Impact of China's Energy Needs,* International Institute for Strategic Studies, Adelphi Paper No. 346 (2002).

30. Kenneth Lieberthal and Mikkal Herberg, China's Search for Energy Security: Implications for US Policy," *NBR Analysis*, vol. 17, no. 1 (2006), pp. 5–42.

31. Erica Downs, "The Chinese Energy Security Debate," *The China Quarterly*, no. 177 (March 2004), pp. 21–41.

32. Jin Zhang, *Catch-up and Competitiveness in China: The Case of Large Firms in the Oil Industry* (London: RoutledgeCurzon, 2004).

33. Xin Ma and Philip Andrews-Speed, "The Overseas Activities of China's National Oil Companies: Rationale and Outlook," *Minerals and Energy*, vol. 21, no. 1, (2006), pp. 1–14.

34. Amy M. Jaffe and Steven W. Lewis, "Beijing's Oil Diplomacy," *Survival*, vol. 44, no. 1 (2002), pp. 115–134.

35. Erica Downs, *The Energy Security Series: China* (Washington, DC: The Brookings Foreign Policy Studies, December 2006); Xin Ma and Philip Andrews-Speed, "The Overseas Activities of China's National Oil Companies: Rationale and Outlook," *Minerals and Energy*, vol. 21, no. 1 (2006); John Mitchell and Glada Lahn, *Oil for Asia* (London: Chatham House, 2007); Trevor Houser, "The roots of Chinese Oil Investment Abroad," *Asia Policy* no. 5 (2008), pp. 141–166.

36. Philip Andrews-Speed, "China's energy policy and its contribution to international stability," in M. Zaborowski (ed.), *Facing China's Rise: Guidelines for an EU Strategy,* EU Institute for Security Studies, Chaillot Paper, No. 94 (2007), pp.71-81; John Mitchell and Glada Lahn, *Oil for Asia* (London: Chatham House, 2007); David Zweig and Jianhai Bi, "China's Global Hunt for Energy," *Foreign Affairs*, vol. 84, no. 5 (2005), pp. 25–38.

37. Linda Jakobson and Daojiong Zha, "China and the Worldwide Search for Oil Security," *Asia-Pacific Review*, vol. 13, issue 2 (2006), pp. 60–73; Ian Taylor, "China's Oil Diplomacy in Africa," *International Affairs*, vol. 82, no.5 (2006), pp. 937–959; Indira Campos and Alex Vines, "Angola and China: A Pragmatic Partnership," Chatham House Working Paper, available at: (http://www.chathamhouse.org.uk/files/11175_angolachina_csis.pdf).

38. John V. Mitchell and Paul Stevens, *Ending Dependence: Hard Choices for Oil-Exporting States,* Chatham House Report, London, June 2008.

Chapter 6

1. *Kommersant GUIDE*, No. 213, November 15, 2006, p. 23.

2. International Energy Agency (IEA), *Russia Energy Survey 2002* (Paris: OECD/IEA, 2008), pp. 66–69.

3. Andrew Kramer, "Russia Volunteers to Join an OPEC Cut in Oil Output," *The New York Times*, December 11, 2008.

4. In this respect we may recollect that in the past 16 years or more the absolute majority of OPEC members (but for Saudi Arabia) have consistently violated development and export quotas fixed by themselves; but after all, this is OPEC's internal business.

5. Bloomberg News, "Russia Ramps Up Oil Exports as OPEC Cuts Back," *The New York Times*, September 9, 2009; "OPEC Accuses Russia for Market Seizure," *Kommersant*, September 14, 2009.

6. "Cool down Iran," *Vremya Novostei*, April 22, 2009; "We like Russian Gas," *Vremya Novostei*, April 28, 2009.

7. Pablo Bustelo, *Energy Security with a High External Dependence: The Strategies of Japan and South Korea*, Elcano Royal Institute Working Paper No. 16/2008 (Madrid: Real Instituto Elcano, 2008), p. 32.

8. Ibid.

9. McCaul, "Oil Price Drop Unevenly affects Floating Production Projects," *Oil and Gas Journal*, February 16, 2009, p. 43.

10. Trevor Morgan, "Running Faster Just to Stand Still," *Petroleum Economist* (February 2009), pp. 14–16.

11. "OPEC Stares into the Abyss," *Petroleum Economist* (April 2009).

12. "Shtokman needs Sacrifices," *Vremya Novostei*, December 10, 2008; "Oil Business Invests," *Expert*, no. 5, February 9–15, 2009, p. 8.

13. Stanley Reed, "Iraq Tries for Oil's Major Leagues," *Business Week*, August 10, 2009, pp. 22–23; "Gas Jealously," *Vremya Novostei*, October 19, 2009.

14. "Study sees Continued Deepwater Expenditure Growth," *Oil and Gas Journal*, vol. 107, no. 7, February 16, 2009, pp. 32, 40–42.

15. *BP Statistical Review of World Energy* (June 2009), pp. 12, 20.

16. "Oil with Barriers," *Vremya Novostei*, October 26, 2009.

17. Op. cit.

Chapter 7

1. For more information on power shortages in the Gulf region and their impact on world oil markets, see A.F. Alhajji, "Power Shortages and Private Generation Will Reduce Oil Exports," *World Oil* (June 2008). See also: "Gulf States' Gas, Power Shortage might Curb Crude Exports during Peak-Demand Season," *Global Insight*, April 4, 2008 (http://www.ihsglobalinsight.com/SDA/SDADetail12118.htm).

2. The use of oil as a weapon to coerce the targeted country has been very common, and has been used not only by the oil producing countries, but by others including the United Nations and the United States. However, defending against the use of oil as a political weapon by some oil producers in 1956, 1967 and 1973 has defined energy security in the consuming countries in the last five decades. For more information, see: A.F. Alhajji, "The Failure of the Oil Weapon: Consumer Nationalism vs. Producer Symbolism," *Bridges* (Spring/Summer 2004).

3. In recent years, several publications have emphasized that energy security is not only about oil and oil imports. For more information, see the World Economic Forum's publication "The New Energy Security Paradigm" (Spring 2006); (http://www.weforum.org/pdf/Energy.pdf).

4. As an example, John Swaine wrote an article in *The Daily Telegraph* on September 17, 2008 entitled: "Reliance on Russian Gas Threatens Britain's Security" (http://www.telegraph.co.uk/news/2977170/Reliance-on-Russian-gas-threatens-Britains-security.html).

5. For details of the dispute between Russia and Ukraine that led to the cutoff of natural gas supplies to Europe, see: S. Pirani, J. Stern and K. Yafimava, "The Russo-Ukrainian Gas Dispute of January 2009: A Comprehensive Assessment," Oxford Institute for Energy Studies (February 2009).

6. For example, see: Larry Ness, *Terrorism and Public Utility Infrastructure Protection* (New York, NY: Wiley, 2006); Peter Avis, "Oil Platform Security: Is Canada Doing All it Should?" in Sukhvinder Kaur Multani (ed.), *Security of Maritime Trade: New Dimensions* (Hyderabad: Icfai University Press, 2008); and Bunn and Bunn "Strengthening Nuclear Security Against Post-September 11 Threats of Theft and Sabotage," *Journal of Nuclear Materials Management* (Spring 2002).

7. For example, see The Council on Foreign Relations, *National Security Consequences of US Oil Dependency,* 2006 (http://www.cfr.org/publication/11683/national_security_consequences_of_us_oil_depend ency.html).

8. Ibid.

9. For the impact of hurricanes in the Gulf of Mexico on oil and gas production, see the 2009 EIA study: "Impact of the 2008 Hurricanes on the Natural Gas Industry" (http://www.eia.doe.gov/pub/oil_gas/natural_gas/feature_articles/2009/nghurricanes08/nghurricanes08.pdf).

10. For more information on the California power crisis, see: Ambit ERisk, "The California Power Crisis 2000–2001" (http://www.erisk. com/Learning/CaseStudies/CaliforniaPowerCrisis2000.asp).

11. McManus, John F., "Federal Obstruction Causes Natural Gas Shortage," *The New American*, December 11, 2006.

12. Energy Information Administration (EIA), op. cit.

13. International Energy Agency (IEA), "A Primer on Gasoline Prices," 2006 (http://www.eia.doe.gov/pub/oil_gas/petroleum/analysis_publications/pri mer_on_gasoline_prices/html/petbro.html).

14. EIA, op. cit.

15. For example, see the web page of the World Coal Institute (http://www.worldcoal.org/coal-society/coal-energy-security).

16. A statement by long time Amoco vice President John Lyman at the Energy and National Security in the Twenty-First Century conference in 1995. The Institute for National Strategic Studies, National Defense University.

17. International Energy Agency (IEA), "Energy Security" (http://www. iea.org/subjectqueries/keyresult.asp?KEYWORD_ID=4103).

18. Russia's oil production has surpassed Saudi Arabia's since September 2008, as the Saudis cut production to comply with OPEC quotas. While Saudi production capacity is higher than that of Russia by about 2 mbpd, Russia's oil production in 2009 was higher than Saudi production by about 1.2 mbpd.

19. A statement by Hisham Nazer, the former Saudi Arabian Minister of Petroleum and Minerals Resources at the 60th Annual Meeting of the Independent Petroleum Association of America in San Antonio, October 31, 1989.

20. The report is posted on the White House website (http://www.whitehouse.gov/energy/index.html)

21. From a brochure published by the "Ethanol Across America" education campaign (http://www.ethanol.org/pdf/contentmgmt/Energy_Security_Issue_Brief.pdf).

22. For the effect of policy contradictions on energy markets see: A.F. Alhajji, "Will US Policy Contradictions Lead to Future Energy Crisis?" *CEPMLP Journal*, vol. 8, no. 10 (April 2001).

23. For a discussion of the reaction of the oil producing countries to the rhetoric of energy independence and the impact on global energy security see: Gavin Longmuir and A.F. Alhajji, "The Need for a Balancing Act: Reducing Oil Dependence without Triggering a Global Crisis," *Geopolitics of Energy*, vol. 29, no. 3 (March 2007).

24. For more information on the relationship between the value of the dollar and oil prices see: A.F. Alhajji, "How Does the Weak Dollar Affect Oil Prices," Project Syndicate (http://www.project-syndicate.org/commentary/alhajji5/English).

25. For more details that show a decline in OPEC production and exports during that period see: A.F. Alhajji, "Invitation to an Energy Crisis," Project Syndicate (http://www.project-syndicate.org/commentary/alhajji6/English).

26. All references to NGP refer to in-house work by NGP Energy Capital Management or its data base.

27. Spare capacity data in this Figure reflects the views before the financial crisis: low spare capacity and continued growth in demand in 2009. The financial crisis changed these views, reduced demand, and increased excess capacity.

28. This section draws on previous work by the author, including: A.F. Alhajji, "The US Énergy Security and Middle Eastern Oil" in Robert Looney (ed.), *A Handbook of US–Middle East Relations* (London: Routledge, 2009); and A.F. Alhajji, "What is Energy Security?" *Middle East Economic Survey*, various issues, 2007–08 (a series of 5 articles).

29. For more information see: A.F. Alhajji, "High Oil Prices Have Not Affected Economic Growth—Yet," *Oil & Gas Journal*, vol. 102, no. 31 (August 2004).

30. For example, improvement in heating and cooling energy efficiency might not lead to lower demand for electricity if incomes increase and people start building larger homes. Similarly, improving the efficiency of automobile engines might not reduce gasoline consumption if people drive longer distances than before.

31. Council on Foreign Relations (CFR), op. cit.

32. The discussion here is focused on policy decisions that limit the transfer of technology. It does not cover patents. For example, a producing country might be willing to pay the right price for a new technology invented in a consuming country, but policy makers in the consuming country might adopt policies that prevent the transfer of such technology.

33. "Lower prices" here are different from "low prices." The idea here is that lower prices are market driven and sustainable in the long run because of technological advances, unlike low prices that are not sustainable in the long run.

34. For some general measures of imports dependence and vulnerability see: A.F. Alhajji and Jim Williams, "Measures of Petroleum Dependence and Vulnerability in OECD Countries," *Middle East Economic Survey*, vol. XLVI, no. 16 (April 2003).

Chapter 8

1. Leonardo Maugeri, *The Age of Oil: The Mythology, History, and Future of the World's Most Controversial Resource* (Westport, CT: Praeger Publishers, 2006), pp. 23–38.

2. Francisco Parra, *Oil Politics: A Modern History of Petroleum* (London: I.B. Tauris & Co. Ltd, 2004), p. 10.

3. Maugeri, op. cit., p. 80.

4. Daniel Yergin, *The Prize: The Epic Quest for Oil, Money and Power* (New York, NY: Free Press, 2009), pp. 215–216.

5. Maugeri, op. cit., p. 104.

6. Ibid., pp. 105, 108.

7. Parra, op. cit., pp. 150–154.

8. Ibid., p. 147.

9. Maugeri, op. cit., p. 112.

10. Ibid., pp. 112, 114.

11. Parra, op. cit., p. 146.

12. Robert Mabro, *A Dialogue between Oil Producers and Consumers: The Why and the How* (Oxford: Oxford Institute for Energy Studies, 1992), p. 1.

13. Maugeri, op. cit., pp. 129–130.

14. Ibid., 136.

15. Ibid., 138-139.

16. Ibid., 145.

17. Parra, op. cit., p. 321.

18. Maugeri, op. cit., p. 141.

19. Arne Walther, "Producer–Consumer Dialogue: The Road Ahead," *Middle East Economic Survey*, February 11, 2002, D2.

20. Mabro, op. cit., p. 9.

21. Walther, op. cit., 2002, D2.

22. Mabro, op. cit., pp. i, 10–11, 25–26.

23. Ibid., p. i.

24. Ibid., p. 11.

25. Ibid.

26. Ibid., p. ii.

27. Ibid., p. 27.

28. Robert Skinner, "Energy Security and Producer-Consumer Dialogue: Avoiding a Maginot Mentality," *Background Paper for Government of Canada Symposium – Energizing Supply: Oil and Gas Investment in Uncertain Times*, October 28, 2005, p. 10 (www.oxfordenergy.org/presentations/SecurityOfSupply.pdf).

29. Walther, op. cit., D2.

30. Arne Walther, "Dialogue for Global Energy Security," delivered to the Board of Executive Directors, World Bank Group, November 7, 2007 (www2.iefs.org.sa/Speeches/Pages/DIALOGUEFORGLOBAL ENERGYSECURITYTheRoleoftheIEF.aspx).

31. Arne Walther, "Producer–Consumer Relations in a New Era," *Middle East Economic Survey*, September 25, 2009 (www.mees.com/postedarticles/oped/v49n39-5OD01.htm).

32. Group of Eight (G-8), "St Petersburg Plan of Action for Global Energy Security," July 16, 2006 (http://en.g8russia.ru/docs/11.html).

33. Noe van Hulst, "Key Messages From The 11th IEF in Rome," April 20–22, 2008, p. 3 (www2.iefs.org.sa/whatsnew/Documents/KEY_MESSAGES_FROM_THE_11th_IEF_IN_ROME.pdf).

34. Ali Aissaoui, "The Oil Price Dimension of the Producer–Consumer Dialogue: A Non-Market Perspective," *Middle East Economic Survey*, September 28, 2009 (http://www.mees.com/postedarticles/oped/v52n39-5OD01.htm).

35. Group of Twenty (G-20), "Communiqué from the Pittsburgh G-20 Summit," September 25, 2009 (http://www.pittsburghsummit.gov/mediacenter/129639.htm).

36. Ibid.

37. Aissaoui, op. cit.

38. Vincent Lauerman and Julian Lee, *Canada's Oil Sands* (London: Centre for Global Energy Studies & Geopolitics Central, 2009), p. 39.

39. John Lewis Gaddis, "Grand Strategy in the Second Term," *Foreign Affairs*, vol. 84, no. 1 (January/February 2005); (www.foreignaffairs.com/articles/60421/john-lewis-gaddis/grand-strategy-in-the-second-term#).

40. Lauerman and Lee, op. cit., p. 39.

41. Ibid., pp. 26–27.

42. Ibid., p. 28.

43. Ibid., p. 29.

44. Ibid.

45. Ibid.

46. Martin Wolf, "Victory in the Cold War was a Start as well as and Ending," *Financial Times*, November 10, 2009 (www.ft.com/cms/s/0/123efa0e-ce2f-11de-a1ea-00144feabdc0.html).

47. Krishna Guha, "World Leaders Unite to Restore Growth," *Financial Times*, November 16, 2008 (www.ft.com/cms/s/0/54f72948-b378-11dd-bbc9-0000779fd18c.html)

48. Group of Twenty (G-20), op. cit.

49. Martin Wolf, "Do not Learn Wrong Lessons from Lehman's Fall," *Financial Times*, September 15, 2009 (www.ft.com/cms/s/0/b24477de-a226-11de-9caa-00144feabdc0.html).

50. Timothy Geithner and Lawrence Summers, "A New Financial Foundation," *The Washington Post*, June 15, 2009 (www.washingtonpost.com/wp-dyn/content/article/2009/06/14/AR2009061402443.html).

51. Patrick Jenkins and Brooke Masters, "Banks Concede Reform is Inevitable," *Financial Times*, February 3, 2010 (http://www.ft.com/cms/s/0/c8ecd5e6-10f6-11df-9a9e-00144feab49a.html).

52. Tom Braithwaite and Francesco Guerrera, "Obama Hammers Wall Street Banks," *Financial Times*, January 21, 2010 (http://www.ft.com/cms/s/0/44f593ee-06a7-11df-b426-00144feabdc0.html).

53. Patrick Jenkins, "Barclays Chief Warns on Regulation," *Financial Times*, October 18, 2009 (www.ft.com/cms/s/0/47fd0f82-bc23-11de-9426-00144feab49a.html).

54. Nathan Gardels, "Stiglitz: The Fall of Wall Street is to Market Fundamentalism what the Fall of the Berlin Wall was to Communism," *The Huffington Post*, September 16, 2008 (www.huffingtonpost.com/nathan-gardels/stiglitz-the-fall-of-wall_b_126911.html).

55. Heather Timmons, "Feeling Powerless, India Blames Speculation," *The New York Times*, July 23, 2009 (www.nytimes.com/2008/07/23/business/worldbusiness/23speculate.html?_r=1&scp=1&sq=timmons%20feeling%20powerless,%20India%20blames%20oil%20speculation&st=cse).

56. Gordon Brown and Nicolas Sarkozy, "Oil Prices Need Government Supervision," *The Wall Street Journal,* July 8, 2008 (http://online.wsj.com/article/SB124701217125708963.html).

57. Ibid.

58. Bassam Fattouh and Christopher Allsopp, "The Price Band and Oil Price Dynamics," *Oxford Energy Comment*, July 2009, pp. 10–12.

59. Aissaoui, op. cit.

60. Fattouh and Allsopp, cit. op., p. 9.

61. Geopolitics Central database.

62. Aaron Smith, "Putting Obama's Energy Plan to the Test," *CNNMoney.com*, August 4, 2008 (http://money.cnn.com/2008/08/04/news/economy/obama_energy/?postversion=2008080417).

63. International Energy Agency (IEA), *Oil Market Report*, February 11, 2010, p. 20.

64. Tom Shanker and Mark Landler, "Putin Says US is Undermining Global Stability," *The New York Times*, February 11, 2007 (query.nytimes.com/gst/fullpage.html?res=9B03E3D61E3FF932A257 51C0A9619C8B63&sec=&spon=&&scp=2&sq=Munich%20Confere nce%20on%20Security%20Policy%20putin&st=cse).

65. Andrew E. Kramer, "Russia Resumes Patrols by Nuclear Bombers," *The New York Times*, August 18, 2007 (http://www.nytimes.com/2007/08/18/world/europe/17cnd-russia.html?sq=russia%20resumes%20strategic%20bomber%20flights&st=cse&scp=1&pagewanted=print)

66. Lauerman and Lee, op. cit., p. 41.

67. Ibid., p. 42.

68. Ibid.

69. Ibid., p. 61–64.

70. Ibid., p. 69–72.

Chapter 9

1. Daniel Yergin, *The Prize: The Epic Quest for Oil, Money and Power* (New York, NY: Simon & Schuster, 1991).

2. Glada Lahn, Valerie Marcel, John Mitchell, Keith Myers and Paul Stevens, "Good Governance of the National Petroleum Sector," 2007, Chatham House Document (http://www.chathamhouse.org.uk/files/9115_ggdoc0407.pdf).

3. Michael L. Ross, "Blood Barrels: Why Oil Wealth Fuels Conflict," *Foreign Affairs*, vol. 87, issue 3 (May/June 2008), p. 2

4. Yergin, op. cit., pp. 12–13

5. Daniel Moran and James A. Russell (eds), *Energy Security and Global Politics: The Militarization of Resource Management* (Abingdon: Routledge Global Security Studies, 2009), p. 2.

6. Michael Klare, *Resource Wars* (New York, NY: Henry Holt and Company, 2001).

7. Ibid.

8. Nader Elhefnawy, "The Impending Oil Shock," *Survival* (June 2008).

9. Moran and Russell, op. cit, pp. 7–8.

10. Ibid.

11. Mary Kaldor, Terry Lynn Karl and Yahia Said, *Oil Wars* (London: Pluto Press, 2007).

12. Ibid., p. 2.

13. David Victor, "What Resource Wars?" *The National Interest* online, November, 12, 2007 (http://www.nationalinterest.org/PrinterFriendly. aspx?id=16020).

14. Klare argues this line in his book *Resource Wars*.

15. Amy Myers Jaffe and Ronald Soligo, "Energy Security – The Russian Connection" in Daniel Moran and James Russell (eds), *Energy Security and Global Politics: The Militarization of Resource Management* (Routledge, 2008).

16. OECD Economic Outlook, July 1981; see also Robert Stobaugh and Daniel Yergin, *Energy Future: Report of the Energy Project at Harvard Business School* (New York, NY: Ballantine, 1980).

17. Amy Myers Jaffe, "The Impending Oil Shock: An Exchange," *IISS Survival,* vol. 50, issue 4 (August 2008), pp. 61–82.

18. Ibid.

19. Clifford E. Singer, "Energy and International War: From Babylon to Baghdad and Beyond," *World Scientific Series on Energy and Resource Economics* vol. 6 (World Scientific Publishing Co., 2008).

20. Ibid., p. 3.

21. Ibid., p. 4.

22. Ibid., p. 10.

23. Ibid.

24. "Hello President. If you wind up freezing and hurt us, we will hurt you," Chavez said in his weekly television and radio address. "Do you know how? We are not going to send oil to the United States," CNN, February 10, 2008 (http://www/cnn.com/2008/WORLD/americas/02/10/venez. exxon/index.html).

25. "Iran Warns US on Oil Shipments," CNN, June 4, 2006 (http://www.cnn.com/2006/WORLD/meast/06/04us.iran).

26. See: "Saudi Aramco: National Flagship with International Responsibilities" (www.rice.edu/energy).

27. Kevin Rosner, "Gazprom and the Russian State," Global Market Briefing, Institute for the Analysis of Global Security (London: GMB Publishing, 2006).

28. Amy Myers Jaffe and Ronald Soligo, "Market Structure in the New Gas Economy: Is Cartelization Possible?" in David G. Victor, Amy Myers Jaffe and Mark H. Hayes, *Natural Gas and Geopolitics: From 1970 to 2030* (Oxford: Oxford University Press, 2006).

29. Peter Hartley and Kenneth Medlock, "Scenarios for Russian Natural Gas Exports: The Role of Domestic Investment, the Caspian and LNG," working paper, James Baker III Institute for Public Policy, Rice University (http://www.bakerinstitute.org/publications/EF-pub-HartleyMedlockRussNatGas-050609.pdf).

30. K. Medlock and A. Jaffe, "The Global Energy Market: Comprehensive Strategies to Meet Geopolitical and Financial Risks," Baker Working Paper Series, May 2008 (http://www.bakerinstitute.org/publications/IEEJtransportation-MedlockJaffe.pdf).

31. Klare, op. cit.

32. US China Economic and Security Review Commission, Report to Congress, November 2006, pp. 7–8 (http://uscc.gov/annual_report/2006/annual_report_full_06.pdf).

33. Moran and Russell, op. cit., p. 8.

34. James D. Hamilton, "Oil and the Macroeconomy Since World War II," *Journal of Political Economy*, vol. 91, no. 2 (1983), pp. 228–248.

35. Peter Ferderer, "Oil Price Volatility and the Macroeconomy," *Journal of Macroeconomics* (Winter 1996), pp. 1–26; and William Nordhaus, "Oil and Economic Performance in Industrial Countries," Brookings Paper on Economic Activity, vol. 2, 1980.

36. Robert B. Barsky and Lutz Kilian, "Oil and the Macroeconomy Since the 1970s," *Journal of Economic Perspectives*, vol. 18, no. 4 (Fall 2004), pp. 115–134.

37. Lutz Kilian, "Exogenous Oil Supply Shocks: How Big Are They and How Much Do They Matter for the US Economy?" *Review of Economics and Statistics*, vol. 90, no. 2 (May 2008), pp. 216–240.

38. Mahmoud A. El-Gamal and Amy Myers Jaffe, *Oil, Dollars, Debt and Crises: The Global Curse of Black Gold* (New York, NY: Cambridge University Press, 2010).

39. H. Minsky, *Stabilizing an Unstable Economy* (New York, NY: McGraw Hill, 1986), and *Can "It" Happen Again: Essays on Instability and Finance* (New York, NY: M.E. Sharpe, 1982).

40. This argument is often made by Edward Morse in various public speaking engagements such as at the Council on Foreign Relations and Baker Institute.

41. Amy Myers Jaffe and Ronald Soligo, "The Role of Inventories in Oil Market Stability," *The Quarterly Review of Economics and Finance* no. 42 (2002), pp. 401–415.

Chapter 10

1. Asian countries are becoming important players in providing services, sometimes technology and even investment to build generation plants or other electricity projects, as part of their efforts to improve ties with Middle Eastern countries. With special financing and other incentives on offer from Asia, and in some cases fuel to supply the power sector,

Middle Eastern countries could have limited incentives to establish open competitive power markets, with the rise of Asian players.

2. These new local actors investing in power assets include examples like TAQA and Liwa Energy (Abu Dhabi), Oman Oil Company and the Gulf Investment Corporation.

3. Shuaiba, in Saudi Arabia, is the largest-oil fired plant worldwide (conventional steam oil 11 x 400MW, operational in 2008). It benefited from integrated design and EPC components as well as from lower operating costs.

4. The aviation industry was an important contributor. The technology that made turbines more efficient came from military aircraft, and efforts toward jet engine cost reduction was an outcome of the US deregulation of airlines.

5. Morocco, for example, still plans to launch its 1320 MW coal independent power project (IPP) at Safi, on a 30 year build–operate–transfer (BOT) basis. According to one study, a clean coal power plant will produce electricity at less than $0.05 per kWh, compared with $0.06 for coal gasification, more than $0.06 for wind, more than $0.08 for marine wave energy, and less than $0.04 for nuclear.

6. In order to calculate these costs, the following formulas and assumptions were used: Capacity cost ($/MWh) = PMT (Discount Rate, Operating Life, Capital Cost [($/KW])/8.76/Capacity factor; O&M cost ($/MWh) = O&M cost ($/KW-yr)/8.76/Capacity factor; Fuel costs are calculated depending on the fuel used or potentially used in each case (gas, heavy fuel oil or coal), CO_2 prices are assumed to be nil. That would have to change in the case of the development of a more comprehensive global framework post-2012 for carbon trading, or additional development of Clean Development Mechanisms. In this calculation, power generation costs consider a 10 percent discount rate and $1.1 per MMBtu, $4 per MMBtu for HFO and $2.75 for imported coal.

7. By way of comparison, Asia-Pacific has 3,493 projects in the pipeline (80 percent of the total CERs in 2012).

8. According to the International Energy Agency (IEA), this investment figure is usually compared with the $545 billion earmarked for the hydrocarbons sector during the same period. Although renewables investments appear to be minimal, it is important to note that several countries in the region are hydrocarbon exporters. Therefore, we argue that the two figures are not comparable.

9. Abu Dhabi's active involvement allowed it to host the headquarters of the International Renewable Energy Agency (IRENA). It pledged to spend $136 million to fund the Agency. Masdar was launched in 2007 and includes a zero-carbon city, large scale solar projects inside (the 100 MW IPP Shams 1 followed by Shams 2 and Shams 3) and outside of the UAE, a 500MW gas fired hydrogen plant, and a pilot carbon dioxide (CO_2) capture project in addition to a CO_2 pipeline network to oilfields (for reinjection). It also has a 20 percent stake in a wind farm project in the UK and an unspecified equity stake in Finnish wind turbine manufacturer WinWinD Oy. The Masdar initiative is driven by the Abu Dhabi Future Energy Company, wholly owned by the Abu Dhabi government through the Mubadala Development Company.

10. For example, the IEA estimates that $80 per barrel is an oil price threshold under which gas-fired electricity generation trumps wind farms, risking delaying projects.

11. Set up under the auspices of the UN Framework Convention on Climate Change and based in Bonn, Germany, the CDM allows developed countries to invest in emission-reducing projects in developing countries. CDM registers the projects and issues carbon credits to those involved. It is one of three mechanisms included in the Kyoto Protocol (with Joint Implementation and emissions trading). The objective is to let the market find the lowest cost options for emissions reductions and determine the value of reduction credits through supply and demand balance, rather than setting a predefined value through taxation.

[407]

12. Most MENA countries, expect Iraq and Palestine, are parties to the Kyoto Protocol. As of May 2007, Egypt and Israel were the only ones who ratified it.

13. Nuclear ambitions are not new to the region. The first efforts date back to the post-World War II period, and some continued during the Cold War. Some were officially linked to power generation; others were suspected to be for less-peaceful purposes.

14. Historical examples include Urenco (a consortium of the British, German, and Dutch governments) and Eurodif (European Gaseous Diffusion Uranium Enrichment Consortium).

15. The PBMR is developed by PBMR Ltd., involving the state-owned South African Industrial Development Corp., South Africa's utility Eskom and Westinghouse who took over British Nuclear Fuel (BNF) shares. Because it could be either dry (Helium) or water-cooled, it does not need to be located near water sites. It may be an appropriate solution given the challenging summer temperatures in the Gulf. Because the PBMR is smaller than traditional reactors, it requires a smaller safety perimeter.

16. The cost of the Saudi marginal barrel of oil is estimated at around $20 per barrel (source CERA). New gas production cost (sour gas in Abu Dhabi for instance) is in the area of $5 per MMbtu.

17. The concept of sustainability is a complex one, but it became widely used after the publication of the Brundtland Commission report (the World Commission on Environment and Development) in 1987. Sustainable development was defined as: "development that meets the needs of the present without compromising the ability of future generations to meet their own needs."

18. The UNDP uses today more than 150 composite indices to measure countries' performance, up from less than 25 before 1985. These indices cover a diverse set of issues including competitiveness, governance, social aspects, human rights, environment and security.

19. The "Dutch Disease," the "Curse of Oil," and the "Paradox of Plenty," among other concepts, have all been extensively analyzed since the 1950s. The expression Dutch Disease was mentioned for the first time in 1977 in *The Economist*, in relation to the debate following oil discoveries in the UK. This syndrome refers to the disappointing economic performance of the Netherlands following the development of the Groningue gas field. Empirical research on low economic performance of resource holding countries really took off in the 1990s.

20. OPEC Annual Statistical Bulletin. Qatar came second in the world after Liechtenstein, straddled by Austria, Germany and Switzerland.

21. Saudi Arabia's population was around 24 million in 2008, while Qatar accounted about 1.64 million inhabitants. The former extends over an area of more than 2,240,000 km², whereas Qatar registers 11,400 km².

22. The oil price assumption in the budget is $37 per barrel.

23. "Saudi Arabia is using its overseas assets to finance domestic requirements specified in its budget for this year ... in other words, the kingdom is channeling part of those funds into domestic development because it apparently does not want to borrow at this stage," Malick Yunus, senior economist at the National Commercial Bank, July 2009.

24. Data from Central Bank and SAMBA.

Chapter 11

1. Eman Ghoneim, "A Remote Sensing Study of Some Impacts of Global Warming on the Arab Region," in Mostafa K. Tolba and Najib W. Saab (eds), *Arab Environment: Climate Change: Impact of Climate Change on Arab Countries* (Beirut: Arab Forum for Environment and Development, 2009), p. 36.

2. UNESCO Institute for Statistics, "Estimates and Projections of Adult Illiteracy for Population Aged 15 Years and Above by Country and by Gender, 1970–2015," July 2002 (http://www.uis.unesco.org/en/stats/statistics/UIS_Literacy_Country2002.xls).

3. *Gulf Industrial Newsletter* vol. 44 (March 2004), p. 2.

4. "Arab Environment Future Challenges: Executive Summary Recommendations: 2008 Report of the Arab Forum for Environment and Development" (Beirut: Arab Forum for Environment and Development, 2009), p. 10.

5. Information and Communication Technology Research Forum (ICTRF); (http://www.ku.ac.ae/ICTRF2009/index.php?page=presentations).

6. Jim Giles, "Oil Rich, Science Poor," *Nature* no. 2 (November 2006), p. 28.

7. For example, "Patents from nine Arab countries registered in the US Patents and Trademarks Office (USPTO) during the period 1980–2000 totaled 370 compared to 16,328 for South Korea. Arab scientists have increased the number of published works and their output has increased at a rate of 10 percent per annum over the last three decades compared to 26 percent increase annually by South Korea over the last two decades. The quality of these publications is limited as there were only four Arab publications in 1987 which were cited more than 40 times compared to 10,481 in the United States." Abdulla Alnajjar, "Networking the Arab Scientific Community can Bring Change to the Arab Countries: Toward Harvesting Outcome of Arab Education System" (http://iie.qf.org.qa/files/pdf/abdalla%20alnajjar.pdf).

8. Cooperation Council for the Arab States of the Gulf (GCC) Secretariat General, "The Economic Agreement between the GCC States," adopted by the CGG Supreme Council (22nd Session; December 31, 2001) in the City of Muscat, Sultanate of Oman.

9. Webometrics, "Ranking Web of World Universities: Arab World," January 2010 (www.webometrics.info/top100_continent.asp?cont=aw).

10. "A Global Perspective on Research and Development," UNESCO Institute for Statistics Estimates, September 2009.

11. Ibid.

12. Ibid.

13. Dow Chemical Company (http://www.dow.com/).

14. Eli Lilly & Co. (http://www.lilly.com/research/).

15. Saudi Arabian Ministry of Foreign Affairs. "Cooperation Council for the Arab States of the Gulf" (http://www.mofa.gov.sa/Detail.asp?In SectionID=5505&InNewsItemID=63566).

16. Cooperation Council for the Arab States of the Gulf (GCC) Secretariat General. *The Economic Agreement between the GCC States*, adopted by the CGG Supreme Council (22nd Session; 31 December 2001) in the City of Muscat, Sultanate of Oman, p. 16.

17. Ibid, p. 18.

18. Ibid, p. 19.

19. Global Investment House, "Global Research – GCC," January 2008 (http://www.gulfinthemedia.com/files/article_en/377920.pdf)

20. Woertz Eckart, "Reflected Glory: The GCC's Future with Renewables," August 19, 2008 (http://gulfnews.com/about-gulf-news/al-nisr-portfolio/gnqfr/articles/reflected-glory-the-gcc-s-future-with-renewables-1.441776).

21. AMEinfo, "Gulf Research Center to Establish the 'EU–GCC Clean Energy Network'" (http://www.ameinfo.com/219791.html).

22. Meena Janardhan, "Middle East: In the Race for Renewable Energy Sources" (http://ipsnews.net/news.asp?idnews=43624).

23. Business Intelligence Middle East (BI-ME), "Renewable energy remains at the core of GCC's long-term energy and sustainability strategy," posted September 17, 2009 11:34am (http://www.bi-me.com/main.php?id=40315&t=1&c=35&cg=4&mset=1011).

24. Qatar Foundation, "Qatar Petroleum Will Open Research Centre at QSTP" (http://www.qstp.org.qa/output/Page2071.asp).

25. Meena Janardhan, op. cit.

26. Qatar Foundation, op. cit.

27. Ghasemali Mohebali and A.S. Ball, "Biocatalytic Desulfurization (BDS) of Petrodiesel Fuels," *Microbiology* no. 154 (2008), pp. 2169–2183; D.R. Lovley, "Bug Juice: Harvesting Electricity with Microorganisms," *Nature Reviews: Microbiology* vol. 4 (2006), pp. 497–508.

Chapter 12

1. United Nations Framework Convention on Climate Change (UNFCCC), "The Kyoto Protocol," 1995 (http://unfccc.int/kyoto_protocol/items/2830.php).

2. Robert Socolow, "Can We Bury Global Warming?" *Scientific American* vol. 293 (July 2005); (http://cmi.princeton.edu/resources/pdfs/bury_globalwarming.pdf).

3. International Energy Agency (IEA). "Technology Roadmap: Carbon Capture and Storage" (2008); (http://www.iea.org/papers/2009/CCS_Roadmap.pdf).

4. Ibid.

5. Advanced Power Generation Technology Forum (APG-TF), "Cleaner Fossil Power Generation in the 21st Century," UK, April, 2009.

6. Ibid.

7. Ibid.

8. B. Metz, O. Davidson, H. de Coninck, M. Loos and L. Meyer (eds), "Intergovernmental Panel on Climate Change (IPCC) Special Report on Carbon Dioxide Capture and Storage (CCS)," (Cambridge: Cambridge University Press, 2005), p. 96.

9. International Energy Agency (IEA), "Capture at power stations and other major point sources – Zero emissions technologies for fossil fuels," Working party on fossil fuels CO_2, (2003); (http://www. iea.org/papers/2003/CO2_Power_Fossil_Fuels.pdf).

10. McKinsey and Company, "Carbon Capture and Storage: Assessing the Economics," McKinsey Climate Change Initiative, 2008 (http://www. mckinsey.com/clientservice/sustainability/pdf/CCS_Assessing_the_Eco nomics.pdf).

11. Data from CIGRE (International Council on Large Electric Systems). CIGRE is one of the leading worldwide organizations on electric power systems, covering their technical, economic, environmental, organizational and regulatory aspects, based in France and founded in 1921. The GCC–CIGRE is Gulf Cooperation Countries regional organization, based in Doha, Qatar.

12. See Intergovernmental Panel on Climate Change (IPCC), "IPCC Special Report on Carbon Dioxide Capture and Storage (CCS)," 2005, p. 34 (http://www.ipcc.ch/publications_and_data/publications_and_data _reports_carbon_dioxide.htm).

13. International Energy Agency (IEA), "CO_2 Emissions from (per kWh) Fuel Combustion Highlights," 2009 (http://www.iea.org/co2highlights).

14. World Energy Council (WEC), "Carbon Dioxide Capture and Storage (CCS): Cleaner Energy Council, Interim Balance," 2007 (http://www.usea.org/programs/CFFS/FINAL CCS Brochure English.pdf).

15. M.A. Yaterlinde, J.R. Ybema and G.H. Martimus, "Long-term Global Energy Developments and their Implications for Europe," ECN Policy Studies, the Netherlands, 2004 (http://130.226.56.153/rispubl/SYS/syspdf/energconf05/session1_ybema.pdf).

BIBLIOGRAPHY

"Arab Environment Future Challenges: Executive Summary Recommendations: 2008 Report of the Arab Forum for Environment and Development." (Beirut: Arab Forum for Environment and Development, 2009).

"Barack Obama's Acceptance Speech." *NPR*, August 28, 2008 (http://www.npr.org/templates/story/story.php?storyId=94087570); and (http://www.whitehouse.gov/issues/energy-and-environment).

"CB Boom." *China Business Weekly*, October 22–28, 2007.

"China Looks to Energy Independence." Xinhua News Agency, Beijing, October 26, 2007.

"China to Produce 500 m cu m of Coal-Bed Methane this Year." Xinhua News Agency, Beijing, November 9, 2007.

"China: New Home of the Hummer?" *Intelligence Report*, vol. 2, issue 10, June 16, 2009 (http://www.secureenergy.org/files/files/1052_SAFEIntelligenceReport21020090616.pdf).

"China's Coal-Bed Methane Industry holds Promise." *Interfax China Energy Report Weekly*, November 6, 2007.

"CNPC Awarded Licenses for Sino-Turkmenistan Natural Gas Project." *Interfax China Energy Report*, vol. VI, issue 32, September 5, 2007.

"Cool Down Iran." *Vremya Novostei*, April 22, 2009.

"Costs stay High Despite Oil-Price Slump." *Petroleum Economist*, February 2009.

"Gas Jealously." *Vremya Novostei*, October 19, 2009.

"Gulf States' Gas, Power Shortage might Curb Crude Exports during Peak-Demand Season." *Global Insight*, April 4, 2008 (http://www.ihsglobalinsight.com/SDA/SDADetail12118.htm).

"Iran Warns US on Oil Shipments." CNN, June 4, 2006 (http://www.cnn.com/2006/WORLD/meast/06/04us.iran/).

"Obama Aims for Oil Independence." *BBC News*, January 26, 2009 (http://news.bbc.co.uk/2/hi/7851038.stm).

"Oil Business Invests." *Expert*, no. 5, February 9–15, 2009.

"Oil with Barriers." *Vremya Novostei*, October 26, 2009.

"OPEC Accuses Russia for Market Seizure." *Kommersant*, September 14, 2009.

"OPEC Stares into the Abyss." *Petroleum Economist*, April 2009.

"President Obama Calls Energy Bill Passage Critical to Stronger American Economy." The White House, June 27, 2009 (http://www.whitehouse.gov/the_press_office/UPDATED-and-FINAL -WEEKLY-ADDRESS-President-Obama-Calls-Energy-Bill-Passage-Critical-to-Stronger-American-Economy/).

"Shtokman needs Sacrifices." *Vremya Novostei*, December 10, 2008.

"Study sees Continued Deepwater Expenditure Growth." *Oil and Gas Journal*, vol. 107, no. 7, February 16, 2009.

"Sustainable US Policy Options to Address Climate Change." Rice University publications, James Baker III Institute for Public Policy, June 2009.

"Text of Bush's State of the Union Speech," *CNN.com*, February 1, 2006 (http://www.cnn.com/2006/POLITICS/01/31/sotu.transcript/).

"We Like Russian Gas." *Vremya Novostei*, April 28, 2009.

Advanced Power Generation Technology Forum (APG-TF). "Cleaner Fossil Power Generation in the 21st Century," UK, April 2009.

Aissaoui, Ali. "The Oil Price Dimension of the Producer–Consumer Dialogue: A Non-Market Perspective." *Middle East Economic Survey*,

September 28, 2009 (http://www.mees.com/postedarticles/oped/v52n 39-5OD01.htm).

Aissaoui, Ali. *Algeria: The Political Economy of Oil and Gas* (New York, NY: Oxford University Press, 2001).

Aizhu, Chen. "China to Add 1.8 mln bbls African Crude to Reserves." Reuters, March 23, 2009.

Al-Sahlawi, M. "GCC Energy Demand Outlook to 2000." *Energy Economics*, vol. 10, no. 1 (January 1988).

Al-Sahlawi, M. and M. Elbek. "An Alternative Oil Pricing Currency to Improve OPEC's Balance of Trade." *The Journal of Energy and Development*, vol. 22, no. 2 (Spring 1997).

Alhajji, A.F. "High Oil Prices Have Not Affected Economic Growth—Yet." *Oil & Gas Journal*, vol. 102, no. 31 (August 2004).

Alhajji, A.F. "How Does the Weak Dollar Affect Oil Prices." Project Syndicate (http://www.project-syndicate.org/commentary/alhajji5/English).

Alhajji, A.F. "Invitation to an Energy Crisis." Project Syndicate (http://www.project-syndicate.org/commentary/alhajji6/English).

Alhajji, A.F. "Power Shortages and Private Generation Will Reduce Oil Exports." *World Oil* (June 2008).

Alhajji, A.F. "The Failure of the Oil Weapon: Consumer Nationalism vs. Producer Symbolism." *Bridges* (Spring/Summer 2004).

Alhajji, A.F. "What is Energy Security?" *Middle East Economic Survey*, various issues, 2007–08.

Alhajji, A.F. "Will US Policy Contradictions Lead to Future Energy Crisis?" *CEPMLP Journal*, vol. 8, no. 10 (April 2001).

Alhajji, A.F. and J. Williams. "Measures of Petroleum Dependence and Vulnerability in OECD Countries." *Middle East Economic Survey*, vol. XLVI, no. 16 (April 2003).

Alnajjar, Abdulla. "Networking the Arab Scientific Community can Bring Change to the Arab Countries: Toward Harvesting Outcome of Arab Education System" (http://iie.qf.org.qa/files/pdf/abdalla%20alnajjar.pdf).

Ambit ERisk. "The California Power Crisis 2000–2001" (http://www.erisk.com/Learning/CaseStudies/CaliforniaPowerCrisis2000.asp).

AMEinfo. "Gulf Research Center to Establish the 'EU–GCC Clean Energy Network'" (http://www.ameinfo.com/219791.html).

Andrews-Speed, Philip, Xuanli Liao and Roland Dannreuther. *The Strategic Impact of China's Energy Needs*. International Institute for Strategic Studies, Adelphi Paper No. 346 (2002).

Andrews-Speed, Philip. *Energy Policy and Regulation in the People's Republic of China* (London: Kluwer Law, 2004).

Barbir, F. and S. Ulgiati (eds). *Sustainable Energy Production and Consumption* (Springer, 2008).

Barsky, Robert B. and Lutz Kilian. "Oil and the Macroeconomy Since the 1970s." *Journal of Economic Perspectives*, vol. 18, no. 4 (Fall 2004).

Bauer M. and C.P. Hanelt. "Security Situation in the Gulf Region involving, Iran, Iraq and Saudi Arabia as Regional Powers: Policy Recommendations for the European Union and the International Community." Discussion Paper, Center for Applied Policy Research and Bertelsmann Stiftung, September 2008.

Berrah, Noureddine, Fei Feng, Roland Priddle and Leiping Wang. *Sustainable Energy in China: The Closing Window of Opportunity* (Washington, DC: World Bank, 2007).

Bloomberg News. "Russia Ramps Up Oil Exports as OPEC Cuts Back." *The New York Times*, September 9, 2009.

BP. *BP Statistical Review of World Energy 2009* (www.bp.com/proeductlanding.do?categoryId=6929 content Id=7044622).

Braithwaite, Tom and Francesco Guerrera. "Obama Hammers Wall Street Banks." *Financial Times*, January 21, 2010 (http://www.ft.com/cms /s/0/44f593ee-06a7-11df-b426-00144feabdc0.html).

BP. *BP Statistical Review of World Energy* (June 2009).

BP. *BP Statistical Review of World Energy 2009* (www.bp.com/ proeductlanding.do?categoryId=6929 content Id=7044622).

BP. *BP Statistical Review of World Energy 2009* (London: BP, 2009).

Brown, Gordon and Nicolas Sarkozy. "Oil Prices Need Government Supervision." *The Wall Street Journal,* July 8, 2008 (online.wsj. com/article/SB124701217125708963.html).

Bunn, M. and G. Bunn. "Strengthening Nuclear Security Against Post-September 11 Threats of Theft and Sabotage." *Journal of Nuclear Materials Management* (Spring 2002).

Business Intelligence Middle East (BI-ME). "Renewable energy remains at the core of GCC's long-term energy and sustainability strategy." Posted September 17, 2009, 11:34am (http://www.bi-me.com/ main.php?id=40315&t=1&c=35&cg=4&mset=1011).

Campos, Indira, and Alex Vines. "Angola and China. A Pragmatic Partnership." Chatham House Working Paper (http://www. chathamhouse.org.uk/files/11175_angolachina_csis.pdf).

Carson. Iain, and Vijay V. Vaitheeswaran. *Zoom: The Global Race to Fuel the Car of the Future* (New York, NY: Twelve, 2007).

Cole, Bernard D. *"Oil for the Lamps of China": Beijing's 21st-Century Search for Energy.* McNair Paper No. 67, Institute for National Strategic Studies, Washington, DC, 2003.

Collier, Paul, et al. "Managing Resource Revenues in Developing Economies." OxCarre Research Paper 15, Oxford Centre for the Analysis of Resource Rich Economies, May 2009 (Revised).

Cooperation Council for the Arab States of the Gulf (GCC) Secretariat General. "The Economic Agreement between the GCC States." Adopted by the GCC Supreme Council (22nd Session; December 31, 2001) in the City of Muscat, Sultanate of Oman.

Cosku, Balamin B. "The EU's Quest for Energy Security and Persian Gulf." 4th Pan-European Conference on EU Politics, University of Latvia, Riga, Latvia, September 25–27, 2008.

Council on Foreign Relations (CFR). *National Security Consequences of US Oil Dependency,* 2006 (http://www.cfr.org/publication/11683/national_security_consequences_of_us_oil_dependency.html).

Davis, Jeffrey M. et al. (ed.) *Fiscal Policy Formulation and Implementation in Oil-Producing Countries* (Washington, DC: International Monetary Fund [IMF], 2003).

Diwan, Kristin Smith, and Fareed Mohamedi. "The Gulf Comes Down to Earth," *Middle East Report* vol. 252 (Fall 2009).

Downs, Erica Strecker. *China's Quest for Energy Security* RAND Report MR-1244-AF, 2000.

Downs, Erica. "The Chinese Energy Security Debate." *The China Quarterly*, no. 177 (March 2004).

Downs, Erica. *The Energy Security Series: China* (Washington, DC: The Brookings Foreign Policy Studies, December 2006).

Eder, Leonty, Philip Andrews-Speed and Andrey Korzhubaev. "Russia's Evolving Energy Policy for its Eastern Regions, and Implications for Oil and Gas Cooperation between Russia and China." *Journal of World Energy Law and Policy*, vol. 2, no. 3 (2009).

El-Gamal, Mahmoud A., and Amy Myers Jaffe. *Oil, Dollars, Debt and Crises: The Global Curse of Black Gold* (New York, NY: Cambridge University Press, 2010).

Elhefnawy, Nader. "The Impending Oil Shock." *Survival* (June 2008).

Energy Information Administration (EIA). "Impact of the 2008 Hurricanes on the Natural Gas Industry," 2009 (http://www.eia.doe.gov/pub/oil_gas/natural_gas/feature_articles/2009/nghurricanes08/nghurricanes08.pdf).

Fattouh, Bassam and Christopher Allsopp. "The Price Band and Oil Price Dynamics." *Oxford Energy Comment* (July 2009).

Ferderer, Peter. "Oil Price Volatility and the Macroeconomy." *Journal of Macroeconomics* (Winter 1996).

Gaddis, John Lewis. "Grand Strategy in the Second Term." *Foreign Affairs*, vol. 84, no. 1 (January/February 2005); (www.foreignaffairs.com/articles/60421/john-lewis-gaddis/grand-strategy-in-the-second-term#).

Gardels, Nathan. "Stiglitz: The Fall of Wall Street is to Market Fundamentalism what the Fall of the Berlin Wall was to Communism." *The Huffington Post*, September 16, 2008 (www.huffingtonpost.com/nathan-gardels/stiglitz-the-fall-of-wall_b_126911.html).

Geithner, Timothy and Lawrence Summers. "A New Financial Foundation." *The Washington Post*, June 15, 2009 (www.washingtonpost.com/wp-dyn/content/article/2009/06/14/AR2009061402443.html).

Ghoneim, Eman. "A Remote Sensing Study of Some Impacts of Global Warming on the Arab Region," in Tolba, Mostafa K. and Najib W. Saab (eds), *Arab Environment: Climate Change: Impact of Climate Change on Arab Countries* (Beirut: Arab Forum for Environment and Development, 2009).

Giles, Jim. "Oil Rich, Science Poor." *Nature* no. 2 (November 2006).

Girdis, Dan, Startos Tavoulareas and Ray Tomkins. *Liquefied Natural Gas in China. Options for Markets, Institutions and Finance* (Washington, DC: World Bank, 2000).

Global Investment House. "Global Research – GCC" (January 2008); (http://www.gulfinthemedia.com/files/article_en/377920.pdf).

Gore, Al. *Our Choice: A Plan to Solve the Climate Crisis* (Emmaus, PA: Rodale Press, 2009).

Group of Eight (G-8). "St Petersburg Plan of Action for Global Energy Security," July 16, 2006 (http://en.g8russia.ru/docs/11.html).

Group of Twenty (G-20). "Communiqué from the Pittsburgh G-20 Summit," September 25, 2009 (http://www.pittsburghsummit.gov/mediacenter/129639.htm).

Guha, Krishna. "World Leaders Unite to Restore Growth." *Financial Times*, November 16, 2008 (www.ft.com/cms/s/0/54f72948-b378-11dd-bbc9-0000779fd18c.html).

Gulf Industrial Newsletter vol. 44 (March 2004).

Hamilton, James D. "Oil and the Macroeconomy Since World War II." *Journal of Political Economy*, vol. 91, no. 2 (1983).

Hamilton, James D. "Understanding Crude Oil Prices." NBER Working Paper No. w14492 (San Diego, CA: University of California, December 2008).

Hartley, Peter, and Kenneth Medlock. "Scenarios for Russian Natural Gas Exports: The Role of Domestic Investment, the Caspian and LNG." Working paper, James Baker III Institute for Public Policy, Rice University (http:// www. bakerinstitute. org/ publications/ EF-pub-Hartley MedlockRussNatGas-050609.pdf).

Higashi, Nobuyuki. *Natural Gas in China: Market Evolution and Strategy* (Paris: OECD/IEA, 2009).

Horsnell, Paul. *Oil in Asia. Markets, Trading, Refining and Deregulation* (Oxford: Oxford University Press, 1997).

Houser, Trevor. "The roots of Chinese Oil Investment Abroad." *Asia Policy* No. 5 (2008).

Hubbert, M.K. "Techniques of Production as Applied to Production of Oil." US Department of Commerce (May 1982).

Intergovernmental Panel on Climate Change (IPCC). "IPCC Special Report on Carbon Dioxide Capture and Storage (CCS)," 2005 (http://www.ipcc.ch/publications_and_data/publications_and_data_reports_carbon_dioxide.htm).

International Energy Agency (IEA). "A Primer on Gasoline Prices," 2006 (http://www.eia.doe.gov/pub/oil_gas/petroleum/analysis_publications/primer_on_gasoline_prices/html/petbro.html).

International Energy Agency (IEA). "Capture at Power Stations and other Major Point Sources: Zero Emissions Technologies for Fossil Fuels." Working party on fossil fuels CO_2, 2003 (http://www.iea.org/ papers/2003/CO2_Power_Fossil_Fuels.pdf).

International Energy Agency (IEA). "CO_2 Emissions from (per kWh) Fuel Combustion Highlights," 2009 (http://www.iea.org/co2highlights).

International Energy Agency (IEA). "Energy Security" (http://www.iea.org/subjectqueries/keyresult.asp?KEYWORD_ID=4103).

International Energy Agency (IEA). "Energy Technology Perspective 2008" (Paris: IEA-OECD, 2008).

International Energy Agency (IEA). "Technology Roadmap: Carbon Capture and Storage," 2008 (http://www.iea.org/papers/2009/CCS_Roadmap.pdf).

International Energy Agency (IEA). *China's Worldwide Quest for Energy* (Paris: OECD/IEA, 2000).

International Energy Agency (IEA). *Developing China's Natural Gas Market. The Energy Policy Challenges* (Paris: OECD/IEA, 2002).

International Energy Agency (IEA). *Oil Market Report*, February 11, 2010.

International Energy Agency (IEA). *Russia Energy Survey, 2002* (Paris: OECD/IEA, 2008).

International Energy Agency (IEA). *Word Energy Outlook 2009* (Paris: IEA/OECD, 2009).

International Energy Agency (IEA). *World Energy Outlook 2008* (Paris: IEA/OECD, 2008).

International Energy Agency (IEA). *World Energy Outlook 2007* (Paris: OECD/IEA, 2007).

International Monetary Fund (IMF). "Sustaining the Recovery." *World Economic Outlook* (October 2009); (http://www.imf.org/external/pubs/ft/weo/2009/02/index.htm).

Jackson, Peter. "The Future of global Oil Supply: Understanding the Building Blocks." Cambridge Energy Research Associates (CERA). World Federation of Scientists Meeting, Erice, Sicily, August 2009.

Jaffe A.M., "Energy Security: Oil – Geopolitical and Strategic Implications for China and the United States." The James A. Baker III Institute for Public Policy, Rice University, July 2005.

Jaffe, A.M. "The Impending Oil Shock: An Exchange." *IISS Survival,* vol. 50, issue 4 (August 2008).

Jaffe, A.M., and Ronald Soligo. "The Role of Inventories in Oil Market Stability." *The Quarterly Review of Economics and Finance* no. 42 (2002).

Jaffe, A.M., and Steven W. Lewis. "Beijing's Oil Diplomacy." *Survival,* vol. 44, no. 1. (2002).

Jakobson, Linda, and Daojiong Zha. "China and the Worldwide Search for Oil Security." *Asia-Pacific Review*, vol. 13, issue 2 (2006).

Janardhan, Meena. "Middle East: In the Race for Renewable Energy Sources" (http://ipsnews.net/news.asp?idnews=43624).

Jenkins, Patrick and Brooke Masters. "Banks Concede Reform is Inevitable." *Financial Times*, February 3, 2010 (http://www.ft.com/cms/s/0/c8ecd5e6-10f6-11df-9a9e-00144feab49a.html).

Jenkins, Patrick. "Barclays Chief Warns on Regulation." *Financial Times*, October 18, 2009 (www.ft.com/cms/s/0/47fd0f82-bc23-11de-9426-00144feab49a.html).

Kaldor, Mary, Terry Lynn Karl and Yahia Said. *Oil Wars* (London: Pluto Press, 2007).

Kanter, James. "In Finland, Nuclear Renaissance Runs into Trouble." *New York Times*, May 29, 2009.

Khatib, Hisham. "Financial and Economic Evaluation of Projects in the Electricity Supply Industry." The Institution of Engineering and Technology, London, 2003.

Khatib, Hisham. *Economic Evaluation of Projects in the Electricity Supply Industry* (Institution of Engineering and Technology [IET], 2003).

Kilian, Lutz. "Exogenous Oil Supply Shocks: How big are they and How Much do they Matter for the US Economy?" *Review of Economics and Statistics*, vol. 90, no. 2 (May 2008).

Klare, Michael. *Resource Wars* (New York, NY: Henry Holt and Company, 2001).

Kommersant GUIDE No. 213, November 15, 2006.

Kotilaine, J.T. "GCC Economics, Thinking Beyond Oil: Renewable Energy & Opportunities in GCC." Carbon Dioxide Information Analysis Center, NCBC Economic Research, October 2009 (http://www.gulfbase.com/site/interface/.../GCC_Energy_Landscape_04102009.pdf).

Kramer, Andrew E. "Russia Resumes Patrols by Nuclear Bombers." *The New York Times*, August 18, 2007 (http://www.nytimes.com/2007/08/18/world/europe/17cnd-russia.html?sq=russia%20resumes%20strategic%20bomber%20flights&st=cse&scp=1&pagewanted=print).

Kramer, Andrew. "Russia Volunteers to Join an OPEC Cut in Oil Output." *The New York Times*, December 11, 2008.

Lackner, Klaus. "A Guide to CO_2 Sequestration." *Science* vol. 300 (June 2003).

Lahn, Glada, Valerie Marcel, John Mitchell, Keith Myers and Paul Stevens. "Good Governance of the National Petroleum Sector." Chatham House Document, 2007 (http://www.chathamhouse.org. uk/files/9115_ggdoc0407.pdf).

Lauerman, Vincent and Julian Lee. *Canada's Oil Sands* (London: Centre for Global Energy Studies & Geopolitics Central, 2009).

Liao, Janet Xuanli. "A Silk Road for Oil: Sino-Kazakh Energy Diplomacy." *Brown Journal of World Affairs* no. 12 (2006).

Liao, Janet Xuanli. *The Politics of Oil Behind Sino-Japanese Relations: Beyond Energy Cooperation* (Stockholm: Institute for Security and Development Policy, 2008).

Lieberthal, Kenneth, and Mikkal Herberg. "China's Search for Energy Security: Implications for US Policy." *NBR Analysis*, vol. 17, no. 1 (2006).

Longmuir, G. and A.F. Alhajji. "The Need for a Balancing Act: Reducing Oil Dependence without Triggering a Global Crisis." *Geopolitics of Energy*, vol. 29, no. 3 (March 2007).

Looney, R. (ed.). *A Handbook of US–Middle East Relations* (London: Routledge, 2009).

Lovley, D.R. "Bug Juice: Harvesting Electricity with Microorganisms." *Nature Reviews: Microbiology*, vol. 4 (2006), pp. 497–508.

Luo, Dongkun, and Youjin Dai. "Economic Evaluation of Coalbed Methane Production in China." *Energy Policy* no. 37 (2009).

Ma, Xin, and Philip Andrews-Speed. "The Overseas Activities of China's National Oil Companies: Rationale and Outlook." *Minerals and Energy*, vol. 21, no. 1 (2006).

[426]

Mabro, Robert (ed.) *Oil in the 21st Century: Issues, Challenges, and Opportunities* (New York, NY: Oxford University Press, 2006).

Mabro, Robert. *A Dialogue between Oil Producers and Consumers: The Why and the How* (Oxford: Oxford Institute for Energy Studies, 1992).

Maliszewski, Wojciech. "Fiscal Policy Rules for Oil Producing Countries: A Welfare-Based Assessment." International Monetary Fund (IMF), WP/09/126 (Washington, DC: IMF, June 2009).

Maugeri, Leonardo. *The Age of Oil: The Mythology, History, and Future of the World's Most Controversial Resource* (Westport, CT: Praeger Publishers, 2006).

McCaul, James. "Oil Price Drop Unevenly affects Floating Production Projects." *Oil and Gas Journal,* vol. 107, no. 7 (February 16, 2009).

McKinsey and Company. "Carbon Capture and Storage: Assessing the Economics." McKinsey Climate Change Initiative, 2008 (http://www.mckinsey.com/clientservice/sustainability/pdf/CCS_Assessing_the_Ec onomics.pdf).

McManus, J.F. "Federal Obstruction Causes Natural Gas Shortage." *The New American*, December 11, 2006.

Medlock, K.B. III and A.M. Jaffe. "The Global Energy Market: Comprehensive Strategies to Meet geopolitical and Financial Risks." Baker Working Paper Series, May 2008 (http://www.bakerinstitute.org/publications/IEEJtransportation-MedlockJaffe.pdf).

Medlock, Kenneth B., and A.M. Jaffe. "US Energy Policy and Transportation." James A Baker III Institute for Public Policy, The Global Energy Market: Comprehensive Strategies to Meet Geopolitical and Financial Risk Working Paper Series, May 2008.

Metz, B., O. Davidson, H. de Coninck, M. Loos and L. Meyer (eds). "Intergovernmental Panel on Climate Change (IPCC) Special Report on Carbon Dioxide Capture and Storage (CCS)"; (Cambridge: Cambridge University Press, 2005).

Mickinsey & Co. "Reducing US Greenhouse Gas Emission: How Much at What Cost?" December 2007.

Middle East Economic Survey (MEES). August 31, 2009.

Mills, Robin M. *The Myth of the Oil Crisis: Overcoming the Challenges of Depletion, Geopolitics, and Global Warming* (Westport, CT: Praeger, 2008).

Ministry of Electricity & Water (MEW). *Annual Statistical Book 2004–2005*, Kuwait, 2006.

Minsky, H. *Can "It" Happen Again: Essays on Instability and Finance* (New York, NY: M.E. Sharpe, 1982).

Minsky, H. *Stabilizing an Unstable Economy* (New York, NY: McGraw Hill, 1986).

Mitchell, J.V. and G. Lahn. *Oil for Asia* (London: Chatham House, 2007).

Mitchell, John V. and Paul Stevens. "Ending Dependence: Hard Choices for Oil-Exporting States" (London: Chatham House, 2008).

Mitchell, John V., and Paul Stevens. *Ending Dependence: Hard Choices for Oil-Exporting States*. Chatham House Report, London, June 2008.

Miyamoto, Akira, and Chikako Ishiguro. *Pricing and Demand for LNG in China: Consistency between LNG and Pipeline Gas in a Fast Growing Market* (Oxford Institute for Energy Studies, Report NG 9, 2006).

Mohebali, Ghasemali, and A.S. Ball. "Biocatalytic Desulfurization (BDS) of Petrodiesel Fuels." *Microbiology* no. 154 (2008), pp. 2169–2183.

Mommer, Bernard. "Oil Prices and Fiscal Regimes." OIES Working Paper 24 (Oxford: Oxford Institute for Energy Studies, May 1999).

Mommer, Bernard. *Global Oil and the Nation State* (New York, NY: Oxford University Press, 2002).

Moran, Daniel, and James A. Russell (eds). *Energy Security and Global Politics: The Militarization of Resource Management* (Abingdon: Routledge Global Security Studies, 2009).

Morgan, Trevor. "Running Faster Just to Stand Still." *Petroleum Economist* (February 2009).

Multani, S.K. (ed.) *Security of Maritime Trade: New Dimensions* (Hyderabad: Icfai University Press, 2008).

Murray, Bill. "Obama's First Year brings Big Changes in US Energy Policy." *International Oil Daily*, December 30, 2009 (http://www.energyintel.com/DocumentDetail.asp?document_id=652346).

National Development and Reform Commission. *China's Medium and Long Term Energy Conservation Plan* (Beijing: NDRC, 2007).

Ness, L. *Terrorism and Public Utility Infrastructure Protection* (New York, NY: Wiley, 2006).

Nordhaus, William. "Oil and Economic Performance in Industrial Countries." Brookings Paper on Economic Activity, vol. 2 (1980).

Organization for Economic Cooperation and Development (OECD) and International Energy Agency (IEA). "Energy Technology Perspectives." 2008.

Organization of the Petroleum Exporting Countries (OPEC). *World Oil Outlook* (Vienna: OPEC, 2009).

Osnos, Evan. "Green Giant: Beijing's Crash Program for Clean Energy." *The New Yorker*, December 21, 2009 (http://www.newyorker.com/reporting/2009/12/21/091221fa_fact_osnos).

Pablo Bustelo. *Energy Security with a High External Dependence: The Strategies of Japan and South Korea*. Elcano Royal Institute Working Paper No. 16/2008 (Madrid: Real Instituto Elcano, 2008).

Parra, Francisco. *Oil Politics: A Modern History of Petroleum* (London: I.B. Tauris & Co. Ltd, 2004).

Petzet, Alan. "SEG: Saleri says Oil, Gas Key in New Energy Era." *Oil & Gas Journal* (October 29, 2009).

PFC Energy. "Global Crude Oil Supply Forecast: Non-OPEC; Historical Summary and Outlook to 2030." *Global Liquids Supply Forecast* (March 2009).

PFC Energy. "Interest in Unconventional Gas Growing Globally." *Upstream Competition Service*, September 21, 2009.

PFC Energy. "New Fuel Efficiency Standards: Ambitious but Attainable." *Downstream Monitoring Service North America*, June 10, 2009.

PFC Energy. "Non-OPEC Decline Rates Accelerate." *Global Liquids Supply Forecast*, February 10, 2009.

PFC Energy. "Outlook for Fundamentals, Politics and Prices, Q4 2009." *Market Intelligence Service*, October 8, 2009.

PFC Energy. "Saudi Arabia: Rising Capacity." *Market Intelligence Service*, July 16, 2008.

Pirani, S., J. Stern and K. Yafimava. "The Russo-Ukrainian Gas Dispute of January 2009: A Comprehensive Assessment." Oxford Institute for Energy Studies (February 2009).

Qatar Foundation. "Qatar Petroleum Will Open Research Centre at QSTP" (http://www.qstp.org.qa/output/Page2071.asp).

Razavi, Hossein. "Natural Gas Pricing in Countries of the Middle East and North Africa." *The Energy Journal*, vol. 30, no. 3 (2009).

Reed, Stanley. "Iraq Tries for Oil's Major Leagues." *Business Week*, August 10, 2009.

Reppy, J. "Report on the Workshop on Energy Security: Arabian Gulf Oil, International Security, and American Strategy." Cornell University, January 2007.

Rosner, Kevin. "Gazprom and the Russian State." Global Market Briefing, Institute for the Analysis of Global Security (London: GMB Publishing, 2006).

Ross, Michael L. "Blood Barrels: Why Oil Wealth Fuels Conflict." *Foreign Affairs*, vol. 87, issue 3 (May/June 2008).

Rubin, E.S. "IPCC Special Report on Carbon Dioxide Capture and Storage." Report presented at the RITE International Workshop on CO_2 Geological Storage, Tokyo, Japan, February 2006.

Saudi Arabian Ministry of Foreign Affairs. "Cooperation Council for the Arab States of the Gulf" (http://www.mofa.gov.sa/Detail.asp?InSectionID=5505&InNewsItemID=63566).

Segal, Paul. "Why Do Oil Price Shocks No Longer Shock?" OIES Working Paper 35 (Oxford: Oxford Institute for Energy Studies, October 2007).

Segal, Paul. "Why Do Oil Price Shocks No Longer Shock?" Oxford Institute for Energy Studies (OIES), WPM 35, October 2007.

Shanker, Thomas. "Despite Slump, US Role as Top Arms Supplier Grows." *New York Times*, September 7, 2009.

Shanker, Tom and Mark Landler. "Putin Says US is Undermining Global Stability." *The New York Times*, February 11, 2007 (query.nytimes.com/gst/fullpage.html?res=9B03E3D61E3FF932A25751C0A9619C8B63&sec=&spon=&&scp=2&sq=Munich%20Conference%20on%20Security%20Policy%20putin&st=cse).

Sheives, Kevin. "China Turns West: Beijing's Contemporary Strategy towards Central Asia." *Pacific Affairs* no. 79 (2006).

Simbolotti, Giorgio. "Beyond Emerging Low-Carbon Technologies to Face Climate Change." World Federation of Scientists 42nd Seminar, Erice, Sicily, August 2008.

Singer, Clifford E. "Energy and International War: From Babylon to Baghdad and Beyond." *World Scientific Series on Energy and Resource Economics*, vol. 6 (World Scientific Publishing Co., 2008).

[431]

Skinner, Robert. "Energy Security and Producer–Consumer Dialogue: Avoiding a Maginot Mentality." *Background Paper for Government of Canada Symposium – Energizing Supply: Oil and Gas Investment in Uncertain Times*, October 28, 2005 (www.oxfordenergy.org/presentations/SecurityOfSupply.pdf).

Smith, Aaron. "Putting Obama's Energy Plan to the Test." *CNNMoney.com*, August 4, 2008 (http://money.cnn.com/2008/08/04/news/economy/obama_energy/?postversion=2008080417).

Socolow, Robert. "Can we Bury Global Warming?" *Scientific American* vol. 293 (July 2005); (http://cmi.princeton.edu/resources/pdfs/bury_globalwarming.pdf).

Steiner, Christopher. "The Road to $20 a Gallon." *Forbes.com*, July 16, 2009 (http://www.forbes.com/2009/07/14/road-to-20-dollar-gallon-business-energy-oil.html).

Stobaugh, Robert, and Daniel Yergin. *Energy Future: Report of the Energy Project at Harvard Business School* (New York, NY: Ballantine, 1980).

Swaine, J. "Reliance on Russian Gas Threatens Britain's Security." *The Daily Telegraph*, September 17, 2008 (http://www.telegraph.co.uk/news/2977170/Reliance-on-Russian-gas-threatens-Britains-security.html).

Swartz, Spencer. "Is China's Oil and Coal Binge Coming to an End?" *Wall Street Journal Blogs*, December 2, 2009 (http://blogs.wsj.com/environmentalcapital/2009/12/02/is-chinas-oil-and-coal-binge-coming-to-an-end/).

Taylor J., and P. Van Doran. "The Energy Security Obsession." *The Georgetown Journal of Law and Public Policy*, vol. 6, no. 2 (Summer 2008).

Taylor, Ian. "China's Oil Diplomacy in Africa." *International Affairs*, vol. 82, no. 5 (2006).

The White House, Office of the Press Secretary. "President Obama Announces National Fuel Efficiency Policy," May 18, 2009 (http://www.whitehouse.gov/the_press_office/President-Obama-Announces-National-Fuel-Efficiency-Policy/).

Timmons, Heather. "Feeling Powerless, India Blames Speculation." *The New York Times*, July 23, 2009 (www.nytimes.com/2008/07/23/business/worldbusiness/23speculate.html?_r=1&scp=1&sq=timmons%20feeling%20powerless,%20India%20blames%20oil%20speculation&st=cse).

UN Development Program (UNDP), UN Department of Economic and Social Affairs (UNDESA), and World Energy Council (WEC). "World Energy Assessment" (2000).

UNESCO Institute for Statistics. "Estimates and Projections of Adult Illiteracy for Population Aged 15 Years and Above by Country and by Gender, 1970–2015," July 2002 (http://www.uis.unesco.org/en/stats/statistics/UIS_Literacy_Country2002.xls).

United Nations Framework Convention on Climate Change (UNFCCC). "The Kyoto Protocol," 1995 (http://unfccc.int/kyoto_protocol/ items/2830.php).

US China Economic and Security Review Commission. Report to Congress, November 2006 (http://uscc.gov/annual_report/2006/annual_report_full_06.pdf).

US Department of Energy (DOE) Energy Information Administration (EIA). *International Energy Outlook* (Washington, DC: EIA, 2009).

US Energy Information Administration (EIA). *International Statistics 2007.*

US Energy Information Administration (EIA). *Projections of International Liquids Production to 2030* (http://www.eia.doe.gov/oiaf/ieo/pdf/ieopol.pdf).

US Geological Survey (USGS). *World Petroleum Assessment* (Washington, DC: USGS, 2000).

van Hulst, Noe. "Key Messages From The 11th IEF in Rome," April 20–22, 2008 (www2.iefs.org.sa/whatsnew/Documents/KEY_MESSAGES _FROM_THE_11th_IEF_IN_ROME.pdf).

Victor, David G., Amy Myers Jaffe and Mark H. Hayes. *Natural Gas and Geopolitics: From 1970 to 2030* (Oxford: Oxford University Press, 2006).

Walther, Arne. "Dialogue for Global Energy Security." Delivered to the Board of Executive Directors, World Bank Group, November 7, 2007 (www2.iefs.org.sa/Speeches/Pages/DIALOGUEFORGLOBALENER GYSECURITYTheRoleoftheIEF.aspx).

Walther, Arne. "Producer–Consumer Dialogue: The Road Ahead." *Middle East Economic Survey*, February 11, 2002.

Walther, Arne. "Producer–Consumer Relations in a New Era." *Middle East Economic Survey*, September 25, 2009 (www.mees.com/ postedarticles/oped/v49n39-5OD01.htm).

Webometrics. "Ranking Web of World Universities: Arab World," January 2010 (www.webometrics.info/top100_continent.asp?cont=aw).

Woertz, Eckart. "Reflected Glory: The GCC's Future with Renewables." August 19, 2008 (http://gulfnews.com/about-gulf-news/al-nisr-portfolio/gnqfr/articles/reflected-glory-the-gcc-s-future-with-renewables -1.441776).

Wolf, Martin. "Do not Learn Wrong Lessons from Lehman's Fall." *Financial Times*, September 15, 2009 (www.ft.com/cms/s/0/ b24477de-a226-11de-9caa-00144feabdc0.html).

Wolf, Martin. "Victory in the Cold War was a Start as well as and Ending." *Financial Times*, November 10, 2009 (www.ft.com/ cms/s/0/123efa0e-ce2f-11de-a1ea-00144feabdc0.html).

World Economic Forum (WEF). "The New Energy Security Paradigm." (Spring, 2006); (http://www.weforum.org/pdf/Energy.pdf).

World Economic Forum. *GCC Countries and the World: Scenarios to 2025* (Geneva: WEF, 2007).

World Energy Council (WEC). "Carbon Dioxide Capture and Storage (CCS): Cleaner Energy Council: Interim Balance," 2007 (http://www. usea.org/programs/CFFS/FINAL CCS Brochure English.pdf).

World Energy Council (WEC). "Deciding the Future: Energy Policy Scenarios to 2050" (London: 2007).

World Energy Council (WEC). "Survey of Energy Resources" (London, 2007).

Yergin, Daniel. "It's Still the One." *Foreign Policy*, September 2009.

Yergin, Daniel. *The Prize: The Epic Quest for Oil, Money & Power* (New York, NY: The Free Press, 1993).

Yergin, Daniel. *The Prize: The Epic Quest for Oil, Money and Power* (New York, NY: Free Press, 2009).

Yterlinde, M.A., J.R. Ybema and G.H. Martimus. "Long-term Global Energy Developments and their Implications for Europe." ECN Policy Studies, the Netherlands, 2004 (http://130.226.56.153/ rispubl/SYS/syspdf/energconf05/session1_ybema.pdf).

Zaborowski. M. (ed.) *Facing China's Rise: Guidelines for an EU Strategy*. EU Institute for Security Studies, Chaillot Paper, No. 94 (2007).

Zha, Daojiong. "China's Energy Security: Domestic and International Issues." *Survival*, vol. 48 no. 1 (2006).

Zhang, Jin. *Catch-up and Competitiveness in China: The Case of Large Firms in the Oil Industry* (London: RoutledgeCurzon, 2004).

Zweig, David, and Jianhai Bi. "*China's* Global Hunt for Energy." *Foreign Affairs*, vol. 84, no. 5 (2005).

INDEX